STUDIES IN EVANGELICAL HISTORY AND THOUGHT

Oxford's Protestant Spy

The Controversial Career of Charles Golightly

STUDIES IN EVANGELICAL HISTORY AND THOUGHT

A full listing of titles in this series
appears at the end of this book

STUDIES IN EVANGELICAL HISTORY AND THOUGHT

Oxford's Protestant Spy

The Controversial Career of Charles Golightly

Andrew Atherstone

Copyright © Andrew Atherstone 2007

First published 2007 by Paternoster

Paternoster is an imprint of Authentic Media
9 Holdom Avenue, Bletchley, Milton Keynes, MK1 1QR, UK
and
PO Box 1047, Waynesboro, GA 30830–2047, USA

13 12 11 10 09 08 07   8 7 6 5 4 3 2 1

The right of Andrew Atherstone to be identified as the Author of this Work
has been asserted by him in accordance with the Copyright, Designs
and Patents Act 1988.

All rights reserved. No part of this publication may be reproduced, stored in a retrieval system, or transmitted, in any form or by any means, electronic, mechanical, photocopying, recording or otherwise, without the prior permission of the publisher or a license permitting restricted copying. In the UK such licenses are issued by the Copyright Licensing Agency, 90 Tottenham Court Road, London W1P 9HE.

British Library Cataloguing in Publication Data
A catalogue record for this book is available from the British Library

ISBN 978–1–84227–364–7

Typeset by the Author
Printed and bound in Great Britain
for Paternoster
by Nottingham Alpha Graphics

STUDIES IN EVANGELICAL HISTORY AND THOUGHT

Series Preface

The Evangelical movement has been marked by its union of four emphases: on the Bible, on the cross of Christ, on conversion as the entry to the Christian life and on the responsibility of the believer to be active. The present series is designed to publish scholarly studies of any aspect of this movement in Britain or overseas. Its volumes include social analysis as well as exploration of Evangelical ideas. The books in the series consider aspects of the movement shaped by the Evangelical Revival of the eighteenth century, when the impetus to mission began to turn the popular Protestantism of the British Isles and North America into a global phenomenon. The series aims to reap some of the rich harvest of academic research about those who, over the centuries, have believed that they had a gospel to tell to the nations.

Series Editors

David Bebbington, Professor of History, University of Stirling, Stirling, Scotland, UK

John H.Y. Briggs, Senior Research Fellow in Ecclesiastical History and Director of the Centre for Baptist History and Heritage, Regent's Park College, Oxford, UK

Timothy Larsen, Associate Professor of Theology, Wheaton College, Illinois, USA

Mark A. Noll, McAnaney Professor of History, University of Notre Dame, Notre Dame, Indiana, USA

Ian M. Randall, Deputy Principal and Lecturer in Church History and Spirituality, Spurgeon's College, London, UK, and a Senior Research Fellow, International Baptist Theological Seminary, Prague, Czech Republic

For Catherine

Contents

Acknowledgements	xiii
Abbreviations	xv
Prologue: Oxford's Spy	1
Chapter 1: A Tractarian Disciple?	7
Huguenot Heritage	7
Eton and Oxford	9
The Unsettled Curate	16
Church in Danger	23
Littlemore	28
The Widening Breach	31
The Hampden Controversy	36
The Final Split	45
Novel and Confused Doctrines	51
Few Can Be Spared	53
Chapter 2: Remembering the Martyrs	57
An Anti-Catholic Scheme?	59
The Inscription	65
Church or Monument?	70
Conclusion	80
Chapter 3: Keeping Oxford Protestant	85
Tract 90	86
A Party Man?	96
The Poetry Professorship	102
Under False Colours	107

The Hampden Affair Revived	118
Pious Frauds	122
The Vice-Chancellorship	132
Degradation and Censure	137
The 'New Test'	141
Requisition Against *Tract 90*	144
A Jesuitical Journal	147
Agag to the Rescue	157
Chapter 4: The Problem of Professor Jowett	**163**
Chapter 5: Bishop Wilberforce and the Spread of Ritualism	**179**
Cuddesdon College	180
The Public Outcry	185
The Archdeacons' Inquiry	189
College Concessions	194
Student Idiosyncrasies and Secessions	195
A Change of Staff	200
The Lavington Case	206
Prosecution	212
Facts and Documents	218
Petitions and Protests	224
A Ritualist Bishop?	230
The Woodard Schools	234
The Oxford Meeting	241
Cold Feet and a Bishop's Inquiry	247
A Predilection for Rome	254
Chapter 6: Protecting the University Pulpit	**263**
Triumph or Defeat?	272
Chapter 7: The Final Campaign	**279**
The Oxford Diocesan Conference	284
Cuddesdon Teaching and Secessions	289
Address from the Laity	293
The English Church Union and the Church Association	295
Re-writing History	299

Epilogue: Partisan or Protestant?	**309**
Sources	**321**
Index of Names	**327**

Acknowledgements

Numerous debts, too many to calculate, have been incurred during the research for this book. Mark Chapman, Vice-Principal of Cuddesdon Theological College, must be named first. I am grateful for his wise counsel and ceaseless good humour during my early work on Charles Golightly's career, which began as a doctoral project. One of the ironies of this research has been happy hours discussing Golightly within the walls of the very institution he dedicated so much energy trying to shut down. Thanks also to Peter Nockles and Mark Smith for their encouragements and for reading drafts of the book. Peter Nockles and Jane Garnett examined the original thesis and offered shrewd comments.[1]

I am grateful to Shirley and Helen Stack, descendants of Charles Golightly's sister, for their warm hospitality and for permission to publish excerpts from documents in their possession. To them belongs the photograph of Golightly on the front cover, the only known image of their illustrious relative. Thanks also to Graham Wason for access to family papers from Cossington Park in Somerset. For permission to publish material from other manuscript collections, I am grateful to the Master and Fellows of Balliol College, Oxford; the Birmingham Oratory; the Bodleian Library; the British Library; the Jowett Copyright Trustees; the Warden and Fellows of Keble College, Oxford; the Trustees of Lambeth Palace Library; Lancing College; the Provost and Fellows of Oriel College, Oxford; the Principal and Chapter of Pusey House, Oxford and the Principal of Ripon College Cuddesdon. Some parts of this study have previously appeared elsewhere, and I am grateful to Oxford University Press, Cambridge University Press and Ashgate Publishing for permission to reproduce the material in revised form here.[2]

---

[1] Andrew C. Atherstone, *Charles Golightly (1807-1885), Church Parties and University Politics in Victorian Oxford* (DPhil thesis, Oxford University, 2000).

[2] 'The Martyrs' Memorial at Oxford', *Journal of Ecclesiastical History* 54 (April 2003), pp. 278-301; 'Benjamin Jowett's Pauline Commentary: An Atonement Controversy', *Journal of Theological Studies* 54 (April 2003), pp. 139-53; 'The Founding of Cuddesdon: Liddon, Ritualism and the Forces of Reaction' and 'Controversy Renewed: Partisan Polemic and the Great Ritualist "Conspiracy"' in Mark D. Chapman (ed.),

My greatest debt of all is to my dear wife, Catherine, who patiently endured my obsession with Golightly during the early years of our marriage. To her this book is dedicated.

Andrew Atherstone
Eynsham, Oxfordshire
January 2007

Ambassadors of Christ: Commemorating 150 Years of Theological Education in Cuddesdon, 1854-2004 (Aldershot, 2004), pp. 23-50, 67-88.

Abbreviations

BCL   Balliol College Library
BL   British Library
BOA   Birmingham Oratory Archives
CCA   Cuddesdon College Archives
LBV   Liddon Bound Volume
LCA   Lancing College Archives
LPL   Lambeth Palace Library
LRO   Lincolnshire Record Office
KCL   Keble College Library
OCL   Oriel College Library
ODP   Oxford Diocesan Papers
ORO   Oxfordshire Record Office
OUA   Oxford University Archives
PHL   Pusey House Library
SUL   Southampton University Library
WCA   Wadham College Archives

PROLOGUE

Oxford's Spy

Between the 1840s and 1860s the following riddle circulated around the University and diocese of Oxford:

My first he does when he walks,
My second comes down from the sky,
My third he does when he talks,
My whole is an Oxford spy.[1]

Those familiar with the local theological scene did not have to work hard for the solution. The answers to the first three parts of the riddle were straightforward, 'Go – Light – Lie'. They added up to the 'Oxford spy', Oxford's home-grown and most notorious ecclesiastical agitator, Charles Golightly. Educated at the University in the 1820s, he spent most of his life in the city, until locked up in a lunatic asylum in the 1880s. During the intervening half a century he played a leading role in many of the theological *causes célèbres* which rocked Oxford and sent tremors around the Church of England.

Golightly first rose to prominence as an aggressive opponent of the Tractarians, leading numerous campaigns against John Henry Newman, Edward Pusey and their disciples. When Tractarianism transmogrified into ritualism, Golightly again led the resistance, attempting to force the closure of Cuddesdon Theological College and the Woodard Schools. Bishop Wilberforce of Oxford and Bishop Gilbert of Chichester came in for a large share of his opprobrium for their tacit support of ritualism within their dioceses. Nor did Golightly spare the theological 'liberals' – he was closely involved in protests against heavyweight Oxford figures like Professor Hampden, Benjamin Jowett and Dean Stanley. Those who clashed swords with Golightly were threatened with being banned from pulpits, dismissed from teaching posts, thrown out of their colleges or their parishes, and even kicked out of the Church of England itself. His campaigns sometimes met with success, more often with failure. Yet he had an unceasing ability to stir up *odium theologicum* and to keep the

---

[1] For example, *Union*, 9 April 1858, p. 232; Brooke Diary, 2 January 1862, Corpus Christi College Archives, Oxford. This riddle was still in circulation in the 1880s: John R. Bloxam to Gibbes Rigaud, 2 October 1881, Bodleian MS Add. B.115, fo. 53.

controversies at fever pitch, whether amongst University dons or parochial clergymen. He set about his task with energy and unique skill.

During Golightly's many high-profile crusades, his Protestant friends urged him forward and praised him for taking a bold stand for gospel truth. In contrast, his enemies dismissed his claims about heresy within the Church and the University as slanderous nonsense. As the above riddle hints, when he opened his mouth they expected only lies to come forth. The riddle also had an alternative conclusion, gleefully passed on by both Newman and Wilberforce, 'My whole is a very Paul Pry' – after the central character in John Poole's 1825 farce, an interfering busybody and eavesdropper who was unable to mind his own business and constantly intruded on other people's affairs.[2] To many of Golightly's opponents, this seemed an accurate parallel. He was labelled 'one of the most notorious Paul Prys of the day', a reputation which was to stick with him throughout life and remains even to the present.[3] He was mocked and vilified from that day to this. The following two denunciations are typical of the vitriol Golightly attracted during his lifetime. The first was published in 1841, when he was aged 34 and just beginning to achieve national fame. It appeared anonymously in the *Oxford Herald*, but was obviously written by someone with access to local intelligence about Golightly's many broken friendships:

> He has voluntarily undertaken the office of an informer. No one can doubt that his position and circumstances most peculiarly fit him for such an occupation. Conceive the case of a clergyman residing in this University, unencumbered by tutorial duties, with scarcely any parochial responsibilities, unshackled by domestic ties, with nothing, in fact, to draw him off from the arduous and painful task of watching and scrutinizing the conduct of his brethren ... conceive this person, without receiving an injury from any one, without even the approach to a quarrel, giving up his private friendships, breaking off from social intercourse solely from the conscientious feelings of public duty – with what regret would he think that he had ever been associated with men whom he now feels bound to accuse – with what delight would he console himself that he was thereby supremely fitted to be their accuser – trace him through six years pursuing his laborious task with ardour and perseverance – he loses no pains to perfect himself in his art – he has fellow-labourers on all sides – he makes the most wonderful collection of tittle-tattle, gossip, and scandal that has been heard of – he seizes hold of every silly tale, fleeting rumour, and vague report, let it come from what quarter it may. But this is not all. He resorts to personal inspection – his favourite haunts are the chancels and vestries of churches – a deacon's stole, a cross on a

---

[2] John H. Newman to F.S. Bowles, 1 May 1845, in *The Letters and Diaries of John Henry Newman* edited by C.S. Dessain, V.F. Blehl, Edward E. Kelly, Thomas Gornall, Ian T. Ker, Gerard Tracy and Francis J. McGrath (31 vols, London and Oxford, 1961-2006), x. p. 644; Samuel Wilberforce to Charles Anderson, 13 February 1858, Bodleian MS Wilberforce d.28, fo. 80. See John Poole, *The Adventures of Paul Pry* (London, 1825).

[3] *Saturday Review*, 9 July 1859, p. 46.

surplice, are chronicled as undoubted evidence of Popery – but he is even yet bolder than this, the holy chalice is not free from his sacrilegious meddling. Such, indeed, are the qualifications of this most remarkable man.[4]

A second typical denunciation appeared in the *Saturday Review* in 1859, when Golightly was aged 52 and at the height of his powers. It resorted to simple mockery:

> Who that knows Oxford has not heard of Mr Golightly, of Holywell-street? He is part of the place. He is the Delator-General, not only of Oxford, but of the whole Church. If anybody is wanted to do a job extremely dirty and offensive, such as signing a protest complaining of a sermon, or denouncing a brother clergyman, Mr Golightly is the man for it. His ears, being particularly acute, are always pricked up and open to the faintest suspicion of heresy. If an anonymous letter is to be written, it is sure to be written; but immediately a whiff and suspicion of Holywell-street, Oxford (not altogether, in respect of unsavoury stories, unlike its London *congener* [Holywell Street, London, a notorious centre of the pornography trade]) expands itself – there is a rustle and a cackle – and Oxford is aware that Mr Golightly is incubating an ecclesiastical egg, and sitting upon some mare's nest of heterodoxy. Is a sermon to be complained of – all men turn at once to Golightly? Has the Vice-Chancellor indulged in a mild Havannah – have any of the doctors, proctors, or professors ordered an additional pipe of port, or keg of whisky – is there a rumour of a flirtation between a canon of Christ Church and the Pope's niece – has a shooting-jacket, a crucifix, or a crinoline been smuggled into the porter's lodge at St Barnabas – is it currently reported that in the long vacation a Bampton Lecturer was found at a casino or a bull-fight – to a certainty a letter will appear in the *Record*; and the curious thing is, that immediately the name of Golightly flits through every common room. Common consent fixes upon the reverend gentleman as the embodied Indignation-Meeting.[5]

Until now, however, little has been known about Charles Golightly. He darts in and out of numerous books on the Church of England in the nineteenth century, with only the briefest of mentions. Historians are unanimous in their negative verdict upon his extreme opinions and extreme methods, and they reserve some of their most colourful language to describe him. To David Newsome, for example, Golightly has an 'astute and scheming mind'.[6] To Peter Nockles he is a 'zealot'.[7] Vivian Green calls him a 'clerical gadfly',[8] and John

---

[4] *Oxford Herald*, 24 December 1841.
[5] *Saturday Review*, 9 July 1859, p. 46.
[6] David H. Newsome, *The Parting of Friends: The Wilberforces and Henry Manning* (1966; reissued Leominster, 1993), p. 194.
[7] Peter B. Nockles, 'Oxford, Tract 90 and the Bishops' in David Nicholls and Fergus Kerr (eds.), *John Henry Newman: Reason, Rhetoric and Romanticism* (Bristol, 1991), p. 41.
[8] Vivian H.H. Green, *Religion at Oxford and Cambridge* (London, 1964), p. 216.

Prest sums him up as the 'self-appointed champion of the established church'.[9] Margaret Crowther speaks of Golightly's 'witch-hunting',[10] while Desmond Morse-Boycott chose the phrase 'Devil's Advocate' (a label he intended to be taken literally).[11] Other historians, like Sheridan Gilley, Marvin O'Connell and Brian Heeney, accurately describe Golightly as 'a militant antipapist',[12] 'the Tractarians' most bitter and relentless enemy'[13] and an 'indefatigable anti-Puseyite'.[14] Most recently Frank Turner has portrayed him as 'a busybody, carrying gossip and generally making himself a thorn in the side of the Tractarians ... a person of neither substance nor standing', who took on the 'role of self-appointed ecclesiastical agent provocateur'.[15]

Of all church historians, perhaps Owen Chadwick knows Golightly the best. In his popular *Victorian Church* Golightly receives a number of dishonourable mentions as 'the sergeant-sniper of the established church', a 'cackling jack-in-the-box' and 'the notorious skirmisher of the age'.[16] Elsewhere Chadwick reflects on his personality and abilities as follows:

> For Tractarian historiography Charles Pourtales [sic] Golightly has always possessed the qualities of Mephistopheles. He was a loyal, sturdy, contentious Anglican who ... believed himself called to the task of resisting every kind of innovation in the Church of England ... a work demanding herculean resolution in an age of change. Affectionate and generous, he laboured under the illusion that sharp public controversy need not loosen the ties of private friendship. ... Golightly went on his way, a man of one idea, uninhibited by the doubts or hesitations which beset the intellectual. ... He was well tutored in stratagems of war, the more formidable because he was unaware that he was a strategist.[17]

Yet who was Charles Golightly? What were his stratagems? What was his driving motivation? How should his theological outlook and his significance be assessed? John Burgon, in his famous *Lives of Twelve Good Men* (1888), describes Golightly as 'one of the most interesting characters in the University

---

[9] John M. Prest, *Robert Scott and Benjamin Jowett* supplement to *Balliol College Record* 1966, p. 11.
[10] Margaret A. Crowther, *Church Embattled: Religious Controversy in Mid-Victorian England* (Newton Abbot, 1970), p. 232.
[11] Desmond L. Morse-Boycott, *They Shine Like Stars* (London, 1947), p. 93.
[12] Sheridan Gilley, *Newman and his Age* (London, 1990), p. 179.
[13] Marvin R. O'Connell, *The Oxford Conspirators: A History of the Oxford Movement 1833-1845* (London, 1969), p. 222.
[14] W. Brian D. Heeney, *Mission to the Middle Classes: The Woodard Schools, 1848-1891* (London, 1969), p. 80.
[15] Frank M. Turner, *John Henry Newman: The Challenge to Evangelical Religion* (New Haven and London, 2002) pp. 365-6.
[16] Owen Chadwick, *The Victorian Church* (2 vols, London, 1966-70), i. pp. 176, 553.
[17] Owen Chadwick, *The Spirit of the Oxford Movement: Tractarian Essays* (Cambridge, 1990), pp. 237-8.

of Oxford ... a most faithfully attached and dutiful son of the Church of England'.[18] Thomas Mozley, in his *Reminiscences Chiefly of Oriel College and the Oxford Movement* (1882), goes further and honours Golightly as 'a considerable personage, exercising ... a quasi-patriarchal jurisdiction over the University and the Diocese of Oxford, and the Church of England.'[19] The following study examines Golightly's controversial career in detail for the first time. It traces him through fifty years of cataclysmic theological debate which changed the face of the Church of England for ever. As will be seen, Golightly well deserves his title as Oxford's ecclesiastical agitator *par excellence*.

---

[18] John W. Burgon, *Lives of Twelve Good Men* (2 vols, London, 1888), i. pp. xxiv-xxv.
[19] Thomas Mozley, *Reminiscences Chiefly of Oriel College and the Oxford Movement* (2 vols, London, 1882), ii. p. 112.

CHAPTER 1

A Tractarian Disciple?

Huguenot Heritage

In Oxford's Holywell Cemetery, the gravestone of Charles Portalès Golightly records that he was 'staunch throughout life to the religious principles for which his ancestors suffered.' He was named after his great-great-grandfather, Charles Portalès (1676-1764), a Huguenot refugee who fled France during the persecution of Huguenot communities by the regime of Louis XIV. Throughout life Golightly used proudly to recount tales of the dramatic exploits of his Huguenot ancestors and displayed their portraits around his Oxford home.

The Roman Catholic persecution of Huguenots began in the 1660s, with a steady erosion of their religious freedoms and personal liberties, culminating in the Revocation of the Edict of Nantes in October 1685. Many fled into exile, abandoning their possessions; others were forced to convert to Roman Catholicism. Protestant ministers were executed, Protestant children were taken from their parents and given to priests or nuns to be brought up as Roman Catholics. Those who were unable to escape were gaoled or became galley slaves. In the midst of these persecutions, Charles Portalès' father was thrown into prison, while his mother and sister were forced to enter a convent. He and his younger brother were smuggled from France into Switzerland in the panniers of an ass, and were brought up by relatives in Holland. Portalès eventually settled in England, one of 50,000 Huguenot refugees who arrived on British shores between 1660 and 1706. He was naturalised as a British subject in 1702 and worked in London as secretary to Armand de Bourbon, Marquis de Miremont, a Huguenot diplomat.[1]

Meanwhile back in France the first Huguenot 'prophets' or 'inspirés' began to appear, often preaching in their sleep about millenarian themes such as judgment, the last days and the imminent parousia. In July 1702, rather than submit to oppressive government legislation, a small group of Huguenots in the Languedoc region took up arms, led by itinerant inspirés. Known as the

---

[1] *Mémoires Inédits d'Abraham Mazel et d'Élie Marion sur la Guerre des Cévennes 1701-1708* edited by Charles Bost (Paris, 1931), preface. On de Miremont, see David C.A. Agnew, *Protestant Exiles from France, chiefly in the Reign of Louis XIV or, the Huguenot Refugees and their Descendants in Great Britain and Ireland* (2 vols, np, third edition, 1886), i. pp. 415-24; P.J. Shears, 'Armand de Bourbon, Marquis de Miremont', *Proceedings of the Huguenot Society of London* 20 (1962), pp. 405-18.

Camisards (soon numbering perhaps 2,000 men and women), they carried out guerrilla warfare for two years in the mountains of the Cévennes against Roman Catholic officials and government militias, before being forced to surrender.[2] The rebels were executed, imprisoned and scattered, but in 1706 three Camisard inspirés arrived in London where they began to attract a fresh Huguenot and English following, nicknamed 'the French Prophets'.[3] The ecstatic pronouncements continued, often accompanied by physical manifestations such as shaking, jumping, gasping and convulsions, and were received with a mixture of awe, respect and suspicion. Both de Miremont and Portalès joined the French Prophet community, and Portalès became one of their scribes, responsible for recording the prophecies of the inspirés and historical accounts of the movement. From first inspiration to last more than five hundred people became French Prophets, spread across England and Scotland, though by 1718 personal feuds, geographical dispersion and death had begun to destroy their unity and cohesion. The movement soon petered out, despite a brief revival during the 1730s under Hannah Wharton, the Birmingham prophetess, and isolated prophecies continued into the 1760s. One of Wharton's disciples was Golightly's great-grandfather, Francis Wynantz, at whose home John Wesley had his famous meeting with the Moravian, Peter Böhler, in February 1738 – a key event in the eighteenth century Evangelical Revival.[4]

This ancestral history was important to Golightly and bearing the name Charles Portalès meant he could not escape constant reminder of his illustrious predecessor. He inherited the French Prophet archive collected by Portalès and his visitors were regularly treated to viewings of old Huguenot manuscripts and interesting family artefacts (such as Portalès' watch, dressing gown, night cap and Bible).[5] During Golightly's infancy, Portalès' daughter resided with the Golightly family, an elderly woman in her 90s but a living link with their Huguenot past.[6] It has been suggested that because of this Huguenot heritage, he had 'something of a sentimental, as well as an academic, dislike of

---

[2] On the Camisard rebellion, see Henri Bosc, *La Guerre des Cévennes, 1702-1710* (6 vols, Montpellier, 1985-93).

[3] On the French Prophets, see Hillel Schwartz, *The French Prophets: The History of a Millenarian Group in Eighteenth-Century England* (Berkeley and Los Angeles, 1980); Schwartz, *Knaves, Fools, Madmen, and that Subtile Effluvium: A Study of the Opposition to the French Prophets in England, 1706-1710* (Gainesville, Florida, 1978).

[4] *The Journal of the Rev. John Wesley* edited by Nehemiah Curnock (8 vols, London, 1938), i. p. 436.

[5] Mozley, *Reminiscences Chiefly of Oriel College and the Oxford Movement*, ii. p. 109; Peter la Trobe to Golightly, 20 July 1863, LPL MS 1808, fo. 45; 'Certain Curiosities at 6 Holywell Street, Oxford', 8 April 1878, Stack MS 16a. The French Prophet archive is now in the possession of the Stack family.

[6] Frances Belchier née Portalès died in 1812, aged 93. See Frances Golightly's memoir, Stack MS 12g; *Gentleman's Magazine* 82 (December 1812), p. 598.

Romanism'.⁷ Certainly his family who laid his gravestone drew a connection between his ancestry and his theological outlook. Anti-Catholicism and anti-Tractarianism were a dominant feature of Golightly's life, and it is likely that this was partly motivated by knowledge of the suffering of his Huguenot forebears under persecution by Roman Catholics. He used often to quote the saying, 'if the Church of Rome be not Antichrist, she hath ill-luck to be so like him.'⁸

Eton and Oxford

Charles Golightly was born at Ham in Surrey on 23 May 1807 to William and Frances Golightly, a wealthy and well-connected couple. Yet he never knew his father, who died in May 1810 leaving four infant children to be brought up single-handedly: Frances (aged 5), William (aged 4), Charles (aged 2) and Edward (aged 1). Charles followed his older brother to Eton and his school-boy journal reveals typical teenage interests: sculling, shooting, debating, fossil hunting, coin collecting, the Italian mistress, visits to local stately homes, trips to museums and theatres, sermons and dancing, alongside wide-ranging academic study dominated by classics and history.⁹ Despite these varied pass-times, Golightly intensely disliked his experience of Eton, which in the 1820s was notorious for ill-discipline and harsh punishments under the rule of its fierce headmaster, John Keate. Golightly had nothing good to say about the school and often spoke in later life of 'the immense amount of evil' learned and practised amongst the boys, caused in part by the neglect of religious instruction.¹⁰ His Eton career was marred by bullying and flogging. One example that stuck in his memory was the time fellow pupils tried to trick him into walking under a bucket of water.¹¹ The bullying became so severe that he decided to leave the school, but was dissuaded out of a sense of obligation to his mother. If he was not being 'drubbed' by pupils, he was being beaten by masters. For example, when the fifth form were confined to their rooms for throwing bread at supper and Golightly ignored the sanction, he was threatened with flogging. On another occasion he was flogged for failing to recite seventy

---

⁷ Berdmore Compton, *Edward Meyrick Goulburn, DD, DCL, Dean of Norwich: A Memoir* (London, 1899), p. 12.
⁸ Mozley, *Reminiscences Chiefly of Oriel College and the Oxford Movement*, i. p. 177; R.W. Hunt, 'Newman's Notes on Dean Church's *Oxford Movement*', *Bodleian Library Record* 8 (February 1969), p. 136.
⁹ Golightly's Eton Journal (1822-23), Stack MS 6a; partially published in *Etoniana*, no. 51 (2 May 1932), pp. 1-7.
¹⁰ E.M. Goulburn, *Reminiscences of Charles Pourtalès Golightly* (Oxford, 1886), p. 10.
¹¹ Charles P. Golightly, *A Letter to the Very Reverend the Dean of Ripon, containing Strictures on the Life of Bishop Wilberforce, Vol.II with special reference to the Cuddesdon College Enquiry and the Pamphlet 'Facts and Documents'* (London, 1881), pp. 53-4.

lines of Homer, but recorded proudly in his journal that he had not shown the pain and remained 'composed in my mind and serene'.[12] After a lifetime of verbal abuse received during his many theological campaigns, Golightly ascribed his survival instinct to the training he gained at Eton: 'my hide is impenetrable, and I account for it in this way. When I was a boy at Eton I suffered much at the hands partly of Dr Keate, partly of bullying school-fellows; ever since which time mere words have produced very little impression upon me.'[13]

Golightly left Eton in mid-1823, aged 16, for private tuition under Henry Ellacombe, curate of Bitton near Bath. Through Ellacombe's mediation he was offered a place at Oriel College, Oxford,[14] where he matriculated in March 1824.[15] Oriel was a college of moderate proportions (18 fellows, 90 undergraduates), but was at the centre of intellectual revival within the University. During the 1820s and 30s an Oriel fellowship was one of Oxford's most prestigious and sought-after honours, granted solely on the basis of a candidate's academic merit rather than his background. As a result Oriel attracted some of the sharpest minds in the University.[16] When Golightly arrived it was led by the moral philosopher, Provost Edward Copleston (Bishop of Llandaff from 1827) and dominated by the 'noetics', an influential network of theologians who placed strong emphasis upon a rational defence of Christianity, seeking to combat the onslaught of deists and Unitarians.[17] The noetic circle included a number of Copleston's famous pupils who had been fellows at Oriel since the 1810s, such as Richard Whately, Renn Dickson Hampden, and Edward Hawkins (Copleston's successor as Provost). Also on the fellowship were John Keble, John Henry Newman and Edward Pusey (Regius Professor of Hebrew from 1828), whose views on politics and religion later took a very different shape.

Golightly overlapped as an undergraduate with a number of young men who afterwards achieved high distinction in political, literary, legal and administrative spheres. His contemporaries came, of course, from a variety of

---

[12] Golightly's Eton Journal (1822-23), Stack MS 6a.
[13] Golightly, *Letter to the Dean of Ripon*, p. 18.
[14] Golightly's Eton Journal (1822-23), Stack MS 6a.
[15] Joseph Foster (ed.), *Alumni Oxonienses: The Members of the University of Oxford, 1715-1886* (4 vols, London, 1887-88).
[16] K.C. Turpin, 'The Ascendancy of Oriel' in M.G. Brock and M.C. Curthoys (eds.), *The History of the University of Oxford*, vol. 6 *Nineteenth-Century Oxford, Part 1* (Oxford, 1997), ch. 6.
[17] On the noetics, see Richard Brent, 'The Oriel Noetics' in M.G. Brock and M.C. Curthoys (eds.), *The History of the University of Oxford*, vol. 6 *Nineteenth-Century Oxford, Part 1* (Oxford, 1997), pp. 72-6; H.C.G. Matthew, 'Noetics, Tractarians, and the Reform of the University of Oxford in the Nineteenth Century', *History of Universities* 9 (1990), pp. 195-225; William Tuckwell, *Pre-Tractarian Oxford: A Reminiscence of the Oriel 'Noetics'* (London, 1909).

theological backgrounds and many chose careers within the Church of England. They included some who later identified with the Tractarian movement, such as Hurrell Froude (fellow at Oriel from 1826), George Prevost, John Christie and Charles Eden (Newman's successor as vicar of the University Church in the 1840s). Three of the sons of William Wilberforce, the great evangelical philanthropist, also passed through Oriel during Golightly's time – Robert (fellow from 1826), Samuel and Henry. Golightly grew 'intimate' with Henry Wilberforce and by his invitation spent a few days with their illustrious father at Highwood Hill.[18] Although he did not get to know Samuel Wilberforce during their undergraduate years 'beyond quite a common acquaintance', this relationship developed after leaving college and they frequently exchanged hospitality.[19] Henry Ryder, the evangelical Bishop of Lichfield and Coventry, also sent four of his sons to Oriel, two of whom overlapped with Golightly.

One close Oriel friend was Thomas Mozley, who decades later fondly recalled the impression Golightly had made as an undergraduate:

> He had abundance of means, of general information and anecdote, and of self-confidence – invaluable at a university. Most freshmen are so overwhelmed by the new world they are brought into, and the bright vision opened to their eyes, that they spend several terms in recovering self-possession and learning to feel at home. They are leaning upon old school acquaintances, timidly courting new ones, nervous about etiquette ... Golightly must have been as much at home and master of a certain position the day he arrived at Oxford, fifty-eight years ago, as he is today.
>
> He was always accessible, companionable, and hospitable, and his own kindness and frankness were diffused among those that met in his rooms and made a social circle. He could criticise the university sermons freely, raise theological questions, and occasionally lay down the law – a very useful thing to be done in the mass of wild sentiment, random utterances, and general feeling of irresponsibility constituting undergraduate conversation.[20]

Mozley's sketch reveals two of Golightly's chief characteristics, already evident in his undergraduate days and which were to stay with him throughout life – fixed opinions and plain-speaking. It was these distinctive character traits which later helped to generate Golightly's many public protests and for which he was both praised and vilified. As an undergraduate, he put his natural frankness to good effect, challenging his friends about their spiritual position. Although their relationship suffered severe strain over the years, Mozley still wanted publicly to affirm: 'I have to acknowledge the greatest of obligations.

---

[18] Golightly, *Letter to the Dean of Ripon*, p. 4. For Golightly's visits to members of the Wilberforce family, see Golightly to Mozley, 11 September 1827 and 28 July 1830, BOA Thomas Mozley Papers.

[19] Golightly to Mozley, 28 December 1830, BOA Thomas Mozley Papers.

[20] Mozley, *Reminiscences Chiefly of Oriel College and the Oxford Movement*, ii. p. 110.

Golightly was the first human being to talk to me, directly and plainly, for my soul's good, and that is a debt that no time, no distance, no vicissitudes, no difference can efface, no not eternity itself'.[21] Similarly another friend from the 1820s, Charles Heurtley (undergraduate at Corpus Christi College), acknowledged that conversation with Golightly had 'done me much good – in matters of no light importance'.[22] He later wrote that Golightly was 'true and constant in his friendships, sparing neither time, nor money, nor exertion, where he might do service, and what is rarer, faithful in reproving where he believed that reproof was called for.'[23]

During his Oriel years Golightly also struck up friendship with a group of undergraduates and young dons identified by Timothy Stunt as 'radical evangelicals'.[24] As John Reynolds has shown, Oxford evangelicalism in the 1820s was diverse and increasingly fragmented. The moderate 'Claphamite' or 'Simeonite' consensus which dominated the movement since the 1790s had begun to disintegrate.[25] Within the University younger, more extreme men gathered around John Hill (Vice-Principal of St Edmund's Hall) as their mentor, and Golightly was often to be found in their company, drinking tea at Hill's home.[26] This circle included Henry Bulteel, the hyper-Calvinist curate of St Ebbe's church whose preaching regularly offended the University and diocesan authorities. Another was Joseph Philpot (fellow of Worcester College), who got into trouble with his college for holding meetings for prayer and Bible exposition in the Senior Common Room. A particular friend of Golightly was his Oriel contemporary, Charles Brenton, who was famous in Oxford for using a contraption with pulleys and a heavy weight to drag the covers from his bed at five o'clock every morning.[27] He also had connections with other 'radicals evangelicals', such as Benjamin Newton, George Wigram and Richard Sibthorp. This network was actively engaged in the Oxford auxiliaries of leading evangelical societies, such as the British and Foreign Bible Society, the Church Missionary Society and the London Society for Promoting Christianity Amongst the Jews. However, Stunt warns that 'it would be wrong to regard this circle of friends as anything more than just that – a group whose friendship grew out of a common piety and a shared seriousness of purpose rather than any doctrinal or theological orientation.'[28] Golightly was

---

[21] Ibid., p. 109.
[22] Heurtley to Mozley, c.15 September 1829, BOA Thomas Mozley Papers.
[23] *Guardian*, 6 January 1886, p. 26.
[24] Timothy C.F. Stunt, *From Awakening to Secession: Radical Evangelicals in Switzerland and Britain 1815-35* (Edinburgh, 2000), ch. 8.
[25] John S. Reynolds, *The Evangelicals at Oxford 1735-1871: A Record of an Unchronicled Movement with the Record Extended to 1905* (Oxford, 1975), ch. 5.
[26] Hill Diary, 14 August 1826, 9 and 27 February 1827, 11 December 1827, 18 January 1828, Bodleian MS St Edmund Hall 67/6.
[27] Mozley, *Reminiscences Chiefly of Oriel College and the Oxford Movement*, ii. p. 116.
[28] Stunt, *From Awakening to Secession*, pp. 209-10.

always on the edge of the group and never felt entirely at ease with them. Despite their friendship, he refused to identify himself as an 'evangelical', let alone a 'Calvinist', and had serious reservations about some of their theological opinions – particularly those of Bulteel, and even of Hill himself.[29] Perhaps this is why he grew closest to Walter Trower (fellow at Oriel from 1828), who had evangelical sympathies and was part of Hill's circle, but shared Golightly's reservations.

Also included within the orbit of this loose evangelical grouping were the Newman brothers – Frank (fellow at Balliol from 1826) and, to a lesser extent, John (fellow at Oriel from 1822). Their evangelical origins are well-known, and as late as March 1829 John Newman was elected co-secretary with John Hill of Oxford's CMS auxiliary, though they soon famously parted company.[30] The Newman and Golightly families had crossed paths in London when the children were small, and now in Oxford the sons renewed the connection.[31] Frank Newman took Golightly on as a private pupil in the Long Vacation of 1826 and they spent a few weeks reading together at Over Worton, a village north of Oxford, alongside Hungerford Hoskyns (another Oriel undergraduate and a future barrister). Newman's verdict was that Golightly was 'most backward in Aristotle' and did not stand much chance of good examination results in classics.[32]

The following summer Golightly read under the direction of John Newman, first at the Newman family home in Brighton and then at Hampstead (where they were joined by Henry Wilberforce).[33] Newman told his mother of his 'great esteem' for Golightly,[34] and one of his sisters thought that Wilberforce was 'very jealous' at Golightly's closeness to him.[35] Golightly later claimed that he and Newman had shared an 'intimate friendship', though it was more a case of the young undergraduate admiring his brilliant tutor, six years his senior, and wanting to impress him.[36] Indeed Golightly described how he 'looked up to' Newman with 'high respect'.[37] This comes across clearly in his bulletins to Thomas Mozley from Brighton and Hampstead:

---

[29] Golightly to Mozley, 26 June 1829, BOA Thomas Mozley Papers.
[30] Timothy C.F. Stunt, 'John Henry Newman and the Evangelicals', *Journal of Ecclesiastical History* 21 (January 1970), pp. 65-74.
[31] Newman to R.W. Church, 6 March 1882, *Newman Letters and Diaries*, xxx. p. 65.
[32] Francis W. Newman to John H. Newman, 21 August 1826, BOA PC 83a; Hill Diary, 14 August 1826, Bodleian MS St Edmund Hall 67/6.
[33] For details of Long Vacation reading, see *Newman Letters and Diaries*, ii. pp. 22-7.
[34] Newman to Mrs Newman, 20 June 1827, *Newman Letters and Diaries*, ii. p. 19.
[35] Maisie Ward, *Young Mr Newman* (London, 1952), p. 128.
[36] Golightly to Richard Bagot, 6 April 1841, PHL LBV 71, fo. 261.
[37] Charles P. Golightly, *The Position of the Right Rev. Samuel Wilberforce, DD, Lord Bishop of Oxford, in Reference to Ritualism, together with a Prefatory Account of the Romeward Movement in the Church of England in the Days of Archbishop Laud. By a Senior Resident Member of the University of Oxford* (London, 1867), p. 83.

> Mr N. is very kind – constantly walking with me and asking me to dinner. I have made out a little list of important subjects, some of which I contrive should take up the greatest part of the conversation, at least, when we are alone.[38]

> Newman has given me great encouragement. But indeed I hope I may say I have gained some improvement of mind besides mere knowledge of books; at least I am sure I ought to have done so. Newman's talents appear in every thing – in his views of History, of a Science &c, in his Sermons, which by the way are most edifying. Wilberforce is here and is in raptures with them.[39]

During the Long Vacation Golightly suffered from various 'doubts', probably related to his Christian faith and lifestyle, and it was to Newman he went for wise counsel. Again, Golightly reports to Mozley that his summer

> would have passed happier but for a hornet's nest of petty doubts, and scruples of conscience, which I dare say you have already observed in me, and which lately have given me terrible annoyance. I scarcely know whether to attribute them to deficiency in intellect, or incorrect views of religion. I trust however by Newman's advice and assistance I know now how to manage them, and have subdued them.[40]

One of the lasting legacies of Newman's spiritual influence upon Golightly – perhaps the only aspect of his teaching for which Golightly held unceasing gratitude – is possibly related to this episode. Newman emphasised the need to make biblical and theological studies devotional in their aim and not merely critical, a principle Golightly tried to carry through life.[41]

Although Golightly came increasingly under the sway of John Newman, he also made a good impression on the rest of the family. Mrs Newman and her three daughters, Harriett, Jemima and Mary, grew fond of Golightly and teased him for his fastidiousness and eccentricity. For example, Harriett declared: 'Golightly is an old friend ... He is a very great favourite of mine, and I enjoy his peculiarities.'[42] Mary reported how they 'laughed at his amusingness, his manner is indescribable'.[43] Likewise Thomas Mozley's sisters spoke of Golightly's 'amusing absurdities' and 'humorous oddity'.[44] He was particularly

---

[38] Golightly to Mozley, 25 July 1827, BOA Thomas Mozley Papers.
[39] Golightly to Mozley, 11 September 1827, BOA Thomas Mozley Papers.
[40] Ibid..
[41] Goulburn, *Reminiscences of Golightly*, p. 20; W.C. Lake in *Guardian*, 20 January 1886, p. 110; Golightly to Mozley, 26 June 1832, BOA Thomas Mozley Papers.
[42] Harriett Newman to Elizabeth G. Newman, 28 November 1829, in Dorothea Mozley (ed.), *Newman Family Letters* (London, 1962), p. 33.
[43] Mary Newman to Jemima Newman, August 1827, ibid., pp. 18-9.
[44] Jane Mozley to Thomas Mozley, 23 February 1830, BOA Thomas Mozley Papers; Anne Mozley (ed.), *Letters and Correspondence of John Henry Newman during his Life in the English Church* (2 vols, London, 1891), ii. p. 102.

attracted to Mary Newman and hinted to Mozley that there might be a possibility of future romance:

> The Newmans I like very much. His sisters I should think are all of them very sensible young women, but the youngest if any of them is the one whom you will see walking with me thro' Oriel quad. She is to my taste very pretty and I think also she is lively and clever.[45]

However, tragedy struck a few months later, in January 1828, when young Mary Newman suddenly died, aged just 18. Golightly came to view women in his house as 'a plague',[46] though Harriett Newman concluded that marriage would be the best thing for him: 'he would be Mr G.'s best friend who could help him to a suitable wife – wh is the only *chance* of his ever being settled and useful'.[47] In the event it was Thomas Mozley himself who married into the Newman family, wedding Harriett in 1836, while Golightly remained a bachelor to his dying day.

Most of Golightly's happy undergraduate friendships were to be shattered by the tumultuous events of later years. John Henry Newman and Samuel Wilberforce both became his *bête noire* and he clashed with them frequently, in the 1840s and 1850s respectively. Few of his other relationships survived, partly because Golightly's theological perspective remained stationary while others moved on. One friend recalled:

> his intellectual gifts were of a peculiar order, and not quite like those of other men. ... There was but little growth or expansiveness in his mind; while he possessed and exhibited considerable mental vigour, the vigour remained what it was originally – did not seem to receive accessions and enlargement as time went on. Still it *was* vigour.[48]

In contrast, Henry Wilberforce and Richard Sibthorp left the Church of England for the Church of Rome. Frank Newman moved towards Unitarianism and Charles Brenton joined the Plymouth Brethren. Even Thomas Mozley, who remained within the Church of England, broke off contact with Golightly in the 1840s when his old friend publicly attacked him in the press. At least two undergraduate friendships did, however, last all life long – those with Walter Trower (Bishop of Glasgow from 1848) and Charles Heurtley (Lady Margaret Professor of Divinity from 1853), who became allies in several of his theological campaigns.

These broken relationships were all in the future and there was no sign of fracture during the early years. Having received a third class in classics,

---

[45] Golightly to Mozley, 25 July 1827, BOA Thomas Mozley Papers.
[46] Harriett Newman to Mozley, 31 July 1836, BOA Thomas Mozley Papers.
[47] Harriett Newman to Mozley, 3 August 1836, BOA Thomas Mozley Papers.
[48] Goulburn, *Reminiscences of Golightly*, pp. 9-10.

Golightly graduated in May 1828 and remained cheerfully in Oxford for the next two years, reading and preparing for ordination.[49] During that period the focus of the University and the country was upon the controversial question of Catholic Emancipation. Political necessity forced Wellington's Tory government to change its hard-line anti-Catholic stance and at the opening of Parliament in February 1829 the King's Speech announced that the laws concerning Roman Catholic disabilities would be reviewed. For twelve years Home Secretary Robert Peel had sat as Tory MP for Oxford University, but now he felt honour-bound to resign and stand for re-election. Immediately the University was thrown into ferment and a bitter political campaign ensued, resulting in Peel's defeat at the hands of Sir Robert Inglis – a victory for the anti-Catholics and a rebuke to Peel's treachery.[50]

Golightly was once described by a friend as 'of all Tories, the most Tory',[51] and he was soon caught up in the election fever. He asked: 'who I should like to know since the opening of Parliament has been able to turn his attention to the ordinary affairs of life? When Peel has turned traitor, Church and State endangered by an influx of Catholics upon the Government, our Loyal University turned upside down ...'. He rebuked Mozley for viewing these vital questions like 'a cold-hearted philosopher' with 'the most provoking indifference', but added: 'Do not suppose me however carried away by such contentions ... I believe I have felt more concern by the non-arrival of an expected bookcase, than by all the disputations about the Catholic qu[estion] since the issuing of the King's Speech.'[52] Golightly predicted that the Established Church would not last more than forty years, whatever Parliament decided about the Roman Catholics, so ultimately it made little difference. Still he was perturbed that the 'cloven foot' had shown itself in the House of Commons and declared: 'I tremble for the house of Lords, or rather for the Bench of Bishops. I fear some of them will disgrace themselves very much.'[53]

The Unsettled Curate

In June 1830, just a week after his twenty-third birthday (the minimum canonical age), Golightly was ordained at St Paul's Cathedral by Bishop

---

[49] C.L. Shadwell, *Registrum Orielense: An Account of the Members of Oriel College, Oxford* (2 vols, London, 1893, 1902), ii. p. 368.

[50] Henry Tristram, 'Catholic Emancipation, Mr Peel, and the University of Oxford', *Cornhill Magazine* 66 (April 1929), pp. 406-18; N. Gash, 'Peel and the Oxford University Election of 1829', *Oxoniensia* 4 (1939), pp. 162-73.

[51] E.A. Knox, *The Tractarian Movement, 1833-1845: A Study of the Oxford Movement as a Phase of the Religious Revival in Western Europe in the Second Quarter of the Nineteenth Century* (London, 1933), p. 127.

[52] Golightly to Mozley, 16 February 1829, BOA Thomas Mozley Papers.

[53] Golightly to Mozley, 20 March 1829, BOA Thomas Mozley Papers.

Blomfield of London.[54] For fives years he would now be absent from Oxford – the only time he lived away from the city between the ages of 16 and 74. It was the first, and last, period in his life when he was involved in full-time pastoral work. Golightly went as curate to Penshurst in Kent, under his uncle the Revd Philip Stanhope Dodd, who came from a family of clergymen – Golightly's great-grandfather, grandfather, great-uncle, uncle and cousin on his mother's side were all ordained. None achieved high office in the Church of England, but his great-uncle, the Revd William Dodd, had gained notoriety as a fashionable and debt-ridden preacher, nicknamed the 'Macaroni Parson'. He had been hung at Tyburn in 1777 for stealing money by forging the signature of his patron, Philip Stanhope, the Earl of Chesterfield.[55] Golightly's uncle was baptised Philip Stanhope Dodd in honour of the Earl, two years before the tragedy occurred, and was stuck with the name for life.

Golightly did not settle easily into the role of curate at Penshurst. He began his clerical career with great optimism and a multitude of new resolutions, such as a determination to pray and praise throughout the day, and to repeat passages from the Bible, from John Keble's *Christian Year* (1827) or from James Montgomery's *Christian Psalmist* (1828) while dressing and undressing.[56] At first all seemed well and after a few weeks he reported to Mozley:

> I am happily, very happily, set out on my course ... My own family so near [living at Southborough], the gentry so very civil and friendly, the parishioners decent and respectful, my own lodgings very agreeable, perfect health, a beautiful country, these independently of spiritual blessings furnish me with abundant matter of thankfulness and praise ...[57]

Yet soon the discontent and uneasiness began to emerge. In his private notebook Golightly laid out his inner doubts and tried to dispel them:

> I am oppressed with fears occasionally about my ministerial conduct – whether I was right in taking orders at all – whether right in coming to Pensh[urst] – whether now preaching fruitfully and exhorting faithfully from house to house – whether right in my behaviour towards our Gentry, Farmers, Poor, evil livers &c. But mostly this is not right for 1. I have a plain promise of wisdom and if I pray for it I shall be certainly guided aright. 2. If I decide on leaving Penshurst, were I ever to think it my duty to renounce my profession, God could show me some

---

[54] Golightly was ordained deacon on 6 June 1830 and priest (again by Blomfield) on 5 June 1831; Archbishop of Canterbury's Act Books, LPL VB 1/15, fos 163, 193; Bishop of London's Registers, Guildhall Library, MS 9531/26, part 2, pp. 4-5, 13-4.
[55] On William Dodd, see Gerald Howson, *The Macaroni Parson: A Life of the Unfortunate Dr Dodd* (London, 1973).
[56] Golightly's private notebook, 2 July 1830, Stack MS 6d.
[57] Golightly to Mozley, 28 July 1830, BOA Thomas Mozley Papers.

other way of Glorifying him, provided I maintain a single eye to his Glory and a readiness to choose and follow any path he may point out to me.[58]

Although Golightly thought his uncle 'the kindest person in the world' they found it difficult to work together, partly because of theological tensions between them.[59] Perhaps Golightly's evangelical friends at Oxford had influenced him more than he cared to admit. His first sermon 'alarmed my uncle exceedingly. My brothers in the pew observed him crossing his legs, taking a pinch of snuff, and showing other marks ... of ill-concealed uneasiness.'[60] Years later he summed up Dodd as 'an old-fashioned High Churchman, who looked with suspicion upon cottage lectures, then a novelty, and any and every deviation from ordinary clerical routine.'[61] Soon he was complaining to friends about the pressures of parish life, with little time to read, and was finding weekly sermon composition difficult. Matters were made worse by his agreement to teach a troublesome and irritating pupil.[62] He felt he was making 'but little progress in true godliness', wondered whether he had been ordained too young and contemplated giving up active duty for further study. Yet Newman and others advised him to stay at Penshurst.[63] Some respite, perhaps, from the unceasing round of parochial duties came in Golightly's appointment as chaplain to the local lord of the manor, Philip Sidney, Baron De L'Isle and Dudley, of Penshurst Place – a role he continued for some years after giving up on Penshurst.[64]

Meanwhile Golightly's 'radical evangelical' friends and associates from Oxford had reached crisis point. During 1831 and 1832 a number of them walked out of the Church of England into various forms of Dissent, flirting with groups such as the Irvingites, the Strict Baptists and the nascent Brethren movement.[65] One of the first to leave was Henry Bulteel who in February 1831 preached a sensational University sermon at St Mary-the-Virgin in Oxford – a diatribe against the worldliness and immorality of the clergy, with an attack upon the Heads of Houses for complicity in the corruption of the church.[66] By

---

[58] Golightly's private notebook, c.1830, Stack MS 6d.
[59] Golightly to Mozley, 28 December 1830, BOA Thomas Mozley Papers.
[60] Golightly to Mozley, 28 July 1830, BOA Thomas Mozley Papers.
[61] Golightly, *Letter to the Dean of Ripon*, p. 7.
[62] Golightly to Mozley, 15 April 1833, BOA Thomas Mozley Papers.
[63] Golightly to Mozley, 26 June 1832, BOA Thomas Mozley Papers; Newman to Golightly, 10 June 1832, *Newman Letters and Diaries*, iii. p. 55.
[64] See title-pages of Charles P. Golightly, *Look at Home, or Short and Easy Method with the Roman Catholics* (Oxford, 1837); *Brief Remarks upon No.90, Second Edition, and Some Subsequent Publications in Defence of It* (Oxford, 1841).
[65] Grayson Carter, *Anglican Evangelicals: Protestant Secessions from the* Via Media, *c.1800-1850* (Oxford, 2001), ch. 7; Stunt, *From Awakening to Secession*, chs 10-11.
[66] Henry B. Bulteel, *A Sermon on I Corinthians II.12 Preached Before the University of Oxford* (Oxford, 1831).

the autumn, the Bishop of Oxford had withdrawn his licence to officiate in the diocese and ejected him from the curacy at St Ebbe's. Soon Bulteel seceded from the Church of England, was baptised by immersion and opened a chapel within the bounds of St Ebbe's parish, which quickly became the largest Nonconformist gathering in Oxford. Others followed suit. William Lambert (a scholar of Corpus Christi College) was thrown out of his college for describing the Church of England as 'the mere result of fleshly wisdom ... involved in deep malignant and inveterate opposedness to the Glory of God and the salvation of Souls'.[67] He seceded shortly after publishing *A Call to the Converted*, appealing for a pure and spiritual church.[68] Golightly's close Oriel friend, Charles Brenton, likewise drifted out of the Church of England, as did Benjamin Newton, though with less drama. Although these men sometimes embroiled Golightly in their theological arguments, he tried to resist being dragged into them – a tendency he described as 'my natural aversion to doctrinal discussion'. Whenever possible he avoided themes on which they differed, in conversation and correspondence.[69]

Golightly grew increasingly alienated from these former friends, and was particularly concerned for Brenton, who had been ordained just a few months before him. In December 1830 he asked Mozley: 'Do you think that his mind may be discordant? I know that he used to be subject to great depression of spirits, and was a martyr to indigestion.'[70] Yet Brenton's instability was due to more than just a digestive complaint. During 1831 he worked as a substitute minister, first for Bulteel at St Ebbe's and then for Joseph Philpot at Stadhampton (a village just south of Oxford), where he provoked hostility by refusing to read the burial service over a notorious drunkard who had been the parish-clerk for forty years.[71] Brenton preached a fiery sermon defending his actions, proclaiming that it was absurd, impious, wicked, blasphemous and hypocritical to use the Prayer Book funeral liturgy for 'baptized infidels'. He lamented that the practice of excommunication was almost extinct, and announced to the congregation his intention to resign his ministry and leave the Church.[72] On hearing the news, Golightly concluded that Brenton was in 'a state bordering closely on derangement'. Yet these dramatic events reinforced in his own mind his theological disjuncture with the evangelical movement. Nothing could be further from his thinking than secession from the Church of

---

[67] Quoted in Stunt, *From Awakening to Secession*, p. 256.
[68] See Timothy C.F. Stunt, 'John Synge and the Early Brethren', *Christian Brethren Research Fellowship Journal* 28 (1976), pp. 39-62.
[69] Golightly to Newman, 10 August 1831, BOA Miscellaneous Letters.
[70] Golightly to Mozley, 28 December 1830, BOA Thomas Mozley Papers.
[71] J.H. Philpot, *The Seceders (1829-1869). The Story of a Spiritual Awakening as Told in the Letters of Joseph Charles Philpot and of William Tiptaft* (2 vols, London, 1930-32), i. pp. 93-5, 181, 251-2.
[72] L.C.L. Brenton, *A Sermon on Revelation XIV.13 Tending to Shew the Absurdity and Impiety of the Promiscuous Use of the Church Burial Service* (Oxford, 1831).

England and he admitted that watching his evangelical friends depart had 'raised my prejudices High Church and High Tory to an unusual height.'[73] When Newman wrote to inquire about Brenton's views, Golightly replied:

> With regard to the opinions of those who are usually termed Evangelical I feel that I differ from them on two points chiefly. 1. Their views of Church Discipline, and Unity. This is my grand quarrel with them. 2. That they appear to me, many of them, to make their *feelings* the test of their growth in grace. When this is the case intercourse is impossible, or at all events very disagreeable.[74]

Unlike most of his evangelical friends, Golightly had strong objections to union with Dissenters of all descriptions. For example, he resigned from the Bible Society because it was non-denominational and even welcomed Unitarians (tensions which resulted in the formation of the Trinitarian Bible Society in 1831).[75] The following year he was 'disgusted' by a Temperance Society meeting at Exeter Hall in London, supported despite their theological disagreements by Anglicans, Roman Catholics, Independents and Baptists. Golightly observed of this alliance, 'Liberalism is making rapid strides', and Newman warned him against the Temperance Society because of its neglect of religious dogma.[76]

Nevertheless Golightly did feel some sympathy with the seceders. He agreed with them in the need to agitate for the revival of godly discipline within the church, though perhaps not drawn as tightly as they would like. He hoped for the abolition of the Establishment, which was a major theme in the sermons of Bulteel, Brenton, Lambert and others during 1830-31, though he saw more room for compromise than they.[77] Golightly also thought there was some justification for Brenton's refusal to read the funeral service over a drunkard and was tempted to follow suit in Penshurst. Yet he believed the right way to campaign for change was with the support of the bishops, not by casting them off. To Mozley, he reflected on Brenton's protest:

> My attention has been lately turned to a subject connected with it – I mean the shameful neglect of discipline in the Church. How can the Church of England expect Xt's blessing when she is living in the daily and deliberate neglect of Xt's commands? Two persons are living together in adultery in my parish and glorying in their crime, and my plain duty is after proper warning to excommunicate them. I would have no temporal disadvantage follow upon the sentence – only the parish

---

[73] Golightly to Mozley, 21 December 1831, BOA Thomas Mozley Papers.

[74] Golightly to Newman, 10 August 1831, BOA Miscellaneous Letters.

[75] On the early tensions within the British and Foreign Bible Society, see Roger H. Martin, *Evangelicals United: Ecumenical Stirrings in Pre-Victorian Britain, 1795-1830* (Metuchen, NJ, 1983), chs 5-7.

[76] Golightly – Newman, 22 May and 10 June 1832, *Newman Letters and Diaries*, iii. pp. 54-6.

[77] Stunt, 'John Henry Newman and the Evangelicals', p. 72.

should be informed that they were no longer members of the fold of Xt and that when they came to die they shd be *refused Xtian interment*. They would *feel that* and their neighbours would feel it and with God's blessing I am convinced that much good would come of it.

I assure you I have been thinking of writing to Newman on this very subject. The question is "What are we – we individual clergy – to do about it?" I answer – petition the Bishops to endeavour to effect some alteration in the Eccles[iastical] Law. If they don't choose to do it the blame lies with them – if they do and their efforts are unsuccessful the blame lies with Parliament – at least in a measure. However, I am persuaded that it will not be long before Ch[urch] and State will be separated and we shall be allowed to do as we like.[78]

Elsewhere he was encouraging his friend:

Oh my dear Mozley, let us beware of worldly conformity, and whilst we are careful, most careful, to give no needless offence, or throw any stumbling-block in the way of the reception of the Gospel but what the cross of Christ presents, let us beware of diluting God's word, or lowering the standard of religion to the practice of a wicked world.[79]

In November 1832 Golightly considered applying for the living of Deddington, a parish between Oxford and Banbury which was expected to fall vacant and was in the gift of the Dean and Canons of Windsor. He was especially attracted by the possibility of moving back nearer his Oxford friends, although on first impressions 'Deddington is a very dreary town situated in a very dreary country, and the parsonage is a very dreary, tasteless, ill-built ugly house.'[80] The existing incumbent, Richard Greaves, was an evangelical with a prominent preaching ministry and his church 'was filled Sunday after Sunday with people who admired Calvinistic doctrine from all the surrounding villages'.[81] Greaves had connections with John Hill and the more radical evangelicals at Oxford, and was part of a well-known and widespread evangelical family (though he eventually moved from his early roots towards mysticism).[82] Having been reminded by recent painful events of his disagreements with the evangelical movement, Golightly anticipated 'hot water' if he were to step into Greaves' shoes. He would be determined to abolish the annual Bible Society meeting held in the church and a prayer meeting held every Sunday ('objectionable under all circumstances but

---

[78] Golightly to Mozley, 21 December 1831, BOA Thomas Mozley Papers.
[79] Golightly to Mozley, 26 June 1829, BOA Thomas Mozley Papers.
[80] Golightly to Mozley, 26 November 1832, BOA Thomas Mozley Papers.
[81] William Wing, *Supplement to Marshall's Deddington* (Oxford, 1879), p. 3.
[82] On Greaves and his siblings, see Timothy C.F. Stunt, 'The Greaves Family: Some Clarifications', *Notes and Queries* 28 ns (October 1981), pp. 405-8; Jacqueline E.M. Latham, 'The Greaves Family: Some Corrections and Further Information', *Notes and Queries* 46 ns (March 1999), pp. 25-7; Stunt, *From Awakening to Secession*, p. 189.

especially so when, as in this case, not superintended by a clergyman'), but he knew such actions would breed hostility:

> The people of course would at once set me down as 'the Devil's Grandchild' and many of the most estimable at once join the Dissenters. I dare say that the first stone of a Dissenting meeting-house would be laid one week after the prayer-meeting was put down. Now under such discouraging circumstances nothing humanly speaking could support me but the cooperation of an efficient curate.

Golightly was also concerned that there was no one of his 'own rank of life' near Deddington – apart from Charles Baring (future bishop of Durham) at Adderbury, but Golightly viewed him with suspicion as 'a Reformer and a Low Churchman'. Without a wife or a curate or pupils, he would therefore feel isolated, stuck away in rural Oxfordshire – near, and yet still too far, from Oxford itself.[83] He invited Edward Blencowe (fellow of Oriel College) to work as his curate at Deddington, but Blencowe declined and Golightly complained to Newman:

> Consider how difficult it is in these days to meet with any young man of *real zeal* who is not Calvinistic, or who has not objections to some of the services of the Church, or some queer notions or other. In short how few young men are there of *real zeal* who care a rush *for authority* and do not think their own opinions worth as much. I do not say as those of any other individual but of the whole Church put together. This is the rock on which Newton, Brenton, and Lambert have split, and to my mind is the most painful feature of the religion of the present day. To have a person for my curate of *such a spirit* would make me wretched.[84]

Unable to find a suitable fellow-worker for Deddington, Golightly decided to remain at Penshurst. In search of a colleague on another occasion, he observed: 'Oh! for an Oxford man! Those monsters from Cambridge. Either careless or half-dissenters.'[85]

As Golightly moved progressively away from his 'radical evangelical' friends, so he remained firmly under Newman's sway. He also began to identify himself more closely with the other leaders of what was to become the 'Tractarian' movement (to give its later label).[86] For example, he claimed to know John Keble's *Christian Year* by heart, perhaps the result of regular

---

[83] Golightly to Mozley, 26 November 1832, BOA Thomas Mozley Papers.
[84] Golightly to Newman, 7 November 1832, BOA Miscellaneous Letters.
[85] Golightly to Mozley, 29 August 1834, BOA Thomas Mozley Papers. However, for Golightly's pleasure at being introduced to Charles Simeon, see Brenton to Mozley, 7 January 1828.
[86] The epithet 'Tractarian' was first coined in 1839, though other labels such as 'Tractite' were common from 1834. For the difficulties of deciding who should be called a 'Tractarian', see Peter B. Nockles, *The Oxford Movement in Context: Anglican High Churchmanship, 1760-1857* (Cambridge, 1994), pp. 36-9.

recitation. He 'devoured' Edward Pusey's *Theology of Germany* (an historical study on the causes of rationalism within German theological writing) as soon as it came out and proclaimed that he had 'never read any work, which gave me a higher opinion of its author.'[87] Later Golightly remarked to Newman, 'I cannot tell you what an influence Pusey's writings and character have had upon me'.[88] It was to be Newman, and increasingly Pusey, who were his chief role-models over the next few years.

Church in Danger

While in Penshurst, Golightly tried to stay in touch with affairs at Oxford. Non-resident members of the University maintained considerable influence through Convocation – the assembly of all MA graduates (whether living in Oxford or not) whose names were on the college books. Until the 1850s, Convocation had significant powers to enact and repeal statutes, appoint University officers and professors, and oversee major issues concerning University administration. Votes had to be cast in person and most matters of business were not considered important enough for non-residents to attend. Nevertheless, when it came to controversial issues (especially concerning the theological outlook of professors, tutors or University preachers) hundreds of MAs gathered in Oxford from around Britain to cast their votes. Golightly was present at several high-profile meetings of Convocation in the 1830s and 40s which became *causes célèbres*, and he quickly learnt to harness the power of non-residents during his theological campaigns.

One of the first minor controversies in which Golightly was involved, while still in Penshurst, was the election of Oxford's first Boden Professor of Sanskrit in March 1832. The two leading candidates were William Mill (Principal of Bishop's College, Calcutta) and H.H. Wilson.[89] Wilson had a good reputation as a scholar, but was neither a clergyman nor a University alumnus, and there were concerns about his religious opinions. It was even reported that he preferred 'the Hindu morals to those of the Gospel', and was living in India 'in a state of notorious concubinage', having had eight or nine illegitimate children with a soldier's wife.[90] Newman was concerned that Wilson might be 'a mere Liberal, and consider the Sanscrit-theology not far inferior to the Christian.'[91]

---

[87] Golightly to Mozley, 5 May 1831, BOA Thomas Mozley Papers; Golightly to Newman, 18 October 1830, *Newman Letters and Diaries*, ii. p. 295.
[88] Golightly to Newman, 3 December 1834, *Newman Letters and Diaries*, iv. p. 375.
[89] W.H. Mill, *Sanscrit Professorship. Dr Mill's Testimonials. Jan. 1832* (London, 1832); H.H. Wilson, *Sanscrit Professorship. Letter of Mr Wilson and Extracts from his Testimonials* (Oxford, 1831).
[90] Bodleian G.A. Oxon b.111 (256).
[91] Newman to John W. Bowden, 15 February 1832, *Newman Letters and Diaries*, iii. p. 16.

Golightly proudly proclaimed that he would 'come up any day against a liberal',[92] and from Penshurst canvassed support for Mill.[93] In the event Wilson was narrowly elected at Convocation by 207 votes to 200, and Mill went on to become Regius Professor of Hebrew at Cambridge.

Golightly also took an active interest in the nationwide debate during 1833 over the controversial Irish Church Temporalities Bill. Nicknamed 'the Spoliation Bill' by its detractors, it was designed to reduce the Church of Ireland by two archbishoprics and eight bishoprics, confiscating £150,000 worth of endowments. There was widespread concern at this interference of Parliament, no longer an exclusively Anglican body, in the affairs of the church. Many in Oxford protested at the bill, not least John Keble in his famous assize sermon, *National Apostasy*, which later assumed mythical status as the starting point of the Oxford Movement.[94] Golightly saw the bill as 'plainly the design of our Infernal enemy' and offered uninvited advice to Bishop Phillpotts of Exeter and Robert M'Ghee (a prominent Dublin clergyman) on how to oppose it – a foretaste of Golightly's many unsolicited letters in later years to bishops and other leading churchmen.[95] When the bill was supported by Parliament's Upper House, he lamented to Mozley:

> Could you have suspected the existence of such flagrant iniquity even in the House of Lords? Could you have expected to find such gross folly proceeding from the lips of so many clever men? ... The establishment is gone – or rather I wish it were. I do not express any fears for *that*, but what a blow to Episcopacy in England! ... Alas for the Protestant Episcopal Church (let us learn to call things by their right names) in these kingdoms.[96]

Bishop Blomfield was a prominent champion of the bill and Golightly mourned:

> The Church is in danger, imminent and immediate danger. ..., *The United Church* appears to me to be in peril chiefly from votes of so many Bishops in favour of the Bill, next from the strange apathy of most of the leading clergy, a remarkable feature of the times, and lastly from the general ignorance of first principles of Ecclesiastical Discipline common I fear to almost all the Clergy. Surely the time is come for a Dissolution of the Union between Church and State. I am anxious to see a party formed among the clergy in opposition on the one hand to the Bp of

---

[92] Newman to Henry Wilberforce, 13 February 1832, ibid., p. 14.
[93] Golightly to Newman, 6 March 1832, BOA B.12.1, fo. 154; Heurtley to Mozley, 12 May 1832, Thomas Mozley Papers.
[94] Mark D. Chapman, 'John Keble, "National Apostasy" and the Myths of 14 July' in Kirstie Blair, *John Keble in Context* (London, 2004), pp. 47-57.
[95] Golightly to Mozley, 2 August 1833, BOA Thomas Mozley Papers. See Golightly to Henry Phillpotts, 24 July 1833; Golightly to Robert M'Ghee, 1 August 1833, LPL MS 1808, fos 139-40, 212-3.
[96] Golightly to Mozley, 23 July 1833, BOA Thomas Mozley Papers.

London and his liberal friends, and on the other to those of the Evangelicals whose views or no views of Eccl[esiastical] Discipline approximate to those of the Dissenters. The Church appears to me in danger from the *union* of those two parties.[97]

From Oxford, Newman encouraged Golightly:

Surely the Church is not lost, when men like yourself show their readiness to act for it and the Lord's sake, and, even if it be lost, yet doubtless the more of its servants play a good part now, the happier for them hereafter. Let us work as knowing we shall have the reward of our labours, elsewhere if not here. ... We have everything against us but our cause. O that we had some bishops for us. The Clergy are dead. ... You can be most useful to us, but we *must* meet.[98]

To others, Newman praised Golightly's activism: 'Golightly has been very zealous in the good cause, and would undertake any thing in support of it';[99] 'G. certainly is in a ferment; and it is a curious phenomenon, to see so staid and precise a person excited, and still precise and staid in the midst of it'.[100] He reported to Hurrell Froude on Golightly's 'most excellent views', though acknowledging that they would not see exactly eye to eye:

He has some private means; and ... he intends to devote them to Apostolical purposes. He would go to Ireland, si jusseris [if you were to command]. He might be useful, tho' not persuasive, among the Evangelicals. If you see him or write, do not frighten him with *your* Apostolical views. He goes so far as to abominate the Erastianism of the Spoliation Bill, and to anathematize τοὺς περὶ βλομφήλιον [Blomfield's party]; but I know not how much further.[101]

Keble in his assize sermon warned that ecclesiastical excitement tends 'to engross the whole mind' and might ruin those who become overly-involved and neglect their ordinary duties.[102] Yet Newman did not think this applied to Golightly who was 'too regular in your habits to be *engrossed* by any thing, even by the activity of zeal.'[103] With the benefit of hindsight, Newman might have regretted giving his future antagonist such encouragement. So might his sister, Jemima, who announced her pleasure that Golightly was

alive to the dangers that surround us and that you are sufficiently at leisure to be able to devote yourself actively in the present alarming struggle. If nothing be left

---

[97] Golightly to Mozley, 2 August 1833, BOA Thomas Mozley Papers.
[98] Newman to Golightly, 30 July 1833, *Newman Letters and Diaries*, iv. pp. 13-4.
[99] Newman to John F. Christie, 6 August 1833, ibid., p. 26.
[100] Newman to Thomas Mozley, 5 August 1833, ibid., p. 24.
[101] Newman to Hurrell Froude, 1 August 1833, ibid., p. 17.
[102] John Keble, *National Apostasy* (Oxford, 1833), p. 26.
[103] Newman to Golightly, 30 July 1833, *Newman Letters and Diaries*, iv. p. 14.

but protestation, that is a duty and will be soothing to those who have done their part ...[104]

Surprisingly, given his later denials of partisanship, Golightly boldly professed to Newman: 'I trust you will find me henceforward a much more active partizan.'[105]

In August 1833, Newman wrote to Penshurst encouraging Golightly to join the society being organised in Oxford to rouse the national clergy, 'with a view to stir up our brethren to consider the state of the Church, & especially to the practical belief & preaching of the Apostolical Succession'.[106] Golightly suggested the name 'Conservative Church Society' – a telling title, again showing his inherent conservatism in matters of both politics and theology. He wanted the chief aims of the society to include Disestablishment and the revival of the Convocations of Canterbury and York, to give the Church of England full responsibility for its own affairs. With the Irish Church Temporalities Act still fresh in his mind, he protested to Newman:

> when the State takes upon herself to decide, and that without consulting the Church, how many Bishops are necessary for the superintendence of the Clergy, and the clergy are cowardly or ignorant enough to submit to her decisions, it appears to me that the time for separation is come.[107]

Returning to his favourite theme of ecclesiastical discipline, Golightly blamed the apathy of clergy in the Church of England to the plight of the Church of Ireland on 'ignorance of the very first principles of Church Discipline forgotten in days of comparative ease and security.' In particular he thought teaching on baptism, liturgy and episcopal authority had been neglected.[108] Revealing again his concern for episcopacy, church order and right doctrine, Golightly hoped to write a pamphlet entitled *Plain and Popular View of the Apostolical Succession*, but it never emerged.[109]

In September, when the first of the *Tracts for the Times* began to be published, Golightly went up from Penshurst to Oxford for conference with Newman, William Palmer (of Worcester College), Thomas Mozley, Charles

---

[104] Jemima Newman to Golightly, 30 July 1833, ibid., p. 15.
[105] Golightly to Newman, 4 November 1833, ibid., p. 85.
[106] Newman to Golightly, 11 August 1833, LPL MS 1808, fo. 184.
[107] Golightly to Newman, 22 August 1833, *Newman Letters and Diaries*, iv. pp. 29-30.
[108] Charles P. Golightly, *A Letter to the Right Reverend Father in God, Richard, Lord Bishop of Oxford, Containing Strictures upon Certain Parts of Dr Pusey's Letter to his Lordship. By a Clergyman of the Diocese, and a Resident Member of the University* (Oxford, 1840), p. 104.
[109] Golightly to James B. Mozley, 12 October 1833, BOA Thomas Mozley Papers.

Marriott (a new fellow at Oriel), William Copeland and others.[110] Although warned by Newman that the Tracts might contain sentiments in which Golightly could not concur, he contributed £50 to their production, 'under the conviction, that exact agreement in every particular of religious opinion was unattainable, and that the tendency of the publication on the whole would be beneficial, as filling up a gap in the then state of Anglican Theology.'[111] Soon the Tracts were being subscribed by a wide range of supporters from across the theological spectrum and Newman was able to inform Charles Girdlestone (a prominent evangelical clergyman in Staffordshire): 'We have been joined by persons of the most opposite sentiments, and I trust may do something towards uniting opposite parties in the Church'.[112] In his *Apologia*, Newman later claimed that he welcomed support from 'high Church or low Church; I wished to make a strong pull in union with all who were opposed to the principles of liberalism, whoever they might be.'[113]

However, Golightly could already see that this alliance was a flimsy one. In January 1834, Thomas Mozley organised a major meeting in Derby on church affairs at which Newman thought Golightly would be particularly useful, because he was 'such an imposing fellow for the Evangelicals'.[114] Yet Golightly wrote to James B. Mozley, only half in jest, prophesying that the evangelicals would discover Newman's true views soon enough and then cast him out. He observed that Newman was under the impression

> that what he is pleased to call my 'Evangelical twang' might conciliate some refractory spirits. However, possessing a lively imagination I shall picture to myself the scene, no doubt a very amusing one, of Newman and Tom labouring awkwardly to wheedle the low church party into a belief that the Apostolical Succession is the only point upon which they are not agreed! How will they set about it? Pray if any Evangelical enters into your house thrust the 'History of Arianism' [Newman's latest book] into the coal-scuttle, and just observe casually that your brother preaches extempore and Newman 'weekday lectures', only taking good care not to tell them what they preach about. However, do what you will, your Evangelicals will find them out and set them down for black sheep if they do not discover them to be wolves in sheep's clothing.[115]

Golightly's prediction proved to be all too accurate. Perhaps he had already begun to guess, though he gives no hint of it yet, that he would also someday

---

[110] Newman Diary, 16-20 September 1833; Newman to Froude, 18 September 1833, *Newman Letters and Diaries*, iv. pp. 50, 53.
[111] Golightly, *Letter to the Bishop of Oxford*, p. 105.
[112] Newman to Charles Girdlestone, 1 November 1833, *Newman Letters and Diaries*, iv. p. 79.
[113] John H. Newman, *Apologia Pro Vita Sua: Being a Reply to a Pamphlet Entitled "What, then, does Dr Newman Mean?"* (London, 1864), p. 111.
[114] Newman to Golightly, 6 January 1834, *Newman Letters and Diaries*, iv. p. 167.
[115] Golightly to James B. Mozley, 16 January 1834, BOA Thomas Mozley Papers.

conclude that Newman was a 'wolf in sheep's clothing'.

Littlemore

In October 1833 Golightly resigned from the curacy at Penshurst to look after his sick mother. His older brother had recently died of small pox, his younger brother was struggling with mental illness, and his sister had sailed to Calcutta to marry an officer in the Bengal artillery, which left him carrying the responsibility of care.[116] However, Mrs Golightly herself died in February 1834, so her son planned to return to his beloved Oxford.[117] Instead he became assistant curate that autumn at Godalming in Surrey, which he described as 'a large, neglected, and awfully wicked parish'. Having travelled around the country for much of the previous year, Golightly was pleased to be settled again, as he reported to Mozley:

> I am glad to find myself at regular work again. Nothing like it, if not for body yet for soul and spirit. It is hard to maintain any settled habits of Scriptural study or a really steady devotional spirit when moving about from place to place. My own frame of mind has suffered extremely.[118]

Golightly's boss in Godalming was 'a sad Low-Church Vicar whom I am sorry to designate by such a title as I trust he is in other respects an estimable man'. The vicar was ill and soon departed for the continent, so was replaced for a while by Golightly's friend, Alfred Menzies, a young fellow of Trinity College, Oxford and probably author of *Tract 14* (on ember days). Menzies was dead within eighteen months, but not before he and Golightly had set about making their parishioners 'Christians and Christian Churchmen'.[119] Golightly remained at Godalming for only a year. He managed to resist suggestions from John Tucker, an old family friend working with CMS near Madras, that he go out as a missionary to India.[120] Yet when Newman offered him the curacy of Littlemore, a village just south of Oxford, it was too good to refuse.

By quirk of medieval history, Littlemore was a neglected part of the parish of St Mary-the-Virgin in Oxford, of which Newman became vicar in November

---

[116] Christie to Thomas Mozley, nd [1833]; Golightly to Thomas Mozley, 15 July 1833; Golightly to James B. Mozley 12 October 1833, BOA Thomas Mozley Papers. For his sister's letters of courtship from her army officer, see George T. Graham to Frances M. Golightly, 1831-34, Cossington MSS.
[117] Christie to Mozley, 12 March 1834, BOA Thomas Mozley Papers.
[118] Golightly to Mozley, 29 August 1834, BOA Thomas Mozley Papers
[119] Golightly to Mozley, 30 September 1834, BOA Thomas Mozley Papers. For Newman's visit to Godalming, see Newman to Jemima Newman, 25 September 1834, *Newman Letters and Diaries*, iv. pp. 333-4. For the Godalming vicar, see Mozley, *Reminiscences Chiefly of Oriel College and the Oxford Movement*, ii. p. 111.
[120] John Tucker to Golightly, 24 February 1835, LPL MS 1811, fos 1-2.

1828. He soon had plans to make it a separate parish, with a chapel of its own, and tried to find a curate to take responsibility for the settlement. Both Robert Wilberforce and Hurrell Froude turned it down,[121] and in January 1830 Golightly (then still based in Oxford preparing for ordination) had resolved to accept the curacy if Newman could find no one else.[122] Instead the post went to J.A. Gower (chaplain of Magdalen College), who remained only a few months, and it was then refused by Edward Blencowe.[123] Some stability was provided by Isaac Williams, who in the spring of 1832 became Newman's curate at St Mary's with responsibility for Littlemore.

In April 1835 Oriel College (patrons of the parish) agreed to provide a site for a chapel in Littlemore and the foundation stone was laid on 21 July. Golightly was one of the contributors to the building project and Newman offered him the curacy, which was immediately accepted.[124] Yet Golightly wanted to be sure this was a secure position and asked:

> The curate I suppose would not be expected to reside there; and you would not send me about my business for anything short of heresy, e.g. if I were to become (not a Calvinist, for that I conceive humanly speaking impossible) but a follower of St Augustine; not that I have at present any leaning that way: – and again that your successor would not be likely to turn me out. ... I am very anxious that I should be in my next station a fixture. A rolling stone gathers no moss. I should feel but little interest in a parish which I might be called upon suddenly to leave. ... Nothing would give me so much pleasure as to take a new Church. My head is full of plans for Littlemore.[125]

Three weeks later Golightly was having second thoughts about whether he and Newman were in sufficient theological agreement, particularly over the question of baptism and new birth, to be able to work together. He wrote to Newman:

> ... do you think that you are acting quite prudently in offering Littlemore to one of whose religious sentiments you know nothing except from casual conversation, and whom you never heard preach in your life? How do you know that you would like my sermons? You indeed are not likely to hear them, but supposing that some fine day Mrs Newman and your sisters [living at Rose Hill, near Littlemore] should, and then the next time they saw you, say, 'Oh John what a peculiar [Golightly's copy of this letter reads 'Evangelical'[126]] you have got at Littlemore.

---

[121] Newman – Wilberforce, 6 and 7 September 1829; Newman – Froude, 11 and 27 September 1829, *Newman Letters and Diaries*, ii. pp. 162-5.

[122] Golightly to Mozley, 12 January 1830, BOA Thomas Mozley Papers.

[123] Newman to J.A. Gower, 1829; Newman – Bagot, 1 and 5 February 1830; Blencowe to Newman, 6 September 1830, *Newman Letters and Diaries*, ii. pp. 194-5, 287.

[124] Newman to Golightly, 30 April 1835, *Newman Letters and Diaries*, v. p. 63.

[125] Golightly to Newman, 5 May 1835, BOA Miscellaneous Letters.

[126] LPL MS 1946, fo. 17.

He certainly preached last Sunday what we thought tantamount to the total corruption of human nature, and told us that we should search and examine ourselves as to whether we were "born again". In short his sermons in tone and spirit are very different to what yours are.'

Now I certainly might express myself on these and other subjects in a way you might not like. I do believe most firmly that O[ur] S[aviour]'s Baptism is the Baptism of the Spirit *generally* (with possible exceptions I have nothing to do) and that congregations are to be addressed as St Paul addresses the Corinthians – 'What, know ye not that ye are the temples of God, and that the Spirit of God dwelleth in you?' But then I conceive that the principle of divine grace is in too many persons so apparently inoperative that we are justified in calling upon them to search and examine themselves whether they have the Sp[irit] of God or not. ...

Again if I am responsible minister at Littlemore I should certainly wish to act upon my own plans – rather I should say that I could not engage to act upon yours at least without knowing before I settle there what they are. You mentioned the other day Baptism by Immersion if parents would consent, and I think frequent Communion. I would gladly adopt either of these; but could you name any others?

Now I think, my dear Newman, that on so important a subject we cannot be too plain with one another. ... Would you like me to put into your hands two or three of my Sermons? *I offer you every satisfaction.* No two persons who think for themselves think alike on all subjects. But the question is, Do our sentiments sufficiently coincide for you to feel justified in entrusting part of your parish to me? Now if when I am established at Littlemore you come to an opposite conclusion you would probably think it your duty to turn me out, which I should not like – nor should I like staying if you disapproved of my ministry. I should much like to be your curate if you take me with your eyes open but I have written this letter to be sure whether they are.[127]

Golightly's preaching about baptism and new birth was the very issue over which the two men clashed a year later, putting an end to their relationship. Golightly never did begin work as Littlemore's curate. His letter to Newman was almost prophetic – except that in the event it was Pusey who heard his suspect sermon, not Mrs Newman and her daughters. At the time, however, Newman brushed away his concerns. Indeed in his *Apologia* he used Golightly's appointment as an example of how he chose colleagues without concern for 'intimate agreement of opinion'.[128]

Therefore in October 1835 Golightly acquired a house in Oxford (No.6 Holywell Street), which he was to occupy for the next 46 years.[129] On discovering that the building occupied the site of an old tavern called the 'The Cardinal's Hat', he adopted that name for his house and painted a cardinal's hat

---

[127] Golightly to Newman, 26 May 1835, BOA Miscellaneous Letters.

[128] Newman, *Apologia Pro Vita Sua*, p. 135.

[129] In the 1850s Golightly added 7 Holywell Street: compare 1851 and 1861 census returns; HO 107/1728, fo. 45; RG 9/893, fo. 106.

over the lintel – a surprising choice, given his strong anti-Catholicism.[130] With clear self-knowledge and insight into his personal moral struggles, he explained to his friend Mozley why he was concerned at living back in the University city:

> I feel that it is a very critical time with me. Every place has its dangers and temptations; but those of Oxford I consider to be of a very peculiar character, though it has also peculiar advantages – the greatest perhaps being the opportunities afforded us of daily public prayer. But alas! how great is the danger of our lapsing into formality, of our being blinded by party feeling to important truth, of *'sins of the tongue'. Here is my great danger* – Unkind and bitter speaking of others, magnifying their blemishes, over-looking their good qualities, needlessly exposing their faults. Oh! could we bear in mind that awful declaration of St James: 'If any man seem to be religious and bridleth not his tongue, that man's religion is vain.'[131]

It was from Holywell Street that many of Golightly's campaigns against Tractarians, ritualists and theological liberals were carefully planned in succeeding decades. His home became the venue for numerous crisis meetings and councils of war amongst Oxford's Protestants. Isaac Williams wrote that Golightly 'was strongly with us, had taken a house in Oxford in which he said he should hide us when persecution arose; but he soon himself became our chief persecutor ... the active watcher and accuser against Church principles'.[132] Years later Newman recalled: 'Without me Golightly would not have come to Oxford, and he was my chief slanderer.'[133]

The Widening Breach

Before Golightly had been back in Oxford a couple of months, deep disagreement with his 'Tractarian' friends and mentors began to show. He was invited to attend meetings of the Theological Society newly established by Pusey, but their doctrinal divergence became increasingly obvious.[134]

The first clash came over Newman's book, *The Arians of the Fourth*

---

[130] The tavern may have been called 'The Cardinal's Cap' or 'The Cardinal's Head': Burgon, *Lives of Twelve Good Men*, i. p. xxvii. There is no further evidence, however, for Thomas Mozley's claim that Golightly visited cardinals at Rome or had a 'lurking tenderness for Cardinals': Mozley, *Reminiscences Chiefly of Oriel College and the Oxford Movement*, ii. p. 109.

[131] Golightly to Mozley, 9 October 1835, BOA Thomas Mozley Papers.

[132] *The Autobiography of Isaac Williams* edited by Sir George Prevost (London, 1892), pp. 100-1.

[133] John H. Newman, *Autobiographical Writings* edited by Henry Tristram (London, 1956), p. 267.

[134] H.P. Liddon, *Life of Edward Bouverie Pusey* edited by J.O. Johnston and R.J. Wilson (4 vols, London, 1893-97), i. p. 337.

Century, a work of historical theology and a thinly-veiled attacked upon the liberalism of the day.[135] Yet what troubled Golightly was Newman's discussion of the *disciplina arcani* (secret discipline) of the early church, otherwise known as the principle of 'economy' or 'reserve'.[136] According to Newman's historical analysis, before catechumens were received into the church by baptism the central truths of the gospel were held back from them. As they prepared over several years to be admitted into full discipleship so their instruction progressed, 'advancing from the most simple principles of natural religion to the peculiar doctrines of the Gospel, from moral truths to the Christian mysteries.'[137] In other words, those outside the church were only taught general ideas about God's existence and the moral law, while the deeper mysteries of salvation – the Trinity, the Incarnation and the Atonement – were reserved until after baptism. Newman contrasted this polemically with the contemporary evangelical practice of preaching about the cross of Christ to all and sundry, pointedly quoting the command of Christ not to cast pearls before swine.[138]

One of the dominant themes in Golightly's writings is a rebuke of duplicity and deceit. He used to teach children the ditty 'Better to die – than to tell a lie' and Bishop Knox reflected that 'above all his characteristics he was distinguished by hatred of falsehood'.[139] On one occasion Golightly tried to prevent the ordination of an undergraduate from St Edmund's Hall who was shown to be 'a liar and an imposter' forging love-letters to impress his friends.[140] Therefore Newman's recommendation of 'economy' with the gospel truths was worrying and Golightly admitted it was a 'shock to his confidence in him'.[141] In particular he highlighted Newman's statement in *The Arians* that Clement of Alexandria 'accurately describes the rules which should guide the Christian in speaking and acting economically. ... He both thinks and speaks the truth; except when consideration is necessary, and then, as a physician for the good of his patients, he will be false, or utter a falsehood'.[142] Golightly lamented: 'Woe worth the Church of England in the day that shall see this

---

[135] Stephen Thomas, *Newman and Heresy: The Anglican Years* (Cambridge, 1991), ch. 2.

[136] For Newman on 'economy', see Raymond Chapman, *The Tractarian Principle of Reserve* (PhD thesis, London University, 1978); Robin C. Selby, *The Principle of Reserve in the Writings of John Henry Cardinal Newman* (Oxford, 1975).

[137] John H. Newman, *The Arians of the Fourth Century, their Doctrine, Temper, and Conduct, Chiefly as Exhibited in the Councils of the Church, between A.D. 325 & A.D. 381* (London, 1833), p. 49.

[138] Ibid., pp. 50-2.

[139] Knox, *Tractarian Movement*, p. 252; Burgon, *Lives of Twelve Good Men*, i. p. xxvi.

[140] Mozley, *Reminiscences Chiefly of Oriel College and the Oxford Movement*, i. pp. 245-6.

[141] Golightly, *Position of Samuel Wilberforce*, p. 83.

[142] Newman, *Arians*, p. 81.

system adopted either into the teaching or the conduct of her ministers!'[143] He compared St Clement's 'most objectionable sentiment' unfavourably with St Paul's proclamation in Scripture: 'We have renounced the hidden things of dishonesty, not walking in craftiness, nor handling the Word of God deceitfully; but by manifestation of the truth, commending ourselves to every man's conscience in the sight of God' (2 Corinthians 4.2).[144]

First Golightly remonstrated in person with Newman, but was fobbed off with a joke: 'I abandon Clemens Alexandrinus to your tender mercies'.[145] Since Newman would not listen, he then did his best to alert others in Oxford to this suspect teaching. Golightly showed the passage in question to Arthur Perceval (author of three of the Tracts), who apparently turned away in disgust with the words, 'Oh! very bad indeed, many of the fathers use such language, and that is how the Jesuits justify their use of pious frauds.'[146] In December 1835 Froude heard that Golightly had 'rebelled', but Newman played down the disagreement:

> As to our being out of joint here, no. Golius would not goliare or γολίζειν, i.e. be golius, unless he acted as he did. At present he goes about declaiming against my patronage of Clem. Alex – my incaution – my strange sayings so very unsatisfactory – such a pity as hurting my influence etc. He is such, as to take a key stone for an excrescence and insist on its removal.[147]

When the theological trajectory of the Tractarian movement later became known, Golightly concluded that Newman's adoption of the principle of 'economy' had led him to practice 'systematic disingenuousness'.[148] He saw a direct line of development to Newman's notorious *Tract 90* and to Isaac Williams' *Tract 80* on *Reserve in Communicating Religious Knowledge*.[149] Newman's dishonesty was a theme to which he regularly returned in his polemical writings in subsequent years.

After criticising Newman's *Arians*, Golightly began to criticise the *Tracts*

---

[143] Golightly, *Letter to the Bishop of Oxford*, p. 87.

[144] Charles P. Golightly, *New and Strange Doctrines Extracted from the Writings of Mr Newman and His Friends, in a Letter to the Rev. W.F. Hook* (Oxford, 1841), pp. 16-8.

[145] Golightly, *Position of Samuel Wilberforce*, p. 84; Golightly to Pusey, 17 May 1836, LPL MS 1808, fo. 220.

[146] *Morning Herald*, 13 January 1843. It was William Palmer (of Worcester College) who first introduced Golightly to Perceval in 1835 as 'a very pleasing intelligent person … a man of good fortune & respectable connexions': Palmer to Perceval, 29 January 1835, PHL LBV 14/13.

[147] Newman – Froude, 21 and 24 December 1835, *Newman Letters and Diaries*, v. pp. 184-5.

[148] John H. Browne to Golightly, 8 November 1842, LPL MS 1804, fo. 98.

[149] Golightly, *Position of Samuel Wilberforce*, p. 84; Golightly, *Letter to the Bishop of Oxford*, pp. 79-87; Golightly, *New and Strange Doctrines*, pp. 16-9.

for the Times themselves. He found little with which to disagree in the early publications and admitted that the Tracts were 'the instruments of recalling public attention to much valuable but neglected truth'.[150] He especially admired Pusey's *Tract 18* (promoting fasting) and Froude's *Tract 9* (against the shortening of church services) and *Tract 59* (against state interference in church matters).[151] Golightly acknowledged that the Tracts had done good in proclaiming that the Church was not 'a creature of the State' but 'a divinely-constituted Society', yet soon concluded that this advantage was outweighed by their 'doctrinal errors'.[152] In particular he believed that the Tracts' teaching on the atonement, the sacraments, sin after baptism and justification was 'sadly fallen from the truth'.[153]

Golightly was especially vocal in his objections to Pusey's teaching on sin after baptism in *Tract 68* on *Scriptural Views of Holy Baptism*, issued in September 1835. In the second of a series of three lengthy tracts on this topic, running to a total of almost 300 pages, Pusey claimed that there was 'no account in Scripture of any second remission, obliteration, extinction of all sin, such as is bestowed on us by "the one Baptism for the remission of sins"'.[154] Sins committed before baptism were automatically washed away by the sacrament, but Pusey insisted that it was much more difficult to obtain forgiveness for sins committed after baptism:

> The fountain has been indeed opened to wash away sin and uncleanness, but we dare not promise men a second time the same easy access to it, which they once had: that way is open but once: it were to abuse the power of the keys entrusted to us, again to pretend to admit them thus: now there remains only the 'Baptism of tears', a Baptism obtained, as the same fathers said, with much fasting, and with many prayers.[155]

These views ran directly counter to contemporary evangelical teaching, which explained that forgiveness of sins was always available for those who truly repented and put their faith in Christ, whether before or after baptism. Pusey's advocacy of a 'baptism of tears' pointed instead to the doctrine of penance, which had been abolished from the Church of England at the time of the Reformation. Critics from across the theological spectrum assailed the Tract's teaching on sin after baptism for undermining the doctrine of justification by faith alone and placing the emphasis upon the works of the sinner (such as

---

[150] *Oxford Herald*, 1 January 1842; Golightly, *Letter to the Bishop of Oxford*, p. 103.
[151] Golightly to Newman, 9 February 1837, BOA Miscellaneous Letters.
[152] *Oxford Herald*, 6 February 1841.
[153] Charles P. Golightly, *Strictures on No.90 of the Tracts for the Times. By a Member of the University of Oxford* (2 parts, Oxford, 1841), part 2, p. 90.
[154] Edward B. Pusey, *Scriptural Views of Holy Baptism* (Tract 68) (London, 1835), p. 54.
[155] Ibid., p. 59.

fasting and prayer) rather than on the works of Christ as sufficient for salvation. It led some early supporters of the Tracts, like F.D. Maurice and Samuel Wilberforce, to distance themselves permanently from the movement.[156]

Golightly was not slow to make his own criticisms known. He complained privately to Pusey that this doctrine was 'utterly subversive of the comfort of a Xtian and putting him in a much worse situation than either the Roman Catholic or the Jew.'[157] In later years he returned to the theme, complaining publicly to the Bishop of Oxford that Pusey was propagating modern-day Novatianism, a revival of the third century rigorist sect who refused to readmit lapsed Christians to fellowship.[158] Golightly believed Pusey's erroneous views about forgiveness were 'calculated to break many a bruised reed' and warned in the *Oxford Herald*: 'I greatly fear that the cause of true religion will be found in the long run to have suffered very seriously at the hands of Dr Pusey and his friends.'[159] His summary of the general thrust of the *Tracts for the Times* was that they tended 'to interfere with the character of the Gospel as a message of Reconciliation, and to throw clouds of darkness around the path of the sinner returning to his God.'[160]

On 31 January 1836 Pusey reiterated his teaching on sin after baptism in a sermon at Christ Church cathedral.[161] The sermon caused something of a stir and although Golightly was not present, he soon heard about it second-hand and began to criticise Pusey in public.[162] Newman told John Christie (another fellow of Oriel): 'Golightly is making himself a great I won't say what. He is going about prosing against Pusey's Sermon – this is worse than his anti-clementismus.'[163] To Pusey, Golightly admitted:

> I must plead guilty to having objected to *your sermon* as often as I heard it mentioned in conversation, and that was *very often indeed* during the first fortnight after its delivery. It excited as you know a great deal of attention. I may

---

[156] F.D. Maurice, *The Kingdom of Christ: or Hints on the Principles, Ordinances, and Constitution of the Catholic Church* (3 vols, London, 1837-38), i. pp. 91-103; Olive J. Brose, *Frederick Denison Maurice: Rebellious Conformist* (Ohio, 1971), pp. 117-32; 'The Penal Consequence of Sin' in Samuel Wilberforce, *Sermons Preached before the University of Oxford, in St Mary's Church, in the Years MDCCCXXXVII, MDCCCXXXVIII, MDCCCXXXIX* (London, 1839), ch. 2.
[157] Golightly to Pusey, 1 February 1837, PHL PUS 127.
[158] Golightly, *Letter to the Bishop of Oxford*, p. 53.
[159] *Oxford Herald*, 6 February 1841. See also Golightly, *Letter to the Bishop of Oxford*, p. 105; Arthur Perceval in *British Magazine* 15 (May 1839), p. 538.
[160] Golightly, *Letter to the Bishop of Oxford*, pp. 105-6.
[161] Mozley, *Reminiscences Chiefly of Oriel College and the Oxford Movement*, ii. pp. 146-9.
[162] Golightly to Philip S. Dodd, 13 February 1836, LPL MS 1805, fo. 127.
[163] Newman to Christie, 14 February 1836, *Newman Letters and Diaries*, v. p. 234.

also have questioned your judgment in advocating such a doctrine, but in no other way can I ever be said to bear a word agt you.[164]

These were signs of an ever widening breach between Golightly and his former friends. It was increasingly evident that their relationships might not stand the strain. In the short term, however, they were reunited by a common foe. Pusey's controversial sermon was suddenly eclipsed by the Hampden controversy.

The Hampden Controversy

During 1834 and 1835 there was increasing political pressure to allow Dissenters into England's ancient universities by abolishing subscription to the Thirty-Nine Articles at matriculation and graduation. In Oxford the campaign was led by one of the Oriel 'noetics', Professor R.D. Hampden who published *Observations on Religious Dissent*, boldly advocating the removal of all doctrinal tests, a work described by Peter Nockles as 'the first breach in Oxford's hitherto united front against her external liberal assailants'.[165] Dozens of pamphlets flowed from the press, many of which attacked Hampden's opinions, such as Henry Wilberforce's *The Foundation of the Faith Assailed in Oxford* and Newman's *Tract 73* (*On the Introduction of Rationalist Principles into Revealed Religion*).[166] However, Hampden's proposals won favour at the Hebdomadal Board, the University's executive body made up of the Heads of Houses, and they planned to substitute a simple test of conformity to the Church of England in place of subscription to the Articles. This radical measure provoked stiff resistance, co-ordinated from Pusey's rooms at Christ Church. Non-resident members of the University were summoned to Convocation in May 1835, where the measure was decisively thrown out by 459 votes to 57.

The following year there was uproar again when Hampden was appointed Regius Professor of Divinity by Lord Melbourne's Whig government, on the death of Professor Burton.[167] The *Standard* saw Hampden's nomination as further progress on 'the march of religious liberalism',[168] and declared: 'The

---

[164] Golightly to Pusey, 17 May 1836, LPL MS 1808, fo. 218.
[165] Peter B. Nockles, '"Lost Causes and ... Impossible Loyalties": The Oxford Movement and the University' in M.G. Brock and M.C. Curthoys (eds.), *The History of the University of Oxford*, vol. 6 *Nineteenth-Century Oxford, Part 1* (Oxford, 1997), p. 215.
[166] Thomas, *Newman and Heresy*, chs 7-11.
[167] For a detailed account of this affair and its background, see David W. Heughins, *R.D. Hampden and the 'Oxford Malignants'; The Hampden Controversy of 1836* (PhD thesis, Minnesota University, 1983). For the connection between the Whig government and the Oriel noetics, see Richard Brent, *Liberal Anglican Politics: Whiggery, Religion, and Reform 1830-1841* (Oxford, 1987), chs 4-5.
[168] *Standard*, 10 February 1836.

Church of England is outraged, insulted, and endangered, by this most scandalous appointment'.[169] Likewise, *John Bull* warned:

> The question now is, whether the established religion of the country shall, or shall not be, CHRISTIANITY. The question now is, not of pounds, or shillings, or pence, of tithes, or rates, or property; but whether infidelity, liberalism, German rationalism, scepticism, and BLASPHEMY, shall or shall not be publicly taught under the KING's authority, and, in his Royal name, to the rising generation of our Clergy.[170]

Now on site in Oxford, Golightly was actively involved behind the scenes in the resistance to Hampden's appointment over the next three months, gaining firsthand experience of extensive theological controversy. The lessons he learnt in 1836 were to stand him in good stead for his campaigns in years to come. It was perhaps the Hampden affair which gave him his first real taste of ecclesiastical dispute. The irony is that Golightly was trained in the best methods of agitation under the tutelage of Pusey, who took a leading role in the affair. Although the fissure between the two men had begun to show, they worked side by side during this crisis – Golightly often acting as the 'runner' who helped turn Pusey's strategy into practical action.

Debate centred upon Hampden's Bampton Lectures of 1832, entitled *The Scholastic Philosophy considered in its relation to Christian Theology*, in which he attempted to distinguish between Christian dogma and Scriptural truth. It was rumoured that the ideas for the lectures had been supplied by the Spanish theologian, Blanco White, who had recently defected to Unitarianism.[171] One critic later spoke of Hampden's 'theological monstrosities', propagated by 'a Church-hating Liberalism, and under the smiles of a Church-destroying Ministry.'[172] Pusey warned against Hampden's 'Sabellian and indefinite teaching' concerning the doctrine of the Trinity and described his Bampton Lectures and the Christian faith as 'two opposite systems, which cannot stand together: the one must ultimately destroy the other, in any Church, wherein both are entertained'.[173] Golightly, who wrote regular bulletins on the controversy for his uncle back in Penshurst, declared: 'The battle we have been fighting has been against the first attempt which has been made to introduce the German system of Theology into England.'[174]

---

[169] *Standard*, 20 February 1836.
[170] *John Bull*, 6 March 1836, p. 76.
[171] Martin Murphy, *Blanco White: Self-banished Spaniard* (New Haven and London, 1989), p. 155.
[172] *Oxford Herald*, 27 August 1842.
[173] Benjamin Harrison, *Dr Hampden's Theological Statements and the Thirty-Nine Articles Compared. By a Resident Member of Convocation. With a Preface* [by E.B. Pusey] *and Propositions Extracted from his Works* (Oxford, 1836), pp. viii, xix.
[174] Golightly to Dodd, 1 March 1836, LPL MS 1805, fo. 129.

However, as Hampden's supporters pointed out, his Bamptons had never been censured at the time, and he had subsequently been appointed both Principal of St Mary Hall and Professor of Moral Philosophy. His opponents responded that the lectures were of such 'length, stupidity, and obscurity', that to have condemned them before would only have increased their circulation.[175] Indeed Arthur Stanley (undergraduate of Balliol College and future Dean of Westminster) thought Hampden had 'the most extraordinary faculty of writing obscurely that any man ever had.'[176]

Unofficial news of Hampden's appointment quickly leaked out. At Oxford on 8 February 1836 a letter was seen at the Post Office addressed to him from Melbourne, which was guessed to be an offer of the vacant Professorship.[177] Owen Chadwick suggests that if the University had been presented with a *fait accompli*, subsequent events would have been different, but a rumour, not yet final, allowed for agitation.[178] Two days later about thirty people met in the Common Room of Corpus Christi College, the first of many meetings to be held there over the next three months, and agreed a protest to King William, to be sent via Archbishop Howley of Canterbury.[179] The *Morning Chronicle* thought Hampden's enemies were 'disgracing themselves by an exhibition of party spirit, of calumnious misrepresentation, of vindictive persecution, which has rarely been matched in the annals of ecclesiastical misdoings.'[180] Yet his opponents insisted they were 'contending, not for party or personal pre-eminence; but for a grand, a vital, and an all-important *principle*.'[181]

Immediately apparent in the controversy was an intertwining of theological and political motivations. Some saw the agitation as a 'torrent of Ecclesiastical Toryism',[182] an attempt to attack Lord Melbourne and the Whigs via Oxford's Regius Professor. For example, the *Leamington Chronicle* declared: 'Under the profession of religious zeal, and an earnest contending for the faith, a political object has been attempted – the sacred character of the Ministry has been dragged into the troubled waters of political agitation – and the name of Jehovah has been prostituted to party purposes.'[183] Likewise an observer writing in the *Globe* (a 'Whig' newspaper) rebuked 'that rancorous spirit

---

[175] J.B. Mozley to Maria Mozley, 13 February 1836, in *Letters of the Rev. J.B. Mozley* edited by Anne Mozley (London, 1885), p. 51.

[176] Arthur P. Stanley to Mary Stanley, nd [1836], OCL Hampden Papers, no. 327.

[177] Hawkins to Whately, 18 February 1836, OCL Miscellaneous Letters, vol. 5, no. 413; Lord Melbourne to Hampden, 10 February 1836, OCL Hampden Papers, no. 25.

[178] Chadwick, *Victorian Church*, i. p. 114.

[179] Golightly to Dodd, 9 February 1836, LPL MS 1805, fo. 125.

[180] *Morning Chronicle*, 21 March 1836.

[181] *Strictures on an Article in the Edinburgh Review; Entitled, 'The Oxford Malignants and Dr Hampden', with Some Observations on the Present State of the Hampden Controversy. By a Member of Convocation* (Oxford, 1836), p. 26.

[182] *Leamington Chronicle*, 17 March 1836.

[183] *Leamington Chronicle*, 24 March 1836.

which, under the cloak of zeal for orthodoxy, conceals the fiercest political hatred against the present cabinet.'[184] However, Hampden's antagonists strongly repudiated the suggestion that they were motivated by party politics. The *Standard* (a 'Tory' newspaper) insisted that the dispute cut across Whig and Tory party lines.[185] Similarly, *John Bull* proclaimed: 'The question is not, whether a man be Whig or Tory – is he a Christian? Is he a Trinitarian?'[186] When the affair was over, Samuel Wilberforce concluded: 'whatever people may say ... there was no political feeling in the matter. It was loose Churchmen against sound Churchmen whatever their politics'.[187] Yet the common cause certainly drew together a wide variety of people, from diverse theological and political backgrounds. Perhaps Baden Powell, who had close connections to the Oriel noetics, offers the best summary of the temporary and fragile alliance:

> The maintenance of the Church, – the denunciation of Socinianism, – the support of the orthodox faith, – create rallying points for numberless partisans, who neither adopt nor even at all apprehend the extreme principles of their leaders; while motives of a different kind operate upon others; – and thus the ranks of the opponents of Dr Hampden *and* the present ministry; – of neologism and whiggery; – of heresy and reform, – are swelled by innumerable recruits of a strange variety of classes and complexions.[188]

Lord Melbourne initially balked at persevering with the appointment, but decided to do so 'for the sake of the principles of toleration & free enquiry', and on 20 February it was formally gazetted.[189] Three days later Golightly met with Pusey to discuss the best form of opposition. Pusey wanted to request the Vice-Chancellor to appoint six Doctors of Divinity to scrutinise Hampden's Bampton Lectures, but feared Hampden might retaliate against his recent sermon on 'sin after baptism'. It might in any case have been difficult to find six DDs who would willingly become embroiled in the dispute. Therefore Pusey concluded: 'Well, let us call another meeting then in Corpus Common Room and be guided by their decision as to the course to pursue ... Only see that members of Convocation have due notice of it that a sufficient number of persons be got together'. Golightly immediately set about 'to concoct the necessary measures', and inform as many people within the University as

---

[184] *Globe*, 16 February 1836.
[185] *Standard*, 18 March 1836.
[186] *John Bull*, 28 February 1836, p. 68.
[187] Wilberforce to Charles Anderson, 31 May 1836, Bodleian MS Wilberforce d.21, fo. 44.
[188] Baden Powell, *Remarks on a Letter from the Rev. H.A. Woodgate to Viscount Melbourne, Relative to the Appointment of Dr Hampden* (Oxford, 1836), p. 3. For Powell's relationship with the 'noetics', see Pietro Corsi, *Science and Religion: Baden Powell and the Anglican Debate, 1800-1860* (Cambridge, 1988), chs 7-10.
[189] Melbourne to Hampden, 13 February 1836, OCL Hampden Papers, no. 28.

possible.[190]

When Hampden's opponents came together again at Corpus, they agreed to ask the Hebdomadal Board to recommend that bishops allow ordination candidates to attend the lectures of the Lady Margaret Professor of Divinity instead of the Regius Professor, because they had no confidence in his doctrinal opinions.[191] Many were content to settle for this petition, but with rumours circulating that Melbourne was about to make Hampden a bishop, a bolder protest seemed necessary.[192] Therefore they also asked that Convocation be given 'an opportunity of disavowing and condemning the evil principles and doctrines' in his works.[193] Vaughan Thomas (chaplain of Corpus) pointed out the precedent from 1690 of Convocation's action against Arthur Bury (Rector of Exeter College) whose book *The Naked Gospel* was found to contain heretical statements and burnt publicly in the quadrangle of the Schools.[194]

However, the Hebdomadal Board remained intransigent and the *Standard* insinuated that the Heads had been bribed by the Whig government with promises of bishoprics.[195] A further meeting at Corpus discussed a memorial to the Heads drafted by Edward Greswell (fellow of Corpus), but most felt that it was 'too much expressed in the language of menace'.[196] Instead they tried to apply personal pressure to individual members of the Board. At Pusey's request, Golightly visited fourteen colleges, persuading friends in each society to deliver to its Head a sheet of suspicious quotations from Hampden laid out in parallel with the Thirty-Nine Articles.[197] Further meetings at Corpus were followed by further public appeals, with little effect.[198] A small committee, consisting of Vaughan Thomas, John Hill, Pusey, Newman, Greswell and William Sewell (fellow of Exeter College) also promised to extract heretical statements from Hampden's writings.[199] Once again Golightly took upon

---

[190] Golightly to Dodd, 1 March 1836, LPL MS 1805, fo. 128.
[191] Bodleian, Bliss B.213 (15).
[192] *Standard*, 24 February 1836.
[193] Bodleian, Bliss B.213 (16). See also Hill Diary, 24-25 February 1836, Bodleian MS St Edmund Hall 67/10.
[194] *Oxford Herald*, 11 June 1842. See also *Latitudinarianism in Oxford in 1690, A Page from the Life of Bishop Bull* (Oxford, 1835).
[195] *Standard*, 1 March 1836.
[196] Hill Diary, 1 March 1836, Bodleian MS St Edmund Hall 67/10.
[197] Golightly to Dodd, 5 March 1836, LPL MS 1805, fos 132-3.
[198] Bodleian, Bliss B.213 (21) and (22).
[199] Hill Diary, 9 March 1836, Bodleian MS St Edmund Hall 67/10. William Palmer (of Worcester College) and one of Greswell's brothers (probably Richard Greswell) were also proposed for the committee, but declined. For Palmer's prominent involvement, see *A Letter to His Grace the Archbishop of Canterbury, Explanatory of the Proceedings at Oxford, on the Appointment of the Present Regius Professor of Divinity. By a Member of the University of Oxford ... With a Letter to the Corpus Committee, by Jortin Redivivus* (third edition, London, 1836), p. 13.

himself the responsibility to ensure that this idea led to practical results. Working feverishly behind the scenes, he declared himself 'quite exhausted ... having been extremely earnest to procure *this pledge* by going in person to the various members of the committee and assuring them of its absolute necessity lest by further protraction of this vexatious business those who have attended our meetings should be worn out and our means of opposing Dr Hampden be exhausted.'[200] Still only in his twenties, Golightly clearly derived pleasure from this close contact with senior men, which gave him a feeling of significance. Although he did not play a vocal part in the Corpus meetings, he was able to dedicate all his energies to the affair, as he reported to his uncle:

> Having had the entire command of my time, and a very large acquaintance in the University of course I have not been idle. I should have been wanting in my duty if I had. But I have made it a rule never to put myself forward at any of our public meetings. On such occasions I have not spoken one word. If I have had any suggestion to offer it has been to some one of older standing than myself who if he thought proper has brought it forward and I have been urgent with those over whom I have any influence of my own standing to let our seniors speak ...[201]

Although he did not speak at the meetings, Golightly had the ear of Pusey and other major players. He also became familiar with a wide range of people across the University, observing: 'Among the singular effects produced by this continued excitement, and frequent public meetings one has been that every body has become acquainted with every body – I myself appear to know half the University.'[202] These personal relationships were to prove of great benefit in later years when he relied on Oxford friends and acquaintances to support his anti-Tractarian campaigns or to supply him with information about Tractarian activities.

Although evangelicals like John Hill were active in opposing Hampden, the prominent role of Pusey and Newman meant that the Tract writers became an obvious target for pro-Hampden polemic. Sewell was also known to be sympathetic to the Tractarian cause. It was asked of these three: 'Are they safe guides to a Protestant public? ... And yet these are the persons who are endeavouring to give the law of orthodoxy to the University!'[203] The report of the Corpus Common Room committee declared that Hampden's publications tended to subvert 'the whole fabric and reality of Christian truth', but it also spoke of 'Christ's Holy Catholic Church' and of 'our ancestors in the faith'.[204] This led Nicholas Wiseman (rector of the English College at Rome and later

---

[200] Golightly to Dodd, 8 March 1836, LPL MS 1805, fo. 135.
[201] Golightly to Dodd, 1 March 1836, LPL MS 1805, fo. 131.
[202] Golightly to Dodd, 8 March 1836, LPL MS 1805, fo. 135.
[203] *Specimens of the Theological Teaching of Certain Members of the Corpus Committee at Oxford* (London, 1836), p. 4.
[204] Bodleian, Bliss B.213 (5), pp. 2, 5-6.

cardinal-archbishop of Westminster) to mock: 'Is this Oxford or Salamanca that speaks? Is it Corpus Christi College or the Sorbonne? ... surely these are not the distinctive principles, and acts, and terms of a Protestant clergy, and a Protestant university!'[205] Hampden's opponents were labelled 'a knot of semipapal Oxonian Divines'[206] and the anti-Catholic theme was continued in a satirical poem by 'Bishop Bonner', celebrating the imminent burning of Hampden and his books.[207] Meanwhile, in the *Edinburgh Review*, Thomas Arnold aggressively assailed 'these High Church fanatics' as 'the peculiar disgrace of the Church of England'.[208]

Continuing this line of attack, a satirical *Pastoral Epistle from His Holiness the Pope* addressed the Tract writers as 'beloved children' and 'our Missionaries'. Attempting to portray Hampden as the honest Protestant, it encouraged them 'to undermine the influence of those, whose writings hold out no hope that they may be won over to the true Church. They are in truth dangerous men, and you should represent them as such. ... Suffer not such men to be the instructors of youth ... denounce them at once as unsound in the faith, as heretics, as Socinians.'[209] In response, Pusey insisted that Hampden was opposed by a broad range of people across the theological spectrum:

> there is in Oxford, happily, far too much thoughtfulness and scrupulousness to be influenced by any party, however powerful: men here form their individual convictions, according to their own consciences ... in truth, individuals of every shade of religious opinion within the latitude left free by our Articles, were united by one feeling of common danger impending over the Church, and that, independently of each other: they met and acted together spontaneously, actuated only by one common apprehension.[210]

Likewise, someone asked:

> *What* party? Look at the Record and the British Magazine. Are they of the same party? Are they likely to agree on any one point if they can possibly help it? Look through the list of names affixed to the various documents. You will find there

---

[205] Nicholas P.S. Wiseman, 'The Oxford Controversy', *Dublin Review* 1 (May 1836), p. 255. See also, *Letter to the Archbishop of Canterbury*, pp. 36-40.
[206] *Letter to the Archbishop of Canterbury*, p. 38.
[207] *Morning Chronicle*, 18 March 1836.
[208] Thomas Arnold, 'The Oxford Malignants and Dr Hampden', *Edinburgh Review* 63 (April 1836), p. 235.
[209] Charles Dickinson, *Pastoral Epistle from His Holiness the Pope to Some Members of the University of Oxford* (London, 1836), pp. 21, 34-5.
[210] Edward B. Pusey, *An Earnest Remonstrance to the Author of the 'Pope's Pastoral Letter to Certain Members of the University of Oxford'* (London, 1836), p. 34.

specimens of the highest of what are termed High Churchmen, and the lowest of those who are designated the Low Church ...²¹¹

The week before Hampden's inaugural lecture, there was at last a minor victory for his antagonists. Bowing to public pressure, the Hebdomadal Board finally agreed to submit a measure to Convocation suspending the University statutes by which the Regius Professor of Divinity, *ex officio*, had a voice in the appointment of select preachers and the trial of sermons charged with heresy.²¹² Golightly responded: 'tho' this is very insufficient – yet still it is a concession to Public feeling, and a public condemnation of *the man* under the University seal. Let us be thankful for this. It is entirely attributable under God's blessing to the energy and perseverance of our meetings.'²¹³ When Hampden stood before the University to deliver his inaugural lecture on 17 March, he complained at the 'cloud of prejudice and clamour' surrounding his appointment, and protested:

> Amongst all charges too the insinuations of heterodoxy, of latitudinarianism, of scepticism, are obviously the most difficult to be removed. They are of so vague a nature that each person adapts to them the chimera of his own fears or fancies, and there is no knowing to what point to address a refutation.²¹⁴

The professor remained defiant: 'to misrepresentation, and clamour, and violence, with God's help, I will never yield'.²¹⁵

Hampden's lecture appeared superficially to be 'sound, orthodox, and even ... evangelical'.²¹⁶ John Lamb (Master of Corpus Christi College, Cambridge) thought it 'must command the admiration of every mind in which party zeal or party rancour has not obscured the reason and quenched every spark of Christian charity.'²¹⁷ Nonetheless the *Standard* accused Hampden of 'duplicity', and likened him to Carneades, the philosopher expelled from Rome for speaking with equal skill and earnestness both for and against the excellence of virtue.²¹⁸ Golightly called the lecture 'a most artful production – containing a strictly orthodox statement of doctrine as far as it goes, but

---

²¹¹ John Chandler, *A Non-Resident MA's Self-Vindication for Attending to Support the Vote of Censure on Dr Hampden's Writings* (Oxford, 1836), p. 12.
²¹² OUA Hebdomadal Board Minutes, 7, 9, and 11 March 1836.
²¹³ Golightly to Dodd, 8 March 1836, LPL MS 1805, fo. 134.
²¹⁴ R.D. Hampden, *Inaugural Lecture read before the University of Oxford in the Divinity School on Thursday, March 17th, 1836* (third edition, London, 1836), p. 26.
²¹⁵ Ibid., p. 29.
²¹⁶ C.R. Cameron, *Does Dr Hampden's Inaugural Lecture Imply Any Change in his Theological Principles? A Letter ... to a Resident Member of Convocation* (Oxford, 1836), p. 3.
²¹⁷ John Lamb to Hampden, 21 March 1836, OCL Hampden Papers, no. 59.
²¹⁸ *Standard*, 19 March 1836.

defective, and *retracting nothing*'.[219] Lest others be taken in by it, he thought an exposé necessary before Convocation's all-important vote. Pusey began composing a pamphlet, entitled *Dr Hampden's Past and Present Statements Compared*, but knowing Pusey was a 'slow writer', Golightly also set to work. He dashed off a short, anonymous, pamphlet entitled *Brief Observations upon Dr Hampden's Inaugural Lecture*, which was distributed *gratis* through college common rooms – the first of many controversial publications during his long career.[220] It argued that Hampden was not to be trusted because his writings contained many statements contrary to Scripture and to the Thirty-Nine Articles, particularly about the Trinity and the atonement. Golightly proclaimed:

> In short, Dr Hampden has retracted *nothing*. Whatever opinions he held before, he holds now. He has not called in one of his obnoxious publications; and, if he has been misunderstood, maintains that the fault lies with his readers ... Why then should the University change their opinion of Dr Hampden as a teacher of Theology, on account of his Inaugural Lecture?[221]

Pusey's more weighty discourse 'was not ready till a day after the fair', Golightly told his uncle, with a hint of satisfaction that he had trumped his old mentor.[222]

Between 400 and 500 non-residents went up to Oxford for the eagerly anticipated Convocation on 22 March 1836, and about four-fifths planned to vote in favour of the statute limiting Hampden's influence within the University. However, before they could do so, the two proctors vetoed the proceedings in what the *Standard* called 'one of the last struggles of the sceptical party against the aroused energies of the Christian clergy and laity of the Church of England.'[223] After this fruitless meeting non-residents gathered at Brasenose College where they were addressed by various dignitaries and petitioned the Vice-Chancellor to renew the censure of Hampden after the Easter vacation.[224] The irony of Lord Kenyon (a veteran anti-Catholic

---

[219] Golightly to Dodd, 24 March 1836, LPL MS 1805, fo. 138.

[220] Ibid., fo. 139; John Miller, *Conspectus of the Hampden Case at Oxford, in a Letter to a Friend* (London, 1836), p. 19.

[221] Charles P. Golightly, *Brief Observations upon Dr Hampden's Inaugural Lecture* (Oxford, 1836), p. 7.

[222] Golightly to Dodd, 24 March 1836, LPL MS 1805, fo. 139. Edward B. Pusey, *Dr Hampden's Past and Present Statements Compared* (Oxford, 1836), is dated 21 March 1836, but may have been printed later.

[223] *Standard*, 25 March 1836. For the report of Convocation, see *Standard*, 23 March 1836. For translation of Vaughan Thomas' Latin speech, see *Oxford Herald*, 26 March 1836.

[224] Bodleian, Bliss B.213 (24); Arnold, 'Oxford Malignants', p. 233; Hill Diary, 22 March 1836, Bodleian MS St Edmund Hall 67/10.

campaigner) speaking to the non-residents alongside Pusey did not pass without notice, but was another sign of the wide spectrum of theological opinion allied against the Regius Professor of Divinity.[225] Convocation was recalled in May and, with new proctors in place, the proposed statute passed overwhelmingly by 474 votes to 94.[226] When re-issuing his Bampton Lectures the following year, Hampden spoke of his distress at seeing 'questions of Truth, of Religious Truth above all, arbitrated, like measures of political expediency, by personal and party influence, by appeals to feelings and prejudices, by the gathering of numbers, and the loudest cry.'[227]

The Final Split

Golightly and Pusey had stood shoulder to shoulder in their opposition to Professor Hampden, but when that affair was over the focus fell again upon their own theological disagreements. Their contretemps over Pusey's controversial sermon on 'sin after baptism' had not been settled and in May 1836, the week that Hampden was censured by Convocation, Golightly preached his own sermon on baptism and new birth, to which Pusey objected. Pusey's sermon had been in Christ Church cathedral; Golightly's was to a non-University congregation, perhaps in a village church outside Oxford. He asked his hearers to examine whether or not they were 'born again'.

Golightly's sermon notes do not survive and it is difficult to discern accurately his opinions on spiritual regeneration and its relationship to baptism. It had long been a topic of dispute within the Church of England, and debates raged over the legitimate interpretation of the church's historic formularies. For example, Article 27 of the Thirty-Nine Articles states that baptism is 'a sign of regeneration or new birth'. The Prayer Book liturgy declares of the baptised infant, with less ambiguity, 'this child is regenerate'. The doctrine of baptismal regeneration, Newman instructed Golightly, meant precisely being 'born again in baptism'.[228] However, evangelicals traditionally argued that 'new birth' is received not through water baptism but through repentance and faith in Jesus Christ, and they interpreted the words of the Prayer Book accordingly.

Golightly's views are difficult to reconstruct. In 1831 he told Newman of his disagreement with his evangelical friend, Charles Brenton, who did not 'consider Regeneration always to accompany Baptism administered in Infancy'.[229] Although Golightly was vocal against Pusey's teaching on sin after baptism, he does not appear to have criticised the teaching on baptismal

---

[225] *Letter to the Archbishop of Canterbury*, p. 40.
[226] *Standard*, 6 May 1836.
[227] R.D. Hampden, *Introduction to the Second Edition of the Bampton Lectures, of the Year 1832* (London, 1837), p. 2.
[228] Newman to Golightly, 6 June 1836, *Newman Letters and Diaries*, v. p. 310.
[229] Golightly to Newman, 10 August 1831, BOA Miscellaneous Letters.

regeneration which dominates *Tracts 67-69*. According to E.M. Goulburn:

> He was always strong on the subject of Baptism, its privileges, and the gift conferred in it; he did full justice to the words of the Catechism respecting the first Sacrament, 'wherein I was made a member of Christ, the child of God, and an inheritor of the kingdom of heaven'.[230]

However, Pusey thought Golightly's sermon of May 1836 was 'altogether inconsistent with Baptismal regeneration', and warned him that 'unless a person very accurately examines his expressions (for a time at least) very many will fall into language which does not convey their meaning.'[231] Keble told his brother: 'Golightly has been slanting off from sound doctrine ... I don't mean any thing very bad, only that he has talked in sermons in a vague way abt new birth & agst Pusey.'[232]

Golightly allowed Newman to see his sermon notes, commenting: 'Between the upper and nether millstone of his [Pusey's] and your criticism I fear it will come off but badly.' In self-defence, he added: 'in addressing an ignorant uncatechized congregation I have always been more anxious to impress upon them the two or three leading ideas of a Sermon, than to weigh with accuracy every particular term wh I made use of in it.'[233] Newman agreed with Pusey that parts of the sermon were 'quite irreconcilable' with Golightly's former avowals of baptismal regeneration and the event raised doubts in his mind about Golightly's suitability for the Littlemore curacy (or at least gave him the opportunity to backtrack on his previous offer). He wrote to explain:

> Having the fullest confidence in the soundness of your formal doctrine, I am no longer certain that you will consistently maintain it in your preaching. To speak openly, I do not see now, how I can take an *irrevocable* step about Littlemore – any step which puts that part of my Parish once and for ever beyond my own superintendance.[234]

In his irritation, Newman penned a sharp rebuke against Golightly's habit of criticising his friends – but deleted the paragraph before sending the letter. It reveals his true feelings at the severe strain put on their relationship and shows that for Newman there was more at stake than merely Golightly's suspect sermon. The expunged sentences read:

> There is something incongruous surely, as I think your own judgment will admit, in your going about talking against Pusey and myself, as you have done. You have a right to do so – but you cannot keep friends on such terms, as it stands to reason.

---

[230] Goulburn, *Reminiscences of Golightly*, p. 22.
[231] Pusey to Golightly, 9 May 1836, LPL MS 1808, fo. 241.
[232] John Keble to Thomas Keble, nd, KCL C14.
[233] Golightly to Newman, 9 May 1836, BOA Miscellaneous Letters.
[234] Newman to Golightly, 15 May 1836, *Newman Letters and Diaries*, v. p. 297.

My dear G. I really think, if you will allow me to speak plainly and seriously you need a little (what is commonly called) sophronizing [being taught moderation and self-control].[235]

Golightly was clearly hurt and angry when told he would no longer be given sole and permanent charge of Littlemore. He responded: 'in the teeth of so strong an expression of want of confidence in my ministry ... accompanied as it is with a refusal to license me I should not be justified as a prudent man in undertaking the charge.'[236] At first Newman was adamant: 'I do not think that your not being at Littlemore is a great loss to me'.[237] The next day, however, he was 'truly sorry and disappointed' that Golightly had refused the curacy. He regretted the loss of 'such a valuable assistant', and offered to license him provided that 'it is understood that you are not forthwith, as I had originally intended and expressed to you, αὐτόνομος in Littlemore in consequence.'[238]

Yet for Golightly there was no turning back. He reckoned Newman's 'general expression of want of confidence' meant it was 'quite hopeless that we should act together with any comfort.' He thought Newman 'precipitate' in offering him the curacy, and concluded (again with insight into his natural conservatism):

> I always doubted whether the plan would do, and felt that my mind was of *too conservative a cast* to suit you. I abandon any views which I have once deliberately taken up with extreme reluctance and look with suspicion at every new view (old perhaps in itself but new to me) which interferes with them. This will account for my talking so much against Pusey's sermon which I suspect, my dear Newman, displeased you more than any particular statement contained in my own, and from the same feelings I might do many things of the same sort which you would equally object to.[239]

To Pusey, Golightly complained:

> This decision puts me to serious personal inconvenience because it has been known that he had asked me to be his curate for at least a year to the Diocese, the University, and my own Family and friends. And of course when I am known to be at issue with an individual of his exalted character whether for piety, genius, or learning, it is not difficult to guess at whose door the blame will be laid. I must needs be the sufferer. ... The long and the short of the matter is that Newman was too hasty in making me his curate at first ... This precipitancy was the less

---

[235] Newman to Golightly, 15 May 1836 (draft), ibid., p. 297.
[236] Golightly to Newman, 2 June 1836, ibid., p. 297.
[237] Newman to Golightly, 2 June 1836, ibid., p. 306.
[238] Newman to Golightly, 3 June 1836, ibid., pp. 307-8.
[239] Golightly to Newman, 6 June 1836, BOA Miscellaneous Letters.

excusable because he has for at least 8 or 9 years charged me with an 'Evangelical leaning'.[240]

Newman recalled: 'He never got over it. We were never friends again.'[241] More sympathetically, Thomas Mozley concluded: 'So there was Golightly cajoled, betrayed, and cast adrift. It was a case of downright folly all round.'[242] He recommended that instead of Littlemore, his friend take charge of St Bartholomew's Chapel, a derelict leper chapel on farmland south of Oxford.[243] In the event Golightly began work as curate in the village of Toot Baldon, sharing the duties initially with A.C. Tait (future Archbishop of Canterbury) and George Johnson (future Dean of Wells), curates of neighbouring Marsh Baldon.[244]

In Oxford, Golightly continued publicly to criticise Newman and Pusey leading to a final and irreparable breach with his former friends and mentors in early 1837. The last straw came when they clashed directly over justification by faith – the doctrine *par excellence* on which the Reformation was built. Golightly complained to Pusey that he and Newman were 'unconsciously doing the work of the ancient disturbers of the Galatian Church', and that their teaching tended 'to mystify the doctrine of Justification by Faith'.[245] He heard that some of their followers thought justification by faith alone should never have been included in the Thirty-Nine Articles, and that another spoke of it as a 'Nauseous Doctrine'.[246] Golightly warned that Newman's views tended 'to confound Sanctification with Justification',[247] and thought his *Lectures on Justification* bore an appropriate motto: 'Who is this that darkeneth counsel by words without knowledge?'[248] He proclaimed that Newman's erroneous

---

[240] Golightly to Pusey, 17 May 1836, LPL MS 1808, fos 218-20.

[241] Newman's memorandum (1860) in Mozley, *Letters and Correspondence of John Henry Newman*, ii. p. 105.

[242] Mozley, *Reminiscences Chiefly of Oriel College and the Oxford Movement*, ii. p. 112.

[243] Thomas Mozley to Maria Mozley, 14 June 1836, BOA Thomas Mozley Papers. See J.H. Parker, 'St Bartholomew's Chapel', *Proceedings of the Oxford Architectural and Historical Society* 2 (1864-71), pp. 177-84; Victoria County History, *A History of the County of Oxford*, vol. 4 *The City of Oxford*, edited by Alan Crossley (Oxford, 1979), pp. 473-4.

[244] Hill Diary, 15 August 1836 and 12 September 1842, Bodleian MS St Edmund Hall 67/11 and 67/13; parish registers; visitation returns (1838) ORO ODP b.41, fos 21-3; 'Records of the Diocese of Oxford, vol. 1: Oxfordshire' ODP b.70, fo. 51; survey of diocese (1846) ODP d.550, fo. 31; 'Records of the Baldons' PAR 13/17/MS2/1, fos 15-8; Samuel Wilberforce – Golightly, 1846, LPL MS 1811, fos 185-205.

[245] Golightly to Pusey, 1 February 1837, PHL PUS 127.

[246] Golightly to Pusey, 3 February 1837, PHL PUS 127.

[247] Golightly, *Letter to the Bishop of Oxford*, p. 33.

[248] Golightly, *Letter to the Dean of Ripon*, pp. 3-4. See also Knox, *Tractarian Movement*, p. 205; Golightly, *New and Strange Doctrines*, pp. 11-6.

A Tractarian Disciple?

interpretation of this 'great fundamental doctrine of Christianity ... opens wide a door for almost every possible heresy on the subject.'[249] In later years Golightly recalled that from the day he discovered Newman believed justification by faith alone was unscriptural, he had 'not hesitated to communicate my alarms to others.'[250]

Instead of answering Golightly's theological questions, Pusey warned him against his habit of criticising other people from a position of ignorance. It was rumoured that Golightly even planned to write a pamphlet against the early church fathers,[251] so Pusey challenged him:

> I cannot but think you in an unhealthy state of mind; talking over or against people is a bad occupation ... I shd think that you were not yourself aware to what extent you do it. ... I wish you wd read a little more of the fathers instead of talking agst them, & that not thro' the glasses of the 19th cent. ... You have involved yourself in modern Divinity, & you have blended in your own mind 2 inconsistent systems (witness the sermon wh I heard). It is the case of a great many in the present day.[252]

Golightly protested that their dispute should remain theological and doctrinal, and not descend into personal jibes. He had objected only to people's opinions, not their characters, and asserted:

> Nor can I see any reason why I should not continue to do so so long as I see certain persons and their followers not content with attempting to revive Monachism [monasticism] and various questionable practices abandoned by our Church, boldly attacking the system of the Church itself, criticising the Liturgy ...

---

[249] Golightly, *Strictures on No.90*, part 1, p. 48.

[250] Golightly's memoranda, LPL MS 1811, fo. 261. See also, E.A. Knox, *Reminiscences of an Octogenarian, 1847-1934* (London, 1934), p. 114. For Newman on justification, see Henry Chadwick, 'The *Lectures on Justification*' in Ian T. Ker and Alan G. Hill (eds.), *Newman After A Hundred Years* (Oxford, 1990), pp. 287-308; Alister E. McGrath, *Iustitia Dei: A History of the Christian Doctrine of Justification* (third edition, Cambridge, 2005), pp. 296-307; José Morales, 'Newman and the Problems of Justification' in Stanley L. Jaki (ed.), *Newman Today* (San Francisco, 1989), pp. 143-64; David H. Newsome, 'Justification and Sanctification: Newman and the Evangelicals', *Journal of Theological Studies* 15 (April 1964), pp. 32-53; J.S. O'Leary, 'Impeded Witness: Newman Against Luther on Justification' in David Nicholls and Fergus Kerr (eds.), *John Henry Newman: Reason, Rhetoric and Romanticism* (Bristol, 1991), pp. 153-93; Thomas L. Sheridan, *Newman on Justification* (Staten Island, NY, 1967); Peter Toon, *Evangelical Theology 1833-1856: A Response to Tractarianism* (London, 1979), ch. 5.

[251] Golightly to Newman, 9 February 1837, BOA Miscellaneous Letters. Golightly later spoke of his 'profound reverence' for most of the fathers: Golightly, *Letter to the Bishop of Oxford*, p. 86.

[252] Pusey to Golightly, 2 February 1837, LPL MS 1808, fo. 233.

and not only objecting to certain of the 39 Articles but also to the whole of them as a burden upon the Church.

He insisted he was not 'a solitary individual setting up my judgment' against Pusey and Newman, but that many people across the country were increasingly concerned by their teaching, 'some of them staunch High Churchmen'.[253] Nonetheless, Pusey continued with his moral advice, telling Golightly to remove the beam from his own eye (that of exaggerated self-opinion) instead of criticising others:

> I must ask you to ask yourself, why it is your vocation, *more than that of others*, to wander about talking agst people's preaching, or the fathers. ... you may be found to be speaking agst the truth, & that is a very earnest thing to think of; so, if you will take in good part my plain advice, I wd read more of the old fathers & speak less. ... I am sure that you are injuring your spiritual state by your present course, & if you see it not so now, I trust that you will see it hereafter. In plain words, you are giving way to what you probably know to be your besetting sin – vanity.[254]

Golightly acknowledged he would try to profit from Pusey's reproof, but complained: 'you have written what in most cases flesh and blood could not bear. To irritate and mortify is not always to mend.'[255] Pusey, still signing himself 'your very *sincere* friend', further advised Golightly 'to observe strictly day by day what symptoms of vanity there are in your words & thoughts, what hardly perceptible risings of it you can see, how often "I" occurs to your thoughts'. He believed Golightly had assumed 'an office for wh you were not qualified, that of criticizing N. whom you do not understand', and warned: 'speaking evil of a person whom you do not understand, & misrepresenting him, because you do not understand him, is (only not wilful) slandering.'[256] Their correspondence ended with Golightly still defiant:

> You have charged me with certain *moral defects*. I have brought no such charge against you or Newman. I have found fault with *your system*, and shall continue to do so. Why am I to pay more deference to your opinions, than you pay to those of the Evangelicals or Dr Hampden? If you find fault with others' systems, what right have you to complain when others find fault with yours? With respect to the charges you have brought against my moral character, however valid they may be, I cannot admit that you were justified in making them either by seniority, or station, or by the terms of our acquaintance.[257]

---

[253] Golightly to Pusey, 3 February 1837, PHL PUS 127.
[254] Pusey to Golightly, 3 February 1837, LPL MS 1808, fos 235-6.
[255] Golightly to Pusey, 4 February 1837, PHL PUS 127.
[256] Pusey to Golightly, 3 and 4 February 1837, LPL MS 1808, fos 235-6, 238.
[257] Golightly to Pusey, 7 February 1837, PHL PUS 127.

Newman concluded: 'I wish the said G. were not so insufferably conceited',[258] and promptly returned Golightly's donation towards the *Tracts for the Times*.[259]

In later years it was a source of constant speculation how a close friend and admirer of Newman and Pusey, an early participant in the Oxford Movement and a subscriber to the *Tracts for the Times* could turn into one of the most vociferous and unceasing opponents of all that savoured of Tractarianism. Some concluded (as Pusey seems to have done) that it was partly due to Golightly's 'pride'. For instance, in the mid-1840s it was rumoured that he had begun to fight the Tractarians because he was 'disappointed in his ambitious aim of being a leader' in the movement. The *English Churchman* claimed that Pusey's recognition as the movement's figurehead was 'a never-ceasing source of envy, hatred, and malice' to Golightly, who viewed the Regius Professor of Hebrew as evil Haman did the godly Mordecai in the Book of Esther.[260] Likewise a satirical poem, addressed to Golightly as 'Agag', spoke of:

> The sceptic ones, who say that wounded pride
> Has been the spur to goad thy jaded side,
> And hint in terms obscure, as if they knew,
> 'Had Jaffier's friends been kind, he'd still be true':
> That all were just the Tracts have sung or said,
> Had they but march'd with Agag at their head;
> Nor once remorse had tingled through thy veins,
> Or paled thy cheek, hadst thou but kept the reins.[261]

From Golightly's perspective, however, it was not a question of pride but a question of truth.

Novel and Confused Doctrines

Within a few years of Golightly's final split with Pusey and Newman, he had begun to criticise Tractarian opinions not just by word of mouth, but in pamphlets (sometimes running to hundreds of pages) and letters to the newspapers. In early 1839 Bishop Bagot of Oxford recommended that Pusey issue a statement 'such as shall stop the accusations of yr being in any degree hostile to the Reformation, – enable your Friends to defend you from such

---

[258] Newman to Henry Wilberforce, 18 February 1837, *Newman Letters and Diaries*, vi. p. 30.
[259] Newman to Golightly, 9 February 1837, ibid., p. 24. See Golightly to Newman, 22 May 1840, *Newman Letters and Diaries*, vii. p. 329.
[260] *English Churchman*, 8 January 1846, p. 24.
[261] *Heroic Epistle from Titus Oates, to his Lineal Descendant, Agag Oates, at Oxford* (London, 1845), p. 6. Jaffier was a central character in Thomas Otway's tragedy, *Venice Preserv'd* (1682), which bore parallels to the Gunpower Plot.

charges – and put to silence the Romanists who wrongly, but boldly claim you as countenancing them.'[262] The result was Pusey's *Letter to the Bishop of Oxford*, in which he argued that the Tract writers taught no new doctrines and simply aimed to tread a 'via media' between the extremes of 'Romanism' and 'Ultra-Protestantism'.[263] Such was the interest in Pusey's pamphlet, that it reached a fourth edition by the summer of 1840.

Golightly replied in May 1840 with his own anonymous *Letter to the Bishop of Oxford*, claiming that in fact the Tract writers were guilty of both 'serious violations of Discipline' and 'Novel and Confused views of Doctrine'.[264] He warned the bishop that he had heard about Tractarians crossing themselves, genuflecting, dating letters by the vigil of Roman festivals, and wearing 'some forgotten portion of the ancient clerical dress' – in direct disobedience to Bagot's wishes expressed in his recent Visitation charge to the Oxford diocese.[265] If such liturgical practices were allowed to be revived because not expressly forbidden by Prayer Book rubric, what would stop the return of anointing with oil, the kiss of peace, white garments and candles at baptism, or infants receiving holy communion? – a clear *reductio ad absurdum*.[266] In particular, Golightly argued that the Tractarian teaching on justification, sin after baptism and 'economy' was not the teaching of the Anglican Church, quoting extensively from divines such as Andrewes, Beveridge, Bingham, Bramhall, Bull, Hall, Hammond, Hooker, Jackson, Pearson, Ussher, Van Mildert and Waterland. He insisted he did not belong to the evangelical party 'or indeed to any party whatsoever', and rebuked Pusey for giving the impression that the Tracts were assailed exclusively by Low Churchmen.[267] Golightly sent a copy of his pamphlet to Pusey, Newman and Isaac Williams, still confident 'that the friendly feeling which subsists between us will not be impaired'. He hoped that Pusey would not again accuse him of 'vanity and presumption' for attacking Tractarian opinions, but such optimism proved naive.[268] Pusey told Golightly that he was 'laboring [sic] under a bias' and guilty of 'a very grievous act of injustice' and 'a very cruel ... misrepresentation'.[269]

---

[262] Bagot to Pusey, 19 January 1839, PHL LBV 39/5.
[263] Edward B. Pusey, *A Letter to the Right Rev. Father in God, Richard Lord Bishop of Oxford, on the Tendency to Romanism imputed to Doctrines held of Old, as Now, in the English Church* (Oxford, 1839), p. 22.
[264] Golightly, *Letter to the Bishop of Oxford*, p. 2.
[265] Richard Bagot, *A Charge Delivered to the Clergy of the Diocese of Oxford ... at his Third Visitation* (Oxford, 1838), p. 19.
[266] Golightly, *Letter to the Bishop of Oxford*, pp. 14-5.
[267] Ibid., pp. 16-8, 110.
[268] Golightly to Pusey, nd, LPL MS 1804, fos 59-60; Golightly to Newman, 21 May 1840, *Newman Letters and Diaries*, vii. p. 328; Golightly to Isaac Williams, nd, LPL MS 1806, fo. 86.
[269] Pusey to Golightly, nd, LPL MS 1808, fos 229, 231.

Pusey's *Letter to the Bishop of Oxford* provoked further responses, such as that in late 1840 from George Miller (Vicar-General of Armagh diocese from 1843). Miller spoke of Pusey's 'association',[270] which was enough to have William Sewell insisting there was no 'secret body' recognising Pusey as head or agreeing to propagate the doctrines of the Tracts. Instead, Sewell declared, the Tract writers were 'singularly independent of each other', not attempting 'to form a new school' but agreeing in 'the duty of guarding against the formation of any party, or setting up the authority of any individual within the Church'. Indeed he thought Pusey's 'most anxious efforts have been directed to obliterate all such parties, and to warn men against trusting to human authority, when compared with divine'.[271] Likewise Arthur Perceval maintained the Tractarians were not involved in some 'secret association, combination, or conspiracy', but simply 'a united effort' to maintain the doctrine of Apostolic Succession and the teaching of the Prayer Book.[272] Golightly retorted with an anonymous letter in the *Oxford Herald* that Sewell was 'apt to mistake his wishes for realities' and that the existence of an 'association' was proved by revelations in the writings of Hurrell Froude. For example, Froude had assumed for himself and his friends a 'party name' ('apostolicals') and had proposed the adoption of 'a party vocabulary' (to be called 'vocabularium apostolicum').[273]

Few Can Be Spared

With sufficient financial resources inherited from his family, Golightly had no need for paid employment.[274] He lived comfortably on his own means, without the urgency of finding work, and only served occasional curacies, such as those in Penshurst, Godalming and Toot Baldon. Nor did he have any teaching position at Oxford University. However, in October 1840 Philip Shuttleworth, the new Bishop of Chichester, invited Golightly to become Principal of Chichester Theological College. The college had been founded the previous year by his predecessor, Bishop Otter, with the encouragement of George

---

[270] George Miller, *A Letter to the Rev. E.B. Pusey, DD, in Reference to his Letter to the Lord Bishop of Oxford* (London, 1840), pp. 8, 70.

[271] *Irish Ecclesiastical Journal* 1 (November 1840), pp. 81-2.

[272] *Irish Ecclesiastical Journal* 1 (January 1841), pp. 110-1.

[273] *Oxford Herald*, 12 December 1840; *Remains of the Late Reverend Richard Hurrell Froude* (4 vols, London, 1838-39), i. p. 329.

[274] For Golightly's various inheritances, see for example, will of William Golightly, proved 23 June 1820, Prob 11/1512 fos 211-3; admon of William Charles Golightly, granted 27 March 1833, Prob 6/209 fo. 205; will of Frances Margaretta Golightly, proved 11 March 1834, Prob 11/1828 fos 397-9; will of Margaret Golightly, proved 24 November 1842, Prob 11/1970 fos 367-70; admon of Edward Richard Golightly, granted 31 December 1856, Prob 6/232 fo. 201. See also probate and financial papers, LPL CM 23 and MSS 4203-8; Golightly to George T. Graham, 26 February 1834; G.T. Graham to Sarah Graham, 14 August 1835, Cossington MSS.

Chandler (Dean of Chichester) and Henry Manning (rector of Lavington and soon to be Archdeacon of Chichester).[275] Otter's first principal was Charles Marriott, who had just three students to teach when the doors opened, rising to seven with a year. However, Marriott suffered through ill health and was expected to retire, presenting Shuttleworth with the opportunity to make his own appointment.

When Golightly first met Marriott in Oxford in 1833, he had nothing but praise for him: 'Such well-toned piety! Sound high church principles united with deep and earnest feeling, and connected with so much practical wisdom and good sense as I have never before discovered in any body under forty.'[276] Yet Marriott had identified himself closely with the Tractarian movement and his fledgling theological college soon gained a reputation for Tractarian bias. Perhaps this is why Shuttleworth, who was suspicious of the institution he had inherited, wanted Golightly to take charge. However, Golightly declined the offer and explained his reasons to the bishop at length. First, he predicted that the theological college experiment was unlikely to succeed, since they were more expensive than the traditional Universities and in small institutions students ran 'the much greater risk of ... receiving a party bias'.[277] Marriott, for instance, had met with little success despite being

> favoured by a large and active party. My own determination would be to connect myself with no party whatever. Consequently I shd not have the support of any, and an institution wh scarcely held together in Mr M.'s hands would immediately crumble to pieces in mine.[278]

Second, Golightly lacked tutorial experience and academic distinction, which meant he would not be best suited to leading a theological college. Yet third, and most importantly, he felt he must decline Shuttleworth's invitation because he was needed in Oxford. Newman and Pusey were gaining an advantage by outlasting their antagonists in the city. Since the late 1820s a number of heavyweight Tractarian opponents had been elevated to the episcopate – such as Edward Copleston (Bishop of Llandaff from 1827), Richard Whately (Archbishop of Dublin from 1831), Edward Denison (Bishop of Salisbury from 1836) and Shuttleworth himself. Other leading Protestant theologians in Oxford had died – such as Charles Lloyd (Bishop of Oxford) in 1829 and Edward Burton (Regius Professor of Divinity) in 1836. Of course, most of these men had left Oxford before the Tractarian movement began, so Golightly was guilty

---

[275] R.S.T. Haslehurst, 'A Short History of Chichester Theological College', *Cicestrian* 10 (Trinity 1939), pp. 82-100 (copy at West Sussex Record Office).
[276] Golightly to James B. Mozley, 16 January 1834, BOA Thomas Mozley Papers.
[277] Golightly to Philip N. Shuttleworth, 22 October 1840, LPL MS 1809, fo. 38. For complaints at the heavy expense of diocesan theological colleges, see also Golightly's private notebook, *c.*1839, Stack MS 6d.
[278] Golightly to Shuttleworth, nd, LPL MS 1809, fo. 42.

of obvious anachronism. Nor had he always welcomed their theological teaching – he was 'woefully disappointed', for example, when Burton became Regius Professor and predicted his lectures would 'revive old heresies, and disseminate Unitarianism'.[279] Yet such scruples were now forgotten as Golightly focussed on the new Tractarian threat. With a sure sense of his own significance, he concluded to Bishop Shuttleworth that he must decline the invitation to Chichester because 'in the present condition of the University few of the friends of genuine and vital religion can conveniently be spared.'[280] R.W. Church commented that Golightly walked around Oxford 'looking as pleased as if he had refused a piece of preferment'.[281] However, when Dean Chandler went up to Oxford to preach, he denied (presumably out of ignorance, rather than malice) that Golightly had been offered the principalship. This left Golightly 'in a flame of indignation' – a tale which Newman was happy to circulate.[282]

During the rest of his life, Golightly never took on full-time employment. Although he had no tutorial position, he was often involved with undergraduates at Oxford University and made an effort to cultivate friendships with them. Just as he had been mentored as an undergraduate by men like John Hill and John Henry Newman, so now he mentored others. E.M. Goulburn (undergraduate at Balliol College and later Dean of Norwich) remembered him as 'a most kind friend and counsellor', with a keen concern for the spiritual welfare of the junior members of the University.[283] In the late 1830s Golightly's young acquaintances included Goulburn, Samuel Waldegrave (later the evangelical Bishop of Carlisle) and Frederick Faber (later a convert to Roman Catholicism).[284] In 1840 Frederick Robertson (undergraduate at Brasenose College) was supervised by Golightly in his pre-ordination reading in early church history and described him as 'a fund of general information'.[285] Likewise in the mid-1840s he grew friendly with Thomas Valpy French (an undergraduate at University College and later Bishop of Lahore). As late as the 1870s Goulburn asked Golightly to take Lord Brooke (undergraduate at Christ Church) under his wing, because his father was nervous about the corrupting influence of University life and would be heartbroken 'if he were to be

---

[279] Golightly to Mozley, 26 June 1829, BOA Thomas Mozley Papers.
[280] Golightly to Shuttleworth, 22 October 1840, LPL MS 1809, fo. 43.
[281] Church to Rogers, 31 October 1840, in M.C. Church, *Life and Letters of Dean Church* (London, 1894), p. 26.
[282] Newman to Rogers, 21 December 1840, *Newman Letters and Diaries*, vii. p. 464.
[283] Goulburn, *Reminiscences of Golightly*, pp. 5, 33.
[284] Mozley, *Reminiscences Chiefly of Oriel College and the Oxford Movement*, ii. p. 112.
[285] Frederick W. Robertson to Sarah Robertson, 1840, in Stopford A. Brooke, *Life and Letters of Frederick W. Robertson* (2 vols, London, 1865), i. p. 36. I am grateful to Christina Beardsley for this reference.

Romanised, and still more if he were to be Rationalised.'[286] At a similar period Golightly grew close to E.A. Knox (a young evangelical fellow at Merton College and later Bishop of Manchester), who was forty years his junior. These relationships with impressionable young men made his concern about the theological teaching at Oxford all the more acute.

It was Golightly's lack of parochial responsibilities, however, which was frequently a source of chagrin to his opponents. They poked fun at his leisured lifestyle and wished he would spend his energies in low-profile but profitable parish work rather than in ceaseless theological agitation. Some felt that Golightly ended up creating mischief because he had too much time on his hands. Certainly his flexible schedule meant he had greater freedom to campaign or write or canvass than those with ministerial or tutorial obligations. Indeed, busy clergymen would occasionally approach Golightly in the hope that he would take up some cause on their behalf. Most of his limited parochial experience was gained through Sunday duty at village parishes near Oxford, either helping friends or replacing non-resident clergy. He admitted that preaching to University audiences was not his *forte*, and preferred to address rural congregations where he was more effective.[287] In 1846, after ten years as part-time curate of Toot Baldon, he laid down that charge and worked at different periods over the next thirty-five years in the parishes of Headington, Marston, Elsfield, Stanton St John and Claydon.[288] Knowing that Golightly would always be remembered as a lover of ecclesiastical controversy, Bishop Knox emphasised that in fact his 'principal joy was pastoral work among the country poor.'[289]

---

[286] Goulburn to Golightly, 9 September 1872, LPL MS 1806, fos 195-6.
[287] Goulburn, *Reminiscences of Golightly*, pp. 26-30.
[288] Parish registers; *Oxford Times*, 26 October 1878, 9 January 1886. For Golightly's ministry at Claydon, see Thomas H. Greene to Golightly, December 1879 – April 1880, LPL MS 1806, fos 292-325.
[289] Knox, *Reminiscences of an Octogenarian*, p. 115. See also Burgon, *Lives of Twelve Good Men*, i. p. xxvi.

CHAPTER 2

Remembering the Martyrs

During the mid-1830s opponents of the nascent Oxford Movement began to portray it as a revival of Roman Catholicism within the Church of England. This form of polemic was evident as early as 1836 during the Hampden crisis, as has been seen. The following year a local clergyman, Peter Maurice (described by William Copeland as 'the precursor of the Golightlys of after days'[1]) stirred up controversy by chastising the teaching of the *Tracts for the Times* as 'the popery of Oxford'.[2] Weight was lent to these claims by the publication by John Henry Newman and John Keble in February 1838 of excerpts from the correspondence and journal of Hurrell Froude, who had died of tuberculosis two years before, aged only 32. Froude's *Remains* provided pithy and startling quotations on a variety of subjects, but particularly on the Reformation:

> I am every day becoming a less and less loyal son of the Reformation.[3]
> As to the Reformers, I think worse and worse of them.[4]
> Really I hate the Reformation and the Reformers more and more ...[5]
> The Reformation was a limb badly set – it must be broken again in order to be righted.[6]

Newman and Keble's revelation of these opinions to the public was intentionally provocative, described by Piers Brendon 'an anti-eirenicon *par excellence*'.[7] The responses were predictably violent. For example, Bishop Sumner of Chester declared: 'the foundations of our Protestant church are undermined by men who dwell within her walls, and those who sit in the

---

[1] R.D. Middleton, *Newman and Bloxam: An Oxford Friendship* (London, 1947), p. 40.
[2] Peter Maurice, *The Popery of Oxford: Confronted, Disavowed, & Repudiated* (London, 1837).
[3] *Remains of Hurrell Froude*, i. p. 336.
[4] Ibid., p. 379.
[5] Ibid., p. 389.
[6] Ibid., p. 433.
[7] Piers Brendon, *Hurrell Froude and the Oxford Movement* (London, 1974), p. 180. See also W.J. Baker, 'Hurrell Froude and the Reformers', *Journal of Ecclesiastical History* 21 (July 1970), pp. 243-59; Piers Brendon, 'Newman, Keble and Froude's *Remains*', *English Historical Review* 87 (October 1972), pp. 697-716.

Reformers' seat are traducing the Reformation.'[8] Froude was called 'a disguised Papist'[9], and the *Christian Observer* proclaimed: 'The battle of the Reformation must be fought once more'.[10] In Oxford the Lady Margaret Professor of Divinity, Godfrey Faussett (described by David Newsome as 'a man whose egregious gift for trouble-making could be challenged only by C.P. Golightly'[11]) preached against 'the revival of Popery'.[12]

Charles Golightly was one of many who objected to the publication of Froude's private papers. He used it as an opportunity to speak further against Newman, as Frederic Rogers reported: 'Dissentiente Golightly ... trumpets to the world such a proof of your breach of confidence'.[13] Golightly criticised Froude's lack of respect for episcopal authority and his extravagant statements against the Reformers,[14] and in contrast considered one of the best ways to do good amongst his friends was to instil in them a love for the Reformation.[15] He later wrote:

> But for these despised Reformers, where would have been the religion of this land? Buried beneath the deadly garb of superstition, fed from the poisoned streams of ignorance and idolatry. But for them, the darkness of Romanism had still benighted the prosperity of England, or infidelity had exalted its unblushing head. We had been as Sodom, we had been like unto Gomorrah. The condition of France and Spain present to our view a fearful counterpart of that fate that awaited us![16]

At the beginning of Michaelmas Term 1838, Golightly was at the heart of plans to build a Martyrs' Memorial in Oxford to commemorate the lives and deaths of bishops Cranmer, Latimer and Ridley who were burned at the stake outside the city walls in the 1550s. Coming so soon after the publication of Froude's *Remains*, it was seen by some as a direct attack upon Tractarian views of the Reformation. Certainly most historians of the Oxford Movement interpret the Martyrs' Memorial as an anti-Tractarian statement. H.P. Liddon's account of the memorial in his *Life of Edward Bouverie Pusey* (1893-97) has long since become authoritative and his claims are often repeated: 'There is

---

[8] J.B. Sumner, *A Charge Delivered to the Clergy of the Diocese of Chester* (London, 1838), p. 2.
[9] 'Papistical Tendency of the Tracts for the Times', *Church of England Quarterly Review* 5 (January 1839), p. 220.
[10] *Christian Observer* (August 1838), p. 507.
[11] Newsome, *Parting of Friends*, p. 284.
[12] Godfrey Faussett, *The Revival of Popery* (Oxford, 1838).
[13] Rogers to Newman, 20 March 1838, BOA PC 10/29.
[14] Golightly, *Letter to the Bishop of Oxford*, pp. 6-9, 18-26; *Oxford Herald*, 6 February 1841.
[15] Golightly's private notebook, *c.*1839, Stack MS 6d.
[16] Golightly, *Strictures on No.90*, part 2, p. 85.

little doubt that it was intended primarily as a protest against Froude's "Remains", and the editors of that book, Newman and Keble. ... It was, and it remained, an expression of hostility to the Oxford writers.'[17]

However, as this chapter will show, Liddon's conclusion is too simplistic. There was also a strong anti-Catholic, as opposed to anti-Tractarian, impulse to the scheme which has been overlooked, largely as a result of interpreting the memorial in the light of subsequent theological developments. Although Froude's *Remains* were a significant stimulus, they do not provide the whole answer. Much of the polemic surrounding the monument was directed exclusively against Roman Catholicism. Although for some subscribers this may have been a rhetorical device, others felt able to be both pro-Tractarian and anti-Catholic.

An Anti-Catholic Scheme?

The need for a permanent monument to the Oxford martyrs was suggested on several occasions long before Hurrell Froude and the Tractarians sprang to prominence. The first known proposal was in 1773 when Edward Tatham (future Rector of Lincoln College) recommended a memorial amongst his architectural improvements for Oxford, in the form of an arch across Broad Street, with statues of Cranmer and Ridley in the pillars on either side.[18] During the late 1810s a memorial was again considered.[19] It was discussed by Philip Shuttleworth, who called it a 'hobby-horsical scheme',[20] Edward Copleston and others, but never got 'beyond after dinner conversation' because of a difference of opinion on where the monument should be placed.[21]

Plans for the Martyrs' Memorial which stands today eventually got off the ground in October 1838, but the original idea occurred more than two years earlier; that is, two years before Froude's *Remains* appeared. In early 1836 a small group of Golightly's friends went up to Oxford to vote in the Hampden affair, and while at dinner at No.6 Holywell Street they discussed why a monument to the Oxford martyrs had never been erected:

---

[17] Liddon, *Life of Pusey*, ii. pp. 65, 68. Elsewhere Liddon suggests the memorial was built by 'Puritanism', p. 290.

[18] Edward Tatham, *Oxonia Explicata & Ornata: Proposals for Disengaging and Beautifying the University and City of Oxford* (London, 1773), p. 5. See engraving in 1777 edition.

[19] For suggestions at this period, see W.M. Wade, *Walks in Oxford* (Oxford, 1817), p. 81; *Gentleman's Magazine* 90 (November 1820), p. 386. Compare also *John Bull*, 17 February 1839, p. 80.

[20] Shuttleworth to Lord Holland, 6 January 1839, BL Add. MS 51597, fo. 153.

[21] Golightly to Heurtley, November 1875, LPL MS 1807, fo. 61; circular, October 1838, Bodleian Gough Maps 233.3. Shuttleworth claimed that a monumental cross had been proposed for the identical site agreed in 1839: *Oxford Herald*, 14 March 1840.

Upon which one of the party, more in earnest than the rest, took his purse out of his pocket, and throwing down a sovereign on the table, exclaimed 'There's my contribution towards it, and I will never take it back till it's done'. Others sitting at the table were impressed, and one of them obtained promises of contributions from friends in the course of the following summer to the amount of £30 or £40. But nothing more came of it either that or the following year.[22]

Although Golightly's relationship with Newman and Pusey was showing signs of strain in 1836, at that period he still considered himself one of their friends. Indeed the curacy at Littlemore had not yet fallen through and Golightly worked as a close ally of Pusey during the Hampden crisis. It is therefore unlikely that this first idea for the Martyrs' Memorial was intended as a protest against the Tractarians. Although Golightly was later famous for his many anti-Tractarian campaigns, he was also capable of launching direct attacks upon Roman Catholicism. For example in 1837, three years before his first pamphlet against Pusey and Newman, he published *Look at Home, or Short and Easy Method with the Roman Catholics*. In reply to Roman Catholic criticisms of the Church of England, he sought to expose the worldly compromise, internal divisions and doctrinal corruption of the Church of Rome. Warning against mariolatry, he accused Roman bishops of holding 'heretical opinions' and declared: 'We can have no Communion with the Roman Pontiff, because HE HAS SET UP ANOTHER GOD.'[23] Appealing for an end to Roman interference in English affairs, Golightly concluded:

> Unhappy Church! We watch not for your halting, we triumph not at your fall. But we say to you, Keep your Theologians at home to heal your own divisions, and send them not to make mischief among us. ... We remember the words of the Angel to Mary, 'Blessed art thou among women', and we would call her with holy Elizabeth 'the Mother of our Lord'; but God forbid that we should ever with you attribute inspiration to her, and exalt her into the place of the Holy Ghost. Awake from this idolatrous delusion! Nor is it in scorn or anger that we fling back upon yourselves the charge of lying prostrate at the feet of the Civil Power. We repeat it. It is no pleasure to us to mark your imperfections and corruptions, and the curse of the Almighty resting upon you for your obstinate adherence to them.[24]

At a similar period, Golightly observed in his private notebook: 'Popery produces different effects upon the National character of different countries, as Intoxication does upon the constitution of different individuals. Some it stupefies and brutalizes like the Spaniards and Italians, others like the Irish it excites into Maniacs.'[25] On another occasion he wrote to the newspapers to

---

[22] Golightly to Heurtley, November 1875, LPL MS 1807, fo. 61.
[23] Golightly, *Look at Home*, pp. 6, 11.
[24] Ibid., p. 34.
[25] Golightly's private notebook, c.1839, Stack MS 6d.

expose Roman Catholic hypocrisy concerning fasting in Lent.[26] It is misleading, therefore, to interpret Golightly as merely an anti-Tractarian campaigner. He was also strongly anti-Catholic and the initial anti-Catholic stimulus behind the Martyrs' Memorial at Oxford should not be overlooked.

The memorial project was revived in 1838 and Golightly's involvement at an early stage is well attested. For instance, an opponent of the memorial attributed it 'to Mr G., of Oriel College, a gentleman well known to all Oxonians ... not free from party bias'.[27] Likewise Newman blamed it on 'goose Golightly and Co'.[28] Golightly's friend, Richard Cotton, was also involved in devising the scheme and together they were appointed secretaries to the Martyrs' Memorial Committee,[29] although Peter Toon is wrong to suggest that Cotton represented the 'evangelicals' and Golightly the 'high churchmen'.[30] Cotton took a less central role, particularly during the latter stages of the project, perhaps because of his increased responsibilities on becoming Provost of Worcester College.

The original idea was to build a martyrs' church in the St Ebbe's district of Oxford, because the parish church was too small for the burgeoning population.[31] Since the inhabitants of St Ebbe's were too poor to pay for an extra church themselves, a committee (including Golightly, Pusey and Newman) was formed in June 1838 to collect subscriptions from the town and University.[32] A few months later it was suggested that this church commemorate Cranmer, Ridley and Latimer, probably an ingenious solution to raise the profile of the venture because fund-raising was not going well. Although Newman and Pusey were promised the return of their subscriptions if the new church became a Martyrs' Church, it is unlikely that the idea was primarily motivated by anti-Tractarianism.[33] Indeed Tractarian sympathisers Charles Marriott, Isaac Williams and Frederick Oakeley had already subscribed to the project.[34] This new proposal may have arisen because workmen digging a drain in Broad Street opposite Balliol College in the spring of 1838 unearthed

---

[26] *Oxford Herald*, 16 October 1841. For amusement at Golightly's mistranslation from a French periodical, see Mark Pattison to Eleanor Pattison, [17 October 1841], Lincoln College Archives, MS/Pat/II/A; *Oxford Herald*, 23 October 1841.

[27] *Morning Post*, 3 January 1839.

[28] Newman to Jemima Mozley, 23 April 1839, *Newman Letters and Diaries*, vii. pp. 66-7. Cf. Newman to Liddon, 22 February 1888, *Newman Letters and Diaries*, xxxi. p. 246.

[29] Walter K. Hamilton to William Gladstone, 20 February 1839, BL Add. MS 44183, fo. 190.

[30] Peter Toon, 'The Parker Society', *Historical Magazine of the Protestant Episcopal Church* 46 (September 1977), p. 325.

[31] Visitation returns (1838), ORO ODP b.41, fo. 172.

[32] *Oxford Herald*, 23 June 1838; Hill Diary, 19 June 1838, Bodleian MS St Edmund Hall 67/12.

[33] H.B.W. Churton to Newman, 12 November 1838, BOA Miscellaneous Letters.

[34] *Oxford Herald*, 30 June 1838.

ashes and burnt sticks. It was assumed they had discovered the actual spot on which the martyrs suffered and a call was made in the *Christian Observer* for a permanent memorial.[35]

Some did think the Martyrs' Memorial was aimed at the Tractarians. One wrote: 'It is well-known that a small faction in Oxford, working by their sophistry on the weak, started the memorial, because they thought by so doing, to annoy the learned and pious writers of the Oxford Tracts.'[36] Pusey thought the proposed memorial 'a mere party-business'[37] and 'nothing but a cut at us'.[38] Likewise Walter Kerr Hamilton (future Bishop of Salisbury) had heard some confess that they were motivated by Froude's *Remains* and believed many others were 'unconsciously influenced' by the book.[39] Benjamin Harrison (author of four of the Tracts) was initially sorry the martyrs were 'made bones of contention in Oxford by this ill-judged zeal',[40] but having found out more about the scheme he was hopeful that Pusey and Newman might join, if only the 'Protestant principles' which were to form the rallying cry could first be carefully defined. Whitaker Churton, the evangelical curate of St Ebbe's, was concerned about the dangers of division if 'an ultra Protestant, or mere Protestant spirit' took up the memorial, leading to 'an evil Reformation spirit' being stirred up.[41]

Pusey still refused to have anything to do with what he saw as 'a very unfortunate business, as was likely, since it originated in wrong and unkind feelings';[42] but Harrison persisted in trying to persuade him that he had misjudged the motives behind the project: 'I could not help feeling that you had a more painful impression as to the feelings in which this proposed Memorial originated than, from what I have seen of different parties in Oxford, I think there is occasion for.'[43] Similarly, Samuel Wilberforce thought Newman and Pusey should subscribe 'just to prevent the tone of party-feeling with which the Memorial will assuredly otherwise become associated.'[44] Nonetheless Pusey

---

[35] *Christian Observer* (June 1838), p. 354.
[36] *John Bull*, 24 February 1839, p. 93.
[37] Pusey to Edward Churton, 26 December 1838, PHL Churton MSS.
[38] Pusey to Benjamin Harrison, 10 October 1838, PHL LBV 90, fo. 409.
[39] Hamilton to Gladstone, 20 February 1839, BL Add. MS 44183, fo. 190. On Hamilton, sometimes called 'the first Tractarian bishop in England', see Kenneth M. Weinert, *Renewal beyond Party: The Career of Walter Kerr Hamilton, Bishop of Salisbury* (PhD thesis, Vanderbilt University, 1993).
[40] Harrison to Pusey, 12 October 1838, PHL LBV 47/27.
[41] Harrison to Pusey, 30 October 1838, PHL LBV 47/29.
[42] Pusey to Harrison, 5 November 1838, PHL LBV 90, fo. 416.
[43] Harrison to Pusey, 6 November 1838, PHL LBV 47/30.
[44] Samuel Wilberforce to W.F. Hook, 7 December 1838, in A.R. Ashwell and R.G. Wilberforce, *Life of the Right Reverend Samuel Wilberforce, Lord Bishop of Oxford and afterwards of Winchester with selections from his Diaries and Correspondence* (3 vols, London, 1880-82), i. p. 131.

wrote to Bishop Bagot of Oxford:

> this plan of a monument was *devised*, only to serve as a party purpose: it was, in fact, (as some of themselves avow) a counter movement against 'Froude's Remains', or, as one of them said, 'it will be a good cut against Newman'. It was intended to set the Reformers against the Fathers, and to set up certain views which some people identify with the Reformers against those of the Ancient Church.[45]

It is noteworthy, however, that several people sympathetic to the Tractarians were also supporters of the memorial. Some suggest that this is because the real motives behind the project were well-disguised. For instance, R.W. Church recorded that 'The appeal seemed so specious that at first many even of the party gave in their adhesion',[46] while Geoffrey Faber wrote: 'The Tractarians were duly embarrassed; Keble and Newman remaining rigidly aloof, while lesser men fell dumbly into the trap.'[47] Most popular introductions to the Oxford Movement follow Faber's lead and reiterate the 'trap' hypothesis.[48] Certainly the memorial caused a crisis of conscience for some, including Pusey himself. He spoke of 'friends in the country' such as George Prevost, who were 'in a state of perplexity, not knowing whether to join the memorial or no', and of 'others who are partly falling into the memorial for want of something better, partly are stigmatized because they do not join. In the N[orth] it is a sort of Shibboleth.'[49]

The subscriptions book reveals support by people from a variety of theological perspectives. There were subscribers usually identified as evangelicals, such as Lord Ashley, Lord Kenyon, the Sumner brothers, Daniel Wilson, G.S. Faber, Edward Bickersteth and Francis Close.[50] There were also subscribers of more liberal persuasion, such as Copleston, A.C. Tait and Thomas Arnold.[51] The names of Tractarian sympathisers are by no means absent, such as Bishop Phillpotts of Exeter, Edward Churton, Francis Paget, Charles Eden (author of *Tract 32*), W.F. Hook, William Gladstone, Harrison

---

[45] Pusey to Richard Bagot, 12 November 1838, PHL LBV 71, fo. 55.
[46] R.W. Church, *The Oxford Movement: Twelve Years 1833-1845* (London, 1891), pp. 192-3.
[47] G.C. Faber, *Oxford Apostles: A Character Study of the Oxford Movement* (1933; reissued London, 1954), p. 372.
[48] For recent examples, see George Herring, *What Was the Oxford Movement?* (London, 2002), p. 59; Michael Chandler, *An Introduction to the Oxford Movement* (London, 2003), p. 48; C. Brad Faught, *The Oxford Movement: A Thematic History of the Tractarians and Their Times* (University Park, Pennsylvania, 2003), p. 90.
[49] Pusey to Keble, 24 January 1839, KCL B6/519.
[50] Subscriptions book, pp. 8-9, 12-13, 23, 28, 45, 64, 74. The subscriptions and committee minute books were held by Golightly until his death, and were given by his great-nephew, Pitt Kennedy, to Wadham College, Oxford in 1900.
[51] Ibid., pp. 3, 20, [84], [89], [100], [102].

and Hamilton.[52] Members of the recently established Parker Society, which Peter Toon has shown had varied theological support, subscribed in the latter stages of the project.[53] Hook thought everyone should support the memorial, since 'we ought to honor [sic] all who have suffered hardship for the Church'.[54] Hamilton disliked the scheme, but had no objection in principle: 'I greatly regret the whole thing, but we must take matters as we find them & I think it would be right for all members of the Church now to assist in the work to save *it* from failure & *themselves* from misconstructions.'[55] Gladstone subscribed despite having famously defended Newman and Keble's involvement with Froude's *Remains* in July 1838 in the House of Commons.[56] Far from indicating the success of any supposed 'trap', such breadth of support instead illustrates that the memorial was not promoted by one section of the Church of England (such as an 'evangelical party') against another. Indeed, Lord Dungannon used the Martyrs' Memorial as evidence that evangelicals had no place in 'Protestant, orthodox and episcopal Oxford'.[57]

The chief motivation for many in supporting the memorial was as a protest against Roman Catholic expansion, not as a protest against the Tractarians. As John Wolffe, Denis Paz and others have shown, anti-Catholicism was particularly strong in the years surrounding the Roman Catholic Relief Act of 1829.[58] For instance, popular organisations were founded to defend Protestant principles, such as the Reformation Society (1827) and the Protestant Association (1835). In October 1835 nationwide celebrations were held to mark the tercentenary of the English Reformation, while between 1837 and 1841 John Foxe's *Acts and Monuments* was republished, the first complete edition

---

[52] Ibid., pp. 11, 17, 27, 34-35, 54, [88].
[53] Ibid., pp. [105-107]; Toon, 'Parker Society'.
[54] W.F. Hook to Pusey, 3 April 1839, PHL PUS 4/14.
[55] Hamilton to Gladstone, 20 February 1839, BL Add. MS 44183, fos 191-2.
[56] *Hansard*, 30 July 1838, pp. 818-9. Cf. W.E. Gladstone to John Gladstone, 22 July 1847, in Perry A. Butler, *Gladstone: Church, State, and Tractarianism. A Study of his Religious Ideas and Attitudes, 1809-1859* (Oxford, 1982), p. 173. On Gladstone's relationship to the Tractarians, see M.J. Lynch, 'Was Gladstone a Tractarian? W.E. Gladstone and the Oxford Movement, 1833-45', *Journal of Religious History* 8 (December 1975), pp. 364-89; Agatha Ramm, 'Gladstone's Religion', *Historical Journal* 28 (June 1985), pp. 327-40.
[57] *Morning Post*, 13 December 1841.
[58] J.R. Wolffe, *The Protestant Crusade in Great Britain, 1829-1860* (Oxford, 1991); D.G. Paz, *Popular Anti-Catholicism in Mid-Victorian England* (Stanford, California, 1992); G.I.T. Machin, *The Catholic Question in English Politics 1820 to 1830* (Oxford, 1964); F.H. Wallis, *Popular Anti-Catholicism in Mid-Victorian Britain* (Lewiston, NY, 1993).

since 1684.⁵⁹ 'No popery' was frequently made an electioneering tool, and was a notable influence in the Conservative revival of the late 1830s which carried Peel to power in 1841.⁶⁰

The Martyrs' Memorial at Oxford should be seen as part of this anti-Catholic movement. Vaughan Thomas, for instance, supported the memorial as 'a public manifestation ... a national expression ... in opposition to the efforts of Romanism to reestablish itself in the United Kingdom'. He hoped that the London clergy with the Duke of Newcastle and Earl of Winchilsea (veteran anti-Catholic campaigners) might support the memorial 'as a defensive measure, a rallying point for the demonstration of the strength of the Church against the open assaults & daring inroads of Popery both in London & the Provinces'. Thomas thought the memorial should be 'taken clean out of our hands, & dealt with far away from the politics & polemics of Oxford', which confused the issue.⁶¹ Likewise the *Oxford Herald* announced:

> The Popery of England, under the guidance of Jesuits, is secretly strengthening its sympathies and multiplying its means of communication and confederacy with the Popery of Ireland, while both, subject alike to the intrigues and machinations of artful emissaries of the various monkish orders, are in gradual but rapid progress of preparation for an extended conspiracy with the Popery of continental Europe against Protestantism wherever it is to be found. ... At such a moment an appeal to the hearts and consciences of the Protestants of Great Britain, reminding them of what they owe to the piety and the courage of Cranmer, Ridley, and Latimer cannot fail to command universal attention, or to evoke a prompt and suitable response.⁶²

The Inscription

In October 1838 a Martyrs' Memorial Committee was set up (including a dozen Heads of Houses) and appealed for the support of 'all well-wishers to the Church',⁶³ but early plans were in a state of disarray. Newman described this initial confusion:

> People are busy here in getting up a Memorial to the Reformers, but whether it is to be an Ultra Protestant or an Anglican testimony – whether a Church or a Cross – whether with the Reformers' names mentioned or not – whether to be set up

---

⁵⁹ D.A. Penny, 'John Foxe's Victorian Reception', *Historical Journal* 40 (March 1997), pp. 111-42; Penny, 'John Foxe, Evangelicalism and the Oxford Movement' in D.M. Loades (ed.), *John Foxe: An Historical Perspective* (Aldershot, 1999), pp. 182-237.

⁶⁰ Peel subscribed to the Martyrs' Memorial: Subscriptions book, p. 56. Wellington refused to subscribe because he thought there were already enough churches in Oxford: Wellington to Macbride, 25 February 1839, SUL Wellington Papers 2/249/116.

⁶¹ Harrison to Pusey, 30 October 1838, PHL LBV 47/29.

⁶² *Oxford Herald*, 1 December 1838. See also *Oxford Herald*, 29 December 1838.

⁶³ Circular, October 1838, Bodleian Gough Maps 233.3.

here and [or] elsewhere – and whether to be supported by Oxford people or strangers, does not appear. There are the most opposite plans. Three prospectuses have come out, or at least three plans, independent of each other and independent of the Committee. I suppose they will manage to put it into shape at last. They say that they got the President of Magdalen's name, by saying it was intended to commemorate the primitive Martyrs – and lost the Vice Chancellor's by saying it was intended as a hit at me.[64]

On 3 November a public meeting, chaired by George Hall (Master of Pembroke College), delegated the task of drawing up a prospectus and an inscription for the memorial to a small committee, chaired by J.D. Macbride (Principal of Magdalen Hall), with Philip Shuttleworth (Warden of New College), J.A. Cramer (Principal of New Inn Hall), William Sewell and Golightly.[65] Golightly's involvement alongside these senior Oxford dignitaries again shows his significance to the project, although he tended to work behind the scenes rather than in the public eye.

The inscription caused heated debate. One onlooker proposed wording which emphasised that the martyrs had 'maintained the orthodox faith' and secured 'the national blessing of a pure and apostolic church'.[66] Although Pusey was determined to have little to do with the project, he nevertheless wrote to Harrison: 'while I keep aloof myself, I shall be very glad if those who can, would mend it: what I should like best, would be a Cross with an inscription ... *without any mention of the names*. I think this might be really in the end, a good; although, (with the turn things are taking) I think it best to keep myself altogether clear.'[67] Recalling Augustine's saying, 'Non martyribus, sed Deo martyrum', he proposed the following wording:

> Deo Opt. Max.
> qui
> persecutionis Marianae
> ignibus
> Ecclesiam suam
> his in terris
> lustravit atq. purgavit.[68]

Keble wrote: 'Anything which separates the present Church from the

---

[64] Newman to Harriett Mozley, 2 November 1838, *Newman Letters and Diaries*, vi. p. 335.
[65] Hill Diary, 3 November 1838, Bodleian MS St Edmund Hall 67/12.
[66] *Oxford Herald*, 10 November 1838.
[67] Pusey to Harrison, 5 November 1838, PHL LBV 90, fos 416-8.
[68] 'To God the Best and Greatest who through the fires of the Marian persecutions purified and purged his church in these lands.' Compare 'Hints Toward a History of Puseyism', *Oxford Protestant Magazine* 1 (February 1848), p. 597.

Reformers I should hail as a great good: & certainly such would in a measure be the effect of a monument of acknowledgement that we are not Papists, without any reference to them.'[69] Pusey's inscription was passed on by Harrison to Sewell,[70] who proposed it to the sub-committee, but it was rejected in favour of the following:

> TO THE GLORY OF GOD,
> AND IN GRATEFUL COMMEMORATION OF HIS SERVANTS,
> THOMAS CRANMER,
> NICHOLAS RIDLEY,
> HUGH LATYMER,
> PRELATES OF THE CHURCH OF ENGLAND,
> WHO NEAR THIS SPOT
> YIELDED THEIR BODIES TO BE BURNED,
> BEARING WITNESS
> TO THE SACRED TRUTHS
> WHICH THEY HAD AFFIRMED AND MAINTAINED
> AND REJOICING
> THAT TO THEM IT WAS GIVEN
> NOT ONLY TO BELIEVE IN CHRIST
> BUT ALSO TO SUFFER FOR HIS SAKE,
> THIS MONUMENT
> WAS ERECTED BY PUBLIC SUBSCRIPTION
> IN THE YEAR OF OUR GOD
> MDCCCXXXIX

Rumours circulated that Golightly had drawn up the inscription,[71] but it was actually written by Macbride and approved with few alterations.[72] Shuttleworth defended it against the charge that it was intended as a protest against the Tractarians: 'Our first resolution was to make the measure *as little offensive as possible* to *all* Parties within the University. It was agreed therefore that nothing, if it could be so contrived, should be introduced into the inscription which Mr Newman or his friends could say was, by any implication, directed against themselves.'[73] The inscription was sent to Bishop Bagot, who approved it and agreed to be patron to the project.

A few days later, however, a complaint was made that 'many sincere Protestants' would be offended because the differences between the Church of England and the Church of Rome were only alluded to in a 'very sparing

---

[69] Keble to Pusey, 18 January 1839, PHL LBV 50/15.
[70] Pusey to Keble, 13 January 1839, KCL B6/503.
[71] *Morning Post*, 3 and 14 January 1839.
[72] Shuttleworth to Henry Martin, 5 January 1839, Bodleian MS Eng.hist.c.1033, fo. 102.
[73] Ibid..

manner'.[74] Therefore a further public meeting was held on 13 November at which the significant phrase 'against the errors of the Church of Rome' was added after 'the sacred truths which they had affirmed and maintained'.[75] Similarly 'a few words about Protestantism' were added to the prospectus, which now spoke both of 'the three revered Prelates, who had so large a share in restoring our own branch of the Catholic Church to primitive Orthodoxy' and of 'the blessings of that Protestant reformed religion'.[76] This public meeting was later described as 'a *hole and corner* meeting, being confined to those who entertained particular views favourable to the object',[77] but Shuttleworth insisted: '*all persons* who chose to attend were admitted'.[78] The main voice of dissent came from Richard Greswell of Worcester College who objected to the word 'Protestant' because it occurred in none of the writings of the three martyrs nor in the Prayer Book.[79]

The added phrase 'against the errors of the Church of Rome' caused considerable contention. One of the casualties was Sewell, who withdrew from the project, believing it wrong 'for one branch of the Church to raise monuments to the sins or errors of another'. Newman commented: 'stomach or conscience could not stand it and he bolted.'[80] James Ingram (President of Trinity College) also provisionally withdrew.[81] Pusey thought the scheme 'unkind to the Church of Rome, in throwing a hindrance to her reforming herself, & healing the schism.'[82] Martin Routh (President of Magdalen College) was concerned that the inscription was untrue, since Cranmer may have died not for religion, but for his political actions against Queen Mary and her mother. Edward Churton thought some of the chief blessings of the Reformation should be mentioned, although as Pusey observed, 'this would require much carefulness and a very judicious hand (else we should go to

---

[74] Ibid..
[75] Hill Diary, 13 November 1838, Bodleian MS St Edmund Hall 67/12.
[76] Hill Diary, 15 November 1838, Bodleian MS St Edmund Hall 67/12; prospectus, November 1838, Bodleian G.A.Oxon.c.54 (132).
[77] *Morning Post*, 3 January 1839.
[78] Shuttleworth to Martin, 5 January 1839, Bodleian MS Eng.hist.c.1033, fo. 102.
[79] *Jackson's Oxford Journal*, 9 February 1839. The Tractarians were said to find the word 'prelates' offensive: W.S. Bricknell, *Resignation and Lay Communion: Professor Keble's View of the Position and Duties of the Tractarians, as exhibited in his 'Letter to the Hon. Mr Justice Coleridge'*, respectfully submitted to the attention of the Members of Convocation, with reference to the approaching vacancy in the Poetry Professorship (London, 1841), p. 15. It was suggested the inscription be written in English, Greek, Latin, Hebrew, German and French: *Oxford Herald*, 27 February 1841.
[80] Newman to Thomas Henderson, 28 December 1838, *Newman Letters and Diaries*, vi. pp. 363-5.
[81] Pusey to Harrison, 21 November 1838, PHL LBV 90, fo. 426.
[82] Pusey to Keble, 13 January 1839, KCL B6/503.

pieces again).'[83]

One observer believed the phrase 'against the errors of the Church of Rome' had been added specifically to include Dissenters, 'making the memorial no longer a *Church of England memorial*, but merely *Anti-Popish*'. He insisted subscribers should withdraw, since 'it is a duty in Churchmen to refuse to fraternise with heretics and schismatics'.[84] Another thought it unfortunate that 'the glory of God' was given only one line, while the martyrs had fifteen lines, and reckoned 'in defence of the Catholic faith' would have been better than 'against the errors of the Church of Rome'.[85] A third offered six reasons not to subscribe, including that it is one's Christian duty 'not designedly to deride the opinions or to wound the feelings of others' but to live 'in the bond of Christian peace and charity'.[86]

When Bishop Bagot heard of the change in inscription, he asked that as a compromise the words 'and in support of the usages of the primitive Church' be added after 'against the errors of the Church of Rome'.[87] With circulars already disseminated and the inscription having been agreed by public meeting, the committee refused his request. Bagot therefore withdrew his patronage of the scheme, and was followed by Archbishop Howley of Canterbury and Bishop Blomfield of London.[88] Shuttleworth wryly commented: 'We have reason to believe that the friends of Mr Newman have been very active in creating this difficulty'.[89]

By early January 1839, however, Bagot had been convinced that the words 'against the errors of the Church of Rome' were not intended to monopolise the project for one section of the Church of England, and again he agreed to be patron to the memorial: 'after a good deal of enquiry I became quite satisfied in my mind that there had *not* been party feeling in the measure'.[90] Immediately Howley and Blomfield renewed their support;[91] 'as a demonstration (I suppose) against Romanism', observed Newman.[92] The following day Bagot attempted

---

[83] Pusey to Harrison, 13 January 1839, PHL LBV 91.
[84] *Morning Post*, 3 January 1839.
[85] *Jackson's Oxford Journal*, 29 December 1838.
[86] Ibid..
[87] Shuttleworth to Martin, 5 January 1839, Bodleian MS Eng.hist.c.1033, fo. 103. Or possibly, 'and in conformity with the principles of the primitive church', Pusey to Keble, 13 January 1839, KCL B6/503.
[88] Newman to Henderson, 28 December 1838, *Newman Letters and Diaries*, vi. p. 364; Shuttleworth to Holland, 30 December 1838, BL Add. MS 51597, fo. 151.
[89] Shuttleworth to Martin, 5 January 1839, Bodleian MS Eng.hist.c.1033, fo. 103.
[90] Bagot to Pusey, 28 January 1839, PHL LBV 39/6. Knox, *Tractarian Movement*, p. 222 is wrong to say Bishop Bagot refused to subscribe; Subscriptions book, p. 48.
[91] Subscriptions book, p. 23. They were soon followed by Archbishop Harcourt of York, ibid., pp. 25, [93].
[92] Newman to Keble, 8 January 1839, *Newman Letters and Diaries*, vii. p. 7. Cf. Newman to Marriott, 8 January 1839, ibid., p. 9.

to persuade Pusey to subscribe to the memorial: 'he was satisfied there were no party feelings in it ... he repeated several times, "it wd be *invaluable* (laying a great stress on the word) to the Church at this moment"'.[93] Pusey therefore suggested an ingenious solution: 'to drop my own private judgment, and to act, not on my individual responsibility, but in compliance with the wishes of my Diocesan ... my name being connected in some way with his, as "the Rev Dr P. by the Rt Rev The Lord Bp of O.".'[94] From Hursley in Hampshire, Keble commented:

> I should require something like episcopal authority to make me subscribe. Do you think the Bishop of Oxford is enough my Diocesan as well as yours, to make it right for me to sacrifice my opinion as you have offered to do? And ought I in any case unless N. does? ... But the great thing is obeying one's superior when one really knows their wishes.[95]

After consulting Archbishop Howley, Bagot decided Pusey should not support the memorial 'merely out of deference',[96] but nevertheless if he could bring himself to subscribe 'good would be silently done'.[97] The fact that Pusey and Keble were prepared even to consider subscribing, indicates that there was a degree of ambiguity behind the Martyrs' Memorial. If it had been simply an attack upon the Tractarians, it is likely they would have remained firmly at a distance.

Church or Monument?

The form which the Martyrs' Memorial should take was difficult to settle. As has been seen, the first idea put forward was a new church for St Ebbe's parish, but opinion fluctuated, and plans were changed to a monument in November 1838, back to a church in January 1839, and finally back to a monument in March 1840.

From the start there were different proposals. In October 1838 Pusey was visited in turn by Sewell (who proposed a cross in Broad Street) and Churton (who proposed a church for St Ebbe's containing statues of the martyrs), upon which he commented: 'Certainly splendid notions for these people to have lighted upon, one, a cross in the midst of the broadest street in the city; the other, a Cathedral with shrines!'[98] However, Pusey replied to his visitors: 'it must not be the Martyrs' Church, canonizing them, that there might be no objection to a cenotaph, provided the inscription were a sound one, but that the

---

[93] Pusey to Keble, 13 January 1839, KCL B6/503.
[94] Pusey to Harrison, 13 January 1839, PHL LBV 91.
[95] Keble to Pusey, 18 January 1839, PHL LBV 50/15.
[96] Bagot to Pusey, 19 January 1839, PHL LBV 39/5.
[97] Bagot to Pusey, 24 January 1839, PHL LBV 39/7.
[98] Pusey to Newman, 23 October 1838, *Newman Letters and Diaries*, vi. p. 332.

Church must be called after someone already canonized, not by individuals', again illustrating that he was not totally opposed to the project.

The first public meeting in November 1838 was 'all but unanimous' in favour of 'a monument merely ornamental', but at another meeting a fortnight later there was 'a much larger minority' in favour of a church.[99] Over the following weeks there were increasing requests for a church to be built, so a third public meeting was called for 31 January 1839 to decide the matter and in the meantime subscribers were asked to indicate whether they preferred a 'monument' or a 'church and monument'.[100]

Debate was intense. Some proposed building a church called 'The Holy Martyrs' in Broad Street, others that St Mary Magdalen's church be pulled down and a new church erected on its site.[101] With St Mary Magdalen's and St Ebbe's parishes both requiring extra seating, one early circular recommended that St Mary Magdalen's church be moved to St Ebbe's and replaced by a larger building, thus solving both problems at once.[102] A poor clergyman who could not afford to subscribe to the memorial, proposed that people offer their services in reading the liturgy or preaching, so an endowment for the church would be unnecessary.[103] However, the *Christian Observer* (with its eye on the Tractarians and Bagot's tolerance of them) warned against building a church:

> there is no adequate security that the pulpit may not be made to defame the doctrines for which those martyrs sacrificed their lives; especially in a diocese, the ecclesiastical ruler of which – melancholy to relate – has for several years been countenancing the doctrines and actions of the most insidious and dangerous body of men that ever obtruded itself within the precincts of the English Church.[104]

One observer, in favour of a monument, considered it wrong to 'mix up a monument with *public utility*' because 'the *honorary* object is lost in the practical *convenience*'. To build a church in commemoration of the martyrs would be like building a Nelson ward at Greenwich Hospital instead of a pillar, or Wellington almshouses at Chelsea instead of a monument, the reason for which would soon be forgotten. He continued: 'If the proposed Church is to have any *special* relation to CRANMER and his holy colleagues, it is mere *Popery* and *idolatry*, and if not, the nominal appropriation is mere *nonsense*. The horns of this dilemma I do not think that Dr SHORT [a member of the

---

[99] *Times*, 7 February 1839.
[100] *Jackson's Oxford Journal*, 8 December 1838.
[101] *Jackson's Oxford Journal*, 1 December 1838; *Oxford Herald*, 8 and 29 December 1838.
[102] PHL BRIC 4/1.
[103] *Oxford Herald*, 19 January 1839.
[104] *Christian Observer* (January 1839), p. 64.

committee] will be able to creep under, nor Dr GOLIGHTLY to overleep.'[105]

Statues of Cranmer, Ridley and Latimer erected in a church was considered by some to be 'the very kind of way in which Idolatry was gradually introduced into the Church of Rome. Dr SHUTTLEWORTH and Dr MACBRIDE will perhaps only stand before the statues to admire them, but their pupils will soon say, "Holy martyrs, *if* you can, pray for us", and the sons of their pupils will leave out the *if*.'[106] Pusey remarked when he heard of the proposed church: 'So we too have begun canonizing only instead of being done by the Church, it is done by one or two individuals, and we are to have Churches of S. [Latimer], S. Cranmer, and S. Ridley. Well το δ' εὐ νικατω [Let it be a good victory].'[107] He also suggested that building a church to the martyrs would be to ignore Jesus' warning against those who 'build the sepulchres of those who their fathers had slain'.[108] On the other hand, Frederic Rogers preferred a church to a monument 'as the farther they went in identifying it with Cranmer, the more intelligible was the ground that one could take against them.'[109]

Alternative forms of memorial were also suggested. One proposal was for an octangular or cruciform building (not a church), containing statues of the martyrs, with a fund for the salary of a porter, so that the memorial could be inspected by visitors free of charge.[110] Another was for almshouses for the widows of clergymen.[111]

The public meeting on 31 January 1839 was arranged to discuss whether a church or monument would be the best memorial to the martyrs. Some also hoped that the inscription would be open for discussion again, despite having been settled (albeit controversially) in November.[112] Pusey's original proposal had been rejected, but he was still hopeful that the inscription might be changed 'from a commemoration of the reformers into a thanksgiving for the blessings of the reformation'. He suggested that 'for the sake of union', Bagot or Howley might send an altered inscription, remarking that even Newman, 'tho he wished not to be committed ... saw no objection to this plan of commemorating the blessings of the Reformation by a tablet in the Church ... provided the inscription be a good one.'[113] Bagot's proposed addition of the words 'and in support of the usages of the primitive Church' was no longer a condition of his

---

[105] *John Bull*, 10 February 1839, pp. 67-8. Cf. *Jackson's Oxford Journal*, 8 December 1838.
[106] *John Bull*, 24 February 1839, p. 93. Cf. *Jackson's Oxford Journal*, 16 February 1839.
[107] Pusey to Harrison, 10 October 1838, PHL LBV 90, fo. 409.
[108] *Oxford Herald*, 1 December 1838; Pusey to Harrison, 21 November 1838, PHL LBV 90, fo. 426; Pusey to Harrison, 13 January 1839, LBV 91; Pusey to Keble, 13 January 1839, KCL B6/503.
[109] Rogers to Newman, 21 January 1839, *Newman Letters and Diaries*, vii. p. 14.
[110] *Oxford Herald*, 10 November 1838.
[111] *Jackson's Oxford Journal*, 5 January 1839.
[112] *Jackson's Oxford Journal*, 29 December 1839.
[113] Pusey to Keble, 13 January 1839, KCL B6/503.

support, but he nevertheless hoped it might be discussed (naively as it turned out).[114]

In late January Pusey learnt from the Memorial Committee that his suggested change to the inscription would not be discussed, so he put forward an alternative plan to build a second church '& so get them or a good portion of them to join us instead of [our] joining them.' The inscription might be:

> This Church was built to the honor [sic] of the Holy Trinity, and in humble acknowledgement of the Good Providence of Almighty God over His Church in this land, and of His manifold blessings, vouchsafed to her at the time of the Reformation, and continued & enlarged at subsequent eras, from that time until now, especially in the restoration of the cup to her laity and of a pure liturgy & His holy word in her native tongue.

He recommended £10,000 be raised, observing: 'The Catholics ought to do things on a better scale than ultra-Protestants.'[115] Keble promised £100 towards Pusey's scheme, and suggested a paper be issued explaining that they had devised it because their 'view of history' did not permit them to subscribe to the Martyrs' Memorial.[116] Newman, Isaac Williams, Arthur Perceval and Sir William Heathcote (patron of Hursley and MP for North Hampshire) were all opposed to the plan, however, and Bagot refused to be patron because it might seem like rivalry to the plan for a Martyrs' Church.[117] Pusey had no choice but to give it up and concluded: 'I do not know but that we shd have appeared to be in a false position, & to be insincere, taking up the Reformation to gain popularity. So I am glad that things have so ended, at least for the present.'[118]

The day before the public meeting on 31 January, a pamphlet was distributed in Oxford addressed to subscribers of the memorial, by the architect and convert to Roman Catholicism, Augustus Welby Pugin. Pugin had quarried the work of Peter Heylyn and other historians of the Reformation for information which displayed the martyrs in a poor light, describing them as a trio 'whose conduct exhibits an almost unrivalled compound of dissimulation, cruelty, and weakness.'[119] That the inscription should mention 'witness to the

---

[114] Bagot to Pusey, 28 January 1839, PHL LBV 39/6; Pusey to Harrison, 3 February 1839, LBV 91.

[115] Pusey to Keble, 24 January 1839, KCL B6/519. Ironically the new church eventually built for the St Ebbe's district was called Holy Trinity, opened in 1845.

[116] Keble to Pusey, 25 January 1839, PHL LBV 50/16.

[117] Ibid.; Bagot to Pusey, 28 January 1839, PHL LBV 39/6; Williams to Newman, nd, LBV 66/1.

[118] Pusey to Keble, 29 January 1839, KCL B6/510.

[119] A.W.N. Pugin, *A Letter on the Proposed Protestant Memorial to Cranmer, Ridley, & Latymer, Addressed to the Subscribers to and Promoters of that Undertaking* (London, 1839), p. 4.

sacred truths', angered Pugin at 'so flagrant an insult to truth'.[120] He continued:

> What a miserable foundation does your establishment stand upon, if such men as these are its pillars! ... This Cranmer memorial is only a party scheme, another deception ... But go on, erect your puny memorial, and when it is done it will cut but a sorry appearance among the venerable remains of ancient days that will surround it. CATHOLIC is indelibly stamped on the very face of your ancient city.[121]

Circulated with Pugin's pamphlet was a satirical handbill, offering a reward for the heart of Cranmer, said to have been found unburnt amongst his ashes, as a rare Protestant relic which could be deposited within the memorial.[122] A stern reply came from Thomas Lathbury (curate of the Abbey Church, Bath) who described Pugin's 'slanderous pamphlet' as 'a tissue of falsehoods from beginning to end'.[123] Pugin aroused such anger in Oxford that in March 1843 he lost the opportunity to work on the rebuilding of Balliol College as a result – partly through the influence of 'that source of all mischief Golightly'.[124] It is ironic that Gilbert Scott, who eventually built the Martyrs' Memorial, recounted: 'I fancy the cross itself was better than any one but Pugin would then have produced.'[125]

At the public meeting on 31 January 1839, Macbride headed off revived discussion of the inscription by stating that if any were there 'from curiosity' but had not yet subscribed, they could not take part in the proceedings.[126] The support of Archbishop Howley and Bishops Bagot and Blomfield had been given on condition that the memorial be a church not a monument, which left little room for debate, and it was agreed to build 'a church near the spot ... commemorative, chiefly by external decorations, of the three martyred prelates'. The non-party nature of the memorial was categorically affirmed by A.T. Gilbert (Principal of Brasenose College and Vice-Chancellor):

---

[120] Ibid., p. 3.

[121] Ibid., pp. 20, 24-5.

[122] Handbill, Bodleian G.A.Oxon.4°365 (2); *Times*, 6 February 1839.

[123] Thomas Lathbury, *The Protestant Memorial. Strictures on a Letter Addressed by Mr Pugin to the Supporters of the Martyrs' Memorial at Oxford* (London, 1839), pp. 4, 8.

[124] J.D. Dalgairns to J.M. Gresley, 3 April 1843, KCL KP 1164. See J.H. Jones, 'The Civil War of 1843', *Balliol College Annual Record* (1978), pp. 60-8; H.M. Colvin, *Unbuilt Oxford* (London, 1983), pp. 105-12; John Bryson, 'The Balliol That Might Have Been: Pugin's Rejected Designs', *Country Life*, 27 June 1963, pp. 1558-61; L.B. Litvack, 'The Balliol That Might Have Been: Pugin's Crushing Oxford Defeat', *Journal of the Society of Architectural Historians* 45 (December 1986), pp. 358-73.

[125] G.G. Scott, *Personal and Professional Recollections* (1879; facsimile edition, Stamford, 1995), p. 90.

[126] *Jackson's Oxford Journal*, 2 February 1839.

It was probably well known to those around him that the undertaking in which they were engaged was characterised as a party and a political one. He thoroughly disavowed every thing of the sort, and regretted that it was ever surmised that such were their motives. It was indeed a sign of the times when Protestants could not assemble to do honour to the memory of those they venerated without being liable to the charge of uniting for party or political purposes.

Professor Faussett proclaimed that the memorial would 'demonstrate to the world the triumph of genuine Protestant principles; which was the more necessary at this moment when the followers of the Church of Rome were making daily exhibitions of their increasing power, rearing edifices, and endeavouring to propagate their errors in every part of the country'.[127]

The main voice of dissent at the meeting (apart from a drunk who was thrown out for being 'exceedingly uproarious'[128]) came again from Richard Greswell. He was concerned that the memorial should not fail, because of 'the revival, namely, of Jesuitism, and the alarming spread of the Roman Catholic Religion in this and other countries', but he described the attempt to raise funds as 'a complete failure', falling far short of the £10,000 given as a target in November.[129] Macbride replied: 'I cannot bring myself to believe that a Protestant University, and a Protestant country, will suffer this church to be a poor memorial unworthy of the men and of the cause which it is to commemorate.'[130] He was confident that subscriptions would flood in so quickly that designs for the church would be chosen by 21 March (the anniversary of Cranmer's death), and the foundation stone would be laid on 16 October (the anniversary of Ridley and Latimer's deaths). His optimism was to prove unfounded. In fact there was a lull in the project, and John Hill records in his diary only five meetings of the committee for the rest of the year (none between March and November), as they waited for subscriptions to trickle in and tried to find an appropriate site for the Martyrs' Church.[131] Newman wrote contentedly in February:

> Golightly is making himself a Scaramouch here. He has got up a project of a Testimonial to Cranmer – but has stuck half way in the important matter of *funds*. The present appearance is as if the existing Subscribers would be obliged to lug out considerably to keep the said concern from being a failure. G. himself is a liberal man in money matters – but I shall have a malicious satisfaction in seeing certain persons obliged, as a point of honour, to come down handsomely. ... This

---

[127] *Oxford Herald*, 2 February 1839.
[128] *Jackson's Oxford Journal*, 2 February 1839.
[129] *Jackson's Oxford Journal*, 9 February 1839.
[130] *Times*, 7 February 1839.
[131] Hill Diary, 9 February, 1 March, 5 and 23 November, 7 December 1839, Bodleian MS St Edmund Hall 67/12.

precious project was mainly devised against me and others – they will pay dear for their frolick.[132]

Similarly he told another friend:

> They reckoned confidently on getting £20,000 or £25,000 for the purpose. Shuttleworth said 'It was hard if the No Popery cry would not yield them that –'. Now they have not got £5,000 yet; and the novelty of the thing over and the Bishops' adhesion. One must not boast – they may have some windfall – but at present things bid fair for their being contented with busts in the Bodleian. You see they are pledged to a *Church* – a Church involves endowment – and they are going to build it where it is not wanted, and to buy land for the purpose. They have a grand scheme of pulling down and rebuilding St Mary Magdalen. Would it not be a remarkable and quite ominous satire on the said Cranmer, if they were obliged to pull down a Church? besides, pulling it down will cost them £5,000, and they will have nothing left to build it up with. I long to see them all, as a point of honour, doubling, trebling, and quadrupling their subscriptions. I long to see old Faussett, Shuttleworth, and Radcliffe pulling out their £100s to build a thing which no one cares for, where no one wants it – and just completing it by the time that all sensible people, convinced by the force of reason and the testimonies of history, have given up Cranmer as a bad job.[133]

St Ebbe's and St Mary Magdalen's parishes must have soon been informed that the Martyrs' Church would not be combined with their own church building projects. St Ebbe's relaunched their building appeal in March 1839,[134] and St Mary Magdalen's began theirs in June.[135] Instead three sites 'near the spot' were considered for the Martyrs' Church, all of which were occupied by houses: a site in front of Trinity College, next to Kettle Hall (but the college rejected the committee's approaches), a site opposite Balliol College (but the leases of the premises had been only recently renewed), and a site on the south side of Beaumont Street opposite that bought for the new Taylorian Institute (now occupied by the Randolph Hotel, but this was too expensive). In addition an Act of Parliament might have been necessary for the second two sites to settle any dispute over compensation.[136]

Subscriptions were received from across Britain, from supporters as far afield as Northampton, Sheffield, Colchester, Bristol, Manchester, Bath, Barnsley, Henley, Worcester, Reading, Glastonbury, Derby, Cheltenham,

---

[132] Newman to M.R. Giberne, 6 February 1839, *Newman Letters and Diaries*, vii. p. 28.

[133] Newman to Woodgate, 3 March 1839, ibid., p. 46. Cf. Newman to Christie, 5 February 1839; Newman to Jemima Mozley, 4 March 1839, ibid., pp. 25, 47-8.

[134] *Oxford Herald*, 9 and 16 March 1839.

[135] St Mary Magdalen, minutes of committee for church enlargement (1839-42), ORO PAR 208/2/A2/2; churchwardens' accounts and vestry minutes (1834-52), PAR 208/4/F1/76.

[136] *Oxford Herald*, 14 March 1840.

Clapham, Cambridge, Aberystwyth and Newcastle,[137] but by December 1839 total subscriptions stood at less than £5,000 and hopes for a Martyrs' Church 'near the spot' had to be abandoned. A proposal to use the funds to erect a church in St Ebbe's parish was yet again considered but rejected. Instead, on 7 December the Memorial Committee agreed to approach St Mary Magdalen's parish about the possibility of erecting a monument at the northern end of their churchyard, and rebuilding and enlarging the north aisle of their church.[138] This proposal was ratified at a fourth public meeting on 5 March 1840. Macbride, who chaired the meeting, again emphasised that 'party' motives were not involved in the scheme:

> The only denomination which it can reasonably be supposed to displease is that which condemned them to the flames, as heretical; and, with reference to Roman Catholics, permit me to observe that our object is not to stigmatise the persecutors, but to honour the persecuted. ... I repeat that we have been influenced by no party motives, we have made no appeal to the passions of prejudices, we have simply proposed to honour departed worth, or rather, I should say, the grace of God, magnified in these Martyrs ...[139]

Before shortage of funds can be put forward conclusively as the reason for abandoning the plan for a Martyrs' Church two further pieces of evidence must be considered. First, when a further appeal for subscriptions was made in October 1840, the committee declared that 'the sums contributed were ample for the original design', but more than £1,000 extra would now be required to meet the expense of 'a Memorial consisting of two parts' (a Martyrs' Aisle and a Martyrs' Monument).[140] It is unlikely that the projected monument and aisle would cost more than an entire church, and the 'ample' funds are most generously interpreted as 'overstatement' by the committee.

Second, Bishop Knox recounted how 'Golightly used to tell with much satisfaction of the defeat of the attempt to side-track the project into the erection of a church. Such a church must necessarily have been built in the slums and condemned from the first to obscurity.'[141] It is hard to imagine how Golightly, who as secretary of the committee was doing his best to raise subscriptions, would consider it a victory if not enough money was collected. Indeed when a church was suggested instead of a monument in December

---

[137] Subscriptions book, passim. Banks were opened for subscriptions in Scotland: *Times*, 1 April 1839.

[138] Hill Diary, 7 December 1839, Bodleian MS St Edmund Hall 67/12; minutes of Oxford Paving Commissioners, 15 January and 3 February 1840, Bodleian Gough Maps 233.2.

[139] *Oxford Herald,* 14 March 1840.

[140] Circular, October 1840, Bodleian Vet.A4.c.128 (2).

[141] Knox, *Tractarian Movement,* p. 221.

1838, he increased his subscription from £10 to £50.[142] Probably, therefore, it was not the erection of a church in general to which Golightly objected, but the erection of a church in the slum district of St Ebbe's (although this may have been his original intention a year and a half before). Moreover, the 'defeat' was possibly a simple boast by Golightly many years after the event to people who could not remember the original circumstances.

The monument was to be a cross, in the Gothic style of the 'Eleanor Crosses' erected by Edward I. On the death near Lincoln of his wife, Queen Eleanor, Edward had erected eleven crosses at the points where her funeral procession stopped on the way to Westminster (Charing Cross). By 1840 only three of these survived, in different geometrical designs, at Geddington (triangular), Northampton (octagonal) and Waltham (hexagonal). The committee decided that the Martyrs' Memorial should be based on the cross at Waltham,[143] and designs were received from seven architects: Gilbert Scott, John Blore, John Derick,[144] M.E. Hadfield (who had designed the monumental cross erected in 1834 at Sheffield's cholera cemetery[145]), G.J.J. Mair (who designed the third storey of the cross open on all sides, 'like a lanthorn', allowing light through the middle), J.C. Buckler and Mr Mitchell (an unknown volunteer). The designs of Scott, Blore and Derick were short-listed, and Scott's was eventually chosen, with thirteen out of sixteen votes.[146] The appropriateness of the fact that Scott was grandson of Thomas Scott, the famous evangelical Bible commentator, did not pass without note.[147]

From this point onwards the erection of the Martyrs' Memorial was much more straightforward. At Scott's recommendation, magnesian limestone for the monument, of the same sort used for the new Houses of Parliament, was brought from Charles Lindley's Mansfield Woodhouse Quarries in Nottinghamshire.[148] In March 1841, Charles Kirk of Sleaford, the county surveyor for Lincolnshire, won the contract for building the memorial, with a

---

[142] Subscriptions book, p. 1.
[143] *Copy of the information and instructions forwarded to the architects who have been invited to favour the committee with designs for the Memorial Cross* (Oxford, 1840); *Gentleman's Magazine* 13 (May 1840), pp. 516-7. Cf. *Oxford Herald*, 15 December 1838.
[144] Derick's design survives at Bodleian MS Top.Gen.a.4, fo. 8.
[145] John Holland, *Cruciana. Illustrations of the Most Striking Aspects under which the Cross of Christ, and Symbols derived from it, have been contemplated by Piety, Superstition, Imagination, and Taste* (Liverpool, 1835), p. 247.
[146] Hill Diary, 20, 27 and 30 May 1840, Bodleian MS St Edmund Hall 67/13; *Oxford Herald*, 6 June 1840; *Times*, 2 July 1840. Blore hoped Wellington and Sir Charles Wetherell would exert their influence with the committee on his behalf: Blore to Earl of Charleville, 23 May 1840, SUL Wellington Papers 2/250/131. See the subsequent spat between Blore and Derick: *Times*, 6, 9 and 16 July 1840.
[147] *Times*, 2 July 1840.
[148] Committee minute book, 9 September 1840.

tender of £4,455,[149] and William Cox from Oxford was appointed the clerk-of-works and principal carver.

The foundation stone of the monument was laid by Frederick Plumptre (Master of University College, who had taken over from Macbride as chairman of the committee) on 19 May 1841.[150] It had been raining most of the day right up until the time of the ceremony, but the rain stopped and the sun broke through the clouds, seen as 'an apt emblem of those clouds which were dispelled by the Reformation'. Vaughan Thomas addressed the gathered crowd on the appropriate timing of the occasion, since it was the tercentenary of Cranmer's achievement in May 1541 of getting the Bible in English distributed throughout the parish churches of England authorised by Henry VIII.

The statues of Cranmer, Latimer and Ridley were carved in London by Henry Weekes, who worked in the studio of the sculptor Sir Francis Chantrey, and arrived complete in Oxford in April 1842. Each statue was designed to convey a theological message, re-enforcing the martyrs' stand 'against the errors of the Church of Rome'.[151] The statue of Cranmer holds a large Bible with 'Maye MDXLI' cut into its cover, illustrating the importance to the Reformation of the Scriptures in the vernacular. Ridley worked to prevent vestiary questions from creating divisions between supporters of the Reformation, and so his statue, unlike the others, is robed in a cope, 'whilst his hands, firmly locked together, erect countenance, and well-balanced stability of body, represent the firmness of his faith'. Latimer's statue was described as

> the very image and representation of pious humility, or rather of old age, stooping under the burden of four-score years, indicating at the same time submissiveness to the will of God, and holy resolution to do it: the arms crossed over the breast greatly aid the expression of humility. There is also the look of that self-possession which enabled the aged Latimer to say to his disputatious Judge ... 'The Popish Church hath erred, and doth err.'[152]

Around the basement storey of the monument were carved various symbols, again illustrating theological points: a crown of thorns and a crown of glory; firebrands and palm branches ('the martyrs' palm of victory'); a chalice, to remind people of the martyrs' role in the eucharistic controversies of the Reformation; and an open Bible with the words 'THE BYBLE IN ENGLYSH AUTHORIZED MAYE MDXLI'. Similar designs were carved along the outside wall of the north aisle of St Mary Magdalen's church. Under each bishop were carved the coats of arms of his family and of his episcopal see. The

---

[149] Committee minute book, 28 January and 20 March 1841. See contract with Kirk and related correspondence, Bodleian MS Top.Oxon.b.112, fos 10-56.
[150] *Oxford Herald*, 22 May 1841, supplement.
[151] *Copy of information to architects*; Henry Weekes to William Buckland, committee minute book, 5 February 1841.
[152] *Oxford Herald*, 4 June 1842, supplement.

arms of Cranmer were considered particularly significant, with the pelican motif indicating his willingness to shed his blood, and a larger pelican was carved underneath his statue.

The Martyrs' Aisle of St Mary Magdalen's church was finally opened on 19 May 1842, containing on permanent display an old door from the Bocardo Prison, reputed to be that of the cell in which the three martyrs were imprisoned.[153] Gilbert (by now Bishop of Chichester) preached on Deuteronomy 13.1-6, drawing parallels between the Church of Rome and the 'false prophet' who entices people to serve false gods. He protested against 'the spiritual despotism usurped by the Roman Church', and condemned 'her discipline ... her unscriptural veneration of names and things and places, her invocation of saints, and Transubstantiation, and pretended infallibility, and the arrogated supremacy of the Pope.'[154] By April 1843 all the work on the Martyrs' Monument and Martyrs' Aisle had finally been completed (except the bronze lettering of the all-important inscription and an ornamental iron railing), but the total cost had escalated to more than £9,000.[155]

Conclusion

From conception to completion the Martyrs' Memorial in Oxford spanned five years of intense theological debate within the Church of England. This fast-moving theological climate has distorted the way in which historians have interpreted the memorial. In his study of anti-Catholicism, John Wolffe argues that during the late 1830s the Protestant societies and press were only incidentally concerned with opposing the Oxford Movement and directed their main attacks against Roman Catholicism, but that after the publication of Newman's *Tract 90* in February 1841, Tractarianism began to come to the forefront of anti-Catholic concerns.[156] In the same way, as the theological climate changed, the original anti-Catholic element of the Martyrs' Memorial was forgotten and it became increasingly identified with anti-Tractarianism.

On the publication of *Tract 90* (examined in the next chapter), Bishop Sumner of Winchester wrote to Golightly: 'It is time indeed that you should

---

[153] This door was rescued by Alderman Fletcher when the Bocardo was demolished in 1771, and moved in 1800 to the lodge of Bridewell prison in Gloucester Green from where it was transferred to the Martyrs' Aisle: Wade, *Walks in Oxford*, p. 430; *Christian Observer* (August 1837), pp. 495-6. The door was given on permanent loan in 1963 to St Michael-at-the-North-Gate, Oxford, where it is on display.

[154] *Oxford Herald*, 4 June 1842, supplement.

[155] Committee minute book, 20 March 1841, 7 April 1843 (loose papers); Hill Diary, 7 April 1843, MS St Edmund Hall 67/14; *Record*, 9 January 1843. Plumptre and Golightly both donated £200 to help defray expenses, and Thomas bought the wooden model of the monument (now in the *Museum of Oxford*).

[156] Wolffe, *Protestant Crusade*, pp. 117-8.

arise & build your Martyrs' Memorial ... The vizor has been dropped.'[157] One pamphleteer writing against *Tract 90* proclaimed that Newman was trampling over 'the charred ashes of Latimer and Ridley' and enticing others into the 'murderous embrace' of the 'Great Harlot'.[158] Another lamented:

> Shades of Cranmer, Latimer, and Ridley, come forth! Come forth, that ye may be stripped of honours which you have long unworthily borne, and of crowns of martyrdom to which you have no claim! Your own Articles of religion are identical, it appears, with the doctrines of Gardiner and Bonner, and you were, therefore, not martyrs but suicides![159]

During the *Tract 90* crisis the following verses circulated Oxford:

> Quoth Dick the other day to Ned,
> 'What zeal the Church shows here!
> To build a Pile to those who bled
> For truths she holds so dear.'
>
> 'Not quite so fast', saith wiser Ned,
> 'I prithee list a minute:
> She builds their Pile *outside the Church*,
> But d__s the doctrines *in it*!'[160]

In the midst of the contest between Isaac Williams and James Garbett for the Poetry Professorship in late 1841, it was observed: 'It is somewhat remarkable that while one party in the University are erecting their misplaced cross to the memory of the martyrs, another party are fostering doctrines that would soon rekindle the fires in Broad-street.'[161] Someone else warned that the Tractarians were 'extinguishing the torch which was kindled in the fires of Latimer and Ridley',[162] and when William Palmer of Magdalen College (not to be confused with William Palmer of Worcester College) anathematized Protestantism, it was suggested the word 'Protestant' be added to the memorial inscription.[163] In 1841 Golightly's friend, W.S. Bricknell (vicar of Grove near Wantage), donated the profits from the sale of his anti-Tractarian sermons to the memorial

---

[157] Charles R. Sumner to Golightly, 12 March 1841, LPL MS 1809, fo. 87.
[158] Charlotte E. Tonna, *A Peep into Number Ninety* (London, 1841), p. 32.
[159] William Thorpe, *A Review of a Letter from the Rev. W. Sewell ... to the Rev. Dr Pusey: to which are added Remarks on Mr Sewell's Treatise on Christian Morals, and also on an Article, attributed to him, entitled 'Romanism in Ireland' which appeared in a Late Number of the Quarterly Review* (London, 1841), pp. 13-4.
[160] *Oxford Chronicle*, 17 April 1841.
[161] *Standard*, 10 December 1841.
[162] *Standard*, 3 January 1842.
[163] *Oxford Herald*, 22 January 1842.

fund.¹⁶⁴ The rapid spread of Roman Catholicism was never far away, and two workmen were reported to have seceded to Rome while employed on the memorial itself.¹⁶⁵

For the *British Critic* of July 1841 Frederick Oakeley wrote a notorious article on Bishop Jewell, questioning whether the Reformers suffered for 'the truth'. He expressed a desire for 'the *unprotestantizing* ... of the national Church', which should 'recede more and more from the principles, if any such there be, of the English Reformation.'¹⁶⁶ The next year George Townsend of Durham published a parody entitled *The Life and Defence of the Conduct and Principles of the Venerable and Calumniated Edmund Bonner* by 'a Tractarian British Critic', in which he wrote: 'Our Ultra-Protestant friends at Oxford have lately erected a monument to Ridley, Cranmer, and Latimer, who were burnt. We hope so to unprotestantize, or to Romanize the nation, that we shall raise a monument to Mary, Gardiner, and to Bonner, who burnt them.'¹⁶⁷ In 1843 the following poem appeared:

> Thou shewest, OXFORD, contrasts sad and strange,
> Here! true to death – The Witness Fathers sealed
> Their evidence in blood! – and from the pile
> Furnished by ruthless Rome, sent through the Isle,
> Light, wherein Truth has since stood clear revealed.
> But while a Nation's thankfulness bids rise
> Their fair MEMORIAL! – thy voice seems to change.
> Some, their time-honoured names at nought do prize,
> Mock at their martyr-service – deem the light
> They died to kindle, shows the truth too bright –
> And through a veil again would have us read,
> The saving verities of Britain's Creed:
> If THESE be right – this Monument deface,
> If THOSE! – why give their poor defamers place?¹⁶⁸

In his novel *Loss and Gain* (1848), Newman linked Tractarian secessions to Rome with a Martyrs' Memorial at Cambridge,¹⁶⁹ and by the tercentenary of Ridley and Latimer's deaths in October 1855, the Martyrs' Monument and

---

¹⁶⁴ W.S. Bricknell, *Preaching: Its Warrant, Subject, & Effects, Considered with Reference to 'The Tracts for the Times'* (London, 1841), frontispiece.
¹⁶⁵ *British Critic* 32 (July 1842), p. 259.
¹⁶⁶ Frederick Oakeley, 'Bishop Jewel; His Character, Correspondence, and Apologetic Treatises', *British Critic* 30 (July 1841), pp. 14, 45. See Browne to Golightly, 18 March 1842, LPL MS 1804, fo. 107. On Oakeley, see Peter Galloway, *A Passionate Humility: Frederick Oakeley and the Oxford Movement* (Leominster, 1999).
¹⁶⁷ George Townsend, *The Life and Defence of the Conduct and Principles of the Venerable and Calumniated Edmund Bonner* (London, 1842), p. 380.
¹⁶⁸ *Letters from Oxford, in 1843: by 'Ignotus'* (Dublin, 1843), p. [3].
¹⁶⁹ John H. Newman, *Loss and Gain* (London, 1848), p. 318.

Martyrs' Aisle were explicitly interpreted as a protest against both Roman Catholicism and Tractarianism.[170] In later years Golightly was best known as a life-long opponent of the Oxford Movement, and Newman as a convert to Rome. It is natural therefore that in the light of subsequent developments, historians have interpreted the Martyrs' Memorial as a simple anti-Tractarian scheme. Yet its original anti-Catholic nature must not be forgotten.

---

[170] John C. Miller, *The Martyrs' Candle: A Sermon Preached at the Commemoration of the Tercentenary of the Martyrdom of Ridley and Latimer* (London, 1855), pp. 19, 21.

CHAPTER 3

Keeping Oxford Protestant

> the Oxford parties ... consist of Hampden and the Arians, Newman and the Tractarians, Palmer and the Retractarians, and Golightly and the Detractarians.
>
> (H.C. Robinson, 1845)[1]

During the early 1840s Charles Golightly established his reputation as one of the leading anti-Tractarian campaigners in Oxford. His knowledge of the local scene and his personal contacts within the University provided him with an unusual fund of information about Tractarian activities. This he used to great effect, sending regular warnings to the church authorities and to the general public about the latest worrying developments within the Tractarian camp. William Copeland, who succeeded where Golightly failed in becoming Newman's curate at Littlemore, called him 'the common informer of the Movement'.[2] R.W. Church named him as one of the Oxford Movement's 'savage enemies'.[3]

Golightly quickly became an expert in harnessing the powers of the press to stir up public feeling in defence of the Protestant heritage of the Church of England and the University of Oxford. However, his unsolicited letters to bishops and archdeacons, and his anonymous newspaper criticisms of fellow clergymen, meant that his enemies found it easy to portray him as a troubler of the church. He was mocked as a telltale and busybody, a lover of gossip who thrived on theological strife. Golightly's reputation as 'Oxford's Protestant spy' grew with every year that passed. Recalling the early 1840s, Church wrote: 'A system of espionage, whisperings, backbitings, and miserable tittle-tattle, sometimes of the most slanderous or the most ridiculous kind, was set going all over Oxford. Never in Oxford, before or since, were busybodies more truculent or more unscrupulous.'[4] Golightly's alarming disclosures about the Tractarians soon became a byword, considered worthy of as much serious notice as the political speeches of the radical Joseph Hume or bawdy ballads from the

---

[1] *Diary, Reminiscences, and Correspondence of Henry Crabb Robinson* edited by Thomas Sadler (3 vols, London, 1869), iii. p. 260.
[2] PHL LBV 72, fo. 9.
[3] Church to Pusey (?), 20 June 1882, PHL LBV 70/112.
[4] Church, *Oxford Movement*, p. 290.

notorious Seven Dials district of London.⁵

Nevertheless, despite his methods, Golightly was not without numerous supporters. Many of his attacks did real damage to the Tractarian cause and had to be taken seriously. Although Golightly often led the way, he had an unfailing ability to mobilize both clergy and laity to join his campaigns. Fellow Protestants wrote to him from around the country with encouragement and praise. William Chambers spoke for many when he applauded the opposition called forth by the *Tracts for the Times* and told Golightly: '*You* at least have done what you cd, & have proved yourself valiant for the truth.'⁶ It was the crisis over the last Tract which thrust Golightly firmly into the limelight.

Tract 90

On 27 February 1841, Newman published his notorious *Tract 90*, entitled *Remarks on Certain Passages in the Thirty-Nine Articles*. The Articles were seen as one of the foundation stones of the Protestant Reformed Church of England, but the Tract was a bold attack upon their exalted status and their universally-accepted Protestant interpretation. Newman's primary aim was to show that although the Articles were 'the offspring of an uncatholic age', they could still be subscribed in good faith and *ex animo*, 'by those who aim at being catholic in heart and doctrine.'⁷ This involved a sometimes tortuous argument about their 'literal and grammatical sense'. For example, Article 21 states that general councils 'may err', but Newman claimed that by the rules of strict grammar this only applied to councils called by princes, not councils called 'in the name of Christ'. Likewise Article 22 rejects the 'Romish doctrine' concerning purgatory, indulgences, the veneration of images and relics, and the invocation of saints as 'a fond thing vainly invented ... repugnant to the Word of God'. In a famous chapter (described by Golightly as 'the most extraordinary part of this most extraordinary production'⁸) Newman tried to prove that 'Romish doctrine' meant only the popular medieval corruption of official Roman Catholic dogma, not the teaching of the primitive church, or contemporary Catholicism, or even the Council of Trent. He freely admitted that he thought it a 'duty' to interpret the Articles 'in the most Catholic sense they will admit' and proclaimed: 'The Protestant Confession was drawn up with the purpose of including Catholics; and Catholics now will not be excluded.'⁹ Elsewhere in the Tract, Newman was less than complimentary about the Articles. He rejected calls for their immediate abolition, but

---

⁵ *English Churchman*, 19 September 1844, p. 597.
⁶ William Chambers to Golightly, 25 April 1844, LPL MS 1805, fo. 9.
⁷ John H. Newman, *Remarks on Certain Passages in the Thirty-Nine Articles* (Tract 90) (London, 1841), p. 4.
⁸ Golightly, *Strictures on No.90*, part 2, p. 14.
⁹ Newman, *Remarks on Certain Passages in the Thirty-Nine Articles*, pp. 80, 83.

continued:

> Till her members are stirred up to this religious course, let the Church sit still; let her be content to be in bondage; let her work in chains; let her submit to her imperfections as a punishment; let her go on teaching with the stammering lips of ambiguous formularies, and inconsistent precedents, and principles but partially developed. We are not better than our fathers; let us bear to be what Hammond was, or Andrews, or Hooker; let us not faint under that body of death, which they bore about in patience; nor shrink from the penalty of sins, which they inherited from the age before them.[10]

These statements were nothing less than revolutionary. The fact that the Tract was issued anonymously, as were all the *Tracts for the Times*, only increased its aura of sedition. Newman's sentiments were calculated to shock.

Early in the battle which exploded over *Tract 90*, the *Times* applauded combatants for avoiding 'the coarse and grovelling vulgarities of sectarian polemics'.[11] Yet such optimism did not last long. Soon pamphleteers and leader writers were regretting the 'vituperative bitterness and exaggeration'[12] and the 'painful degree of excitement' which greeted the Tract.[13] Robert Scott (fellow of Balliol College) was alarmed by the 'want of moderation, and prejudice on both sides, both in Oxford and elsewhere',[14] while young Frederick Temple (an undergraduate at Balliol) told his mother: 'if you trust one party the Tract is a piece of the most complete Jesuitical juggling, if the other nothing can be more fair.'[15] Some who had previously defended the *Tracts for the Times*, like William Sewell, now quickly distanced themselves from the movement. He advised that the series be immediately discontinued, in order to avoid 'the possibility of a schism'.[16] Yet others saw the conflict as an inevitable consequence of the deep theological fault lines running through the Church of England. For example, Frederick Oakeley privately professed to Pusey: 'I have long apprehended that, sooner or later, there must be a struggle between the maintainers of two entirely opposite *principles*, however much in other respects united'.[17] Meanwhile Newman's sister encouraged him to stand his ground:

---

[10] Ibid., p. 4.
[11] *Times*, 18 March 1841.
[12] Thomas Ridley, *Strictures on Party and Controversy in Religion; with reference to the Church of England, Romanism, Infidelity, Presbyterianism, the Dissenters, and the Oxford Tract System* (London, 1841), p. 34.
[13] *Morning Post*, 1 April 1841.
[14] Scott to Tait, [15 March 1841], LPL Tait Papers, vol. 77, fo. 22.
[15] Frederick Temple to Dorcas Temple, 15 March 1841 in E.G. Sandford, *Frederick Temple: An Appreciation* (London, 1907), p. 59.
[16] William Sewell, *A Letter to the Rev. E.B. Pusey ... on the Publication of No.90 of the Tracts for the Times* (Oxford, 1841), p. 12. Sewell made a similar appeal in *Irish Ecclesiastical Journal* 1 (March 1841), p. 141.
[17] Oakeley to Pusey, 15 March 1841, *Newman Letters and Diaries*, viii. p. 95.

'The tug of war must come some day'.[18]

One of the central figures who aggravated the controversy over *Tract 90* was Golightly. Of all his many theological protests, it was his assault upon that Tract which was most remembered in later years. His reputation as an anti-Tractarian campaigner was encapsulated by his hostile actions during the crisis. Forty-five years later, Golightly's close friend, E.M. Goulburn, attempted to defend him in the pages of the *Guardian*, but felt unable to justify his response to *Tract 90*. Goulburn could only offer the extenuating circumstances of mental instability:

> Golightly sometimes lost himself in controversy. ... And, in bar of a harsh judgment upon certain things which he did and said in the heat of controversy, I may observe that *I do not think he was quite himself at that period.* His mind, harassed and excited by what he conceived to be the disingenuousness of the Tract, and the danger to which the Church would be exposed, should such a method of dealing with the formularies prevail and find acceptance, was momentarily thrown off its pivot. One night ... he (quite seriously, for indeed he was in no frame for joking) expressed his apprehension that at some street corner a party of Tractarians might be lying in wait for him, with the view of doing him some grievous bodily harm. All my laughing at him did not seem to dispel the illusion. He had Tract XC on the brain.[19]

Others drew attention to the malevolent anger of Golightly and his Protestant allies. For instance, Oakeley recalled:

> At Oxford, especially, there were persons who hunted down the leading Tractarians with implacable fury and unwavering pertinacity. They acted the part of jackals to the nobler beasts of prey. They had their emissaries in the suspected colleges, and their eyes were intent upon every action, and even gesture, from which the purposes of those whom they regarded as the enemies of religion could be collected or conjectured. There is the best reason for believing that the opposition to Tract 90 was fostered, if not set on foot, by one of these active subordinates; and the partial success of that effort was such as to encourage the repetition of similar attempts as the occasion for them arose.[20]

As Oakeley hints, the *Tract 90* affair may have given Golightly a fresh taste for ecclesiastical warfare. His anti-Tractarian campaigning was raised to a new level of intensity and the crisis saw the start of five years of ceaseless agitation.

When John Keble visited Oxford in early March 1841 he 'found the fat all in

---

[18] Harriett Mozley to Newman, 14 March 1841, ibid., p. 67.
[19] Goulburn, *Reminiscences of Golightly*, pp. 30, 32.
[20] Frederick Oakeley, *Historical Notes on the Tractarian Movement (A.D. 1833-1845)* (London, 1865), pp. 84-5.

the fire ... Golius had been stirring every body up'.²¹ Others described Golightly as 'in high agitation'²² and 'in high glee'.²³ In the heat of the controversy, Newman identified him as the chief cause of the storm, lamenting to his friends:

> Do you know I am in a regular scrape about that Tract 90? – *all* through Golius – who has solely proprio marte [by his own efforts] stirred up the world, who else would have slept.²⁴

> people are taking it up very warmly, thanks (I believe) entirely to Golightly ...²⁵

> Golightly ... is *the* Tony Fire-the-Faggot of the affair, and ... would be pleased to know I felt him to be so ...²⁶

> Golightly was the *sole* concoctor of the whole matter and has the thanks of four Bishops in his pocket.²⁷

Likewise Church explained that Golightly's

> genius and activity have contributed in the greatest degree to raise and direct the storm. He saw his advantage from the first, and has used it well. He first puffed the Tract all over Oxford as the greatest 'curiosity' that had been seen for some time: his diligence and activity were unwearied; he then turned his attention to the country, became a purchaser of No.90 to such an amount that Parker [the bookseller] could hardly supply him, and sent copies to all the Bishops, etc. In the course of a week he had got the agitation into a satisfactory state, and his efforts were redoubled. He then made an application to the Rector of Exeter [Joseph Richards] to be allowed to come and state the case to him with the view of his heading a movement, but he was politely refused admittance; he had better success with the Warden of Wadham [Benjamin Symons]. ... The row, which has

---

[21] John Keble to Elizabeth Keble, 14 March 1841, quoted in R.H. Greenfield, *The Attitude of the Tractarians to the Roman Catholic Church 1833-1850* (DPhil thesis, Oxford University, 1956), p. 324.
[22] E.C. Woollcombe to Robert Scott, nd, PHL SCO 1/46/1.
[23] Church to Newman, 10 March 1841, *Newman Letters and Diaries*, viii. p. 66.
[24] Newman to Henry Wilberforce, 11 March 1841, ibid., p. 67.
[25] Newman to Harriett Mozley, 9 March 1841, ibid., p. 61.
[26] Newman to Perceval, 12 March 1841, ibid., pp. 68-9. 'Tony Fire-the-Faggot' is the nickname given in Scott's *Kenilworth* to Anthony Forster of Cumnor Place. Scott portrays him as a religious hypocrite and accomplice to murder, the only man prepared to provide a light for Latimer and Ridley's pyre since 'he liked as well to see a roasted heretic, as a roasted ox': Walter Scott, *Kenilworth* (1821; Penguin Classics edition, London, 1999), p. 13.
[27] Newman to Henry Wilberforce, 22 March 1841, *Newman Letters and Diaries*, viii. p. 113.

been prodigious they say, has made Golly a great man ...²⁸

Church added sarcastically: 'It is supposed that a niche will be left for him among the great Reformers, in the Memorial, and that his life will be put in Biographical Dictionaries.'²⁹

As Church indicates, Golightly's principal tactic was to bring the Tract to the attention of as many people as possible, in the hope that senior churchmen would pronounce against it. He posted the publication to a number of bishops he knew would be sympathetic to the anti-Tractarian cause, including Bishop Blomfield of London, Bishop Shuttleworth of Chichester and the two evangelical Sumner brothers, John (Bishop of Chester) and Charles (Bishop of Winchester). Blomfield responded: 'It is really hardly possible to believe that the writer of such a Tract can be of the Reformed Church'³⁰ Shuttleworth encouraged Golightly that *Tract 90* was 'obviously calculated to do much mischief if not checked.'³¹ Charles Sumner hoped 'the tocsin will not have been rung in vain in the ears of the University.'³² Golightly also sent the Tract to Bishop Phillpotts of Exeter, who had begun to show his dislike of Tractarian teaching and deplored Newman's 'rashness, and culpable indiscretion'.³³ In July 1841 Oakeley praised the moderation of the bishops, despite those who were 'endeavouring, by clamour, to provoke them to some authoritative interference', though the pronouncements soon came in a flood of episcopal charges denouncing *Tract 90*.³⁴ Golightly also tried to form a bond with George Miller in Ireland by sending him a copy of the Tract. Miller was shocked by Newman's opinions and expressed his disgust 'that any man above the lowest class of pettifogging practitioners of the law should descend to chicanery so disreputable'.³⁵

---

[28] Church to Rogers, 14 March 1841, ibid., pp. 109-10.
[29] From a conflated version of the above letter, in Church, *Dean Church*, p. 31.
[30] Blomfield to Golightly, 11 March 1841, LPL MS 1804, fo. 52.
[31] Shuttleworth to Golightly, 10 March 1841, LPL MS 1809, fo. 57.
[32] Charles R. Sumner to Golightly, 12 March 1841, LPL MS 1809, fo. 87.
[33] Phillpotts to Golightly, 1 April 1841, LPL MS 1808, fo. 214. Golightly also possibly sent *Tract 90* to Archbishop Howley: Shuttleworth to Golightly, 10 March 1841, LPL MS 1809, fo. 56. See 'A Member of Convocation' (Golightly?) in *Standard*, 25 March 1841; Edward B. Pusey, *The Articles Treated On in Tract 90 Reconsidered and their Interpretation Vindicated in a Letter to the Rev. R.W. Jelf* (Oxford, 1841), p. 151.
[34] Frederick Oakeley, *The Subject of Tract XC Examined, in Connection with the History of the Thirty-Nine Articles, and the Statements of Certain English Divines* (London, 1841), p. 9. See W.S. Bricknell, *The Judgment of the Bishops upon Tractarian Theology. A Complete Analytical Arrangement of the Charges Delivered by the Prelates of the Anglican Church, from 1837 to 1842 inclusive; so far as they Relate to the Tractarian Movement* (Oxford, 1845), pp. 532-71; Nockles, 'Oxford, Tract 90 and the Bishops', pp. 55-63.
[35] Miller to Golightly, 12 March 1841, LPL MS 1808, fo. 91.

Meanwhile in Oxford itself Golightly set out to generate local hostility towards the Tract. According to Archbishop Tait's biographers, on the day *Tract 90* was published William Ward (fellow of Balliol College) burst excitedly into Tait's rooms at Balliol and threw the pamphlet down on the table with the words, 'Here is something worth reading!'[36] However, Golightly also claimed responsibility for recruiting the future archbishop for the opposition. He used to enjoy recounting how at a particular spot in Holywell Street he called Tait's attention to the Tract, saying 'Have you read Tract XC? No? Then go home and read it.'[37] Indeed, Church wrote at the time that Tait was 'merely a skirmisher set on to rouse people by Golightly'.[38]

On 8 March, less than ten days after Newman's Tract appeared, a council of war was held at Wadham College in the rooms of Edward Cockey. In attendance was a small group of men brought together by Golightly – Tait, John Griffiths (Sub-Warden of Wadham), Thomas Brancker (fellow of Wadham), T.T. Churton (Vice-Principal of Brasenose) and H.B. Wilson (fellow of St John's).[39] He had also tried to recruit Charles Eden, Travers Twiss (fellow of University College and later Regius Professor of Civil Law), Robert Hussey (Regius Professor of Ecclesiastical History from 1842), Edward Hansell (of Magdalen College) and George Johnson (Golightly and Tait's fellow curate at the Baldons), but without success.[40] Tait had drafted a public address about *Tract 90*, which described it as 'highly dangerous', tending 'to mitigate, beyond what charity requires, and to the prejudice of the pure truth of the Gospel, the very serious differences which separate the Church of Rome from our own'. It rebuked the Tract's 'new and startling views' about the liberty allowed in interpreting the Church of England's historic formularies, which would lead to Roman doctrine being taught in lecture rooms and pulpits.[41] The meeting agreed that the address should be signed by Tait, Griffiths, Churton and Wilson, who became known as the 'Four Tutors' – 'gentlemen who had scarcely the happiness of each other's acquaintance till Golly's skill harnessed them together.'[42] Cockey and Brancker did not add their names in case the remonstrance appear to originate from Wadham College, nor did Golightly since he held no college or University post.[43] Once again Golightly proved

---

[36] Randall T. Davidson and William Benham, *Life of Archibald Campbell Tait, Archbishop of Canterbury* (2 vols, London, 1891), i. p. 78.
[37] Knox, *Tractarian Movement*, p. 253.
[38] Church to Rogers, 14 March 1841, *Newman Letters and Diaries*, viii. p. 109.
[39] Liddon, *Life of Pusey*, ii. p. 167.
[40] Church to Rogers, 14 March 1841, *Newman Letters and Diaries*, viii. p. 109. Cf. E.C. Woollcombe to Scott, 17 March 1841, PHL SCO 1/46/3.
[41] *Certain Documents, &c &c Connected With Tracts for the Times, No.90* (Oxford, 1841), pp. 5-6. See draft at LPL Tait Papers, vol. 77, fos 1-6.
[42] Church to Rogers, 14 March 1841, *Newman Letters and Diaries*, viii. p. 109.
[43] Liddon, *Life of Pusey*, ii. p. 167. E.C. Woollcombe considered adding his name to the address: Tait to Golightly, [6 March 1841], LPL MS 1809, fos 112-3.

himself a master at enticing significant figures within the University to put their reputations on the line and publicly challenge the Tractarians, while he remained behind the scenes co-ordinating the protests.

Having come forward boldly to criticise Newman, the Four Tutors now left themselves open to public opprobrium. For example, Henry Bulteel (who had seceded from the Church of England in 1831) argued that 'if the Semipapist is not consistent in his Subscription, neither is the Arminian, nor is the Evangelical'. Therefore he doubted that the Four Tutors could 'consistently cast the first stone at the accused'.[44] Another critic warned the Four Tutors that they were supported in their protest by an amalgam of theological radicals:

> Infidels, Semi-infidels, Heretics, Schismatics, false Churchmen, and, alas! Ministers who scruple not themselves to alter the Church Services ad libitum, and point-blank to contradict from the pulpit her express declarations, *these* all hail the Four Tutors as allies; for *them* you fight; and for *them*, if you succeed, you conquer. ... your most numerous friends and applauders are the worst enemies of the Church ... you minister arms and strength to their unholy or unhappy fury.[45]

John Griffiths replied that Newman had been rebuked not merely 'by young and shallow and flippant critics, but by persons of matured experience, of sober judgment, of tempered feelings, of guarded language, persons actuated by no party spirit, but staunch and sincere and zealous supporters of the Church of England'.[46]

Having been kick-started by Golightly, the public protests against Newman and his Tract now quickly began to gather momentum. Within a week of the Four Tutor's address, *Tract 90* also received a formal censure from the University's Heads of Houses. As well as his attempts to rouse the Warden of Wadham, it was said that Golightly 'struck up a great intimacy' with the Provost of Oriel, Edward Hawkins, who had to suffer his 'pertinacious prosing.'[47] Likewise Vice-Chancellor Wynter was urged in a private interview 'with an active and highly respectable member of Convocation' to bring the Tract before the Hebdomadal Board.[48] Hinting at Golightly's influence, one observer wrote that the Heads '*went lightly* forward', following 'the blind track of ill-digested popular prejudice'.[49] The Rector of Exeter planned to present the Heads with a letter by William Palmer (of Worcester College) in praise of *Tract 90*, but concluded 'it would have been like throwing "cold water on red-hot

---

[44] *Oxford Chronicle*, 20 March 1841.
[45] John Griffiths, *Two Letters Concerning No.90 in the Series Called the Tracts for the Times* (Oxford, 1841), pp. 7-8.
[46] Ibid., p. 24.
[47] Church to Newman, 11 March 1841, *Newman Letters and Diaries*, viii. p. 66.
[48] Wynter Memoir, PHL LBV 135/79. Liddon identified this member of Convocation as Golightly: Liddon, *Life of Pusey*, ii. p. 170.
[49] *Morning Post*, 24 March 1841.

iron".'⁵⁰ Instead the Board agreed, by nineteen votes to two, to appoint a committee to draw up a censure of the Tract.⁵¹ Newman asked for time to publish an explanation, but was refused.⁵² Responding to the public mood (or as Church put it, 'driven frantic by Golightly and the "Standard"'⁵³) the Board resolved on 15 March that the 'modes of interpretation' suggested by *Tract 90*, 'evading rather than explaining the sense of the Thirty-nine Articles, and reconciling subscription to them with the adoption of errors which they were designed to counteract', were against the University statutes.⁵⁴ Pusey later claimed the Heads had 'acted under panic and excitement, produced by misconception and misrepresentation',⁵⁵ and that their statement looked 'like the vent of a long-pent-up wish to be free of us.'⁵⁶ Thomas Mozley lambasted them for 'tyranny', lamenting that the Hebdomadal Board had 'degenerated from the arbiter of justice into an accomplice of party'.⁵⁷ Meanwhile Arthur Stanley appealed to Tait: 'do not draw these Articles too tight, or they will strangle more parties than one. I assure you when I read the resolution of the Heads I felt the halter at my own throat.'⁵⁸

Some wanted to go even further and summon Convocation, so that the University *en masse* could pronounce a public censure of *Tract 90*.⁵⁹ One observer warned, however, that this would only 'proclaim aloud to the world the want of unity among our brethren, and ... give the enemy a cause to blaspheme.'⁶⁰ Even Golightly balked at this step. Not afraid in future years to

---

⁵⁰ Palmer to Newman, 9 March 1841; Church to Newman, 10 March 1841, *Newman Letters and Diaries*, viii. pp. 63, 65.

⁵¹ OUA Hebdomadal Board Minutes, 12 March 1841. The two who voted against this decision were Joseph Richards (Rector of Exeter College) and E.A. Dayman (one of the proctors). See Griffiths, *Two Letters*, pp. 13-4; John H. Newman, *Tract XC On Certain Passages in the XXXIX Articles ... With a Historical Preface by the Rev. E.B. Pusey, DD and Catholic Subscription to the XXXIX Articles Considered in Reference to Tract XC by the Rev. John Keble, MA* (revised preface, Oxford, 1866), p. xvi.

⁵² Newman to Hawkins, 14 March 1841, *Newman Letters and Diaries*, viii. pp. 72-3. See Newman, *Tract XC* (1865 edition), pp. xii-xiii; (1866 edition), pp. xvi-xviii. Hawkins – Pusey, January – March 1866, OCL Newman Letters, nos 1033-46; Newman to Hawkins, 1 January and 8 April 1866, *Newman Letters and Diaries*, xxii. pp. 124-5, 206-7; R.D. Middleton, *Newman at Oxford: His Religious Development* (London, 1950), pp. 244-70.

⁵³ Church to Rogers, 14 March 1841, *Newman Letters and Diaries*, viii. p. 109.

⁵⁴ *Certain Documents, &c &c Connected With Tracts for the Times, No.90*, p. 3.

⁵⁵ Pusey, *Articles Treated On in Tract 90*, p. 150.

⁵⁶ Newman, *Tract XC* (1865 edition), p. xiv.

⁵⁷ Thomas Mozley, 'The Oxford Margaret Professor', *British Critic* 30 (July 1841), p. 232.

⁵⁸ Stanley to Tait, 30 March 1841, LPL Tait Papers, vol. 77, fo. 29.

⁵⁹ *Record*, 5 and 12 April 1841. See Golightly to Blomfield, 15 April 1841, LPL MS 1804, fos 56-7.

⁶⁰ *Oxford Herald*, 17 April 1841.

harness the power of Convocation during his campaigns, he admitted in this case it would be fruitless, tending 'to stir up party excitement and party feeling on a matter in which all feelings should be absorbed in love and truth. ... High Church and Low Church principles, as they are called, would guide some, the party influence others. Popery or Presbyterianism might terrify others from recording their vote according to the principles on which, under other less exciting circumstances, they might act.'[61]

In the face of intense hostility, Newman attempted to stand his ground. In self-defence, he explained that *Tract 90* had been misunderstood and was intended merely 'to keep members of our Church from straggling in the direction of Rome'.[62] However, before the end of March he issued a *Letter to the Bishop of Oxford*, conceding to Bagot's request that the Tracts be discontinued.[63] William Palmer (of Worcester College) was dismayed by this weak yielding to public pressure, and complained privately to Pusey:

> all is concession to popular error, and to hostile *party* ... in the meantime *nothing* is done to save Church principles – *nothing* is done to remove popular mistakes – *nothing* is done to encourage Churchmen – and some of the most deserving men in the country are trampled under foot. On the one side all is triumph and ferocity, and on the other all is timidity, and apology, and humiliation. Is this a proper position for the great and influential body who hold Church principles?[64]

Palmer drew up a Declaration, published in the *Oxford Herald*, in praise of the *Tracts for the Times*,[65] but it was abandoned for fear it would provoke Counter-Declarations and result in 'a quasi-Schism'.[66]

The *Tract 90* controversy continued to boil over for many months. Throughout 1841 a torrent of pamphlets poured off printing presses across the country, some applauding the Tract, others abusing it. Amongst the first and the longest responses was Golightly's *Strictures on No.90*, which appeared in two parts and ran to a total of 170 pages (the longest publication of his life), signed simply 'A Member of the University of Oxford'. Part 1 was published as early as 24 March and Part 2 in mid-April.[67] In a sustained historical and theological

---

[61] Golightly, *Strictures on No.90*, part 2, p. 95.
[62] John H. Newman, *A Letter Addressed to the Rev. R.W. Jelf, DD, Canon of Christ Church, in Explanation of No.90, in the Series Called the Tracts for the Times* (Oxford, 1841), p. 29.
[63] John H. Newman, *A Letter to the Right Reverend Father in God, Richard, Lord Bishop of Oxford, on Occasion of No.90, in the Series Called the Tracts for the Times* (Oxford, 1841).
[64] Palmer to Pusey, 1 April 1841, in Liddon, *Life of Pusey*, ii. p. 205.
[65] *Oxford Herald*, 3 April 1841. For earlier plans for a Declaration, see Pusey to Keble, 17 March 1841, *Newman Letters and Diaries*, viii. p. 96.
[66] R.W. Jelf to Newman, 18 March 1841, ibid., p. 90.
[67] Golightly, *Strictures on No.90*, part 2, pp. 92-4.

critique, Golightly set out to prove that the teaching of *Tract 90* was 'neither Anglican nor scriptural'.[68] Addressing each of Newman's points in turn, he showed how they were contradictory to the statements of classical 'Anglican' works such as the Homilies, John Jewell's *Apology of the Church of England*, Richard Hooker's *Laws of Ecclesiastical Polity*, Alexander Nowell's *Catechism*, Joseph Hall's *No Peace with Rome*, James Ussher's *Body of Divinity* and Jeremy Taylor's *Dissuasive from Popery*. The other authorities quoted in the *Strictures* ranged from Augustine and Chrysostom, via Bishop Nicholas Ridley, to seventeenth and eighteenth century divines such as Bramhall, Beveridge, Burnet, Waterland and Secker. As well as attempting to prove that Newman was un-Anglican, Golightly went further and called him an 'apologist' of the Church of Rome, 'that apostate Church'.[69] He claimed that the tendency of *Tract 90* was 'not to reconcile Romanists to our Church, but members of our Church to communion with Rome. So to lessen the distance, by drawing us to them, not them to us; palliating their errors, and over-shadowing our truths'.[70] He showed the similarity between Newman's teaching and that of the Lateran Council, the Tridentine Council, the Roman Breviary and the scholastic theologian Peter Dens (often quoting at length from these authorities in Latin).

Of all Golightly's pamphlets, his *Strictures on No.90* has the best claim to theological scholarship. Only his *Letter to the Bishop of Oxford* (1840) and his *Brief Account of the Romeward Movement in the Church of England in the Days of Archbishop Laud* (1867) reveal a similar depth of reading and historical research. Together they support Goulburn's bold assertion that Golightly

> deserved to be called a *divine*; he had a fair (not, I think, an extraordinary) knowledge of the Fathers, was well versed in the works of Calvin, and of the great English theological writers, and had made himself perfect master of the Roman controversy, to which he seemed to have a natural attraction. ... history was a most congenial study to him. He did not travel perhaps over a very wide area of it (his method of study on all subjects was slow), but what periods he did know he knew thoroughly and accurately, and had his historical resources at command whenever they were wanted.[71]

However, this was scholarship with a sharp polemical edge. The country was more alarmed by *Tract 90* than any previous Tract, but Golightly warned that it contained 'no new statement of the views of the party, nothing more erroneous in doctrine than has before repeatedly been published by the Tractarians.'[72] He

---

[68] Ibid., part 1, p. 48.
[69] Ibid., part 2, p. 60.
[70] Ibid., part 2, p. 91.
[71] Goulburn, *Reminiscences of Golightly*, pp. 22-3.
[72] Golightly, *Strictures on No.90*, part 2, p. 90.

observed, 'how far sophistry and argumentative conviction may prevail, I know not; but of one thing I am fully conscious, that if their principles of interpretation prevail, we may have all doctrine preached in our pulpits, but that which is scriptural, catholic, and true.'[73] Returning to his favourite theme of Tractarian deceit, he also questioned Newman's '*honesty* and fair play'.[74] Golightly concluded this *magnum opus* with a passionate plea that 'No peace with Rome' must remain

> the watchword of our Church, if she wish not again to sink under the bondage of ecclesiastical tyranny, whether the seat of supremacy be the city whose merchants are princes [Babylon-Tyre in the Bible], or her whose foundation is upon seven hills. To the Lord alone can we look up, in these perilous times, for deliverance and peace. He stilleth the madness of the people, He sitteth above the water-flood, He remaineth King for ever! Yet our duty is obvious. Let us gird up the loins of our mind, be sober, be vigilant; watch and pray, that we enter not into temptation. 'From all false doctrine, heresy, and schism, from hardness of heart, and contempt of thy word and commandment; Good Lord deliver us.'[75]

A Party Man?

Golightly's first anti-Tractarian pamphlet, *A Letter to the Bishop of Oxford*, claimed that Newman and his curate at Littlemore mixed water and wine at holy communion, in 'clear violation' of the Prayer Book rubrics.[76] Therefore Newman took the opportunity of his own *Letter to the Bishop of Oxford* during the *Tract 90* crisis, to explain that he mixed water and wine at the University Church in Oxford so as not to upset the stomachs of early-morning communicants.[77] Golightly was far from satisfied. He thought Newman had dodged the issue by overlooking the practice at Littlemore, so he wrote privately to Bagot in April 1841 reiterating his accusation and raising questions about Newman's honesty (a favourite line of attack). However, the bishop refused to have anything to do with the matter unless it was brought before him as an official charge.[78]

Fearing 'a fresh outbreak of needless agitation and war of pamphlets', Bagot asked Bishop Blomfield to have a quiet word with Golightly to recommend peace. Bagot knew Blomfield was more likely to be heard, and explained:

---

[73] Ibid., part 1, p. 18.
[74] Ibid., part 2, p. 15.
[75] Ibid., part 2, p. 95.
[76] Golightly, *Letter to the Bishop of Oxford*, pp. 12-14.
[77] Newman, *Letter to the Bishop of Oxford*, p. 42. See G.C. Berkeley to Bagot, 4 April 1841, PHL LBV 71, fos 256-7.
[78] Golightly – Bagot, 6, 7 and 8 April 1841, PHL LBV 71, fos 258-69. See Golightly, *Strictures on No.90*, part 2, pp. 93-4; *Brief Remarks*, pp. 7-8.

> Mr Golightly, though an excellent man, is one who certainly, in Oxford at least, is too fond of troubled waters – and he has for some years past (they *once were* great friends) felt and shewn a personal hostility to Mr Newman which is perhaps greater than he is himself aware of. In short he would I think prefer agitation with a chance of triumph, to peace if it entailed silence.[79]

Therefore Blomfield wrote to Golightly, without mentioning Bagot's name, expressing his hope that Newman's concession to discontinue the Tracts would mean an end to the agitation in Oxford. He exhorted his young correspondent:

> I am extremely desirous that no further controversy should be raised at the present moment. Individuals on both sides will, of course, give utterance to their opinions; which I trust will be done temperately and charitably: but I strongly deprecate any thing like a combined effort to put down the supporters of the Tract writers ... Enough has been done, to direct the attention of the Church to what is dangerous or questionable in the Tracts, and more, no doubt, will be done, by repeated discussion: but it would be most injurious to the Church, that *parties* should be more distinctly separated *from*, and ranged *against* each other, than they now are. The errors, whether of doctrine or discipline, which are imputed to Mr Newman and his friends, may now, I think, be left to the vigilance & discretion of the Bishops.[80]

Golightly immediately reassured the bishop that he knew of no planned campaign against the Tractarians, although he admitted that it was difficult to view Newman as 'an ingenuous or even an honest man'.[81] With the conflict balanced precariously on a knife edge, Blomfield was not confident that his letter would keep Golightly permanently in check. He lamented to Bagot: 'I am sorry to see that Dr Hook and others are most unwisely fanning the flame which might otherwise be kept under; and if they continue to do so, it will be impossible to keep their opponents quiet.'[82] Such, indeed, proved to be the case.

In 1838, appealing for unity between members of the Church of England, W.F. Hook (vicar of Leeds) had rebuked those who mistook 'party spirit for Christian zeal' and who formed 'hostile confederacies within the Church ... waging a worse than civil war with the deadly weapons of theological hatred.'[83] He asked, 'is this a time to divide our house, and to form parties and factions? Is this the season for discord?',[84] and concluded:

---

[79] Bagot to Blomfield, 12 April 1841, PHL LBV 71, fos 270-2.
[80] Blomfield to Golightly, 14 April 1841, LPL MS 1804, fos 54-5.
[81] Golightly to Blomfield, 15 April 1841, LPL MS 1804, fo. 57.
[82] Blomfield to Bagot, 14 April 1841, PHL LBV 72, fo. 3.
[83] W.F. Hook, *A Call to Union on the Principles of the English Reformation. A Sermon, preached at the Primary Visitation of Charles Thomas, Lord Bishop of Ripon* (London, 1838), p. 23.
[84] Ibid., p. 43.

> I hate party names, which often make distinction between persons where there is no difference. I believe that, in real principle, a more united body of men never existed than the Clergy of England at the present time, and the attempt to make them suppose themselves at variance cannot certainly be of God. But if men *will* divide us – be it so.[85]

The *Tract 90* affair, however, made Hook reconsider the benefits of partisanship. He had intended to publish a critique of the Tract, but when it was condemned by the Hebdomadal Board he decided instead to support Newman.[86] In March 1841, he wrote to Newman: 'Our Enemies force us into the position of a Party and as a Party we must be prepared to act: by which I mean, that in any ulterior proceedings little minor points of difference must be forgotten and we must act as one man in asserting our general Principles.'[87]

At a meeting of the SPCK in Leeds, Hook proclaimed, in what was called 'a formal declaration of war',[88] that is was no longer possible to ignore 'the lamentable fact that the Church of England is now divided into two parties.' He continued:

> A party has been found acting in a party spirit, and on party tactics, in various parts of the country; and in self-defence a party now must be formed to meet it. (Cheers.) We can no longer halt between two opinions; we cannot attempt to hunt with the hounds and to run with the hare; we must take our part; and as far as I am concerned I will nail my colours to the mast of High Principle, and blow high or blow low, come sunshine or come storm, through the Grace of God, I will adhere to them. (Loud applause.)[89]

Bishop Longley of Ripon, who was chairing the meeting, interrupted Hook to call him to order, so Hook expanded on his thesis in a *Letter to the Bishop of Ripon*. He asserted:

> It is a fact, an undeniable fact, that there are two Parties in the Church of England; the High Church Party and the Low Church Party. And the act of the Hebdomadal Board renders it absolutely necessary for us to range ourselves on the one side or on the other. That is to say, we must join that party with which in general principles we agree, and not desert it merely because we may think that a few individuals may have expressed themselves on some points incautiously, or have been hurried into acts which a colder and a calmer judgment may condemn. ...

---

[85] Ibid., p. 173.
[86] W.F. Hook, *Letter to the Right Reverend the Lord Bishop of Ripon, on the State of Parties in the Church of England* (London, 1841), pp. 5-6.
[87] Hook to Newman, 17 March 1841, *Newman Letters and Diaries*, viii. p. 98.
[88] Thomas Kennion, *Letter to the Rev. Walter Farquhar Hook, DD, Vicar of Leeds, with Observations upon his Letter addressed to the Right Reverend, the Lord Bishop of Ripon* (London, 1841), p. 3.
[89] *Leeds Intelligencer*, 3 April 1841.

We cannot halt between two opinions. We must take our side. Minor differences must be forgotten when our general principles are attacked. High Churchmen have always been averse from such a proceeding. We have hitherto repudiated all idea of Party. I myself have done so very zealously. But we are opposed by a Party; and a Party, too, feared by our rulers; and, in self-defence, we also must form ourselves into a Party; and not refuse to support one another merely because we may not all agree in respect to a few non-essentials. ... The Low Church party have declared a war of extermination against High Church Principles, and peace will not be restored to the Church until it is made quite clear that we are too strong to be put down by clamour.[90]

Nevertheless, Hook maintained that bishops should 'moderate between parties without declaring themselves for either'.[91]

Golightly warned Bishop Blomfield that Hook's Letter would cause 'serious and extensive mischief'.[92] He thought it 'most injudicious ... highly injurious ... likely rather to widen the breach, than to restore us to a state of "unity and concord"',[93] and responded with an anonymous pamphlet entitled *New and Strange Doctrines Extracted from the Writings of Mr Newman and His Friends, in a Letter to the Rev. W.F. Hook*, signed by 'One of the Original Subscribers to the Tracts for the Times'. Golightly challenged Hook's claim that the fault of the Tract writers was merely 'the want of a little care and caution'.[94] As evidence, he pointed to violent Tractarian attacks upon the Thirty-Nine Articles, the Prayer Book, the Reformation and the bishops. This was followed with examples of the 'novelty and strangeness' of Tractarian teaching on subjects like justification, sin after baptism, reserve, the Council of Trent, tradition, the adoration of images, the invocation of saints, the sign of the cross, and the sinlessness and assumption of the Virgin Mary. Far from being 'incautious' expressions, Golightly insisted that the Tractarians were making 'calculated efforts to shake the confidence of the youthful and unwary in the existing system of the Anglican Church, and to prepare them for the reception of another system – what, – Mr Newman is not yet prepared to say.'[95] He

---

[90] Hook, *Letter to the Bishop of Ripon* (third edition), pp. 5-6, 14.
[91] Ibid., p. 13. Other authors at this period divided the Church of England into three parties: R.M. Milnes, *One Tract More, or the System Illustrated by 'The Tracts for the Times', Eternally Regarded. By a Layman* (London, 1841), p. 3; G.A. Poole, *The Present State of Parties in the Church of England: with especial reference to the Alleged Tendency of the Oxford School to the Doctrines and Communion of Rome* (second edition, London, 1842), pp. 4-6; *Noah's Ark. A Satire. Dedicated to the Readers of the 'Tracts for the Times'. By a Graduate of the University of Oxford* (Oxford, 1841), pp. 9-12; Robert Montgomery, *The Three Parties: or, Things as They Are in the Church of England* (London, 1845); William Goode in *Christian Observer* (1847), pp. iii-viii.
[92] Golightly to Blomfield, 15 April 1841, LPL MS 1804, fo. 57.
[93] Golightly, *Strictures on No.90*, part 2, p. 94.
[94] Golightly, *New and Strange Doctrines*, p. 7.
[95] Ibid., p. 25.

concluded his pamphlet with a direct rebuke to Hook, proclaiming that people should be told

> not to join a party, but avoid one; and instead of calling any man master, in all their religious perplexities to look to Him for guidance who has promised his Holy Spirit to all who ask Him, and has given us by the mouth of his prophet, the following all-important exhortation; 'Trust in the Lord with all thine heart, and lean not to thine own understanding: in all thy ways acknowledge Him, and He shall direct thy paths.'[96]

There were a number of other similar responses to Hook in subsequent months, which chastised him for advocating partisanship. For instance, Francis Hill of Cheltenham asked:

> Party men! what is a party man? One who, from short-sighted views of human expediency, suppresses his conscientious conviction of the errors of his *party* – one who ranges himself upon all occasions, right or wrong, with a particular set – a man who is the slave of confederacy, instead of a champion for the truth ... A party man is a *factious* man, whatever be the object of contention.[97]

Likewise F.D. Maurice stated that the notion of party was '*the* great anti-Church doctrine', and lamented that what was once considered a 'sin' was now proclaimed a 'duty'.[98] Moreover he objected to Hook's categorisation of everyone into 'High Church' or 'Low Church' as far too simplistic.[99] *Fraser's Magazine* also challenged Hook's thesis:

> It must not be supposed that Dr Hook's division is correct. He has magnified the importance of the Tractarians too much. Nor must it be imagined that the members of the Hebdomadal Board and the *four tutors* are low churchmen. Those gentlemen are *sound* churchmen, but not *low* churchmen; and with them are ranged the great mass of the clergy. ... In our estimation, the term *high churchmen*, by being applied to and assumed by the Tract writers and their supporters, will henceforth become a term of reproach – a term to designate a mere section of the clerical body; while some other expression must be devised to

---

[96] Ibid., pp. 26-7.
[97] Francis Hill, *A Letter to Dr Hook, in Reply to his Letter to the Bishop of Ripon; with Proofs of the Failure of Mr Newman's Defence of the 90th Tract* (Cheltenham, 1841), p. 3.
[98] F.D. Maurice, *Reasons for Not Joining a Party in the Church. A Letter to the Ven. Samuel Wilberforce, Archdeacon of Surrey: suggested by the Rev. Dr Hook's Letter to the Bishop of Ripon, on the State of Parties in the Church of England* (London, 1841), pp. 8-9.
[99] Ibid., pp. 12-18. For Maurice's views of church parties, see C.R. Sanders, 'Coleridge, Maurice, and the Church Universal', *Journal of Religion* 21 (January 1941), pp. 31-45; Sanders, 'Was Frederick Denison Maurice a Broad-Churchman?', *Church History* 3 (September 1934), pp. 222-31.

characterise the majority of the clergy. ... The majority of the clergy are neither *high* nor *low churchmen*, as these terms are understood by Dr Hook, but they are TRUE, SOUND, AND ORTHODOX CHURCHMEN![100]

According to Maurice's son, Hook acknowledged he was wrong and withdrew his pamphlet.[101] By 1842 he had returned to distinguishing between 'High Churchmen of the old school, the Church-of-England men' (such as himself) and 'the Oxford Divines'.[102]

Meanwhile Golightly continued to look for opportunities to attack the Tractarians in Oxford. A.T. Gilbert (Principal of Brasenose College) encouraged him in the duty of 'keeping an unsleeping watch and the careful abstinence from all inadvertent compromise.'[103] During the spring and summer of 1841, Newman's friends and allies published detailed and passionate defences of *Tract 90*. For example, at the start of April, Keble offered *The Case of Catholic Subscription to the Thirty-Nine Articles Considered*. Pusey came out in May with a typically massive pamphlet, running to over 200 pages, entitled *The Articles Treated On in Tract 90 Reconsidered and Their Interpretation Vindicated*. These were followed in July by Frederick Oakeley's *The Subject of Tract XC Examined*. Most provocative of all was William Ward who published *A Few Words in Support of No.90* and *A Few More Words*, arguing that the Thirty-Nine Articles might be subscribed in their non-natural sense.[104] He spoke of the 'defective state', 'decayed condition' and 'present degradation' of the Church of England, which was responsible for leaving its members 'buried in the darkness of Protestant error'.[105] Protestants might view *Tract 90* as 'a wanton exercise of ingenuity', but Ward described it as 'a most important step towards claiming for all members of the Church of England a full right to that *substratum* of Catholic doctrine on which Catholic feeling and practice may be reared up.'[106] He looked forward to the day when the Church of

---

[100] 'The Tracts for the Times, No.90', *Fraser's Magazine* 23 (June 1841), pp. 636-7.

[101] Frederick Maurice, *The Life of Frederick Denison Maurice, chiefly told in his own Letters* (2 vols, London, 1884), i. p. 304.

[102] W.F. Hook, *Reasons for Contributing Towards the Support of an English Bishop at Jerusalem, stated in a Letter to a Friend* (London, 1842), p. 38. When taunted in 1850 with having deserted the ranks of High Churchmen, Hook declared: 'Although I have not left any party, or joined any party, but remained stationary, I cannot be blind to the fact that many who are now reputed Low Churchmen, are what would have been called thirty years ago High Churchmen': *The Nonentity of Romish Saints, and the Inanity of Romish Ordinances* (third edition, London, 1850), p. 9.

[103] Gilbert to Golightly, 30 May 1841, LPL MS 1806, fo. 4.

[104] William G. Ward, *A Few Words in Support of No.90 of the Tracts for the Times, partly with reference to Mr Wilson's Letter* (Oxford, 1841); *A Few More Words in Support of No.90 of the Tracts for the Times* (Oxford 1841).

[105] Ward, *A Few More Words*, pp. 29-30.

[106] Ibid., p. 79.

England would be 'restored to active communion with the rest of Christendom' as 'the united Catholic Church'.[107]

Golightly was an avid reader of these pamphlets and sent a copy of *A Few More Words* to Bishop Bagot, proclaiming that Newman and Ward were 'convinced that the Council of Trent is orthodox'. He also reported that Ward was hoping for the reunion of the Church of England with the Church of Rome, and that some of Newman's undergraduate disciples had begun to attend the local Roman Catholic chapel in Oxford.[108] At the start of the new academic year, in October 1841, Golightly issued some *Brief Remarks Upon No.90, Second Edition, and Some Subsequent Publications in Defence of It*. He pointed to inaccuracies in the pamphlets of Pusey, Ward and Oakeley, and complained that Newman had been allowed to produce a second edition of *Tract 90* despite his promise to the bishop that the *Tracts for the Times* would be discontinued. As at the time of their irrevocable split in 1837, Pusey responded to these criticisms by offering Golightly some moral advice:

> for a long time past, others as well as myself have seen that you are (unconsciously, I trust) influenced by a secret grudge or dislike of Newman. Whether it be owing to yr having been annoyed in the O[riel] C[ommon] room, or to whatever other ground, certain it is, that while you speak kindly of myself, you speak very differently of him, who is every way far my superior. ... If, as is probable, you are not conscious of it, I wish for your own sake, you wd try to divest yourself of every painful feeling about him. It wd be, I trust, to your endless welfare. ... If we had more love & holiness, we shd understand each other better.[109]

However, George Miller praised Golightly's *Brief Remarks* as 'brief, but pungent',[110] and the *Morning Herald* thought that if his pamphlet did not 'awaken the Protestant mind of England to a wholesome sense of the danger, the insidious advances and the ultimate objects of *Puseyism*, we should despair of the cause of the noblest institution, religious and civil, that has ever adorned and solaced civilised society.'[111]

The Poetry Professorship

John Keble's ten-year term as Oxford's Professor of Poetry reached its conclusion in 1841. Isaac Williams appeared to be a natural successor, well-

---

[107] Ibid., p. 91.
[108] Golightly to Bagot, 27 May 1841, PHL LBV 72, fos 7-11.
[109] Pusey to Golightly, 23 October 1841, LPL MS 1808, fo. 242.
[110] Miller to Golightly, 25 October 1841, LPL MS 1808, fo. 115. In June 1841 Golightly had planned to publish *A Letter to George Miller*: Miller to Golightly, 4 June 1841, LPL MS 1808, fo. 104.
[111] *Morning Herald*, 18 November 1841.

known as a poet through his *The Cathedral* and *Thoughts in Past Years*. However, Williams was also notorious for his part in the Tractarian movement, especially as author of *Tract 87* on *Reserve in Communicating Religious Knowledge*. Like Newman's *Arians*, this Tract advocated the principle of 'economy' with the gospel truths, so was anathema to evangelicals and other traditional Protestants. As a result the election for the new professor was hotly-contested. Williams was put forward by Trinity College as their official candidate, while Brasenose College (headed by Principal Gilbert) proposed James Garbett, rector of Claydon in Sussex. As early as June 1841, Golightly's co-belligerent, W.S. Bricknell, warned the public that Williams would be a candidate and denounced his teaching.[112] By mid-September Pusey was already claiming the election was 'made a party question'.[113]

The contest intensified in Michaelmas term. On 5 November Golightly was invited to preach the annual Bonfire Night sermon before the University. He spoke from the Old Testament about the Gibeonite deception of Joshua, 'tracing the evil of the principle of doing evil that good may come'.[114] The notes for his sermon do not survive, but Golightly probably drew a parallel between the Gibeonites and the Tractarians – just as the Gibeonites hid the full facts from the Israelites, so he believed the Tractarian principle of 'reserve' was an 'evil' deception. Less than a fortnight later, on 16 November, a circular from Wadham College proclaimed that if Williams was elected it would be seen as Convocation's endorsement of Tractarianism.[115] The next day a second circular (attributed to Golightly[116]) insisted that the theological views of the poetry professor were important, as proved by recent words in the *British Critic*: 'Give us ... this divine auxiliary [poetry] on our side, and we will let you dictate, denounce, proscribe and even persecute, as you please. Providence has placed in our hands powers that laugh to scorn your petty dominion.'[117] Indeed Keble had wound up his last lecture as professor 'with a strong protest in favour of the connection of religion and poetry.'[118] The *Morning Herald* warned: 'The doctrines of "Reserve" and the "*Disciplina arcani*" will never be so attractive as in a song or sonnet – and this is the atmosphere in which the bats and owls of

---

[112] Bricknell, *Resignation and Lay Communion*, pp. 26-36. See also *Oxford Herald*, 22 January 1842.
[113] Pusey to Hook, 14 September 1841, PHL LBV 95/25.
[114] Hill Diary, 5 November 1841, Bodleian MS St Edmund Hall 67/13.
[115] *Times*, 7 December 1841; WCA Symons Papers.
[116] *Morning Post*, 20 December 1841.
[117] *Oxford Herald*, 20 November 1841; *British Critic* 30 (October 1841), p. 466.
[118] J.B. Mozley to Maria Mozley, 30 October 1841, *Letters of the Rev. J.B. Mozley*, p. 123. See John Keble, *The Case of Catholic Subscription to the Thirty-Nine Articles Considered: with especial reference to the Duties and Difficulties of English Catholics in the Present Crisis: in a Letter to the Hon. Mr Justice Coleridge* (London, 1841), p. 17.

Puseyism love to expatiate.'[119] Some of Williams' friends appealed for theological issues to be kept out of the contest, but they were quickly derided: 'The candidate's poetic genius, his classic taste, his critical accuracy – these we should do well to inquire into; but his religious opinions we are to put out of sight! Why, Sir, what would the veriest Neologian wish more than this?'[120]

On 17 November Pusey came forward in public support of Williams, professing his hope that the University would not make 'all its elections matters of party strife'.[121] In response, Gilbert insisted that Garbett was proposed by Brasenose College not as a rival theological candidate, but for his merits in poetry:

> it may unfortunately be true, that what was begun in generous rivalry may be assuming, more or less, the character of religious division. But we deny that we are responsible for this, either generally, or now in particular. We have not sought such an issue; we have encouraged no step towards it.[122]

Not being a member of Trinity College, Pusey's obvious connection with Williams was via the *Tracts for the Times*. He was therefore blamed for initiating a theological contest. Newman told Keble that Pusey's circular was 'considered a failure – it looks like hoisting the flag of party',[123] and Williams recalled in his autobiography that as a result 'the opposite party had promises pouring in on all sides, and many, who had been with us, held aloof, and some withdrew their promises. A regular reign of terror set in.'[124] Frederic Rogers thought Pusey was 'most outrageously injudicious' and had 'knocked Williams's chance on the head'.[125]

So the battle was joined and the stakes were high. Soon some were asserting: 'the *real* question *now* at issue ... is not whether Mr Williams or Mr Garbett shall become Professor of Poetry, but whether the University of Oxford shall or shall not hereafter be considered a Protestant University.'[126] Likewise G.S. Faber told Golightly: 'The impending struggle is no mere contest between two

---

[119] *Morning Herald*, 29 November 1841.
[120] *Standard*, 4 December 1841. For suggestions of a theological disclaimer at Convocation, see *Morning Post*, 20 December 1841 and 7 January 1842. See also the planned declaration by W.F. Hook, Edward Churton and John Miller, 31 December 1841, LPL Williams Dep.5.
[121] *Oxford Herald*, 20 November 1841.
[122] *Standard*, 22 November 1841.
[123] Newman to Keble, 25 November 1841, *Newman Letters and Diaries*, viii. p. 351.
[124] *Autobiography of Isaac Williams*, p. 139.
[125] Frederic Rogers to Sophy Rogers, 21 November and 12 December 1841, in *The Letters of Frederic Lord Blachford* edited by George E. Marindin (London, 1896), pp. 106, 108.
[126] *Standard*, 31 December 1841.

men, but between two sets of antagonist *Principles*.'[127] Golightly did not agitate publicly about the poetry professorship, but his friend Bricknell fired off several pamphlets. He proclaimed that the election was 'a contest for the maintenance of the pure principles of our Protestant Faith', and asked: 'are the Members of Convocation to look calmly on, and see the poison spread, and make no effort to administer the antidote which they possess? Shall they commit the suicidal act of yielding, without a struggle, a post which is confessedly of such great importance?'[128] On the other side, Newman declared: '*We must strain every nerve*. If we are defeated, at least if we do not show a large minority, it will hasten the catastrophe of men going to Rome.'[129]

As the controversy continued to gather pace, *John Bull* complained that 'the voice of reason is drowned amid the noise of party'.[130] Some portrayed the election in simplistic terms as a dispute 'between Protestants and Puseyites',[131] or between 'the High Church and the Low Church parties'.[132] Henry Woodgate, for instance, claimed that the evangelicals had adopted Garbett as their party champion and were resorting to the 'low carnal weapons of dishonourable rivalry'.[133] However, the official sponsors of Williams and Garbett did their best to distance themselves from the charge of 'extreme or party bias'.[134] The supporters of both candidates were drawn from a wide theological spectrum. Indeed the *Morning Post* spoke of 'an unhallowed alliance of Radicals and Infidels, with Conservatives and ultra-Protestants' arrayed against Williams – an alliance for which it suggested the name 'Golightlyism'.[135]

---

[127] Faber to Golightly, 14 December 1841, LPL MS 1805, fo. 235.

[128] W.S. Bricknell, *'Is There Not a Cause?' A Letter to the Rev. E.B. Pusey ... occasioned by his Circular in Support of the Rev. Isaac Williams ... as a Candidate for the Poetry Professorship* (Oxford, 1841), p. 21. See also W.S. Bricknell, *'Horae Canonicae': The Liturgy As It Is, or the Liturgy As It Was? A Second Letter to the Rev. E.B. Pusey ... occasioned by his Circular in Support of the Rev. Isaac Williams ... as a Candidate for the Poetry Professorship* (Oxford, 1841); W.S. Bricknell, *The 'Tracts for the Times' Continued. An Attempt to Elucidate the Theology of the Rev. Isaac Williams by a Comparison of the Ninety-First Number of the 'Tracts for the Times', (A Recent Pamphlet on Various Points of Faith and Practice), with No.86 of the Original Series; in a Letter to the Honourable and Right Reverend the Lord Bishop of Oxford* (Oxford, 1842).

[129] Newman to Thomas Mozley, 29 October 1841, *Newman Letters and Diaries*, viii. p. 312.

[130] *John Bull*, 8 January 1842, p. 19.

[131] *Morning Herald*, 29 December 1841.

[132] *Morning Post*, 20 December 1841.

[133] Henry A. Woodgate, *A Brief Analysis of the Tracts on Reserve in Communicating Religious Knowledge, in the Series called Tracts for the Times: with Remarks on the Same* (Oxford, 1842), p. 4.

[134] *Standard*, 13 December 1841.

[135] *Morning Post*, 10 and 13 December 1841. For another description of the wide variety of people arrayed against Williams, see *Oxford Herald*, 8 January 1842.

Throughout December 1841 appeals were regularly made in the press for both Williams and Garbett to stand down and make room for a neutral candidate.[136] Amongst those suggested as an alternative poetry professor were the great 'Lake Poet', William Wordsworth;[137] the editor of the *Quarterly Review*, John Lockhart;[138] William Sewell;[139] and Thomas Claughton (eventually poetry professor in 1852 and future Bishop of St Alban's).[140] In January 1842 James Tyler (rector of St Giles-in-the-Fields, London) and William Gladstone organised an appeal asking both candidates to withdraw, signed by 260 non-residents, including six bishops.[141] However, it was said of these signatories (who included W.F. Hook, William Gresley, Robert and Henry Wilberforce, and Edward Churton) that 'not a few were known full-grown Tractarians and zealous party men; others were Tractarians half-fledged'.[142] The *Standard* rejected the proposed compromise:

> Of real peace we are sincere friends: but of exciting passions to the full, and then, by an ingenious and one-sided artifice, withdrawing the decision for the time, and leaving the fires of party spirit to smoulder until a more convenient opportunity occur, we are most determined enemies.[143]

Another asserted: '*the battle must be fought*, and the sooner it is fought and decided who is on the Lord's side the better it will be for the purity and peace of the Church.'[144] Gilbert refused to let Garbett withdraw,[145] but in order to avoid calling up non-residents to Convocation, a comparison of votes was agreed. On 20 January 1842, one week before the election was due, 921 promised votes were counted for Garbett and 623 for Williams, so Williams withdrew.[146] However, the *Standard* lamented the large minority: 'Why *two-fifths*? why *one-fifth*?, or *one-fiftieth*? ... The contemplation of this rapid

---

[136] *Times*, 7 and 11 December 1841; *John Bull*, 11 December 1841, p. 594. See also the appeals by F.D. Maurice, *Morning Post*, 14 December 1841, and W.D. Conybeare, *Standard*, 23 December 1841.
[137] *Morning Post*, 15 December 1841.
[138] *Oxford Herald*, 15 January 1842; John Williams to Tait, 20 December 1841, LPL Tait Papers, vol. 77, fos 123-4.
[139] *Oxford Herald*, 8 January 1842.
[140] *Times*, 11 December 1841; *Morning Post*, 23 December 1841; *Autobiography of Isaac Williams*, p. 138.
[141] *Times*, 14 January 1842; Butler, *Gladstone: Church, State, and Tractarianism*, pp. 179-82.
[142] *Christian Observer* (February 1842), p. 126.
[143] *Standard*, 30 December 1841.
[144] *Standard*, 5 January 1842.
[145] *Standard*, 30 December 1841.
[146] *Standard*, 20 January 1842.

growth of the Romanist sect is painful. May Heaven grant that it prove monitory!'[147]

At the next vacancy on the episcopal bench, it was suggested in all seriousness that Prime Minister Peel would make Golightly a bishop, for 'his invaluable services in the cause of Protestantism, and also on account of his pure orthodoxy'.[148] Instead, on Shuttleworth's sudden death in January 1842, Peel named Gilbert as the new Bishop of Chichester – an appointment announced immediately after the conclusion of the poetry professor contest and widely interpreted as a reward for Gilbert's part in resisting the Tractarians at Oxford. The *Standard* thought the nomination proof of 'the care of Providence for the Protestant Church',[149] but *John Bull* was less content: 'Sir ROBERT might have done worse certainly. He might have placed the mitre on the head of SYDNEY SMITH, or on that of Mr GOLIGHTLY. But he might have likewise done better.'[150]

Under False Colours

Concurrent with the controversy over the poetry professorship, Golightly was involved in renewed attacks upon the Tractarians which further raised the profile of the troubles at Oxford. Departing from his usual method of writing pamphlets, he sent a series of letters to national newspapers between November 1841 and February 1842, which highlighted a whole variety of concerns over Tractarian theology and practice. The dominant theme was again about Tractarian dishonesty, especially in their relationship with the Church of Rome.

In the closing months of 1841, four people who had been influenced by the *Tracts for the Times* seceded to Roman Catholicism. The most prominent was Richard Waldo Sibthorp (fellow of Magdalen College, Oxford), formerly an evangelical, of whom Golightly once held a 'high opinion'.[151] Other lesser-known seceders were also hunted down and exposed to public disgrace – F.D. Wackerbarth (alumnus of Queens' College, Cambridge), a pupil at Shrewsbury School (about whom Golightly wrote to the Bishop of Lichfield),[152] and John

---

[147] *Standard*, 21 January 1842.
[148] *Standard*, 21 December 1841.
[149] *Standard*, 22 January 1842.
[150] *John Bull*, 29 January 1842, p. 55.
[151] Golightly to Mozley, 26 June 1829, BOA Thomas Mozley Papers. On Sibthorp, see Michael Trott, *The Life of Richard Waldo Sibthorp: Evangelical, Catholic and Ritual Revivalism in the Nineteenth-Century Church* (Brighton, 2005). Pusey was forced to deny that the secession of Sibthorp and others was due to the influence of the *Tracts for the Times*: Edward B. Pusey, *A Letter to his Grace the Archbishop of Canterbury, on Some Circumstances Connected with the Present Crisis in the English Church* (Oxford, 1842), pp. 35-6.
[152] James Bowstead to Golightly, 28 December 1841, LPL MS 1804, fos 77-8. See also B.H. Kennedy, *A Letter to the Right Reverend the Lord Bishop of Lichfield, Visitor of*

Gooch (a tradesman from Oxford).[153] The *Standard* warned:

> The danger, the real danger, under which the Church now suffers, is not that of *losing* the services of men of Mr Sibthorp's mind, but of *retaining* them. Let us find all Romanists at heart *under their own proper banner*, and we shall know where and how to meet them. It is when they hide themselves among our own men that they excite a real and well-founded alarm.[154]

Golightly saw his opportunity and wrote anonymously to the newspaper from Oxford, to confirm these suspicions:

> there is good ground for supposing that there are about 10 members of this University, who, instead of fighting 'under their proper banner', have hoisted the flag of Anglicanism, and under these false colours are taking advantage of their respective positions as fellows of colleges, and clergymen of the Established Church, to propagate 'Romanism', and *oppose* 'primitive views'.[155]

In secret Golightly then requested his allies, G.S. Faber and Bishop Shuttleworth, to write to the *Standard* asking for this shocking claim to be substantiated.[156] When their letters appeared in print, Golightly duly obliged with an answer, proclaiming that he belonged 'to no party whatever' but was 'deeply attached to the University, and to the existing system of the Church of England'.[157] In contrast, he tried to show that many of the Tractarians were sympathetic to the Church of Rome. He reported that, according to William Ward, the Tractarians were now 'divided into disciples of Mr Newman and disciples of Dr Pusey – the latter opposed, THE FORMER NO LONGER OPPOSED TO ROME.' Similarly he claimed that William Palmer (of Magdalen College), recently returned from a year's visit to the Russian Orthodox Church, was surprised to find 'that a great change had taken place in the opinions of certain of his friends; that the *via media* was deserted, that Rome was no longer regarded as a schismatical community, and that there was a strong desire for re-union with her.'[158] Golightly reserved his most stinging

---

Shrewsbury School, on Public School Discipline in General, and with special reference to a Late Anonymous Imputation upon the Religious Teaching of the School, with a Portion of the Correspondence, and Other Documents (Shrewsbury, 1842).

[153] *Oxford Herald*, 15 January 1842.

[154] *Standard*, 6 November 1841. See *Morning Post*, 11 November 1841.

[155] *Standard*, 13 November 1841.

[156] *Standard*, 24 November 1841. See Faber to Golightly, 22 November 1841, LPL MS 1805, fos 233-4; Shuttleworth to Golightly, 23 November 1841, MS 1809, fos 47-8. See also, Miller to Golightly, 23 November 1841, MS 1808, fos 117-8.

[157] *Standard*, 29 November 1841.

[158] Palmer wrote: 'there has been a change indeed here since I left England, or else I was very much in the dark before': Roundell Palmer, *Memorials* (2 vols, London, 1896), i. p. 315.

rebukes for the *British Critic*, the editorship of which had recently passed from Newman to Thomas Mozley. He suggested that the contributors to the *British Critic* were 'in heart and spirit Roman Catholics' and that a recent article by Mozley was 'more worthy of Maynooth than Oxford'.[159] He also reported that Ward had visited Bishop Nicholas Wiseman at Oscott College (a Roman Catholic seminary near Birmingham); that John Bloxam (fellow of Magdalen College) had introduced Sibthorp to Wiseman; and that a Roman Catholic bishop had been visited by members of the University at Oxford's Mitre Inn (this was Thomas Walsh, vicar apostolic of the midland district). Golightly continued:

> A Fellow of Exeter has expressed his belief that seven years hence the Churches of England and Rome will be re-united; some cross themselves in public worship, others make genuflections, others openly praise the Jesuits, talk of *Saint* Ignatius Loyola, have plans for taming refractory bishops, and talk over what they shall do in their day of triumph with the clergy who reject their views.

Immediately apparent in Golightly's letter is his 'scatter-gun' method of attack, linking together a wide variety of isolated facts and snippets of reported conversations (for which he relied on local informants and Protestant friends in college common rooms). His approach proved remarkably successful and was impossible to defend against. On their own, each revelation was of little consequence, but they were difficult to deny without the accused parties doing themselves more damage. By naming individuals, Golightly hoped to provoke a response and draw them into the fray, thus prolonging the controversy.

Golightly followed up his letters by publicising an excerpt from a French Roman Catholic periodical, *L'Ami de la Religion*, which praised the pro-Roman habits and opinions of Wackerbarth. The *Standard* hoped it would 'open the eyes of the most obstinate *connivers* as to the real designs of the *miso-Protestant Tractarians*',[160] but the *Morning Post* was derisory:

> what does the French publication bring forward, after all, but some personal gossip and tittle-tattle, meet enough, perhaps, for the scandal of an 'evangelical' tea-table, where silly women bring forward their penny subscriptions, and their embroidered kettle-holders, in honour of their 'minister', but totally unworthy of the notice of any manly mind, which has been stored with erudition, and has learned the value of evidence and argument.[161]

Golightly's letters had a significant negative impact upon his reputation and his relationships. His public accusations against Thomas Mozley and the *British*

---

[159] See further, Simon A. Skinner, 'Newman, the Tractarians and the *British Critic*', *Journal of Ecclesiastical History* 50 (October 1999), pp. 716-59.
[160] *Standard*, 31 December 1841.
[161] *Morning Post*, 5 January 1842.

Critic finally put an end to whatever shreds remained of their old undergraduate friendship.[162] Yet John Christie encouraged Mozley that people would soon grow tired of Golightly and 'must begin to doubt whether it is quite gentlemanly, not to say Christian, to report private conversations &c as he does.'[163] John Keble called Golightly's letter 'the wildest of all his freaks' and 'almost incoherent'.[164] Nevertheless Keble had planned to preach that those discontent with the Church of England should resist secession to the Church of Rome and saw it as 'providential' that Newman had dissuaded him. Such a sermon would only have increased Protestant suspicions.[165] Likewise Bloxam's Roman Catholic friend, A.W.N. Pugin, abandoned his plans to visit Oxford after reading Golightly's letters. He explained:

> the protestant party seem to catch at anything and when a chance call on Dr Walsh is magnified into popish Bishops receiving members of the university if I was seen gliding into your rooms I might be suspected of plotting some desperate sort of Guy Fawkes deed.[166]

Meanwhile Mark Pattison (fellow and future Rector of Lincoln College) wrote: 'Poor Golly is almost distracted with excitement'.[167] Edward Churton thought Golightly a 'silly booby' who deserved to be prosecuted for defamation.[168]

Even Golightly's friends and family thought he had made a false move. His uncle, Philip Dodd, believed writing to the newspapers was 'imprudent' and would bring 'much Trouble': 'Your ability and (above all) Honesty of Purpose will carry you through, but I wish you had contented yourself with Pamphlet writing.'[169] Faber had been a willing collaborator, but thought Golightly had over-stretched himself: 'it is better to stick to fewer matters which can be distinctly verified, than to take a wider scope, which, for whatever reason, cannot be distinctly established.'[170] He advised: 'on the principle of boxing, you should hit close, and not let an adversary break in by throwing your arms too

---

[162] See Thomas Mozley to J.B. Mozley, 3 December 1841, *Letters of the Rev. J.B. Mozley*, p. 125; Harriett Mozley to Jemima Mozley, 6 December 1841, in Mozley, *Newman Family Letters*, pp. 114-5.
[163] Christie to Mozley, nd, BOA Thomas Mozley Papers.
[164] John Keble to Thomas Keble, 30 November 1841, KCL C15.
[165] Newman – Keble, 25 November and 2 December 1841, *Newman Letters and Diaries*, viii. pp. 351-2. See 'Endurance of Church Imperfections' in John Keble, *Sermons, Academical and Occasional* (Oxford, 1847), ch. 12.
[166] A.W.N. Pugin to John R. Bloxam, 19 December 1841, in Margaret Belcher (ed.), *The Collected Letters of A.W.N. Pugin* (2 vols, Oxford, 2001-03), i. p. 301.
[167] Mark Pattison to Eleanor Pattison, nd, Lincoln College Archives, MS/Pat/II/D.
[168] Churton to Pusey, 9 December 1841, PHL LBV 41/9.
[169] Dodd to Golightly, 30 November 1841, LPL MS 1805, fos 140-1.
[170] Faber to Golightly, 10 January 1842, ibid., fo. 237.

wide.'[171] However, Archdeacon Browne of Ely thought Golightly had conferred obligation 'on all enlightened adherers of the Reformation' by his 'bold and intrepid manner ... in this portentous conflict between truth and error'.[172]

Golightly's attack upon men known to have a close connection with Isaac Williams was seen as an attempt ('utterly contemptible' and 'equally *mean and unchristianlike*') to bias the election for the poetry professorship.[173] One member of Convocation protested: 'If Mr Golightly thinks it his duty to blow the trumpet of alarm in the ears of those in authority, let them, if they wish, submit to it; but let us, who wish to record our votes independently of party feeling, be allowed to do so.'[174] Robert Wilberforce spoke of 'Golly's foolish interference',[175] and another of Williams' supporters acknowledged that 'the Golightly delusion' affected the way people planned to vote.[176] The *Morning Post* called him 'One of the prominent agitators in the ultra-Protestant prosecution'.[177] Meanwhile the other poetry candidate, James Garbett, privately applauded Golightly: 'The thanks of all true Churchmen are due to you for your indefatigable *watch* on the Tractarian Camp.'[178]

Having written to the press, it was primarily through the columns of the newspapers that Golightly was judged. It is easier to fire off a letter than compose a pamphlet, so day after day his character was assessed and assailed from all sides. Protestant allies writing in the *Standard* heaped praise upon him:

> Mr Golightly has laid bare a system elaborately contrived and well adapted to Romanise the United Church ...[179]

> Mr Golightly has, indeed, deserved well of our University, Church, and country, by boldly coming forward as the denouncer of those among us who are in correspondence with Rome, and are covertly labouring to overthrow all that Protestant minds hold dear and sacred.[180]

> Mr Golightly's letter seems to have fallen among the Romanist conspiracy like a shell upon a powder magazine, and it may be hoped that the flame it has kindled will not expire before it has consumed the whole fortress of Romish trumpery,

---

[171] Faber to Golightly, 14 December 1841, ibid., fo. 236.
[172] Browne to Golightly, 19 January 1842, LPL MS 1804, fo. 92.
[173] *Oxford Herald*, 27 November 1841. See *Correspondence Relative to the Professorship of Poetry in the University of Oxford* (Oxford, 1841), a pamphlet possibly compiled by Golightly.
[174] *Oxford Herald*, 11 December 1841.
[175] Robert I. Wilberforce to Newman, 9 December 1841, *Newman Letters and Diaries*, viii. p. 374.
[176] Richard Ward to Newman, 20 December 1841, ibid., p. 381.
[177] *Morning Post*, 11 December 1841.
[178] Garbett to Golightly, 15 November 1841, LPL MS 1806, fo. 2.
[179] *Standard*, 3 December 1841.
[180] *Standard*, 8 December 1841.

fabricated for our destruction.[181]

He was called a 'good and faithful watchman on our walls',[182] and Bricknell spoke of his 'very manly, Christian, and effective line of conduct'.[183] Others lauded his 'Christian eloquence' and 'Protestant energy'.[184] It was even suggested that money be raised to present him with a collection of plate, as a token of esteem for having 'struck terror and dismay into the hearts of the Tractarians'.[185]

By many others, however, particularly through the pages of the *Morning Post*, Golightly's methods were strongly criticised:

> Mr Golightly, instead of giving information to his Bishop, that ten of his clergy were treasonable, denies them all justice whatever – at once seats himself on a bishop's throne, and issues forth a Papal Bull of Excommunication. He does not inform them even privately of his intention, but proclaims at once to all England and to the world that they are traitorous and infamous. Is this to be endured?[186]

He was scornfully described as the 'champion of all that is Protestant',[187] a 'mountain-in-labour' whose letters were a 'muscipular abortion'[188] and 'a long rigmarole diatribe … in favour of himself'.[189] He was denounced for 'the canting hypocrisy, or the monomania that endeavours to spread such alarm through the country against this awful *bugbear*',[190] and one observer hoped for the day when 'those who are now clamouring against *primitive and fixed* principles as conservative of the Church from the fraternal hatred of Romanism and dissent, will not *go lightly* all the days of their lives, but rather, as Hezekiah did, more softly in the bitterness of their souls.'[191] Letters parodying Golightly's own mocked his methods of gathering intelligence and his claims to belong to no party. 'Standhard Goheavy' declared: 'I am, Sir, one of those men who fearlessly perform what they know to be their duty, and never suffer their judgment to be perverted by any prejudice or party feeling of any kind whatsoever.'[192] Likewise 'A Man of no Party' poked fun at Golightly's leisure, self-indulgence and lack of logic.[193] Before James Guillemard (vicar of

---

[181] *Standard*, 13 December 1841.
[182] *Oxford Herald*, 1 January 1842.
[183] Bricknell, *'Horae Canonicae'*, p. 4.
[184] *Morning Herald*, 21 December 1841.
[185] *Standard*, 21 December 1841.
[186] Quoted in *Morning Post*, 22 January 1842.
[187] *Morning Post*, 19 January 1842.
[188] *Morning Post*, 21 December 1841.
[189] *John Bull*, 11 December 1841, p. 594.
[190] *Morning Post*, 22 December 1841.
[191] *Morning Post*, 20 December 1841.
[192] *Morning Post*, 16 December 1841.
[193] *Morning Post*, 20 December 1841.

Kirtlington near Oxford) visited Golightly in November 1841, he wrote: 'I hope you will occasionally *examine the cellars*, and see that no suspicious looking persons are admitted on any pretence. A good "blowing up" from the party is what *you* must expect; but I have no anxiety to be puffed off no one knows where, with No.90 powder.'[194]

One unforeseen consequence of the negative publicity surrounding Golightly's letters to the *Standard* was that he began to isolate some of his natural allies in Oxford. Although urged forward by senior Protestants who remained in the background, friends began to distance themselves from his actions. *John Bull* maintained that Oxford's anti-Tractarian leaders like Gilbert, Tait and Edward Cardwell (Principal of St Alban Hall and Camden Professor of Ancient History) were 'too sound Churchmen to have any feelings in common with Mr GOLIGHTLY – or his friend the editor of the *Standard*.'[195] Just nine months before, at the height of the *Tract 90* crisis, Golightly had been able to rely on the support of young dons like Tait, but now Tait wrote to warn him:

> I think it will be a great pity for you to act without considering how younger men view these matters. The Seniors in this place live so much in a set of their own, that they are not good judges of the common feeling. ... I think you must be on yr guard agst their being very glad to find you disposed to what they want to have done, but do not exactly like to undertake themselves. ... pray remember that any appearance of bitterness or a persecuting spirit, is not only wrong in itself; but if shewn on the right side will be sure in the present ticklish state of opinions in Oxford to drive many persons who are now doubtful into the wrong.[196]

Another insider wrote:

> I do not believe he (G.) would have written any letter of himself without the strong urging and vehement backing up of certain persons whom he reveres beyond expression, who are base enough to make him their tool, and mean enough to shrink from acknowledging their hatred of Newman's views ...[197]

Newman commented: 'Poor Golightly's friends (entre nous) are seriously alarmed for his mind – He is said to be the tool of others. ... this poor unhappy fellow has left his true and natural friends to worship asses.'[198] To J.W. Bowden he wrote: 'Golightly has happily so little tact, as to have disgusted his own friends by his ultra statements.'[199] Another declared:

---

[194] James Guillemard to Golightly, [30 November 1841], LPL MS 1807, fo. 1.
[195] *John Bull*, 22 January 1842, p. 43.
[196] Tait to Golightly, [16 November 1841], LPL MS 1809, fos 114-5. Drafts at Tait Papers, vol. 77, fos 54-5.
[197] Quoted by Newman to Samuel Rickards, 1 December 1841, *Newman Letters and Diaries*, viii. p. 360.
[198] Newman to Jemima Mozley, 5 December 1841, ibid., p. 364.
[199] Newman to J.W. Bowden, 28 February 1842, ibid., p. 475.

... many sensible persons of the same way of thinking *in the main* as Mr Golightly himself, are utterly ashamed of his charge; that they have already began [sic] to cry, '*Save us from our friends*'. Really it may be all very well to be so frightened at the *Pope*, but the *Pope* will never do us so much harm as those who thus *inconsiderately* and *without foundation* attack the fellow-members of their own Catholic and Apostolic Church. When Mr Golightly feels this fear again, let him consider whether one of old George Herbert's '*Jacula Prudentum*' does not somewhat apply to him – '*Here is a talk of the Turk and the Pope, but my next neighbour doeth me more harm than either of them both*'.[200]

Only two individuals named in Golightly's letters to the *Standard* came forward publicly to defend themselves. The first was William Ward, who wrote an open letter to Pusey complaining at Golightly's habit of 'recording what passes in free and unsuspicious conversation'.[201] The second was William Palmer (of Magdalen College) who issued a controversial *Letter to the Rev. C.P. Golightly*, explaining his views on the *via media* and the Roman Church. Intending to provoke, Palmer proclaimed:

I am for no middle ways ... I utterly reject and anathematize the principle of Protestantism as a heresy, with all its forms, sects, or denominations. And if the Church of England should ever unhappily profess herself to be a form of Protestantism (which may God of his infinite mercy forbid!) then I would reject and anathematize the Church of England, and would separate myself from her immediately as from a human sect, without giving Protestants any unnecessary trouble to procure my expulsion.[202]

In reply, 'A Protestant Catholic' insisted that 'the Church of England is *both* Catholic and Protestant'. Golightly ('violent in the extreme against Catholic views'), he argued, would not say 'I believe in the Holy Protestant Church' during the Apostles' Creed; nor would Palmer ('violent against Protestantism') admit the supremacy of the Pope, the doctrine of transubstantiation, or the Tridentine Decrees. He reasoned: 'It is therefore quite possible for both these gentlemen and their friends to hold their own opinions, without in the slightest degree endangering the safety of the Established Church. Each bears to an opposite side of the road, but neither wishes to leave it.'[203] Palmer responded with *A Letter to a Protestant-Catholic*, observing that to protest against Rome did not make one a 'Protestant' (the Greek Church, for instance, was not Protestant). Rather, he defined Protestants as those who insisted on the 'right of

---

[200] *Oxford Herald*, 18 December 1841.
[201] *Standard*, 9 December 1841.
[202] William Palmer, *A Letter to the Rev. C.P. Golightly, occasioned by his Communication to the Standard Newspaper, charging Certain Members of the University of Oxford with dishonestly making use of their positions within the pale of the established church in order to propagate popery* (Oxford, 1841), pp. 9-10.
[203] *Oxford Herald*, 11 December 1841.

private interpretation' of Scripture, independent of the 'dogmatic or traditive authority lodged in the Episcopate'.[204] Protestantism, in that sense, he anathematised as 'the most subtle, the most contagious, and the most corrosive heresy'.[205]

Newman humorously called Palmer's outburst a 'Golightliad',[206] and the *Morning Post* maintained that Palmer's *Letter to Golightly* 'ought to make Mr GOLIGHTLY go heavily enough for many a day, and in penitent sackcloth mourn for the mischievous rashness of himself and his party. But men who try to discourage reverence are not likely to be thus affected.'[207] The newspaper took issue, however, with Palmer's definition of 'Protestantism': 'If all the rabid ravings of anti-Popish zealots be Protestantism, then every man of accuracy, discretion, and moderation, who receives part of the Church revenues, may be described as a hater of Protestantism. But no one of common sense can countenance such absurdity.'[208] Similarly, the *Britannia* stated that arguments over names were of little use:

> We shall not pause to mark the cobweb of subtleties in which the new school involves the plainest of all questions in definitions of Orthodoxy and Heterodoxy, High Church and Low Church, Anglican and Catholic. The true question is, whether England shall forget that the very principle of her Reformation was a *protest* against the corruptions of Popery ...[209]

Calls were made for Palmer's dismissal from his tutorship at Magdalen,[210] and it did not go unnoticed that he was brother of Roundell Palmer (future Lord Chancellor Selborne), acting at the time as secretary of Isaac Williams' London Committee for Oxford's poetry professorship.

Towards the end of January 1842, after the issue of the poetry professor had been settled and the University began to calm down again, it was rumoured that Golightly would

> retire from Oxford to some sequestered spot, where he may have no affairs but his own to meddle with; where, like Napoleon, in his island prison, he may mourn over the ill success of his misguided ambition for notoriety, and atone for his

---

[204] William Palmer, *A Letter to a Protestant-Catholic* (Oxford, 1842), pp. 15-18, 33.
[205] Ibid., p. 19. See in reply F.D. Maurice, *Three Letters to the Rev. W. Palmer, Fellow and Tutor of Magdalene College, Oxford, on the Name 'Protestant'; on the Seemingly Double Character of the English Church; and on the Bishopric at Jerusalem* (London, 1842).
[206] Newman to Church, 24 December 1841, *Newman Letters and Diaries*, viii. p. 384.
[207] *Morning Post*, 10 December 1841.
[208] *Morning Post*, 15 January 1842.
[209] *Britannia*, 15 January 1842, p. 41.
[210] *Standard*, 21 and 30 December 1841; R.D. Middleton, *Dr Routh* (Oxford, 1938), pp. 93-4.

short-lived and unenviable fame, 'The world, forgetting, by the world forgot'.[211]

In fact it was Newman who was soon to retire from Oxford. He moved out in February 1842 to a row of cottages near his church at Littlemore, partly in an attempt to escape the ceaseless controversy in Oxford, and there his Anglican lifeblood began to flow away. Keble was no longer poetry professor and spent most of his time secluded in his parish at Hursley in Hampshire, which left Pusey increasingly prominent as the leader of the Tractarian movement. Yet in Golightly's mind it was Newman who remained the most serious threat and it was Newman who continued to receive the brunt of his attacks. He explained: 'Mr Newman is the real leader of the party, not Dr Pusey, who is no more entitled to give a name to it, than Americus Vespucius was to give a name to the new world.'[212]

In early 1842, as most people were trying to return to a degree of normality after the poetry professor debacle, Golightly was still busy considering a requisition to the Vice-Chancellor to call Convocation to condemn *Tract 90*.[213] Advised against this, he instead issued another letter to the newspapers, this time the *Morning Herald*, giving his view of affairs at Oxford, which had absorbed the nation's attention for the previous three months:

> To judge by the newspapers which advocate tractarian views, it might be supposed that Oxford is torn to pieces between a high church and a low church party. But alas! sir, the melancholy truth is, that we have but one party, of which Dr Pusey is the nominal, Mr Newman the actual leader, wearing out the university with systematic and untiring agitation. The body of the university act solely on the defensive.[214]

Once again Golightly resorted to the 'scatter-gun' method of attack. He described Newman's pulpit at St Mary-the-Virgin Church as 'the grand engine of mischief', propagating Tractarian views throughout the University. He complained that Archdeacon Manning had been appointed a select preacher by the University and that Francis Paget (a Tractarian sympathiser) had been appointed chaplain by Bishop Bagot.[215] He protested that *Tract 90* had reached a third edition and that some undergraduates were known to possess the Roman Breviary – all while the authorities of the University and diocese refused to act. Indeed, Golightly suggested that Bagot had postponed his triennial charge in

---

[211] *Morning Post*, 19 January 1842.
[212] Charles P. Golightly, *Correspondence Illustrative of the Actual State of Oxford with Reference to Tractarianism, and the Attempts of Mr Newman and his Party to Unprotestantize the National Church* (Oxford, 1842), p. 27.
[213] James R. Hughes to Golightly, 22 January 1842, LPL MS 1807, fos 231-2.
[214] *Morning Herald*, 14 February 1842.
[215] Paget later spoke of 'Golightly and such like cattle': F.E. Paget to Robert Eden, 24 January 1879, PHL, 'Introduction to the Bishop Bagot Correspondence', fo. 33.

order to avoid having to express an opinion on the subject.[216] He proclaimed:

> Newspapers, tracts, volumes, periodicals, weekly, monthly, and quarterly, decrying the reformers and the reformation, running down the Prayer Book, complaining of our church's isolation from the Greek and Roman churches, stealthily attacking Protestantism with the very same weapons with which Voltaire and Gibbon attacked Christianity, are perpetually issuing from the press, and infusing the most dangerous opinions into the minds of the youth of the university, by the mere frequency of their repetition. ... But if Romanism should prevail among us, infidelity will soon follow in its rear. But may we not anticipate our church's downfall? Such a result is probable, and, unless effectual measures are taken to stem the progress of corruption, inevitable. Year after year, out of this poisoned fountain there will be poured forth upon the country a torrent of insolent, assuming, fanatical, Jesuitical young clergy, who will bring themselves and the church of England into odium wherever they go.[217]

Since the faith of a majority of studious undergraduates had been 'seriously corrupted', Golightly recommended parents send their sons not to Oxford, but to Cambridge – remarkable advice from a loyal Oxford graduate and resident. G.S. Faber feared that parents should have been left to draw their own conclusions, because

> in our liberal age, persons are so ready to affix the charge of *partizanship* and then compendiously to disregard whatever is said, that, purely for the sake of not weakening the effect of what we may say, I think it prudent to avoid giving, as much as possible, any plausible ground for such a charge.[218]

However, George Miller spoke of Golightly's 'honest boldness',[219] and James Hughes (fellow of New College) encouraged him to adopt 'every lawful mode of resistance'.[220] Another observer hoped Golightly would continue such campaigning, since he was the only person with 'a plain, manly, scriptural mind in either of the Universities, in the Church, or out of it – the *Record* only excepted – at all commensurate with the evil itself of what is called Puseyism, or the dangers of its advance, at once so insidious and so audacious.'[221]

Golightly's four newspaper letters between November 1841 and February

---

[216] When Archdeacon Clerke denied this claim, Golightly stopped the sale of *Correspondence Illustrative of the Actual State of Oxford* and offered to alter or destroy remaining copies: Clerke – Golightly, 7 and 8 March 1842, LPL MS 1805, fos 65-7. Perhaps this was just diplomatic, or perhaps it is another example of Golightly's earnest desire to always speak truth.

[217] *Morning Herald*, 14 February 1842.

[218] Faber to Golightly, 17 February 1842, LPL MS 1805, fo. 239.

[219] Miller to Golightly, 17 February 1842, LPL MS 1808, fo. 125.

[220] Hughes to Golightly, 18 February 1842, LPL MS 1807, fo. 233.

[221] *Record*, 28 February 1842.

1842 were so successful in generating sustained controversy and in exposing Tractarian developments to public censure that writing to the press became a dominant motif in his campaigns over subsequent decades. These early letters were published together as *Correspondence Illustrative of the Actual State of Oxford with Reference to Tractarianism, and the Attempts of Mr Newman and his Party to Unprotestantize the National Church*, but Golightly did not published another pamphlet for seventeen years. His lengthy theological critiques of Tractarian teaching in works such as *A Letter to the Bishop of Oxford* and *Strictures on No.90* had not been widely read and did not provoke much response. So now Golightly began to write short communications with the latest Tractarian intelligence, usually sent to sympathetic editors at the *Standard*, the *Morning Herald*, the *Record*, or the *Oxford Herald*. These had all the advantages of immediacy, brevity and the hint of scandal, and often drew forth a flurry of further letters and revelations. Golightly's newspaper letters were mostly anonymous, signed perhaps 'An Oxford Master of Arts', 'A Member of Convocation', 'Academicus' or 'A Senior Member of the University of Oxford'. Although some can be proved as his, others (perhaps dozens or even hundreds) remain unidentifiable. In this letter-writing campaign, Golightly encouraged Protestant friends to follow his example: 'I am resolved not to be the sole party in the University to expose Tractarianism, for of course in that case, whether I give my name or not, I am suspected of every thing.'[222] Nonetheless, it was a duty to which he felt particularly called, as he explained in late 1843:

> whatever is to be done in the *ordinary way* in opposing Tractarian error, I must be the doer of it, or it is not done at all. On great occasions the Vice Chancellor and the Heads of Houses will come forward vigorously enough; but if any thing relative to the state of things here is to be communicated to the public thro' the medium of the daily papers ... I have the sole charge of the Alarm-bell.[223]

The Hampden Affair Revived

In May 1842 new professorial chairs in Ecclesiastical History and Pastoral Theology were established at Oxford, and the five theology professors were formed into a theology board with the Regius Professor of Divinity as *ex officio* chairman. However, the existing Regius Professor, R.D. Hampden, remained under Convocation's censure of 1836, so the Hebdomadal Board considered this an appropriate opportunity to recommend the censure's repeal and summoned Convocation to vote on the matter.[224] Bishop Copleston rejoiced at

---

[222] Golightly to Bricknell, 9 March 1843, PHL BRIC 1/9.
[223] Golightly to Sandys Wall, 22 November 1843, LPL MS 1806, fo. 92.
[224] OUA Hebdomadal Board Minutes, 16 and 23 May 1842 (proposed by J.A. Cramer). Shuttleworth and Hawkins had recommended the censure's repeal at the Hebdomadal

this 'healing measure', a 'tardy act of justice'.[225] Yet *John Bull* thought that to raise the issue again was 'like a wanton tearing open of a wound which had been cicatrised by time.'[226]

Since his appointment as professor, Hampden had gained a reputation as one of the chief adversaries of Tractarianism within Oxford.[227] Many who had opposed him before, now gave him their support, united against a common foe. For example, John Hill, the only evangelical on the Corpus Common Room Committee of 1836, now supported repeal of the censure 'as being most charitable & the least of two evils.'[228] Although Hampden had retracted none of his former teaching, it was said that 'six years of zealous and irreproachable services ought to be sufficient to efface all preceding dislikes or doubts.'[229] Someone observed that the cause in 1836 had been 'orthodoxy against unsoundness', but in 1842 it was now 'the Reformation against innovations of Popish tendency'.[230] Likewise, another argued that because the chief danger to the church had changed, a different defence was necessary:

> Look round on the state of parties in 1836 and that in 1842. Then the government was believed to be both able and willing to make serious attacks upon the Church; a censure upon the Regius Professor was of course a heavy blow to any such designs. The struggle was thought to lie between the Ministry, supported by the Roman Catholics and Dissenters on one side, and the Church of England on the other. Now a fresh division and reconstruction of parties has taken place; a sect, then comparatively unknown, is now in the full vigour of its existence; the busiest and most proselytizing in all ecclesiastical history ...[231]

The *British and Foreign Review* thought the dispute revealed 'the antagonism of two great principles': 'The fight is again between authority and reason, between the free, but humble and responsible exercise of that gift, and its subjugation to an ambitious and aspiring priesthood.'[232] *John Bull*, however, objected: 'In a logical University this would be considered a singular enthymem [sic] – "I object to Mr NEWMAN's teaching, and therefore I agree with Dr HAMPDEN's"; yet, in point of fact, this *is* the very reasoning upon

---

Board in December 1839: Gilbert to Wellington, 27 December 1839, SUL Wellington Papers 2/250/67.
[225] Copleston to Hampden, 4 June 1842, OCL Hampden Papers, no. 9.
[226] *John Bull*, 28 May 1842, p. 259.
[227] *Record*, 26 April and 29 May 1841. See W.S. Bricknell, *Ten Reasons for Repealing the Hampden Statute. By a Member of Convocation who Voted for the Passing of that Statute in 1836* (Oxford, 1842), p. 3; *A Letter to Certain Members of Convocation* (Oxford, 1842), p. 4.
[228] Hill Diary, 7 June 1842, Bodleian MS St Edmund Hall 67/13.
[229] *Standard*, 1 June 1842.
[230] *Standard*, 3 June 1842.
[231] *Letter to Certain Members of Convocation*, pp. 7-8.
[232] 'Oxford and Dr Hampden', *British and Foreign Review* 15 (1843), pp. 173, 188-9.

which members of Convocation have been called to act.'²³³

Golightly was one of the few prominent anti-Tractarians who thought the censure of 1836 should remain. He warned his friend and fellow Protestant campaigner, W.S. Bricknell:

> What better means could have been devised for rallying around the Newmanites, standing forward on this occasion as the champions of orthodoxy, High Churchmen of every shade of opinion, and reuniting to them the Hooks, Gresleys, and id genus omne [all that sort] who had fallen from them? ... I greatly dread a union of the Evangelicals and Latitudinarians in Dr H.'s favour under the idea that in so doing they would strike a blow at Tractarianism ...²³⁴

Bricknell, however, thought Hampden should not be 'shackled' in his efforts to combat Tractarianism and uphold the teaching of the Reformation.²³⁵ Returning to his *bête noire*, William Palmer (of Magdalen College) argued that Hampden and the evangelicals shared a common attachment to 'Protestantism', that 'fundamental principle of all heresy and error'.²³⁶

After a meeting on 26 May at Magdalen College (chaired by F.A. Faber), a request was made that Vice-Chancellor Wynter withdraw the measure to repeal Hampden's censure. When Wynter refused, members of Convocation were asked to come to Oxford to vote against Hampden, because 'the character of the University both for consistency and for orthodoxy is at stake'.²³⁷ The signatories to these appeals were slated in the *Standard* as 'either tractarians and advocates of Tract 90, or ... scarcely distinguishable from tractarians in their attachment to the principles of that school of theology'.²³⁸ Certainly the names of known Tractarian sympathisers were present, such as Pusey, Newman, Bloxam, Copeland, Marriott, Williams and others.²³⁹ Yet they stood alongside men like Golightly, Tait and Vaughan Thomas, so Hampden's opponents were more accurately said to 'represent many shades of theological opinion – perhaps, indeed, all that exist in Oxford'.²⁴⁰ Attempting to explain away the embarrassment of finding Golightly's name on these petitions, one Protestant commentator observed: 'He is a conscientious man, *but* on this occasion has, unlike many others, thought more of apparent, than of real consistency.'²⁴¹ Pusey remarked wryly to Keble: 'It made one's heart sink, to

---

²³³ *John Bull*, 11 June 1842, p. 283.
²³⁴ Golightly to Bricknell, 1 June 1842, PHL BRIC 1/3.
²³⁵ Bricknell, *Ten Reasons*, p. 5.
²³⁶ William Palmer, *A Letter to the Rev. Dr Hampden, Regius Professor of Divinity in the University of Oxford* (Oxford, 1842), pp. 8-9.
²³⁷ *Morning Post*, 1 June 1842.
²³⁸ *Standard*, 30 May 1842.
²³⁹ *Oxford Herald*, 28 May 1842.
²⁴⁰ *Times*, 3 June 1842.
²⁴¹ *Standard*, 7 June 1842.

have to think Golightly's name an accession.'[242]

At the beginning of June, six days before Convocation, Hampden pointedly chose to lecture on the Thirty-Nine Articles. He criticised *Tract 90* and claimed in contrast diligently to have taught the doctrines of the Articles 'as they are simply read, without diminution or extenuation, or any accommodation whatever.'[243] He appealed for the support of any 'still Protestant members of the Church', and in an attempt to influence the forthcoming vote by portraying his opponents as 'an ambitious aspiring party', proclaimed:

> I have formed no party around me. I have not studied to proselytize any. I have stood alone, except so far as my teaching might associate me with other members of our common faith and common Church. Look to those by whom I am opposed. There you see a compact body, understanding each other, ready to act with each other, to join their names and their hands at the first signal from their leaders. ... But I have formed no party. I have given no name to any followers. Then, I pray you, test me by this criterion, and test my adversaries too. And you will then readily discern who are the disturbers of the peace of the Church – who are the innovators – who are the persons to be suspected and feared.[244]

In response, one pamphleteer complained that Hampden

> plays off the Evangelical school against the Tractarian, and between both maintains his own Latitudinarianism unmoved. He assumes the high position of *perfect orthodoxy, and no recantation*; and he fortifies himself in it by this balance of principles and this play of parties.[245]

Another insisted that the contest was actually between '*Dr Hampden on the one side ... the Church and University on the other.*'[246] Vaughan Thomas printed letters of support sent in 1836 to Hampden's opponents in Oxford, to show that the agitation did not originate in 'party feeling, or personal dislike'.[247] Similarly Thomas Mozley wrote in the *British Critic*:

> certain people, have thought fit to raise the cry of 'party', to bandy nicknames, and denounce 'agitators', and convert every University question into a war of

---

[242] Pusey to Keble, 31 May 1842, KCL B6/547.
[243] R.D. Hampden, *The Thirty-Nine Articles of the Church of England. The Eleventh of the Public Course of Lectures, in Trinity Term, Read before the University, in the Divinity School, Oxford, June 1, 1842* (second edition, London, 1842), p. 43.
[244] Ibid., pp. 44, 48.
[245] *The Lecture of the Regius Professor of Divinity Considered* (Oxford, 1842), p. 6.
[246] *The Censure of 1836 Still Necessary* (Oxford, 1842), p. 8.
[247] Vaughan Thomas, *Letters Addressed by Large Bodies of the Clergy to those Members of Convocation who met in the Common Room of Corpus Christi College, During the Controversy of 1836, together with the answers returned to the same* (Oxford, 1842), p. [3].

principle and opinion, till at last they have actually succeeded to a very great extent in silencing and driving from the arena of public affairs in Oxford a very considerable portion of the University ...

He warned that to silence the Tractarians would leave the field open for 'latitudinarians in religion, and liberals in politics':

Country gentlemen, town clergymen, and watering-place ladies, may be frightened enough at the name of Catholicism, and may be glad to hear that it is discountenanced at Oxford; but if they should happen to find that, Catholicism banished, the professors or tutors are industriously instilling into the rising generation of Englishmen, the principles of free trade, republicanism, religious indifference, and every thing that is either anti-ecclesiastical, or anti-patriarchal, they will begin at last to compute the benefit of the exchange.[248]

When Convocation met on 7 June 1842, the proposed repeal of Hampden's censure was defeated by 334 votes to 219.[249] So the professor's influence in Oxford remained permanently constricted until his nomination as Bishop of Hereford five years later. The *British Critic* rejoiced and concluded:

On the one side were the evangelicals allied with the latitudinarians, the Puritans of the seventeenth century with the establishment party of the eighteenth; on the other were the modern representatives of the strictest and at the same time the most authoritative divinity of our Church. It is satisfactory to see the battle reduced to so simple a form.[250]

However, as Golightly's alliance with his Tractarian opponents shows, the battle was in fact far from simple. The anti-Hampden coalition was an effective one, but strictly temporary.

Pious Frauds

In December 1842 there was another high-profile secession to the Church of Rome – that of Bernard Smith, rector of Leadenham in Lincolnshire and former fellow of Magdalen College, Oxford.[251] However, Smith's conversion was

---

[248] Thomas Mozley, 'New Oxford Theological Statute, and Revival of the Hampden Question', *British Critic* 32 (July 1842), pp. 168-70.
[249] *Oxford Herald*, 11 June 1842; *Times*, 8 June 1842; *Standard*, 8 and 11 June 1842. For J.G. Phillimore's speech, see *Morning Chronicle*, 10 June 1842.
[250] 'New Defenders of the Faith', *British Critic* 32 (October 1842), p. 435.
[251] R.D. Middleton, *Magdalen Studies* (London, 1936), pp. 231-67; R.W. Ambler, 'The Conversion to Roman Catholicism of Bernard Smith of Leadenham, 1842', *Lincolnshire History and Archaeology* 14 (1979), pp. 57-61; 'Ornaments of the Church of Leadenham, disallowed by the Bishop of Lincoln, 1842', KCL I164.

denied in a hoax letter to the *Morning Herald*.[252] This immediately raised suspicions about Tractarian dishonesty and whether Roman opinions were being held secretly within the Church of England. A neighbouring clergyman in Lincolnshire thought Smith was 'acting the part of a Jesuit, believing that he can serve the Papists' cause best by continuing Rector'.[253] From Oxford, Golightly drew the case to the attention of Bishop Kaye of Lincoln,[254] and was quick to demand an answer from Smith through the columns of the newspaper – was he, or was he not, a Roman Catholic? Golightly had heard of a proposal that a Tractarian clergyman in Leicestershire join the Church of Rome and yet retain his living and conform outwardly to the Church of England. Was Smith another example of a 'pious fraud', following the teaching on 'economy' as given in Newman's *Arians*?[255] Golightly declared:

> For myself, I confess that I was very glad to hear of Mr Smith's conversion, and hoped that many others might follow his example. I do not say that every individual embracing Roman Catholic opinions ought necessarily to leave the Church of England; but at all events let them in common honesty give up their preferment, their fellowships, and livings, which they have obtained upon the faith of subscription to Articles which they no longer believe, and cease to officiate in the pulpits of a Protestant church.[256]

Golightly asked why Keble and Newman, as Tractarians holding Roman Catholic opinions, had not yet resigned their livings,[257] and the *Record* complained at Tractarians 'hushing up' their true views.[258] The *Oxford Chronicle* went further, proclaiming that Newman 'the arch-perverter' with his 'leprous and soul-tainting immorality' should be dismissed from the church.[259] Newman was forced to deny that he had recommended Smith retain his living.[260] He was often on the receiving end of this sort of 'exposure' in the newspapers, and later bewailed to his sister:

> It is astonishing what little feeling certain people have. Golightly and the Newspapers would think it wrong to put out a statement on doubtful authority to the effect that I had broken my leg – yet they have no remorse in circulating what is calculated to shock friends indefinitely more. But the said G. is a man literally

---

[252] *Morning Herald*, 5 January 1843. See *Morning Herald*, 13 January 1843.
[253] Robert Simpson to Kaye, 6 January 1843, LRO Cor. B5/1/9.
[254] Golightly to Kaye, 7 and 14 January 1843, LRO Cor. B5/1/10 and B5/1/13.
[255] *Morning Herald*, 13 January 1843. For the Leicestershire clergyman, see Golightly to Bricknell, 7 January 1843, PHL BRIC 1/6; *Record*, 2 February 1843.
[256] *Morning Herald*, 7 January 1843.
[257] *Oxford Herald*, 11 February 1843.
[258] *Record*, 9 January 1843.
[259] *Oxford Chronicle*, 14 January 1843.
[260] Newman, *Apologia Pro Vita Sua*, pp. 299-304; Middleton, *Magdalen Studies*, pp. 256-67.

without bowels. I doubt whether he has any inside, or is more than a walking and talking piece of mechanism.[261]

Elsewhere Newman complained: 'Golightly has known me only to lift up his hand against me and to accuse me of many things of which I am guiltless.'[262]

Golightly took the opportunity of national attention to publicise his local dispute with R.E. Bridges, vicar of Holywell parish in Oxford. Bridges had recently resigned the post and arranged for his brother to serve there until a successor began, but Golightly was told by a friend that this brother held Roman Catholic views. Although Bridges declared that 'he saw no reason why persons holding Romanist opinions should not officiate', the arrangement was soon dropped.[263] Bridges complained that Golightly lacked facts and relied only on private conversation, to which Golightly responded in typical 'scatter-gun' style through the pages of the *Oxford Herald*, under the anonym 'A Master of Arts':

> Why, Sir, facts indicative of the Romeward tendencies of parties, who continue to officiate in our Church, obtrude themselves upon me at every turn; Romish Bishops walking about the streets of Oxford, and receiving visits from members of the University, young men frequenting Roman Catholic chapels, a Jesuit missionary here only last October, calling upon the leaders of the party, and protesting himself highly delighted with the spread of Romanist opinions among the young men; – these facts speak volumes. And, Sir, if I had not these, what could be more decisive than the conversion of ten individuals from Tractarianism to Romanism during the last sixteen months? *Facts* indeed![264]

One Holywell parishioner rebuked clerical 'wolves in sheep's clothing', and another observer asked:

> Is it possible that men should be found, who eat the bread of the Church, and yet would willingly destroy her? Can there be, dwelling in *Oxford*, the scene of Martyrdom for the Protestant faith, those who under the garb of Priests of our Holy Church, are labouring to work her ruin? Yes, it is even so.[265]

Edward Bickersteth (the evangelical rector of Watton in Hertfordshire) thanked Golightly for helping 'to expose these most antichristian proceedings

---

[261] Newman to Jemima Mozley, 24 November 1844, BOA Jemima Mozley Papers. The copy in *Newman Letters and Diaries*, x. p. 434, omits the phrase 'on doubtful authority'.
[262] Newman to Henry Wilberforce, 27 April 1845, *Newman Letters and Diaries*, x. p. 641.
[263] *Morning Herald*, 7 January 1843; *Record*, 30 January 1843.
[264] *Oxford Herald*, 11 February 1843. Golightly named these ten seceders in *Morning Herald*, 16 January 1843.
[265] *Oxford Chronicle*, 21 January 1843.

which are now threatening to overthrow our Reformed Church',[266] and praised his 'plain honesty and Christian boldness'.[267] Archdeacon Browne thanked him for rendering 'such essential service to our beloved Church.'[268] By others, however, Golightly was criticised for his 'idle rumours' and 'slanders', and for recounting 'second-hand gossip, such as one would expect to hear only at the tea-tables of persons who eschew dancing and are addicted to the *Record*.'[269] He was challenged:

> Is it right to labour, as he does, to rouse *mere* suspicion against his brethren? ... If there is one thing more than another that drives men into Romanism, it is the conduct of those who carp and cavil at expressions beyond their understanding, and at modes of life which are the outward form of earnestness ... Whoever, therefore, rips up old sores, and forces upon others, whether they will or not, the contemplation of our divisions, in an unkind spirit, does more mischief to the Church, and damage to the University, than our bitterest enemies could ever bring upon us from without.[270]

One observer said Golightly was not acting 'the part of a watchman who gives warning of the approach of an enemy, but of a scavenger who collects whatever is offensive and casts it on the road side to stink in the nostrils of the people.' Another remarked: 'Truly we have reason to be thankful that the "Master of Arts" is not a Grand Inquisitor, and that his rules of evidence are not received in our courts of justice.'[271] From Oscott, a Roman Catholic complained that Golightly seemed 'to talk with the most inimitable sang-froid of every atrocious sentiment, when coming from the mouth of a "Papist", as if it were all a matter of course.'[272] Golightly's methods were further denounced:

> We are not living in perpetual fear of any sudden irruption of fierce invaders – we have no alarm lest another St Bartholomew's-day should deluge the streets of Oxford with Protestant gore, or the dagger of Jesuits from St Oscott's terrify us in our halls and common rooms – we do not even feel any anxiety about the probability of a Guy Fawkes conspiracy to blow up the next meeting of Convocation. ... If we are to believe ourselves in a country of open or concealed enemies – if we are to be surrounded by clerical police in plain clothes, who will gather our scattered fragments of conversation, and then publish them in newspapers with a charge against our character, the natural result will be, that we

---

[266] Edward Bickersteth to Golightly, 13 February 1843, LPL MS 1804, fo. 31.
[267] Edward Bickersteth, *The Divine Warning to the Church, at this Time, of our Enemies, Dangers, and Duties, and as to our Future Prospects* (London, 1843 edition), p. 256.
[268] Browne to Golightly, nd, LPL MS 1804, fo. 101.
[269] *Oxford Herald*, 28 January 1843.
[270] *Oxford Herald*, 21 January 1843.
[271] *Oxford Herald*, 18 February 1843.
[272] *Oxford Herald*, 21 January 1843.

shall be obliged to place the seal of silence on our lips whenever we are anywhere in other society than that of well-known friends: the knowledge that we are surrounded with informers will generate universal suspicion, and the openness and frankness which ought to be the peculiar characteristic of Oxford society will be at once and altogether destroyed.[273]

Jemima Mozley described Golightly as 'boiling over', but Newman thought Oxford remained comparatively calm: 'Golightly is writing for friends in the country; in Oxford he either cuts people or is cut by them.'[274] Golightly himself was content: 'I believe that the party are mad with me "beyond the experience of former ages".'[275]

Within a week, Newman's 'calm' in his Littlemore refuge had been shattered. The focus of public attention shifted from Smith and Bridges back on to Newman and Pusey. Golightly did not pause in his campaign, but doggedly continued to ask questions about Tractarian honesty. In January 1843 Newman issued a paper recanting various harsh epithets he had used in print against the Church of Rome. For example, in some of the early *Tracts for the Times* and other publications in the mid-1830s he had denounced Roman Catholicism as 'heretical', 'the cause of Antichrist', 'a pestilence', 'a lie', 'corrupt', 'a mystery of iniquity', 'unscriptural', 'profane', 'impious', 'blasphemous', 'gross', 'monstrous', 'cruel'. These statements and others like them Newman now retracted. His paper was significant since is showed a major change in his theological views, but it first appeared anonymously in an obscure periodical, the *Conservative Journal*. Arthur Stanley later likened it to the slave of King Midas 'whispering ... his secret into the reeds'.[276] Newman explained:

> If you ask me how an individual could venture, not simply to hold, but to publish such views of a communion so ancient, so wide spreading, so fruitful in saints, I answer that I said to myself, 'I am not speaking my own words, I am but following almost a *consensus* of the divines of my Church. They have ever used the strongest language against Rome, even the most able and learned of them. I wish to throw myself into their system. While I say what they say, I am safe. Such views, too, are necessary for our position.' Yet I have reason to fear still, that such language is to be ascribed, in no small measure, to an impetuous temper, a hope of approving myself to persons' respect, and a wish to repel the charge of Romanism.[277]

This paper was soon picked up by other journals and newspapers, and provided

---

[273] *Oxford Herald*, 18 February 1843.
[274] Jemima Mozley – Newman, 20 and 21 February 1843, *Newman Letters and Diaries*, ix. pp. 247-8.
[275] Golightly to Bricknell, 1 February 1843, PHL BRIC 1/7.
[276] Arthur P. Stanley, 'The Oxford School', *Edinburgh Review* 153 (April 1881), p. 313.
[277] *Conservative Journal*, 28 January 1843, p. 5; reprinted in *Dublin Review* 14 (February 1843), pp. 271-5.

Golightly with fresh material to fuel his public denunciations of Tractarianism.

In Newman's defence, William Palmer (of Worcester College) claimed that 'we have no right to infer that such retraction ... was intended to apply to the *general view* which had been taken of the Romish system: it seems only to relate to particular modes of expression.' Indeed, Palmer insisted that the Tract writers were '*opposed to Rome and its corruptions*, and *favourable to the Reformation.*'[278] Golightly, however, thought Newman's paper 'most extraordinary', and asked: 'Why should not any young man say, "I do not much like the thirty nine articles but *almost a consensus of our divines* have subscribed them. I am not using my own words. Again if I want a fellowship or living, this is the way to get one. *Such views are necessary for my position*".'[279] William Goode (later editor of the *Christian Observer*) had never seen a 'more thoroughly & transparently Jesuitical production',[280] and Archdeacon Browne proclaimed:

> It would, I should think, be difficult to find, even in the archives of your Bodleian, such a παλινωδια [recantation] as Newman's, as, indeed, it would in any protracted controversy to meet with a parallel to the φενακισμος [deception] practised by the Tractarians. This extraordinary production of Newman's affords a clue to the disingenuousness which has so eminently characterised their writings.[281]

On receiving a copy of Newman's paper from Golightly, Bishop Copleston responded: 'Mr N. seems fast approaching the crisis long expected – and in my opinion the sooner he reaches it the better – his influence being now much more pernicious than it will be when he is an avowed instead of a disguised Romanist.'[282]

Golightly decided to write an anonymous letter to Newman, signed simply 'A Member of Convocation' and circulated throughout college common rooms.[283] He asked how Newman could with any integrity say his expressions against Rome were not his own words but simply those of others: 'Is this οἰκονομία [economy] or φενακισμὸς, to speak Greek, or, in plain English, is it common honesty?' According to Golightly, Newman had 'shifted from point to point through every stage of your erratic course. First those who agreed with you were Anglo-Catholic, now they are Catholic; those who differed from you

---

[278] William Palmer, *A Narrative of Events Connected with the Publication of the Tracts for the Times, with Reflections on Existing Tendencies to Romanism, and on the Present Duties and Prospects of Members of the Church* (Oxford, 1843; reissued with introduction and supplement, London, 1883), pp. 41, 43.
[279] Golightly to Bricknell, nd, PHL BRIC 1/10.
[280] William Goode to Golightly, 27 February 1843, LPL MS 1806, fo. 106.
[281] Browne to Golightly, 28 February 1843, LPL MS 1804, fo. 104.
[282] Copleston to Golightly, 1 March 1843, LPL MS 1805, fo. 72.
[283] *Oxford Herald*, 25 February 1843; *Oxford Chronicle*, 25 February 1843.

were ultra-Protestant, now Protestant; first the Council of Trent was "atrocious", then only "unhappy", at last quite orthodox.' He concluded that Newman had fulfilled Nicholas Wiseman's prediction of 1841 of laying-up 'the pain and regret, of having beforehand branded with opprobrious and afflicting names, that which you discover to be good and holy'.[284] It amused Golightly that some thought his anonymous letter was written by a Roman Catholic, and that all were generally agreed it was not by him: 'The Tractarians say that it is too well done to be my composition.'[285]

During the Hampden Controversy of 1836, Pusey had remonstrated against insinuations that Tractarian criticisms of the Church of Rome were insincere.[286] Therefore at Golightly's request Bricknell wrote anonymously to Pusey through the pages of the *Oxford Herald*, calling himself 'Another Member of Convocation'. He challenged Pusey to distance himself from Newman's retractions, 'unless you would dispute his claim to be considered the most accomplished adept in the revived arts of "economy" and "phenacism".'[287] Golightly also wrote again to Newman, warning that his principle of hiding behind the consensus of the Church was 'dangerous to the morality of the University' and reminiscent of 'the casuistry of the Jesuits'. It would be better for Newman 'that a millstone were hanged about his neck, and he cast into the sea', than that he lead his younger followers to sign the Thirty-Nine Articles dishonestly.[288] As Golightly wrote at a later date: 'Better cut off your right hand, than subscribe what you do not believe'.[289]

Once again letters of support came flooding into No.6 Holywell Street from around the country. C.S. Bird of Gainsborough praised Golightly for 'the contest you carry on for the truth',[290] and Joseph Mendham of Sutton Coldfield thanked him for his 'vigorous, opportune & effectual efforts ... against the unnatural, &, we may now add, unprincipled, as well as ignorant assaults of the enemy in our camp.'[291] Likewise George Miller wrote from Ireland to encourage Golightly's attempts at 'stemming the tide of opinion in Oxford about this odious perversion of our common church.'[292] In contrast, the *English Churchman* called Golightly a 'spiritual Don Quixote' whose letters were as injurious to the Church as if he himself were 'consciously dishonest'.[293]

---

[284] Nicholas P.S. Wiseman, *A Letter Respectfully Addressed to the Rev. J.H. Newman, upon some passages in his Letter to the Rev. Dr Jelf* (London, 1841), p. 30.
[285] Golightly to Bricknell, 24 February 1843, PHL BRIC 1/8.
[286] Pusey, *Earnest Remonstrance*, pp. 32-3.
[287] *Oxford Herald*, 18 March 1843. See Golightly to Bricknell, nd, PHL BRIC 1/10.
[288] *Oxford Herald*, 1 April 1843. Golightly and Bricknell's letters were published in Bricknell, *Judgment of Bishops*, pp. 669-75.
[289] Golightly, *Position of Samuel Wilberforce*, p. 85.
[290] Charles S. Bird to Golightly, 3 March 1843, LPL MS 1804, fo. 40.
[291] Joseph Mendham to Golightly, 14 March 1843, LPL MS 1808, fo. 77.
[292] Miller to Golightly, 4 April 1843, LPL MS 1808, fo. 134.
[293] *English Churchman*, 23 March 1843, p. 184.

Throughout 1843 Golightly kept up his pressure on the Tractarians, both in public and behind the scenes. For example, he wrote privately to Professor James Scholefield at Cambridge with copies of prayers to the Virgin Mary which afforded 'a fearful specimen of the progress of rank Popery amongst the disciples of Newman.'[294] He informed Bishop Kaye of Lincoln that Newman and his followers had been in contact with the Pope, and later wrote again to warn him about the series of 'Lives of the English Saints' written by Tractarian authors.[295] Likewise he cautioned Bishop Gilbert about the teaching at Chichester Theological College.[296] In Oxford, Bishop Bagot had learnt to ignore Golightly's private letters – there was a total breakdown of communication between the two men. Just as Bagot had once asked Bishop Blomfield of London to speak to Golightly during the *Tract 90* crisis, so now Golightly asked Blomfield to intercede with Bagot over the case of Thomas Chamberlain, the Tractarian vicar of St Thomas', Oxford, who had refused Christian burial to the child of a Dissenter.[297] Golightly did not want his name mentioned and perhaps the Bishop of London never let the two men realise they had chosen the same go-between.

The campaign to bring suspicious Tractarian teaching and practices to public attention also continued apace. Golightly printed handbills offering information on Tractarian secessions to Rome and with quotations from Roman Catholic authorities supportive of Tractarianism.[298] He circulated offensive passages from Newman's sermons, against which he and Bricknell debated taking legal action.[299] He planned an exposure of misquotations in the *Tracts for the Times* and the *British Critic*, as another example of Tractarian dishonesty,[300] and considered advertising the fact that Sir James Graham and Edward Stanley (future Lord Derby and Prime Minister) had removed their sons' names from

---

[294] Browne to Golightly, 18 January 1843, LPL MS 1804, fo. 99.
[295] Golightly to Kaye, 5 September 1843 and 24 May 1844, LRO Cor. B5/1/19 and B5/1/22.
[296] Gilbert to Golightly, 9 September 1843, LPL MS 1806, fos 5-6.
[297] Golightly to Blomfield, 8 October 1843, LPL MS 1804, fos 66-7; *Oxford Chronicle*, 30 September 1843. See P.G. Cobb, 'Thomas Chamberlain – a Forgotten Tractarian' in Derek Baker (ed.), *The Church in Town and Countryside*, Studies in Church History 16 (Oxford, 1979), pp. 373-87.
[298] PHL BRIC 1/25 and 1/27.
[299] Golightly to Bricknell, nd, PHL BRIC 1/21 and 1/26; Hodgson to Bricknell, 6 February 1844, BRIC 4/58 and 4/59.
[300] Golightly to Bricknell, 10 August 1843, PHL BRIC 1/15; Goode to Golightly, 30 August 1843, LPL MS 1806, fo. 114. See 'G.' (Golightly?) in *Record*, 20 March 1843: 'What a sorrowful consideration it is, that persons like Dr Pusey can imagine that God's blessing can rest on such trifling with truth and common honesty as this kind of quotation exhibits.'

Oxford to avoid Tractarian influence.[301]

Before the year was out, Golightly was on the war-path again with still more anonymous letters to the newspapers. In September 1843, William Palmer (of Worcester College) published his famous *Narrative of Events*, in which he aimed 'to clear those who uphold Church principles from the imputation of approving certain recent tendencies to Romanism.'[302] It was a bold attempt to drive a wedge between the originators of the Oxford Movement of 1833 and their pro-Roman successors in the next generation. Palmer insisted that the *Tracts for the Times* aimed 'simply to draw attention to *neglected* truths – to appeal to the Church itself as their standard; to be of no other party.'[303] While thus defending Newman, Pusey and Keble, he launched a vociferous attack upon their younger, more radical followers, particularly against the 'Romanizing tendencies' of the *British Critic*. The journal had become increasingly extreme and anti-authoritarian in its views, dominated by the writings of Thomas Mozley (as editor), William Ward and Frederick Oakeley. Palmer proclaimed:

> there is danger of party-spirit amongst some few of the younger adherents of their cause ... there is too implicit an adoption of the views of individuals; too little tolerance for different opinions; too little respect for constituted authorities ... it is unlawful to array ourselves under any banner, or unite ourselves in any combination, but that of Jesus Christ, and of his Church.[304]

Furthermore, Palmer suggested there were some 'who are secretly convinced of the duty of uniting themselves to Rome ... who remain in the Church, only with a view to instil doctrines which would otherwise be without influence – to gather adherents who would otherwise be safe from temptation.' While not wanting to believe that 'such disgraceful and detestable treachery and hypocrisy can exist', he admitted that appearances seemed to justify this belief.[305]

Golightly was ecstatic and wrote excitedly to Bricknell:

> I consider the publication of W. Palmer's pamphlet the most Important event which has occurred in the history of the University during the last two years. Of course the British Critic party are frantic. Poor Palmer! The clouds are gathering

---

[301] Golightly to Bricknell, 28 October 1843, PHL BRIC 1/20; Bricknell to Golightly, 2 November 1843, LPL MS 1804, fo. 86.

[302] Palmer, *Narrative of Events*, p. v. See William S. Adams, 'William Palmer's *Narrative of Events*: The First History of the "Tracts for the Times"', in J.E. Booty (ed.), *The Divine Drama in History and Liturgy* (Allison Park, Pennsylvania, 1984), pp. 81-106.

[303] Palmer, *Narrative of Events*, p. 34.

[304] Ibid., p. 35.

[305] Ibid., pp. 67-8.

in the distance, and a clap of thunder has been already heard.[306]

To another correspondent he proclaimed: 'The Tractarians are in a state of extreme agitation, and I am myself anticipating the secession to Rome of Newman and some twenty or thirty of the foremost of the party, probably at no distant period.'[307] Indeed Newman had just resigned as vicar of St Mary-the-Virgin because he was rapidly losing confidence in his position within the Church of England. At Littlemore at the end of September 1843 he preached his last sermon as an Anglican, poignantly entitled 'The Parting of Friends'.[308] Seeking to hasten this dramatic crisis within Tractarian ranks, Golightly took the opportunity offered by Palmer's *Narrative of Events* to write another series of letters to the *Standard*. Again signing himself simply 'A Master of Arts', he crowed:

> A very remarkable occurrence has just taken place here. Tractarianism is fairly upon the rocks. Mr Palmer, Dr Hook, Mr Perceval, Mr Gresley, Archdeacon Manning, Mr Paget, &c ... have jumped into the long boat without consulting the leaders of the party, and are pulling away from the wreck.[309]

Although Palmer's disclosures about Roman Catholic views held within the Church of England were little different to Golightly's own claims, they were important as 'the reluctant, the very reluctant, admissions of a partisan.'[310] Palmer's attempt to shield Newman at the expense of his disciples deserved 'the severest reprobation', and Golightly insisted that Newman still approved of the sentiments of the *British Critic*, despite having handed over the editorship to Mozley. He also took the opportunity to attack the theory of doctrinal development propounded in Newman's final University sermon a few months earlier. Golightly thought it was no more than 'a scheme for proving anything out of anything, and throwing overboard the testimony of antiquity and the Word of God'.[311] He rebuked the Tractarians' 'miserable attempts to reconcile Romish opinions with Protestant preferment' and concluded:

---

[306] Golightly to Bricknell, 28 October 1843, PHL BRIC 1/20.
[307] Golightly to Wall, 22 November 1843, LPL MS 1806, fo. 93.
[308] John H. Newman, *Sermons Bearing on Subjects of the Day* (London, 1843), sermon xxvi.
[309] *Standard*, 26 October 1843.
[310] Ibid..
[311] *Standard*, 31 October 1843. John H. Newman, 'The Theory of Developments in Religious Doctrine' in *Sermons, Chiefly on the Theory of Religious Belief, Preached before the University of Oxford* (London, 1843), pp. 311-54. See further, John H. Newman, *An Essay on the Development of Christian Doctrine* (London, 1845); Owen Chadwick, *From Bossuet to Newman* (1957; second edition, Cambridge, 1987); Jan-Hendrik Walgrave, *Newman the Theologian: The Nature of Belief and Doctrine as Exemplified in His Life and Works* (1957; translation, London, 1960).

It is lamentable to think that from this unhappy movement our Church is losing character every day. The foreign Protestant draws arguments from it against Episcopacy, the latitudinarian against creeds and articles, the Dissenter against an Established Church; and spirits are given to the Romanists to attempt the destruction of the Church of England by sap, and the Church of Ireland by assault.[312]

Under these pressures, though more as a result of Palmer's attacks than Golightly's, the *British Critic* was closed down in October 1843. The extreme wing of Tractarianism was in disarray. The final nail in the coffin of Golightly's former friendship with Newman and Mozley had been hammered home. Nor did he have much respect for 'moderates' like Palmer, whose 'powers of self-deception are unlimited'. Although Palmer had momentarily proved a useful ally, Golightly described him a few months later as 'a person of very violent temper, and carried away to a very lamentable extent by party feeling.'[313]

The Vice-Chancellorship

By custom, each Vice-Chancellor served the University of Oxford for four years, and his annual nomination by the Chancellor was usually agreed by Convocation as a matter of course.[314] In October 1844, however, when the term of Philip Wynter (President of St John's) came to an end, the nomination of Benjamin Symons (Warden of Wadham) received strong opposition. Once again the dispute revealed the deep theological fault-lines at Oxford.

From June 1844 a series of controversial letters appeared in the *English Churchman* by a Tractarian sympathiser who signed himself 'N.E.S.'. He painted Symons as a partisan who stood 'plainly against what the Church has ever accounted Christianity', and called Wynter 'unjust, tyrannical, an oppressor of the innocent, unconstitutional, unprincipled, through weak-mindedness the tool of others'.[315] Those familiar with the Oxford scene tried to discover the identity of the author – some guessed at JohN DobreE DalgairnS,

---

[312] *Standard*, 7 November 1843.
[313] Golightly to Kaye, 15 February 1844, LRO Cor. B5/1/20.
[314] Gilbert's re-nomination as Vice-Chancellor was opposed in 1839 by G.R.M. Ward and T.W. Lancaster, but passed by 46 votes to two: Gilbert to Wellington, 8 October 1839, SUL Wellington Papers 2/250/46. See also T.W. Lancaster, *An Earnest and Resolute Protestation against a Certain Inductive Method of Theologizing, which has been Recently Propounded by the King's Professor of Divinity in Oxford* (London, 1839); G.R.M. Ward, *An Appeal to the Bishop of Winchester, Visitor of Trinity College, Oxford, on the Misappropriation of the Endowments of that Society, with Hints towards a History of 'The Poor Man's Church' in the University of Oxford* (Oxford, 1839), pp. 6-10.
[315] *English Churchman*, 27 June 1844, pp. 407-8.

resident with Newman at Littlemore, but it turned out to be JohN BrandE MorriS, a fellow of Exeter College.[316] Soon Morris' theme was picked up by others. For example, the *Christian Remembrancer* (supposedly a more 'moderate' successor to the *British Critic*) declared: 'No greater academical criminals than the President of St John's and the Warden of Wadham can by any possibility exist: they have exhausted the class. ... Dr Hampden himself, were his nomination possible, must pass without a murmur, if Dr Symons is to be spared.'[317]

The central charge against Symons was that he was one of the six Doctors of Divinity who had done 'their best to set the mark of the beast on the Church of England' by condemning as heretical Pusey's sermon on *The Holy Eucharist a Comfort to the Penitent* in June 1843.[318] Pusey had been formally accused of heresy by Professor Godfrey Faussett, was found guilty, and was now in the middle of a two-year ban from preaching before the university. It was therefore recommended in the *English Churchman* that the six DDs responsible for this outrage be refused university office of any sort, and that not only Symons be opposed as Vice-Chancellor, but also the Heads of Houses next in turn, Frederick Plumptre (Master of University College) and Richard Cotton (Provost of Worcester College).[319] The *Standard* thought this campaign against Symons was an 'anarchical movement ... based upon principles subversive to all academic order and government'.[320] The *Oxford Chronicle* called the attacks 'literary ruffianism' and 'downright blackguardism and blasphemy', intended 'to bully and intimidate'.[321] Meanwhile Bishop Gilbert of Chichester told Golightly:

> These reckless men will bring a Visitation upon the University, if they are not stopped ... if the violence and distraction continue, and the University is unable, or unwilling, to coerce the offenders, and stay the Tumult, or the Church does not interfere ... the Civil Power will.[322]

Symons himself could not understand the purpose of the opposition to his appointment: 'It really seems to me such a wild-goose game, that I cannot but suppose the object of the agitation is simply to *annoy* – and to have a vent-hole to get rid of their spleen.'[323] The Tractarians had taken a number of hits in recent months and here was an obvious opportunity to retaliate and to

---

[316] *Standard*, 21 September and 2 October 1844.
[317] 'Dr Symons and the Vice-Chancellorship', *Christian Remembrancer* 8 (October 1844), p. 540.
[318] *English Churchman*, 29 August 1844, p. 549.
[319] *English Churchman*, 11 July and 22 August 1844, pp. 441, 536.
[320] *Standard*, 11 October 1844.
[321] *Oxford Chronicle*, 21 September 1844.
[322] Gilbert to Golightly, 20 September 1844, LPL MS 1806, fos 8-9.
[323] Symons to Bricknell, 7 September 1844, PHL BRIC 2/113.

demonstrate their strength.

With Oxford deserted during the Long Vacation and Symons on holiday in Boulogne, Golightly was worried lest 'the University be taken by surprise'. Through the columns of the *Standard* he publicly sounded the alarm, calling non-residents to come up to Oxford and vote in Symons' favour.[324] He was concerned that Wadham College had foolishly taken Symons' election for granted, failing to organise a committee to canvas support.[325] Similarly, the *Morning Herald* warned that although Symons' opponents were 'a mere minority', their strength lay in their 'superior organisation, sympathy, and party spirit.'[326] The *Record* declared it 'essential that *every Protestant* should be at his post',[327] while another asserted: 'The snake must be scotched by one heavy and conclusive stroke – this new head of the "beast" should be destroyed by an overwhelming blow.'[328] Golightly was energetically involved behind the scenes and complained to Bricknell: 'We have had to work like horses, those of us who are here.'[329]

Symons' theological views were the main focus of the argument. Wadham College had a reputation for evangelicalism and it was rumoured that Symons wanted Tractarian opinions 'exterminated' and 'crushed'.[330] The *Christian Remembrancer* complained:

> Under favourable auspices we have had despotism, tyranny, and every sort of injustice, a tolerable augury for a rule which it is known does not even aim at impartiality. The present Vice-Chancellor, Dr Wynter, was not a pledged man, had never committed himself, set up according to some accounts for a High-Churchman, according to all reports sought to pass for one of the old orthodox, Church and State, Establishment men, and yet what his rule has been everybody knows. What, then, are we to anticipate from one who is notoriously the reverse of all this? Active, enterprising, and polemical – pledged and committed against the most eminent men in the University; one who has already with curious dexterity succeeded in reducing his own college to a congenial uniformity, which presents a strange and ominous contrast to all other societies ... a Low-

---

[324] *Standard*, 18 September 1844. For Golightly's authorship, see Golightly to Bricknell, [20 September 1844], PHL BRIC 1/34.

[325] For Symons' committee, when eventually organised, see *Morning Herald*, 2 October 1844.

[326] *Morning Herald*, 25 September 1844.

[327] *Record*, 26 September 1844.

[328] *Morning Herald*, 30 September 1844.

[329] Golightly to Bricknell, [20 September 1844], PHL BRIC 1/34. For Golightly's work behind the scenes, see Golightly to Hawkins, 16, 19 and 25 September 1844, OCL Miscellaneous Letters, vol. 1, nos 44, 48, 50.

[330] John Griffiths, *Letters with a Few Remarks concerning rumours which have lately been in circulation calculated to prejudice the appointment of the Warden of Wadham College to the Vice-Chancellorship* (Oxford, 1844), p. 7; T.W. Allies in *Times*, 4 October 1844.

Churchman of the most extreme type.[331]

Likewise, the Duke of Wellington (Oxford's Chancellor) was warned that Symons was 'notoriously a religious partisan – a warm and vehement member of what is called the Low Church party',[332] although Golightly had recently asserted that 'There is no Low Church party in Oxford'.[333]

Symons' supporters, in contrast, accused his opponents of partisanship. Edward Hawkins (Provost of Oriel) told Golightly that it was 'the most factious proceeding of a very factious party, who deceive themselves sadly, & do very wrong things under the notion of Religion, & High Church Principles.'[334] Similarly, John Griffiths (Sub-Warden of Wadham) encouraged members of his college to resist this 'unprecedented effort of party spirit'.[335] The *Times*, however, thought for Griffiths 'to talk of wanton disturbance, and faction, and uncalled-for violence, is really like a child who stamps on a dog's tail and is angry when he growls, or throws gunpowder into the fire and abuses the explosion.'[336] One correspondent warned Griffiths: 'The Claim that Power shd be conferred irrespective of Party implies a Promise that it will be exercised irrespective of Party.' He would only vote for the Warden if it was Symons' intention to act 'with perfect Judicial Impartiality between the so-called Evangelicals & Tractarians'.[337]

The controversy was not, however, a simple contest between evangelicals and Tractarians. Many who disagreed with Symons' theological principles nonetheless supported his nomination. Even those who identified closely with the Tractarian movement could not agree about the best course of action. Lydia Symons, the Warden's wife, thought the Tractarians were 'without any Centre of unity',[338] and Symons' opponents were warned to

> beware, lest, like the viper biting the file, the blood they draw should be their own. They are deceiving themselves if they think that the majority even of those who have adopted some of their notions and conformed to some of their practices will, therefore, follow their lead to do what is disorderly, revengeful, unacademical, and unchristian.[339]

---

[331] 'Dr Symons and the Vice-Chancellorship', pp. 536-7.
[332] *Times*, 25 September 1844.
[333] Golightly to Kaye, 21 February 1844, LRO Cor. B5/1/21. Compare *Oxford Chronicle*, 28 September 1844.
[334] Hawkins to Golightly, 18 September 1844, OCL Miscellaneous Letters, vol. 1, no. 45.
[335] *Standard*, 5 October 1844.
[336] *Times*, 3 October 1844.
[337] J.W. Awdry to Griffiths, 28 September 1844, WCA Symons Papers.
[338] Lydia Symons to Bricknell, 3 October 1844, PHL BRIC 2/118.
[339] *Morning Herald*, 30 September 1844.

Similarly the short-lived *Churchman's Newspaper* thought the 'factious partisanship' against Symons was 'successfully defeating its own object':

> We have heard of a number of sound, faithful, earnest-minded Catholics, who are so disgusted with the factious character and objects of the greater part of the opposition to him, that they are determined not to vote at all. And some who are opposed to Dr Symons's principles have resolved, in consequence of the conduct of those restless persons, to go and vote in his favour.[340]

The day before Convocation, W.F. Hook published an influential letter in the *Times* explaining that he would not vote. Although he doubted Symons' 'fitness for an office where equal-handed justice is the most essential virtue', and feared that 'on many questions his party feelings might prejudice his judgment', still he refused to join the protest lest he be regarded as favouring 'the extreme opinions of ... the Romanizing party', represented by William Ward and other radicals.[341] The *Churchman's Newspaper* agreed that a careful distinction was needed 'between the great body of sound-hearted English Catholics, and the semi-popish party',[342] but the *Standard* criticised Hook's retreat as a 'jesuitical attempt ... to break the fall of his Tractarian allies'.[343] Similarly the *Record* proclaimed:

> A more miserable exhibition than Dr Hook has made on this occasion, it is hardly possible to conceive. He becomes, as it were, the natural leader and representative of that very numerous class in the Church, which makes no secret of its fondness for Tractarianism; but at the same time only follows the Tractarian standard so far as *prudence* and *expediency* may counsel. A class which, though from its numbers it may be feared by all parties, can be respected by none.[344]

Many followed Hook's lead. Amongst those Tractarian sympathisers who either decided to vote for Symons or to stay at home, were Henry Manning, Edward Churton, William Gresley, Robert Wilberforce, Charles Eden, Walter Hamilton, Frederick Oakeley, William Gladstone and others.[345]

As polling-day approached, Golightly was confident that effective campaigning would see Symons' nomination agreed: 'I trust we shall get a good majority *with pains*. ... The party seem nearly at their wit's *end*.'[346] Convocation met on 8 October 1844 with hundreds of non-residents present,

---

[340] *Churchman's Newspaper*, 4 October 1844.
[341] *Times*, 7 October 1844.
[342] *Churchman's Newspaper*, 8 October 1844.
[343] *Standard*, 12 October 1844.
[344] *Record*, 7 October 1844.
[345] *English Churchman*, 17 October 1844, p. 665. For further details of voters, see *Oxford Chronicle*, 12 October 1844.
[346] Golightly to Bricknell, [28 September 1844], PHL BRIC 1/35.

and Symons was appointed by 882 votes to 183, an overwhelming majority.[347] The *Record* celebrated this 'total and crushing' defeat, yet remained cautious:

> The Tractarians made a great blunder in the battlefield they chose. They fought at a great disadvantage. Many of those who are substantially with them, refused to go to Oxford on an expedition of contumacy and rebellion. Many, too, who went there to oppose them, for the sake of supporting lawful authority, would hesitate as to their vote, if the question concerned the doctrines of the Reformation. Hence this vast majority presents to our view an unsafe, because substantially untrue, view of the relative strength of the two parties.[348]

The *English Churchman*, which was responsible for starting the agitation, agreed: 'the ultra-Protestants have not gained a victory over the Catholics: there were sound Catholics on both sides, but A saw a cloud arising in the north, and B saw one in the south, and each acted accordingly.'[349] With bold confidence, it continued:

> The precedent is set, the parent of future victories. On the one side was arrayed a majority, not six of whom agreed in the chance-medley motives which brought them for once, and by a happy hazard, together; on the other, a minority, not six of whom differed in material points, as far as regards the Academical question, or in their fixed abhorrence of the wickedness practised against Dr Pusey. ... The one is a growing, the other a withering body.[350]

Degradation and Censure

During the early 1840s William Ward (fellow of Balliol College) became increasingly extreme in his religious opinions and increasingly daring in his expression of them. He was a leader of the younger, radical, 'Romanizing' group amongst the Tractarians and first rose to prominence in 1841 with two notorious pamphlets in support of Newman's *Tract 90*. Ward lost his college lectureships as a result, but continued to develop his radical line of thought. Between 1841 and 1843 he published several articles in the *British Critic* suggesting that the Roman Catholic Church was the model for the one true church, which brought upon him the wrath of William Palmer's *Narrative of Events*, as has been seen. In the furore which followed the *British Critic* was forced to close, but still Ward would not remain silent. In June 1844 he defended his views in *The Ideal of a Christian Church*, a lengthy tome which contained many provocative and offensive statements. For instance, he spoke of

---

[347] For Wynter's and Symons' speeches at Convocation, see *Standard*, 10 October 1844; *Morning Herald*, 10 October 1844.
[348] *Record*, 10 October 1844.
[349] *English Churchman*, 17 October 1844, p. 660.
[350] *English Churchman*, 10 October 1844, pp. 644-5.

the Anglican system as 'corrupt to its very core',[351] and rebuked 'the emptiness, hollowness, folly, laxity, unreality, of English Protestantism'.[352] He described the Reformation as 'wholly destitute of all claims on our sympathy and regard',[353] and spoke of his 'deep and burning hatred' for 'that miserable event'.[354] In contrast, he claimed to regard the Roman Church 'with affection and reverence',[355] and celebrated: 'oh most joyful, most wonderful, most unexpected sight! we find the whole cycle of Roman doctrine gradually possessing numbers of English Churchmen'.[356] He insisted the Church of England should be taught to 'appreciate the plain marks of Divine wisdom and authority in the Roman Church, to repent in sorrow and bitterness of heart our great sin in deserting her communion, and to sue humbly at her feet for pardon and restoration.'[357] Most provocatively, Ward maintained: 'Three years have passed, since I said plainly, that in subscribing the Articles I renounce no one Roman doctrine: yet I retain my Fellowship which I hold on the tenure of subscription, and have received no Ecclesiastical censure in any shape.'[358]

The *Record* stated that if Ward's *Ideal* was consistent with the principles of an Anglican clergyman, 'then a thief is an honest man – an Infidel is a religious man – and a courtezan is a virtuous woman.'[359] Likewise the *Times* said his work was 'below contempt, whether we regard his facts, his history, his arguments, or his style: it is the work of a man of superficial knowledge, of no powers of thought, or habits of reflection, but an intemperate vehemence of expression'.[360] Another reviewer concluded: 'The real nature of the movement is ... now confessed. Puseyism is popery – nothing less.'[361]

Benjamin Symons privately described Ward's approach to subscription as 'a flagrant instance of double-dealing'.[362] He had only been Vice-Chancellor for a couple of months, but it now fell to the Hebdomadal Board under his leadership to push for a public censure of the book. On 13 December 1844, having been

---

[351] W.G. Ward, *The Ideal of a Christian Church considered in comparison with Existing Practice, containing a Defence of Certain Articles in the British Critic in Reply to Remarks on them in Mr Palmer's 'Narrative'* (London, 1844), p. 61.
[352] Ibid., p. 565.
[353] Ibid., p. 45.
[354] Ibid., p. 44.
[355] Ibid., p. 100.
[356] Ibid., p. 565.
[357] Ibid., p. 473.
[358] Ibid., p. 567.
[359] *Record*, 16 December 1844.
[360] *Times*, 21 January 1845.
[361] George Redford, 'Tractarian Theology. Ward's Ideal of a Christian Church', *British Quarterly Review* 1 (February 1845), p. 39.
[362] Symons to Wellington, 16 December 1844, SUL Wellington Papers 2/254/106.

urged on by Archbishop Whately and Bishop Copleston,[363] the Heads of Houses issued two propositions to be submitted to Convocation. The first declared passages in Ward's *Ideal* to be 'utterly inconsistent' with the Thirty-Nine Articles and his 'good faith' in subscribing to them. The second proposed that since Ward was admitted to his BA and MA degrees on the condition of subscription, he should now be stripped of them.[364] Richard Harington (Principal of Brasenose) and Joseph Richards (Rector of Exeter) opposed these suggestions, but an anonymous correspondent to the *Standard*, possibly Golightly, came to their defence. Attempting to drive a wedge between radicals (like Ward) and more moderate Tractarian sympathisers, he explained of Harington and Richards:

> Their disorder is not Asiatic but English cholera; they are Anglo-Catholics, not Roman Catholics; Tractarians not of the Ward and Newman, but of the Hook and Manning school. They denounced Mr Ward's dishonesty, it is said, as strongly as anybody; and the only members of the Hebdomadal Board who did not do so were the two proctors, both decided party men.[365]

Because of the Christmas vacation, Convocation would not meet to vote on these propositions until early February. That allowed plenty of time for fierce argument, through pamphlets, periodicals, newspapers and petitions.

Ward's opponents were frequently denounced for being 'blinded by prejudice and party feeling',[366] and rebuked for their efforts 'to commence the purgation of the English Church by a one-sided persecution'.[367] Numerous authors adopted this form of polemic. George Moberly (headmaster of Winchester College) agreed Ward's book was 'violent, unjust, undutiful, and mischievous', but was concerned it would 'throw the University out of all sober-minded self-possession, and drive it, in a paroxysm of anger, to an act of unprecedented severity, of more than doubtful legality, and of apparent one-

---

[363] OUA Hebdomadal Board Minutes, 4 and 11 November 1844; Whately to Hawkins, 6 and 13 November 1844; Copleston to Hawkins, 6 and 13 November 1844; Whately to J.T. O'Brien (Bishop of Ossory), 8 November 1844, OCL Miscellaneous Letters, vol. 1, nos 53-7.

[364] OUA Hebdomadal Board Minutes, 13 December 1844. For Ward's self-defence, see W.G. Ward, *An Address to Members of Convocation in Protest Against the Proposed Statute* (London, 1845). See in reply, F.D. Maurice, *Thoughts on the Rule of Conscientious Subscription, on the Purpose of the Thirty-Nine Articles, and on our Present Perils from the Romish System: in a Second Letter to a Non-Resident Member of Convocation* (Oxford, 1845)

[365] *Standard*, 18 December 1844. For Golightly's use of the anonym 'Academicus', see *Standard*, 10 December 1844, with Golightly to Bricknell, 9 December 1844, PHL BRIC 1/46. For the reply by Harington and Richards, see *Standard*, 19 December 1844.

[366] *English Churchman*, 13 February 1845, p. 100.

[367] *English Churchman*, 27 February 1845, p. 133.

sidedness and partizanship'.[368] Similarly Keble complained that the proceedings were 'inexcusably partial and one-sided', since men such as Professor Hampden continued unquestioned: 'If the "Via Media" is to be defended by something like the sword of excommunication, at least it should be two-edged, and cut both ways.'[369] Meanwhile Hook encouraged Pusey: 'we must take care to prevent the Church of England being transformed into a nasty narrow-minded Protestant Sect.'[370]

Despite being portrayed as a narrow sect, Ward's antagonists were in fact drawn from a wide theological spectrum. Frederick Oakeley claimed that his friend was left as 'a prey to the combined fury of "evangelicals", rationalists, indifferentists, and short-sighted "churchmen".'[371] Likewise in the *Christian Remembrancer*, J.B. Mozley rebuked the temporary theological coalition he saw forming:

> A Liberal school and an Evangelical one, combining and mingling, and gathering reinforcements from different quarters, where distrust of the Church movement happens to prevail, will only see in the Church of England the reflex of themselves, and identify her wholly with their own theology.[372]

Another observer described the 'motley crew' who would vote against Ward:

> All low Churchmen, who conscientiously believe that Puseyism is Popery, and Popery, Antichrist. All Establishmentarians, who love the Establishment more than the Church, and are looking for promotion from the great ones of the earth. All holders of pluralities, who *fleece*, not *feed*, the flock. All lovers of popularity, who measure truth by success. All expediency men, who sacrifice eternal truth for temporary gain. All lovers of ease, whose motto is, 'Leave well alone – it will last our time.' All who wish to escape the imputation of Popery, by fostering the imputation upon others.[373]

The severest criticisms were reserved for the Hebdomadal Board, who had begun the agitation. Their proceedings were variously called 'wanton and capricious persecution',[374] 'a tyrannical act of arbitrary power',[375] 'mob-

---

[368] George Moberly, *The Proposed Degradation and Declaration, Considered in a Letter Addressed to the Rev. the Master of Balliol College* (Oxford, 1845), pp. 4, 14.
[369] John Keble, *Heads of Consideration on the Case of Mr Ward* (Oxford, 1845), pp. 9, 11.
[370] Hook to Pusey, 22 February 1845, PHL PUS 4/53.
[371] Frederick Oakeley, *A Few Words to Those Churchmen, being Members of Convocation, who Purpose Taking No Part in Mr Ward's Case* (London, 1845), p. 22.
[372] James B. Mozley, 'Recent Proceedings at Oxford', *Christian Remembrancer* 9 (April 1845), p. 564.
[373] *English Churchman*, 16 January 1845, p. 46.
[374] Oakeley, *A Few Words*, p. 29.

worship',[376] and 'a cruel mockery ... unwise, unjust, illegal, and suicidal'.[377] The *English Churchman* said of the Heads: 'they are the dagger of retaliation, rather than the sword of justice; their law is of Lynch, rather than Lincoln's Inn',[378] and a pamphleteer proclaimed: 'The enemies of the Church and of the University chuckle in their sleeves at our suicidal madness.'[379] Pusey felt that if the measures were passed it would be 'hypocrisy on a great scale',[380] but meanwhile Golightly was celebrating: 'Let us make hay while the sun shines'.[381]

The 'New Test'

In addition to the two censures against Ward, the Hebdomadal Board proposed a change in the statute governing subscription to the formularies, so that they must now be signed in the sense in which the Thirty-Nine Articles were '*et primitus editos ... et nunc ... ab Universitate propositos*' (both originally published and now proposed by the University).[382] This new statute would have the effect of severely limiting the breadth of interpretation which could be attached to the Articles by Oxford graduates and tutors. One supporter insisted this was no 'new test', but simply an attempt to halt 'Ecclesiastical Fraud' and restore the value of subscription before it was 'jesuitically poisoned by systematic deceit'.[383] Bishop Copleston commented, 'I don't think that even Newman could devise an evasion',[384] but another observer was less optimistic and wrote of Ward: 'No subscription, no declaration, will hold such a man. A theological O'Connell, he will at once drive his triumphal car through every act of Convocation.'[385]

The new statute came under severe criticism from all sides. Pusey thought it would restrain 'that liberty which Archbishop Laud won for us',[386] while another declared: 'Every Oxonian must henceforth solemnly and publicly

---

[375] W.F. Donkin, *A Defence of Voting Against the Proposition to be Submitted to Convocation on Feb. 13, 1845* (Oxford, 1845), p. 4.

[376] 'The Proposed Oxford Test. Subscription to the Articles', *Christian Remembrancer* 9 (January 1845), p. 200.

[377] W.W. Hull, *MDCCCXLV. The Month of January. Oxford* (London, 1845), p. 16.

[378] *English Churchman*, 30 January 1845, p. 72.

[379] R.C. Sewell, *A Letter to the Members of the Venerable House of Convocation, in the University of Oxford* (London, 1845), p. 12.

[380] Pusey to Tait, 31 January 1845, LPL Tait Papers, vol. 77, fo. 301.

[381] Golightly to Bricknell, 10 December 1844, PHL BRIC 1/47.

[382] OUA Hebdomadal Board Minutes, 13 December 1844.

[383] Circular, PHL pamphlet no. 70712.

[384] Copleston to Hawkins, 22 November 1844, OCL Miscellaneous Letters, vol. 1, no. 58.

[385] *Standard*, 4 February 1845.

[386] *English Churchman*, 19 December 1844, p. 799.

profess himself a Cranmerite.'[387] The *Christian Remembrancer* rebuked the Hebdomadal Board's inconsistency:

> To suit the latitudinarianism of 1835, they could have trampled on every article, from 1 to 39, – to suit the equally fatal bigotry of 1845, they cannot endure even the most evanescent shade or difference of possible thought, though in the interpretation of a single clause in a single article. O fickle fortune's wheel! – 'the principles of the Reformation' in 1835 were unscientific, and adverse to theological growth; now a Cranmer's very commas are sacred.[388]

The journal complained that the new statute would give to the Vice-Chancellor 'an instrument of the most grinding and oppressive tyranny to the conscience, which has been heard of since the days of the Solemn League and Covenant and the Westminster Assembly.'[389] Another warned that the statute 'sanctions a vexatious system of "Delations"', with more scope 'for frivolous and trifling informations, whether by interested parties or by busybodies.'[390] Newman believed that Golightly would be quick to play the role of such a busybody, and remarked:

> If the Test passes, the state of things will be as miserable as can be conceived – some men ejected, others straining their conscience – and suspicion, distrust, reserve, dissimulation, everywhere. It would in fact be the reign of the Inquisition. The Vice Chancellor would be able, and would not scruple, to summon a Tutor before him for his Lectures on the Articles, on the information of his Pupils! It would be the reign of Golightlyism. The Statute should have contained another clause, creating a new office for a personage to be called the Oculus Vice-cancellorii – and nominating Golightly to the place.[391]

With years of bitter experience, Newman told Pusey that he was considering a public protest against 'the wretchedness of gossiping, talebearing, prying, delating – in short, of Golightlyism.'[392] That very month Golightly had been stirring up trouble with an anonymous letter to the *Standard* denouncing Pusey's republication of the Jesuit Surin's *Foundations of the Spiritual Life*.[393]

---

[387] *English Churchman*, 9 January 1845, p. 29.

[388] 'The Proposed Oxford Test', pp. 190*-191*.

[389] Ibid., p. 200.

[390] *Mr Ward and the New Test; or, Plain Reasons why those who Censure Mr Ward should not Vote for the New Statute, which Limits the Thirty-Nine Articles; in a Letter to a Friend. By MA* (Oxford, 1845), p. 8.

[391] Newman to Elizabeth Bowden, 27 December 1844, *Newman Letters and Diaries*, x. pp. 473-4.

[392] Newman to Pusey, 16 December 1844, ibid., p. 464.

[393] *Standard*, 6 December 1844. See Golightly to Bricknell, 29 November 1844, PHL BRIC 1/42; J.J. Surin, *The Foundations of the Spiritual Life: Drawn from the Book of the Imitation of Jesus Christ* adapted by E.B. Pusey (London, 1844).

Rare support for the new statute came from William Palmer (of Worcester College), who lamented that the question was 'discussed on party grounds, and not on its own merits.'[394] James Garbett, also in favour, argued that to condemn Ward but oppose the statute was inconsistent and simply made Ward 'a scapegoat'. Although he warned that Convocation must not listen 'to party feelings and theological jealousies', he claimed the statute was not a 'narrow or sectarian scheme ... no school of opinion or shade of doctrine, ever acknowledged within the pale of the Church, is proscribed.'[395] Meanwhile Tait campaigned against the 'new test', believing that 'wielded by irreligious hands, [it] may become an engine of destruction, that will crush at some future day, the very parties who now support it.'[396] He argued that 'Low Churchmen' (the school of Arnold, Thirlwall and Maurice) would not support the measure because they wanted to keep interpreting the Athanasian Creed in a loose sense.[397] Likewise, evangelicals would not want restrictions placed on their own interpretation of the Prayer Book baptismal liturgy.[398] Preaching before the University at the beginning of February 1845, Tait cautioned his hearers not to press on others 'a greater resemblance to ourselves than the Bible requires' nor to 'confound our own prejudices with Christ's all-comprehensive truth'.[399]

The *Morning Post* considered the 'new test' 'one of the clumsiest and most mischievous makeshifts of a bungling legislature and a pusillanimous executive.'[400] William Gresley thought it was even more indefinite than the notorious *et-cetera oath* for which Archbishop Laud was ridiculed in the 1640s.[401] He described it as 'the commencement of a *bellum internecinum* – a war of extermination', and warned:

> do not, on account of the extravagance of a few, forge a weapon, and place it in

---

[394] *Oxford Herald*, 18 January 1845.

[395] James Garbett, *The University, the Church, and the New Test. With Remarks on Mr Oakeley's and Mr Gresley's Pamphlets. A Letter to the Lord Bishop of Chichester* (London, 1845), pp. 49, 51, 58.

[396] A.C. Tait, *A Letter to the Rev. the Vice-Chancellor of the University of Oxford, on the Measures Intended to be Proposed to Convocation on the 13th of February, in Connexion with the Case of the Rev. W.G. Ward* (London, 1845), p. 15.

[397] Maurice retorted, 'if I belong to the school he has described, I must be its most ill-taught and refractory pupil', *Thoughts on the Rule of Conscientious Subscription*, p. viii. Likewise Edward Churton rejected the idea that Arnold was part of a Low Church 'party'; Churton to William Gresley, 27 January 1845, PHL GRES 3/7/50.

[398] Golightly retorted, 'you really cannot know what intelligent Evangelicals have to say'; Golightly to Tait, 15 January 1845, LPL Tait Papers, vol. 77, fo. 281.

[399] A.C. Tait, *Variety in Unity. A Sermon, Preached at St Mary's, Before the University of Oxford, on Sunday, February 2, 1845* (London, 1845), p. 30.

[400] *Morning Post*, 18 January 1845.

[401] William Gresley, *Suggestions on the New Statute to be Proposed in the University of Oxford* (London, 1845), p. 8.

the hands of those who may be wise and discreet men, but who may also be tyrannical and filled with party-spirit, – a weapon whereby they may lop off the most vigorous shoots from the body of the Church, and deprive her of those whose services she most needs.[402]

Meanwhile the *English Churchman* threatened: 'There is sufficient love of fair play left to make this censuring books a double-edged sword, which may cut the fingers of those who try to wield it.'[403] Indeed one 'Anti-Puseyite' in the *Record* warned that since the majority of Convocation and Heads of Houses were High Churchmen, 'every member of the University, professing Protestant, or "Evangelical" principles, will be liable at any moment to instant expulsion.'[404] On 23 January 1845, as a result of these objections from across the theological spectrum, the Hebdomadal Board finally withdrew the disputed measure,[405] leaving the *English Churchman* to celebrate: 'University and the Church – high and low – liberals and bigots – have disclaimed once and for all the doctrines of subscription held alone in the world by the Heads of Houses.'[406]

Requisition Against *Tract 90*

In place of the 'new test', Golightly's co-campaigner, W.S. Bricknell, had the idea of substituting a censure of Newman's *Tract 90*. This had the advantage of being less vague than the 'new test', while still sending out a clear message that there were limits to a legitimate interpretation of the Thirty-Nine Articles. So Bricknell drew up a Requisition asking the Hebdomadal Board to let Convocation vote on a censure of *Tract 90*, and he immediately set about collecting signatures.[407] Edward Cockey, John Griffiths and H.B. Wilson, who were all involved in the Four Tutors' censure of *Tract 90* in 1841, refused to sign the Requisition, and even Golightly was initially cautious.[408] However, once Professor Faussett and Edward Ellerton (an elderly fellow of Magdalen College) agreed to be the Requisition's official promoters, Golightly's concerns were allayed.[409] Soon he and W.H. Cox (Vice-Principal of St Mary Hall) were also energetically collecting signatures. J.B. Mozley publicly exposed these men in the *Christian Remembrancer*:

---

[402] Ibid., p. 12.
[403] *English Churchman*, 5 December 1844, p. 775.
[404] *Record*, 9 January 1845.
[405] OUA Hebdomadal Board Minutes, 23 January 1845.
[406] *English Churchman*, 30 January 1845, p. 68.
[407] See correspondence at PHL BRIC 2 and BRIC 3.
[408] Golightly to Bricknell, [23 January 1845], PHL BRIC 1/50; Cockey to Bricknell, 23 January 1845, BRIC 2/13; Wilson to Bricknell, 23 January 1845, BRIC 2/168.
[409] Bricknell – Faussett, 20 and 21 January 1845, PHL BRIC 2/50 and 2/51.

they are not names that have hitherto carried either awe or weight with them, in University movements. If an unusual and irregular step was to be taken, – if the University was to put aside order, gravity, and *prima facie* equity on any occasion, we should have wished it to have been done upon some other authorities than these.[410]

To his sister, Mozley commented: 'Golightly is in thick communication with Dr Ellerton, and is coming in and going out of College every day. He, and E., and F. are the trio on the subject.'[411] Later he added: 'If the University chooses to accept the guidance of such men as G. and E. and F., it is welcome, and much good may it do it. I cannot admire people's taste.'[412] R.W. Church recalled: 'The mischief-makers were at work, flitting about the official lodgings at Wadham and Oriel. ... The temptation [to censure Newman] was irresistible to a number of disappointed partisans – kindly, generous, good-natured men in private life, but implacable in their fierce fanaticism.'[413]

Bricknell's Requisition eventually received 528 signatures, headed by those of Bishop Copleston, Bishop Gilbert and Lord Ashley.[414] With only a week left before Convocation was due to meet, Vice-Chancellor Symons thought the request was '*impossible*, both *formally* & *morally*'.[415] Nevertheless under pressure the Hebdomadal Board agreed on 4 February 1845 that Convocation should vote upon whether *Tract 90* was guilty of 'evading rather than explaining the sense of the Thirty-nine Articles' and was thus inconsistent with the University statutes.[416] The *Standard* reckoned this condemnation 'must drive the Tractarians from the University, or if they remain, gibbet them there in a light so contemptible, as to render their continued connection with that learned body comparatively harmless.'[417] In retaliation Hook proposed a Requisition asking for the degradation of Archbishop Whately.[418]

Newman's friends came quickly to his defence. Charles Marriott complained that the censure of *Tract 90* was simply 'the Test in a new dress',[419] while

---

[410] Mozley, 'Recent Proceedings', pp. 552-3.
[411] J.B. Mozley to Anne Mozley, 1 February 1845, *Newman Letters and Diaries*, x. p. 518.
[412] J.B. Mozley to Anne Mozley, 5 February 1845, ibid., p. 522.
[413] Church, *Oxford Movement*, pp. 328-9.
[414] W.S. Bricknell, *Oxford: Tract No.90: and Ward's Ideal of a Christian Church. A Practical Suggestion Respectfully Submitted to Members of Convocation* (fifth edition, Oxford, 1845), pp. 70-6; OUA Hebdomadal Board Minutes, 3 and 4 February 1845. Bishop Phillpotts was supportive, but felt unable to sign: Phillpotts to Bricknell, 30 January 1845, PHL BRIC 2/96.
[415] Lydia Symons to Bricknell, 24 January 1845, PHL BRIC 2/122.
[416] OUA Hebdomadal Board Minutes, 4 February 1845.
[417] *Standard*, 27 January 1845.
[418] Hook to Pusey, 6 February 1845, PHL PUS 4/51.
[419] *Oxford Herald*, 15 February 1845.

Frederic Rogers thought it 'a mere substitution of one firebrand for another ... ungenerous in its circumstances, disingenuous in its form, most mischievous in its results'.[420] Charles Eden rebuked this 'unheard-of *precipitancy*',[421] and Mozley exclaimed: 'Nothing can well be supposed more undignified than such a sudden step, at such an impulse, for such an object.'[422] One pamphleteer considered the proposition

> idle in its conception, powerless in its operation – rancorous but not rational – violent but not vigorous. Dictated by party spirit, but totally unguided by prudence, it must defeat its own purpose. It may give importance to error; it may obstruct, but never will it strengthen the cause of truth. It may gratify the excited passions of party, but it will be at the expense of the dignity and authority of the University.[423]

Others termed it 'a factious and a vindictive proceeding',[424] 'an ambuscade',[425] 'a very tardy and impotent afterthought'.[426] The *English Churchman* declared: 'It is war to the knife: it is a contest of extermination'.[427]

After two months of intense argument about Ward's *Ideal*, Newman's *Tract 90* and the role of the Thirty-Nine Articles within the University, Convocation finally met to vote on these matters on 13 February 1845. Once again hundreds of non-residents went up to Oxford to take part in proceedings which were described by the *Tablet* as 'sad enough to make Democritus weep, and farcical enough to make Heraclitus split with laughter.'[428] Mozley termed it 'a sham court',[429] while Stanley later called the meeting 'the great battle of Armageddon'.[430] Allowed to speak in English instead of Latin, Ward appealed for members of different parties in the church to 'cease from this disastrous civil war, and turn their united weapons against the common enemy.'[431] Nevertheless, Convocation agreed by 777 votes to 386 that Ward's *Ideal* was 'utterly inconsistent' with the Articles. He was then stripped of his degrees by 569 votes to 511.

---

[420] Frederic Rogers, *A Short Appeal to Members of Convocation, upon the Proposed Censure of No.90* (London, 1845), pp. 6, 9.
[421] Bodleian, G.A. Oxon. 8° 77 (10).
[422] Mozley, 'Recent Proceedings', p. 555.
[423] Sewell, *Letter to Members of Convocation*, p. 13.
[424] 'Romish Subscription to the Articles', *English Review* 3 (March 1845), p. 178.
[425] *English Churchman*, 6 February 1845, p. 85.
[426] Ibid., p. 87.
[427] Ibid., p. 85.
[428] *Tablet*, 22 February 1845, p. 113.
[429] Mozley, 'Recent Proceedings', p. 528.
[430] Stanley, 'Oxford School', p. 321.
[431] *Times*, 14 February 1845. For further reports of Convocation, see *English Churchman*, 13 February 1845, p. 100. For Anthony Grant's amendment, see *English Churchman*, 20 February 1845, p. 122.

When it came to the third climactic vote, however – the proposed condemnation of *Tract 90* – it was vetoed by the two proctors, H.P. Guillemard and R.W. Church, because of the 'unseemly haste' of the proceedings.[432] Golightly had been talked of in some circles for the proctorial office in 1844, when it was the turn of Oriel College to nominate someone for the post, but was disqualified by having been an MA for more than a decade.[433] Church was nominated by Oriel instead, but if Golightly had been proctor in February 1845 this *cause célèbre* would have ended very differently. A vote of thanks to the proctors for imposing their veto was signed by 544 members of Convocation, from diverse theological viewpoints.[434]

Vice-Chancellor Symons told the Duke of Wellington that he hoped the University might now experience some peace, although he was concerned that 'the disturbing party, whose object is to revolutionize the University and the Church, is restless and perpetually aggressive.'[435] Some Protestants were also restless. Bricknell, Cox, Faussett and Ellerton promoted a second Requisition to the Hebdomadal Board, asking that Convocation be summoned again to condemn *Tract 90* when new proctors were in place. Unusually, Golightly refused to sign this appeal, considering it unwise to call yet another meeting of Convocation,[436] and Cox complained that Golightly was 'nothing doing – and the enemy very active'.[437] Although the second Requisition was larger than the first, receiving 541 signatures, this time it was rejected by the Hebdomadal Board in May long after the debate had died down.[438] Indeed only a month after Convocation, Golightly could conclude that there was 'a lull in the storm of religious controversy'.[439] Over the next few months, Ward, Oakeley, Newman and others slipped quietly out of the Church of England into the Church of Rome, putting themselves beyond reach of their Protestant critics. Yet before the year was out, the theological storm in Oxford was brewing again.

A Jesuitical Journal

Between 1842 and 1845 Sir Robert Peel's government came under critical examination from four young backbench MPs known as the 'Young England Party' – Benjamin Disraeli, George Smythe, Lord John Manners and Alexander

---

[432] Church, *Oxford Movement*, p. 330.
[433] Golightly to Bricknell, 14 February 1844, PHL BRIC 1/31.
[434] *English Churchman*, 13 March 1845, pp. 163-4.
[435] Symons to Wellington, 14 February 1845, SUL Wellington Papers 2/254/118.
[436] Golightly to Bricknell, [17 March 1845], PHL BRIC 1/55.
[437] Cox to Bricknell, [17 February 1845], PHL BRIC 2/26.
[438] OUA Hebdomadal Board Minutes, 5 May 1845. See also, Requisition drafted by C.A. Ogilvie, OUA NW21/8, nos 44-5.
[439] Golightly to Bricknell, [17 March 1845], PHL BRIC 1/55.

Baillie Cochrane.[440] The aims of this group were to revitalise national politics and culture, and redefine the role of the monarchy, aristocracy and national church. They believed that government should depend less on rationalism and utilitarian economic theory, and more upon imagination and faith. The Young Englanders wanted to develop closer links between the different social strata, to relieve the labouring classes from the tyranny of manufacturers and employers (such as through legislation regulating the hours and conditions of factory workers), and to teach the aristocracy to show proper concern for the welfare of the masses. Disraeli's celebrated trilogy, *Coningsby*, *Sybil* and *Tancred* (1844-46) elaborated on these ideas, acting as a form of Young England manifesto.

A revitalised Church of England (in Tractarian dress) was seen as crucial to many of the Young Englanders' reforms. Manners and Smythe became friends of Frederick Faber, whose Tractarian sympathies Manners in particular eagerly adopted. His poem *England's Trust* (1841), an early elucidation of the Young England philosophy, lamented Henry VIII's break with Rome because it led to

> the countless sects that rend
> Our once united isle from end to end.[441]

He spoke of

> our ceaseless struggles to restore
> Back to the Church her purity of yore[442]

and looked for a return to pre-Reformation religion:

> So now the purer faith of purer days
> Peeps through the mould that hides the good old ways,
> And struggling through this chilly age's gloom,
> Gives fairest presage of a glorious bloom.[443]

For the Young Englanders, the church was to take a central role in restructuring society. They favoured a conciliatory Irish policy, and supported the Roman Catholic church in Ireland because they saw it as the church of the people. Manners encouraged the revival of monastic institutions in urban centres, to enable a combination of resources in giving aid to the needy; and promoted the restoration of 'national holy-days', to provide regular refreshment for

---

[440] On the Young Englanders see Richard Faber, *Young England* (London, 1987); John Morrow (ed.), *Young England: The New Generation. A Selection of Primary Texts* (London, 1999).
[441] John Manners, *England's Trust and Other Poems* (London, 1841), p. 6.
[442] Ibid., p. 5.
[443] Ibid., p. 14.

labourers.[444] The influence of Tractarianism on the Young Englanders was frequently noted. A comic ballad spoke of their movement as born in Oxford and 'tinctured with Puseyite leavening'.[445] Likewise the *Morning Herald* commented: 'that tomfoolery is the political offshoot of Tractarianism. Mental dandyism is its chiefest characteristic.'[446]

A short-lived weekly newspaper, *Young England, the Social Conditions of the Empire*,[447] was replaced as the chief organ of the movement in July 1845 by the newly established *Oxford and Cambridge Review*. The first two numbers of the *Review* carried an evaluation of *Sybil* by Manners, and an article on Lord Grey by Smythe,[448] which according to Disraeli 'made a great noise & quite established the Review'.[449] In September an unexceptional article was published defending the Jesuits against the misrepresentations of Eugène Sue's *Le Juif Errant* (The Wandering Jew). It derided Sue as 'the scribbler of obscene stories' and declared: 'animosity is his bread, sarcasm is his dinner, and he sups on slander.'[450] In contrast to Sue, the author verged on panegyric when describing the Jesuits: 'Paraguay, under the Society of Jesus, was the realization of Utopia'.[451] This led the Roman Catholic *Tablet* to praise the *Review* as 'remarkable for impartiality and discrimination', and this article on the Jesuits as a 'just eulogium'.[452] The *Morning Post* applauded: 'A bolder or a more enthusiastic champion the Society of Jesus could not have desired.'[453]

On 1 November, however, the *Tablet* broke the anonymity of the *Oxford and Cambridge Review* and unwittingly provoked a fresh storm of protest led from Oxford by Golightly, when it announced that the defence of the Jesuits had been written by a Roman Catholic – Miles Gerald Keon, a young trainee lawyer and an alumnus of the Jesuit college at Stonyhurst.[454] The editor was quick to defend his periodical, maintaining that Keon's article was inserted 'not with any reference to the creed of the writer, but as a paper displaying ability and eloquence, pregnant with Christian sentiment, and which might have been

---

[444] John Manners, *The Monastic and Manufacturing Systems. By Anglo-Catholicus* (London, 1843); Manners, *A Plea for National Holy-Days* (London, 1843).
[445] Alexander Baillie-Cochrane, *In the Day of the Dandies* (London, 1906), pp. 149-50.
[446] *Morning Herald*, 20 July 1843.
[447] Faber, *Young England*, pp. 144-5.
[448] John Manners, 'The Policy of the New Generation', *Oxford and Cambridge Review* 1 (July 1845), pp. 1-11; George Smythe, 'Earl Grey', *Oxford and Cambridge Review* 1 (August 1845), pp. 195-219.
[449] Benjamin Disraeli to Sarah Disraeli, 23 August 1845, in *Benjamin Disraeli Letters* edited by M.G. Wiebe et al. (6 vols, Toronto, 1982-97), iv. p. 185.
[450] M.G. Keon, 'The Jesuits', *Oxford and Cambridge Review* 1 (September 1845), pp. 225-6.
[451] Ibid., p. 239.
[452] *Tablet*, 6 September 1845, pp. 562-3.
[453] *Morning Post*, 1 September 1845.
[454] *Tablet*, 1 November 1845, p. 691.

written by a Protestant as well as by a Roman Catholic.'[455] This did not stop Golightly, however, from remonstrating in the pages of the *Standard* on 5 November (the date was a handy coincidence):

> And so, sir, this is the way in which this treacherous party are sapping and mining the faith of the Universities. Christ Church and Stonyhurst Colleges, Lord John Manners and Mr Keon, Romish writers in professedly Protestant reviews ... I would hold up, sir, this miserable trickery to the gaze of the public, and feel confident that there is still honesty enough left in Old England to repudiate the Jesuitism of Young England with the abhorrence that it deserves.[456]

Once again Golightly's dominant theme was Protestant truth and Tractarian duplicity. He found the editor of the *Review* guilty of 'as base a fraud as he could possibly have perpetrated'.[457]

Soon the dispute began to escalate. The *Standard* declared: 'Our valuable correspondent, Mr GOLIGHTLY, has brought the proofs together in a manner to leave the parties implicated without a loop-hole of escape'. It predicted the extinction of the *Oxford and Cambridge Review*, now 'detected in the contraband trade of circulating Romish tracts, of the manufacture of Stonyhurst, under the honoured brand of Oxford and Cambridge', and optimistically proclaimed: 'We think that it is "the beginning of the end" of Tractarianism.'[458] The *Church and State Gazette* said of the *Review*: 'the pie-bald periodical in question, not half so honest, yet twice as dull, as the defunct *British Critic*, which Puseyism strangled, is, in fact, a snare and a delusion'.[459] An article was said to have been commissioned from William Ward (by now a convert to Roman Catholicism) for the December issue, and Messrs. Deighton of Cambridge declined to continue as publisher.[460] It was also rumoured that Oxford men had visited Stonyhurst, and that 'the cause of the Jesuits is openly and boldly espoused in some of the common and combination rooms of the Universities, on the part of those who have not seceded, with Messrs. Newman, Oakeley, and Ward, from their Protestant emoluments'.[461] Pusey, for instance, was rebuked for circulating Jesuit literature in Oxford.[462] Echoing Golightly's protest, Francis Close (the leading evangelical clergyman in Cheltenham) asked: 'How long shall we expect honest dealings from men of dishonest principles? *Fraud* is *sanctioned, consecrated, canonized* in the Church of Rome! It would not be the mystery of iniquity if it were otherwise – nor bear

---

[455] *Morning Post*, 4 November 1845.
[456] *Standard*, 5 November 1845.
[457] *Standard*, 11 November 1845.
[458] *Standard*, 11 November 1845.
[459] *Church and State Gazette*, 14 November 1845, p. 728.
[460] *Church and State Gazette*, 28 November 1845, p. 761.
[461] *Church and State Gazette*, 7 and 14 November 1845, pp. 713, 729.
[462] *Standard*, 10 November 1845; Surin, *Foundations of the Spiritual Life*, p. [253].

the faithful impress of its founder the "Father of lies".[463]

Golightly was praised in the *Standard* for 'his unflinching exposure of the Jesuit intrigue',[464] and his 'most important service to the cause of truth, and of pure and undefiled religion'.[465] He was thanked for having 'exposed a most shameful artifice',[466] which entitled him 'to the gratitude of the Church of England for protecting her children'.[467] Joseph Mendham told Golightly: 'Every faithful son of the church, & especially those who are more openly engaged in the same holy warfare with yourself, are eminently indebted to you for the present service, which none could so effectually execute as yourself.'[468] Close applauded him as 'a truly Protestant Brother'.[469]

The *Tablet* pointed out that in receiving a Roman Catholic contributor, the *Oxford and Cambridge Review* did nothing more than periodicals such as *Blackwood's Magazine* and *Fraser's Magazine* had been doing for years. Indeed *Fraser's* original popularity was partly established by the lively 'Reliques of Father Prout', contributed between 1834 and 1836 by Francis Mahony, a Roman Catholic priest and former Jesuit.[470] Golightly, however, saw signs within Keon's article that it was written intentionally by 'a Romanist in the disguise of a Protestant'.[471] For instance, it admitted to 'the bias of our northern notions and northern prepossessions', of 'our preconceived impressions' and 'popular prejudices'.[472] Keon insisted this was not to give the impression he was a Protestant, but was a result of his natural dislike of Spaniards who constituted the majority of early Jesuits.[473] Even though Keon had trained at Stonyhurst, his article spoke only of 'an occasional personal meeting with members of this great order'[474] – in defence he professed that since leaving the college his contact with the Jesuits had indeed been 'exceedingly casual'.[475] The *Morning Herald* was not persuaded by these explanations and asked: 'When Keon writes ... in the character of a Protestant, what is to prevent a Dervish from doing the same?'[476] Keon claimed to have struck a 'hearty blow in the cause of justice and of truth',[477] to which Golightly

---

[463] Francis Close, *The 'Mystery of Iniquity'* (London, 1845), p. 19.
[464] *Standard*, 10 November 1845.
[465] *Standard*, 27 November 1845.
[466] Dodd to Golightly, 12 November 1845, LPL MS 1805, fo. 152.
[467] Bird to Golightly, 15 November 1845, LPL MS 1804, fo. 45.
[468] Mendham to Golightly, 20 November 1845, LPL MS 1808, fo. 80.
[469] Close, *Mystery of Iniquity*, p. 18.
[470] *Tablet*, 8 November 1845, p. 712. See *Morning Post*, 10 November 1845.
[471] *Standard*, 11 November 1845.
[472] Keon, 'Jesuits', p. 227.
[473] *Morning Herald*, 19 November 1845.
[474] Keon, 'Jesuits', p. 247.
[475] *Morning Herald*, 19 November 1845.
[476] *Morning Herald*, 12 November 1845.
[477] Keon, 'Jesuits', p. 247.

responded: 'Astonishing precocity!'[478]

The October issue of the *Oxford and Cambridge Review* had carried a second piece by Keon, in praise of George Canning (Tory prime minister in the 1820s).[479] Keon insisted, however, that there was nothing 'stealthy or dissimulative' in his conduct, since both articles were written at the request of the editor, who knew he was a Roman Catholic.[480] The editor categorically denied he had solicited the articles,[481] which left the *Church and State Gazette* triumphant: 'It is an old-fashioned, time-honoured maxim, that, when certain persons fall out, honest men are sure to reap the advantage. A division among conspirators is always the prelude to an unveiling of the plot.'[482] Nevertheless, Keon showed little concern and described the *Review* as 'a trumpet through which I have blown no timid note',[483] proclaiming: 'I glory in the very sentiments which have called forth such an uproar.'[484]

The editor of the *Review* rebuked the 'uncalled-for and intemperate conduct of those who claim for themselves the merit of exclusive Protestantism', but promised that in future articles would only be accepted from those who were alumni of the two Universities ('Well, under this proviso, Mr Ward, Mr Oakeley, and Mr Newman, might write the whole of the next number!'[485]) and members of the 'English Catholic Church'.[486] The *Morning Herald* ruminated:

> We have heard of the Church of England, the Church of France, the Church of Rome, and the Church of Russia; but an 'English Universal Church' – for *universal* is, we suppose, the meaning of *Catholic* – we never before heard of. Is Mr Oakeley a member of 'the English Catholic Church' or not? Or is this new Church nothing else than that same half-way house to Rome, which has been established in Oxford for the last ten years?[487]

It is in the nature of anonymous reviews that the names of neither the editor nor the contributors are generally known, and therefore it would have been possible for others involved in the *Oxford and Cambridge Review* to remain incognito, simply waiting for Golightly's protest to pass, with no harm to

---

[478] *Standard*, 11 November 1845.
[479] M.G. Keon, 'George Canning', *Oxford and Cambridge Review* 1 (October 1845), pp. 399-420. This article was mistakenly attributed to Smythe by his sister-in-law, followed by historians of the Young Englanders: George Smythe, *Angela Pisani: a novel* (3 vols, London, 1875), i. p. xvi; Faber, *Young England*, p. 76; Morrow, *Young England*, p. 152. See *Morning Post*, 7 and 10 November 1845.
[480] *Morning Post*, 10 November 1845.
[481] *Morning Post*, 11 November 1845.
[482] *Church and State Gazette*, 14 November 1845, p. 728.
[483] *Morning Post*, 10 November 1845.
[484] *Morning Herald*, 19 November 1845.
[485] *Morning Herald*, 18 November 1845.
[486] *Morning Post*, 8 November 1845.
[487] *Morning Herald*, 18 November 1845.

themselves. However, the editor announced that the contributors to the *Oxford Magazine* (which was discontinued after only one number in May 1845) had joined the *Review*.[488] Acting on intelligence from Oxford, and again hoping to draw a response by naming individuals, Golightly publicly singled out three young fellows of Exeter College who had contributed to the *Oxford Magazine*: S.J. Rigaud, J.A. Froude (brother of Hurrell Froude) and George Rawlinson.[489] Although strictly speaking these men were linked by Golightly only to the *Oxford Magazine*, the effect was to tar them with the same brush as used on the *Review*. The editor of the *Oxford Magazine* wrote from Leeds to defend his contributors, so was assumed to be one of the party who had gone to Yorkshire with Pusey for the consecration of St Saviour's, Leeds.[490] He was rumoured to be John Morris, another fellow of Exeter College (the notorious 'N.E.S.' who attacked Wynter and Symons in the *English Churchman*), a convert to Roman Catholicism in January 1846.[491] It was suggested the *Oxford and Cambridge Review* be renamed the *Stonyhurst and Exeter College Review*.[492]

Froude remained silent, and avoided newspaper attention. Rigaud categorically denied any involvement in the *Oxford and Cambridge Review*,[493] charged Golightly with 'slander' and 'gross calumny', and considered bringing the matter before the University authorities.[494] On behalf of his colleagues, Joseph Richards (Rector of Exeter College and himself a contributor to the *Review*[495]) attempted at the Hebdomadal Board to initiate a prosecution against Golightly for slander, but according to one observer his motion 'fell to the ground by the weight of its own absurdity'.[496]

Rawlinson did not escape so easily. He accused Golightly of 'mere gossiping', and demanded an apology, but Golightly encouraged Rawlinson, if he were able, to disavow any connection with the *Oxford and Cambridge Review* and to denounce the editor for publishing Keon's article. Rawlinson retorted: 'You are the very last person in the University whose advice I would

---

[488] *Oxford and Cambridge Review* 1 (November 1845), p. 560.

[489] *Standard*, 5 November 1845. See S.J. Rigaud, 'The University Galleries', *Oxford Magazine* (May 1845), pp. 58-70.

[490] *Standard*, 11 and 12 November 1845.

[491] *Church and State Gazette*, 14 November 1845, p. 729.

[492] *Church and State Gazette*, 7 November 1845, p. 713.

[493] *Standard*, 11 November 1845; circular by Rigaud, 12 November 1845, LPL MS 1809, fo. 34.

[494] Rigaud to Golightly, 8-12 November 1845, LPL MS 1809, fos 31-5; *Church and State Gazette*, 14 November 1845, p. 728.

[495] M.G. Keon, 'The Catholic Man of Letters in London; A History of Nowadays. Inscribed to the New Generation', *Dolman's Magazine* 3 (March 1846), p. 240.

[496] *Standard*, 27 November 1845. See *Church and State Gazette*, 14 and 28 November 1845, pp. 729, 761; *Oxford Herald*, 22 November; *Standard*, 22 November 1845.

take on any matter.'[497] He protested against 'the unwarranted intrusion into my private affairs, and the liberty taken with my name, by a person occupying no position of authority either in the Church or the University, and so with no call that I can see to interfere with my doings.' Rawlinson thought Golightly's naming of the three young fellows was 'calculated to excite the most cruel suspicions against us, and to be of the greatest detriment to our prospects in life', and hoped members of the University would 'one and all join in condemning and discountenancing it.'[498] The *Standard* thought Rawlinson's equivocation 'a shuffling and mock-angry defence, quite in the Stonyhurst style; a defence, however, which is in truth equivalent to a plea of guilt.'[499] Fears were expressed for the undergraduates at Exeter College if they continued under Rawlinson's teaching, and a call was made for his resignation.[500]

Rawlinson admitted he had read Keon's article before joining the *Oxford and Cambridge Review*, and had complained against its 'tone', but did not know it was written by a Roman Catholic and thought it 'such an article as Mr Macaulay might have written if he had taken it into his head to praise the Jesuits.'[501] Nevertheless, the *Morning Herald* asked: ' *"Can one touch pitch and not be defiled?"* Surely, Mr Rawlinson must blame chiefly his own indiscretion (to give it the mildest name) for the disagreeable exposure which has followed.'[502] It was then discovered that in Rawlinson's contribution to the *Oxford Magazine* he had praised the Tractarian Movement as

> the mightiest impulse which man's intellect has received since the era of the Reformation, that at which all around the aged and the timid shake and quail, but which causes the heart of the young to glow and their frame to thrill with expectation and with hope ... Shallow politicians incapable of appreciating it, think to check its progress by withholding patronage; feeble authorities, tyrannical from a sense of their own weakness, seek to put a stop to it by a system of petty persecution; dull intellects deem that it has passed away because it has ceased to be noisy; but it advances all the while with a mighty force not to be resisted.[503]

Such statements only increased the pressure upon Rawlinson. He was rebuked for his derogatory phrase, 'the so-called Reformation',[504] and few were

---

[497] Rawlinson to Golightly, 7 November 1845, LPL MS 1809, fos 3-5; *Standard*, 10 November 1845.
[498] *Morning Herald*, 18 November 1845.
[499] *Standard*, 11 November 1845.
[500] *Standard*, 13, 17 and 19 November 1845; *Church and State Gazette*, 14 November 1845, p. 729.
[501] *Morning Herald*, 18 November 1845. See the letter from the editor of the *Oxford Magazine* in *Standard*, 11 November 1845.
[502] *Morning Herald*, 18 November 1845.
[503] George Rawlinson, 'Reform of the Universities. Mr Christie's Motion', *Oxford Magazine* (May 1845), p. 98.
[504] *Standard*, 17 and 19 November 1845; *Oxford Herald*, 22 November 1845.

convinced by his explanation that he meant merely that the word 'Reformation' was 'inadequate to express the depth and vastness' of such an era.[505] Worse, perhaps, was the language he had used to describe the Heads of Houses, as part of his argument for University reform. For example, he had called the Hebdomadal Board

> a body of well-meaning but most incompetent men, without either firmness or judgment, whose acts, even in trivial matters, Convocation daily rejects with scorn, and whose name is become, throughout the country, a by-word for imbecility. ... Powerless, yet grasping the reins of power – would-be leaders, whom none follow, they occupy a position ridiculous in itself, discreditable to them, and disgraceful to the University.[506]

Bricknell objected to these 'indecent scurrilities',[507] but Rawlinson warned that free discussion would be stifled if names of anonymous authors were always 'hunted out' in this way.[508] He insisted he would continue as a contributor to the *Oxford and Cambridge Review*,[509] and pointed to his article on the recent establishment of the German Catholic Church as illustrative of his true religious opinions. Attacking unreformed rituals within Roman Catholicism (the *Tablet* thought him 'quite unequal to his subject'[510]), it spoke of 'contempt for the more indefensible parts of the Romish system' and of 'all the grossest errors and worst corruptions of Popery'.[511]

By the beginning of December 1845, after a month of controversy, the storm of protest over the *Oxford and Cambridge Review* had blown itself out. Nonetheless, during the Christmas vacation, when preaching before the University, Rawlinson harangued Golightly and Wynter in a sermon lasting an hour and a quarter, on the text, 'Let your moderation be known unto all men'.[512] Golightly's young friend, T.V. French (an undergraduate at University College), knew he would be used to 'such unsparing opposition'.[513] Ultimately, Rawlinson's prospects did not suffer from the affair. He resigned his fellowship at Exeter College in July 1846 on his marriage, but returned to the University in 1861 as Camden Professor of Ancient History, in which capacity he served for almost thirty years.

Froude, whose name did not reappear in the newspapers after Golightly's

---

[505] *Oxford Herald*, 29 November 1845.
[506] Rawlinson, 'Reform of the Universities', pp. 100-1.
[507] *Oxford Herald*, 22 November 1845.
[508] *Oxford Herald*, 29 November 1845.
[509] *Morning Herald*, 18 November 1845.
[510] *Tablet*, 8 November 1845, p. 712.
[511] George Rawlinson, 'Religious Movements in Germany', *Oxford and Cambridge Review* 1 (November 1845), pp. 462, 468.
[512] *Church and State Gazette*, 26 December 1845, p. 825.
[513] T.V. French to Golightly, 3 January 1846, LPL MS 1805, fo. 188.

original letter, wrote at the beginning of December to Charles Kingsley (himself possibly a contributor to the *Oxford and Cambridge Review*):

> I quite agree with you that the editor of the *Oxford and Cambridge Review* has shown himself a very unwise person. At the same time I think it better to go on hoping by and bye that he will see clearly (as he has begun to see dimly) his insufficiency, and that we shall be able to provide ourselves with a better. I do not like 'fresh starts'. If there are many of them people laugh, and that is at least unpropitious The more people hate us the more we rise, and I cannot but augur well of the abuse which has already assailed the *Oxford and Cambridge*.[514]

Having been barred from further contribution to the periodical, Keon went on to edit *Dolman's Magazine* (a Roman Catholic monthly), in which he mocked the Young Englanders but reserved his severest language for the editor of the *Oxford and Cambridge Review* and Golightly: 'Their juvenile Review, accompanying the Quarterlies, "*haud passibus aequis*" [with unequal steps], was, perhaps, too easily frightened by a Low-Church intermeddler of a brain so notedly restless, that had he possessed sounder abilities, he would, at some time or other of his life, have commanded public respect'.[515] The *Oxford and Cambridge Review* responded by calling Keon's writings 'the sycophantic, absurd inventions of an itinerant writer', of which Disraeli could 'make mincemeat enough ... to satisfy the most inordinate consumer of Christmas dainties for generations to come.'[516]

By 1846, however, the Young England movement was a spent force, having lost its cohesion. It has been suggested that this disintegration was partly due to the effect of the Tractarian conversions to Rome,[517] and on Frederick Faber's secession in November 1845 the *Oxford and Cambridge Review* lamented, 'very few are there who can supply his place.'[518] However, several other factors were involved: Disraeli had become increasingly absorbed in the battle with Peel for leadership of the Conservative Party; Smythe had been appointed Under Secretary of State in the Foreign Office; and Cochrane had lost his seat in the House of Commons. At the General Election of 1847 Manners came bottom of the poll in Liverpool after being accused of Puseyism.[519] The *Oxford*

---

[514] J.A. Froude to Charles Kingsley, 8 December 1845, in W.H. Dunn, *James Anthony Froude: A Biography* (2 vols, Oxford, 1961-63), i. pp. 101-2.

[515] Keon, 'Catholic Man of Letters', p. 240.

[516] 'The Catholic Man of Letters in London', *Oxford and Cambridge Review* 2 (April 1846), pp. 271, 273.

[517] Philip Mennell, *Lord John Manners. A Political and Literary Sketch, comprising some account of the Young England Party and the Passing of the Factory Acts. By a Non-Elector* (London, 1872), pp. 70-2.

[518] 'The Recent Secessions – Mr Faber', *Oxford and Cambridge Review* 2 (January 1846), p. 60.

[519] Faber, *Young England*, pp. 155-6.

and Cambridge Review finally folded in December 1847. Keon meanwhile went on to become Russian correspondent for the *Morning Post*, and in 1859 was appointed Colonial Secretary in Bermuda.

Agag to the Rescue

One of Golightly's many nicknames amongst his Oxford contemporaries was 'Agag', because according to 1 Samuel 15, Agag king of the Amalekites 'came delicately'. This epithet was picked up by an anonymous pamphlet, published towards the end of 1845, entitled *Heroic Epistle from Titus Oates, to his Lineal Descendant, Agag Oates, at Oxford*. It did not directly mention Golightly or his fellow anti-Tractarian campaigners by name, but those who knew the Oxford scene could easily interpret the satirical references. Golightly was mocked for his stupidity, dishonesty and malice in ceaselessly searching out pro-Roman sympathisers. 'Titus Oates' offered his blessing to 'young wild Oates' and encouraged him to go

> As though Guy Fawkes had mined thy path below,
> To watch at Mary's porch, and well count out
> Those bad young Sophs, that dare to be devout;
> Thence hastening to inform, with busy pains,
> Those reverend Heads, so destitute of brains,
> Who know not yet, that all at dawn who rise
> To matin prayer, are Jesuits in disguise.
> Live long, and be thy painful toils repaid;
> And, Oxford, live, while Agag lives to aid! ...
> Awake, arise, and rouse the slumbering might
> Of plundering Protestants to march by night,
> And scare each Roman wizard where he dwells,
> Break his weird wand, and scatter all his spells,
> His books o'erthrow, and make full end at once
> Of Bellarmine, new Möhler, and old Duns ...
>
> ... but falter not,
> Denounce aloud those 'stiflers of the plot',
> Who speak of peace, when war thy zeal would bring,
> And plead that Conscience is a sacred thing.
> Go, arm thy front with brass, and from thy heart,
> (Heart sure thou hast), bid modest shame depart;
> Take each prov'd comrade, whose plebeian mind
> Bids him be coarse, because he can't be kind ...
> And all who preach, and teach, and rail, and write,
> Against each gleam of ancient Truth and Light;
> And shew the world how Protestants should prove
> Their Faith, by hating him whom all men love!

> Woe to the few whose brains are yet un-turn'd,
> Who scorn to live and learn what thou hast learn'd ...
> Go on, hunt out the thieves that walk the fold,
> And Fortune pay thy pains with Treasury gold.
> Why shouldst thou doubt? Thou hast my virtues all,
> True likeness of thy great original ...
> Who dares assert that Agag e'er did lie?
> He tracks the coverts of futurity;
> And if not yet the Romish fox appear,
> No matter, – 'twill be there another year.
> Hearts that not yet to mischief feel inclin'd,
> Like the bold pirate's, will, if put in mind;
> And each new convert helps the crowd to bless
> Thy pious rage, and herald thy success. ...
> Speak kind advice to each rash foe you slay,
> As pitying wolves howl meekly o'er their prey;
> And my poor gibbering ghost shall joy to see
> Its deeds, and sufferings, all outdone by thee.

'Titus Oates' concluded his epistle with a prediction that 'Agag' would join him in limbo, alongside other religious persecutors such as Tomás de Torquemada (Spain's first Inquisitor-General), Bishop Bonner (burner of English Protestants), Matthew Hopkins (East Anglia's witch-hunter) and John Endicott (scourge of Quakers in New England). Edward Churton remarked that if this mockery did not silence Golightly, he ought to be given 'a few more kicks and cuffs of the same kind'.[520]

However, Golightly would not yet be silenced. The start of 1846 brought the opportunity for one more high-profile attack upon the Tractarians, this time against Pusey. As so often before, his recurrent theme was Tractarian disingenuousness. Indeed Archdeacon Browne encouraged Golightly to expose Pusey's 'flagrant and atrocious dishonesty'.[521] Pusey's two year ban from preaching before the University was about to come to an end, but Golightly aimed to prevent his return to the University pulpit. The excuse he needed was a recent statement by Pusey in the columns of the *English Churchman* that he was one of those who did not

> formally accept what is now looked upon as distinctive Roman doctrine, yet neither would they formally reject it, for fear, if it should prove to be true, they might be rejecting the truth. Such would, *e.g.* neither reject the invocation of saints, nor yet do they actually practise it; they do not make a definite doctrine 'of a purifying process with pain after death' a part of their belief, nor yet do they

---

[520] Churton to Gresley, 10 January 1846, PHL GRES 3/7/58.
[521] Browne to Golightly, 6 December 1845, LPL MS 1804, fo. 108.

disbelieve it.[522]

Therefore in January 1846 Golightly appealed to Vice-Chancellor Symons to summon Pusey to sign Article 22 of the Thirty-Nine Articles (concerning purgatory and the invocation of saints) before he be allowed to return to the University pulpit.[523] Golightly also drew attention to Pusey's claim that Newman on seceding to the Church of Rome was not 'so much gone from us, as transplanted into another part of the Vineyard';[524] and to Pusey's support for Frederick Oakeley, who had recently admitted his aim as a member of the Church of England had been 'to infuse the Roman spirit into the Anglican body'.[525]

Browne was pleased Golightly was attempting to save the University from 'the disgrace of having its members addressed by such an utterly dishonest heretic as Pusey',[526] while Charles Heurtley thought him entitled 'to the thanks of the university, however it may exasperate some of her members.'[527] Henry Hoper (vicar of Portslade near Brighton) praised him for giving 'utterance before the whole World, to the feelings wh must be raised in the Soul of every sound Protestant'.[528] Likewise Golightly's old Oriel friend, Charles Brenton (who had seceded from the Church of England in 1831), commented: 'Dr P. is I suppose now your *Clodius* and you are sometimes sanguine in the hope of driving him and his faction from the University.'[529] The *English Churchman*, however, asked:

> has Mr GOLIGHTLY no friends to warn him of the un-Christian course which he is pursuing? Is he indeed alone in the University – a disappointed, isolated plotter of mischief? Surely, for the sake of the University, someone should interfere and prevent these periodical outbursts of uncharitableness or imbecility.[530]

Pusey himself privately rebuked Golightly for his long campaign against the Tractarians: 'nothing but an extreme prejudice agst us cd … account for the readiness with which you uniformly believed every report in some colored [*sic*] form, & then circulated it without ascertaining what mt have been ascertained.'

---

[522] *English Churchman*, 9 October 1845, p. 642.
[523] *Standard*, 6 January 1846.
[524] *English Churchman*, 16 October 1845, p. 661.
[525] Frederick Oakeley, *A Letter on Submitting to the Catholic Church. Addressed to a Friend* (London, 1845), p. 34.
[526] Browne to Golightly, 8 January 1846, LPL MS 1804, fo. 112.
[527] Heurtley to Golightly, 13 January 1846, LPL MS 1807, fo. 32.
[528] Henry Hoper to Golightly, 14 January 1846, LPL MS 1807, fo. 191.
[529] Brenton to Golightly, 29 January 1846, LPL MS 1804, fo. 84. Clodius, a Roman politician, was accused of various outrages, including trying to commit adultery with Julius Caesar's wife, Pompeia.
[530] *English Churchman*, 8 January 1846, p. 24.

Nonetheless he hoped that 'however sadly separated in this life, we wish each other well in Christ.'[531]

Pusey considered offering an explanation of the sense in which he subscribed to the Articles, if summoned by Symons, but J.B. Mozley advised him: 'we should lose ground considerably by appending any kind of explanation to our *act of subscription*. ... it would be taken for a dishonest reservation, and a concession on our part, that we had not the same right to sign the Articles ἁπλῶς [naturally] that others have.'[532] If Symons extended Pusey's ban, Mozley thought it would be 'a consummate act of despotism which would be simply claiming the pulpit all the year round for the V.C.'s own friends.'[533] In the event, the Vice-Chancellor concluded that calling Pusey to subscribe to the Articles would be 'worse than useless', since by the principles of *Tract 90* subscription might be made 'by the partisan of any erroneous doctrine whatever.' Instead he suggested Golightly should first see if error was preached, and then take action.[534] The *Morning Herald* agreed: 'The canons of subscription set forth in Tract XC would allow a Mahometan to subscribe the Articles, or Dr PUSEY to declare his belief in the Koran.'[535] Privately Symons warned Pusey that much of his writing was 'plainly and directly at variance with several Articles of the church and with the actual engagements of anyone who had pledged himself to the office of a Teacher in it', and might lead others to 'the sacrifice of moral integrity as well as of christian simplicity.'[536] Meanwhile Samuel Wilberforce (newly appointed Bishop of Oxford) recommended Golightly go further and prosecute Pusey in the Vice-Chancellor's Court.[537]

Pusey boldly stood up to his opponents. When he entered the University pulpit on Sunday, 1 February 1846, he continued exactly where he had left off two and a half years before, with his well-known sermon, *Entire Absolution of the Penitent*.[538] The *Standard* mourned:

> How long, we ask, is Dr PUSEY to be permitted to *poison* the minds of University students? The Romish tendency of the new school can no longer be doubted. If, then, Oxford is to continue a Protestant University, it must be weeded of Romanist teachers, or otherwise, it will only be preparing disciples for Oscott

---

[531] Pusey to Golightly, 6 January 1846, LPL MS 1808, fo. 245.
[532] J.B. Mozley to Pusey, 12 January 1846, PHL PUS 128.
[533] J.B. Mozley to Anne Mozley, 16 January 1846, *Letters of the Rev. J.B. Mozley*, p. 175.
[534] *Standard*, 16 January 1846. See also Whately to Hawkins, 19 January 1846, OCL Miscellaneous Letters, vol. 3, no. 260.
[535] *Morning Herald*, 19 January 1846.
[536] Symons to Pusey, 14 January 1846, PHL LBV 37/45.
[537] Wilberforce to Golightly, 16 January 1846, LPL MS 1811, fo. 181.
[538] Edward B. Pusey, *Entire Absolution of the Penitent* (Oxford, 1846).

and the popish colleges on the Continent.[539]

The *Church and State Gazette* observed: 'It is almost difficult to say what Dr Pusey *does* hold in common with the English Church, *except his canonry*'.[540] Meanwhile the *Oxford Chronicle* argued that the University authorities should take further action against Pusey, to decide 'whether Oxford is to be considered a *Protestant College* or an ally of Rome'.[541]

Yet nothing came of these recommendations. Newman, Ward, Oakeley, Faber, Morris and others had been forced out of the Church of England, but Professor Pusey was determined to stay put. He continued to preach and to grow in stature as the figurehead of the Tractarian Movement. Many of Golightly's campaigns during the previous five years of intense theological conflagration had done real damage to the Tractarians and helped to strengthen the Protestant cause in Oxford. Yet this final attempt to get the better of his old mentor and antagonist ended in failure. It was to be twenty years before Golightly tried again. The nation's attention soon returned to other matters, such as the railway investment 'mania' of 1845-47, as G.V. Cox recalled: 'Controversy had worn itself out ... Instead of High Church, Low Church, or Broad Church, they talked of high embankments, the broad gauge, and low dividends: Brunel and Stephenson were in men's mouths instead of Dr Pusey or Mr Golightly'.[542]

---

[539] *Standard*, 19 January 1846.
[540] *Church and State Gazette*, 10 January 1846, p. 25.
[541] *Oxford Chronicle*, 7 February 1846.
[542] G.V. Cox, *Recollections of Oxford* (London, 1868), p. 338.

CHAPTER 4

The Problem of Professor Jowett

After the Tractarian secessions to Rome in the mid-1840s there was a brief hiatus in the intense series of theological controversies which had embroiled Oxford University for more than a decade. When the Warden of Wadham came to the end of his four-year term as Vice-Chancellor in 1848, one commentator observed that it marked the close of an epoch: 'It began in storm and contest: it has ended, we hope, in peace and goodwill. Much that then embittered the feelings has since passed away; many sources of distrust have, though in sadness, been dried up'.[1] Golightly's pen fell silent for a few years, but soon there was a new danger to attract his attention. In place of the theological vacuum left by retreating Tractarians, there took place what W.R. Ward calls a 'liberal revival' within the University.[2] Men of a different sort rose to prominence, eager to reform both University politics and Christian dogma. They exposed the archaic religious restrictions and poor educational standards in University life, humorously portrayed in Cuthbert Bede's *Adventures of Mr Verdant Green* (1853-57) and humiliatingly analysed in the Blue Book (1852).[3] They also began to question the limits of traditional orthodoxy and some experienced a dramatic 'loss of faith'. For example, J.A. Froude, a disillusioned disciple of Newman, published *The Nemesis of Faith* in 1849 and then resigned his fellowship at Exeter College before it could be taken from him. Mark Pattison, once a contributor to the *British Critic* and the *Christian Remembrancer*, also managed to escape what he called 'the whirlpool of Tractarianism'.[4] He went on to become a leading advocate of theological exploration and administrative reform as fellow and later Rector of Lincoln College. Reflecting on the radical changes of the period, Pattison proclaimed in his *Memoirs*: 'If any Oxford man had gone to sleep in 1846 and had woke up

---

[1] *Guardian*, 12 July 1848, p. 450.
[2] W.R. Ward, *Victorian Oxford* (London, 1965), ch. 7. See also W.R. Ward, 'From the Tractarians to the Executive Commission, 1845-1854' in M.G. Brock and M.C. Curthoys (eds.), *The History of the University of Oxford*, vol. 6 *Nineteenth-Century Oxford, Part 1* (Oxford, 1997), ch. 10.
[3] M.C. Curthoys and C.J. Day, 'The Oxford of Mr Verdant Green' in M.G. Brock and M.C. Curthoys (eds.), *The History of the University of Oxford*, vol. 6 *Nineteenth-Century Oxford, Part 1* (Oxford, 1997), ch. 8.
[4] Mark Pattison, *Memoirs* (London, 1885), p. 171.

again in 1850 he would have found himself in a totally new world.'[5]

Balliol College was at the centre of much of Oxford's progressive thinking.[6] A succession of Thomas Arnold's brightest pupils from Rugby School passed through the college, such as Arthur Stanley, W.C. Lake, A.H. Clough and Matthew Arnold. A.C. Tait and Frederick Temple were on the fellowship, both going on to follow Arnold as headmasters of Rugby and then reach the pinnacle of the Church of England as Archbishops of Canterbury. However, the rising star at Balliol was Benjamin Jowett. In 1854 he narrowly failed in his attempt to become Master, defeated by a single vote by the lexicographer and opponent of reform, Robert Scott. Nevertheless, Jowett's influence in Oxford continued to grow. He combined with other leading 'liberals', like William Gladstone and Henry Liddell (Dean of Christ Church from 1855), in pushing forward the University Reform Act of 1854. Amongst its many revolutionary provisions, the Act dealt a death blow to the historic bond between the Church of England and the University, abolishing subscription to the Thirty-Nine Articles upon matriculation and graduation, and opening many fellowships to laymen.

These friends and collaborators were famous for their desire to 'broaden' the theological limits of University education and Anglican life, so began to be known collectively as 'broad churchmen'. The phrase 'broad church' was in circulation in the late 1840s,[7] but Stanley is responsible for its first known appearance in print, during the Gorham controversy of 1850. He explained in the *Edinburgh Review* that both Bishop Phillpotts of Exeter and his evangelical critic, G.C. Gorham, could be included within the Church of England because the church was 'not High or Low, but Broad'.[8] Four months later the *Times* asserted: 'the Church of England is not so much *High* or *Low* as *Broad* ... she secures the greatest amount of religious freedom because her formularies admit of extreme diversity of opinion'.[9] It was William J. Conybeare's famous *Edinburgh Review* article in 1853, however, that first popularised the term not just as a description for the Church of England, but as the title of a distinctive 'church party'. He explained: 'It is called by various names; Moderate, Catholic, or Broad Church, by its friends; Latitudinarian or Indifferent by its enemies. Its distinctive character is the desire of comprehension. Its watchwords are Charity and Toleration.'[10] A commentator later in the century

---

[5] Ibid., p. 244.
[6] J.H. Jones, 'Balliol: From Obscurity to Pre-eminence' in M.G. Brock and M.C. Curthoys (eds.), *The History of the University of Oxford*, vol. 6 *Nineteenth-Century Oxford, Part 1* (Oxford, 1997), ch. 5.
[7] A.P. Stanley, 'Subscription', *Macmillan's Magazine* 43 (January 1881), p. 209; W.C. Lake, 'More Oxford Memories', *Good Words* (December 1895), p. 829.
[8] A.P. Stanley, 'The Gorham Controversy', *Edinburgh Review* 92 (July 1850), p. 266.
[9] *Times*, 11 November 1850.
[10] W.J. Conybeare, 'Church Parties' (1853), edited by Arthur Burns, in Stephen Taylor (ed.), *From Cranmer to Davidson: A Church of England Miscellany*, Church of England Record Society 7 (Woodbridge, 1999), p. 340.

wrote: 'The High Church would cast out the Low Church, and the Low Church the High, and both would cast out the Broad; but the Broad desires to retain both, – it is *Comprehensive*.'[11] Pietro Corsi suggests that Stanley and Jowett inspired Conybeare to create the label 'broad church',[12] and Golightly tried to protect the University of Oxford from the corrosive influence of both these men.

It was Jowett who first felt the vehemence of Golightly's resistance – not for his desire to improve academic standards, but for his undermining of traditional Christian orthodoxy. The opportunity for agitation came in 1855 when Jowett published a commentary on part of the New Testament. It met with a torrent of negative criticism, and Golightly pressurised the authorities to have Jowett dismissed from his post at Balliol and thrown out of the University for heretical teaching. The account of this turmoil given by Evelyn Abbott and Lewis Campbell, Jowett's friends and his first biographers, is sketchy, partisan and littered with errors.[13] However, subsequent writers such as Geoffrey Faber and Peter Hinchliff, have tended to rely on Abbott and Campbell's version of events.[14] A fresh analysis of this important episode, and Golightly's part in it, is therefore necessary.

In his *Life* of Thomas Arnold, issued in 1844, Stanley noted his mentor's intention of undertaking a 'Rugby edition' of St Paul's Epistles.[15] Shortly afterwards he and Jowett began to work together on the New Testament and continued the project even when Stanley left Oxford in 1851 to become a canon at Canterbury.[16] In June 1855 the first fruits of their labour was published – a commentary by Jowett on 1 and 2 Thessalonians, Galatians and Romans, alongside one by Stanley on 1 and 2 Corinthians.[17] In September they were discussing further commentaries on Ephesians, Colossians, Philippians and Philemon.[18] However, the project immediately ground to a halt – perhaps because that month Jowett was appointed Regius Professor of Greek, with new

---

[11] Hugh R. Haweis, 'The Broad Church; or, What's Coming?', *Contemporary Review* 57 (June 1890), p. 902.

[12] Corsi, *Science and Religion*, p. 199.

[13] Evelyn Abbot and Lewis Campbell, *The Life and Letters of Benjamin Jowett* (2 vols, London, 1897), i. pp. 233-40.

[14] Geoffrey C. Faber, *Jowett: A Portrait with Background* (London, 1957), pp. 218-26; Peter Hinchliff, *Benjamin Jowett and the Christian Religion* (Oxford, 1987), pp. 62-4.

[15] Arthur P. Stanley, *The Life and Correspondence of Thomas Arnold* (2 vols, London, 1844), i. p. 194.

[16] Abbot and Campbell, *Life of Jowett*, i. pp. 99-100, 141-4, 160-2.

[17] Benjamin Jowett, *The Epistles of St Paul to the Thessalonians, Galatians, Romans: with Critical Notes and Dissertations* (2 vols, London, 1855); Arthur P. Stanley, *The Epistles of St Paul to the Corinthians: with Critical Notes and Dissertations* (2 vols, London, 1855).

[18] Jowett to Stanley, 24 September 1855, BCL IIIS/74; Stanley to Jowett, 26 September 1855, MS 410.

teaching commitments, or perhaps because his first commentary was already raising a storm. Stanley and Jowett's volumes were published together and both followed a similar pattern, but their reception was markedly different. Stanley's detailed historical approach was uncontroversial, but Jowett attracted attention by the bold theological essays interspersed throughout his work. As Hinchliff points out, 'For the most part, his actual commentary, even when it was theological or devotional rather than philological, was mild and inoffensive', but the essays 'hardly help to uncover the theology of St Paul: they are outspoken and radical comments on contemporary orthodoxy.'[19] Particularly contentious were the essays on 'Natural Religion', 'Righteousness by Faith', 'Predestination and Freewill' and 'The Doctrine of the Atonement'.[20] It was this last upon which Jowett's opponents concentrated their attacks.

The doctrine of the atonement had not formed a prominent part of Tractarian debates in the 1830s and 40s, and could be described in 1849 as a subject of 'universal accord and tranquil acceptance'.[21] The Bampton Lectures of 1853, delivered by William Thomson (future Archbishop of York), were the first devoted to the atonement for almost sixty years and uncontroversial.[22] Shortly afterwards, however, F.D. Maurice published his notorious *Theological Essays* (1853), which led to his dismissal from King's College, London for his statements on hell.[23] In these *Essays* he claimed that a traditional understanding of the atonement 'outrages the conscience',[24] and his next book, *The Doctrine of Sacrifice* (1854), raised further suspicions about his heterodoxy.

Howard Murphy, Susan Budd and others argue that 'loss of faith' in the mid-nineteenth century was not simply due to intellectual concerns over increasing scientific knowledge or biblical criticism, but often involved questions of morality.[25] As in Maurice's case, there was a growing repugnance

---

[19] Hinchliff, *Jowett*, pp. 55-6.

[20] However, Stanley mischievously suggested circulating the essay on 'Righteousness by Faith' as an anonymous tract amongst Lord Shaftesbury's circle, to see if they would notice: Stanley to Jowett, 26 December 1856, BCL MS 410.

[21] Quoted in A.J. Boyd Hilton, *The Age of Atonement: The Influence of Evangelicalism on Social and Economic Thought, 1785-1865* (Oxford, 1988), p. 288.

[22] For Thomson's response to Jowett, see William Thomson, 'The Death of Christ' in William Thomson (ed.), *Aids to Faith; a Series of Theological Essays* (London, 1861), pp. 323-66.

[23] Geoffrey Rowell, *Hell and the Victorians: A Study of the Nineteenth-Century Theological Controversies concerning Eternal Punishment and the Future Life* (Oxford, 1974), pp. 76-89.

[24] F.D. Maurice, *Theological Essays* (Cambridge, 1853), p. 138.

[25] Howard R. Murphy, 'The Ethical Revolt against Christian Orthodoxy in Early Victorian England', *American Historical Journal* 60 (July 1955), pp. 800-17; Susan Budd, *Varieties of Unbelief: Atheists and Agnostics in English Society 1850-1960* (London, 1977), ch. 5; Josef L. Altholz, 'The Warfare of Conscience with Theology', in Gerald Parsons (ed.), *Religion in Victorian Britain* 4 (Manchester, 1988), pp. 150-69.

towards the apparent ethical implications of Christian doctrines such as election and reprobation, eternal punishment, and vicarious sacrifice, which were seen as 'morally barbarous and a relic of primitive society'.[26] This moral concern was evident, too, amongst biblical scholars such as Bishop Colenso who decided the massacre of Midianites under Moses was non-factual, because it was even more morally reprehensible than the Cawnpore massacre during the Indian mutiny of 1857.[27] Similarly, Jowett in his commentary rejected the traditional teaching that the atonement was vicarious sacrifice. He denounced this idea as 'horrible and revolting' and 'inconsistent with truth and morality'.[28] He asked, 'Was it that God was angry, and needed to be propitiated like some heathen deity of old? Such a thought refutes itself by the very indignation which it calls up in the human bosom. ... God, if He transcend our ideas of morality, can yet never be in any degree contrary to them.'[29] Jowett described sacrificial atonement as a 'human invention' and concluded, 'Not the sacrifice, nor the satisfaction, nor the ransom, but the greatest moral act ever done in this world – the act, too, of one in our likeness – is the assurance to us that God in Christ is reconciled to the world.'[30]

Jowett's volumes were dedicated to his Balliol friend, Frederick Temple, who cautioned him, in one of the few letters which has survived the burning of Jowett's correspondence, against being too antagonistic:

> You seem to me much too controversial, and, when engaged in controversy, very unmerciful. ... I miss in you something of that 'economy' whereby Maurice manages to express his doctrines in the phraseology of the Articles. You run to the opposite extreme and insist upon expressing all that you have to say in words as unlike those of your opponents as you can find.[31]

In early reviews Jowett was charged with 'subtle metaphysical speculation',[32] and his commentary was said to be 'poisonous' and 'a seductive delusion of Satan'.[33] He was pronounced unable to defend himself against those who 'share his principles and laugh at his piety'.[34] W.J. Conybeare (a rival biblical

---

[26] Budd, *Varieties of Unbelief*, p. 111.
[27] Peter Hinchliff, *God and History: Aspects of British Theology, 1875-1914* (Oxford, 1992), p. 29.
[28] Jowett, *Epistles of St Paul*, ii. p. 474.
[29] Ibid., p. 472.
[30] Ibid., pp. 481-2. For Jowett's insistence, with Johann Semler, on the centrality of morality, see Peter Hinchliff, 'Ethics, Evolution and Biblical Criticism in the Thought of Benjamin Jowett and John William Colenso', *Journal of Ecclesiastical History* 37 (January 1986), pp. 95-7.
[31] Temple to Jowett, nd, BCL IE5/2, fo. 1.
[32] *Clerical Journal*, 8 October 1855, p. 452.
[33] *Record*, 12 and 17 December 1855.
[34] *Literary Churchman*, 30 June 1855, p. 105.

commentator as well as a theorist on 'church parties') called Jowett's work 'a retrograde step in biblical literature' whose result was 'to reduce the Christian revelation to the level of a human philosophy'.[35] He observed that Jowett's 'metaphysical distinctions' were

> far too refined to be appreciated by the practical understanding of his countrymen; and that the somewhat aërial barriers by which his position is fenced and limited were too intangible to be perceived by grosser eyes. ... It is evident that the author is incapable of placing himself intellectually in the position of his readers, and of estimating the inevitable result of his statements upon minds less transcendental than his own.[36]

Negative reviews continued for many months.[37] Another declared: 'Poor Oxford, torn first by Romanism scarcely disguised, and next by Rationalism quite as naked! Church of the Reformation, ancient bulwark of the Protestant faith! strange children are nurtured in thy bosom.'[38]

Rare support came from Unitarian journals like the *Christian Reformer* which called Jowett's commentary 'a precious boon to the Church'.[39] James Martineau, the Unitarian leader, also praised Jowett and Stanley's volumes:

> They show how effectually we have escaped from the morbid religious phenomena represented by Simeon at Cambridge, and the counter-irritants applied by John Henry Newman at Oxford; and come as the returning breath of nature to those who have witnessed the fevers of 'Evangelical' conversion or the consumptive asceticism of 'Anglican' piety.[40]

---

[35] William J. Conybeare, 'The Neology of the Cloister', *Quarterly Review* 98 (December 1855), pp. 152, 185. The 'ignorance' of Conybeare's review was said to be equalled by its 'pretentious audacity': J. Llewelyn Davies, *St Paul and Modern Thought: Remarks on Some of the Views Advanced in Professor Jowett's Commentary on St Paul* (Cambridge, 1856), p. 3.

[36] William J. Conybeare, 'School Sermons', *Quarterly Review* 97 (September 1855), p. 337.

[37] For example, 'Jowett on the Epistles', *Christian Observer* (January 1856), pp. 18-43; 'Stanley and Jowett on the Epistles', *Christian Remembrancer* 31 (April 1856), pp. 445-92; 'Professor Jowett on the Epistles to the Thessalonians', *Journal of Sacred Literature and Biblical Record* 3 (April 1856), pp. 1-52; 'Jowett on the Epistles of St Paul', *United Church Journal* 1 (April and May 1856), pp. 100-8, 143-50; James H. Rigg, 'Rationalism in the Church of England', *London Quarterly Review* 7 (October 1856), pp. 1-51.

[38] 'Jowett on the Pauline Epistles', *British and Foreign Evangelical Review* 5 (January 1856), p. 215.

[39] 'Jowett on the Epistles of St Paul', *Christian Reformer* 12 (July 1856), p. 428. See also the American Unitarian *Christian Examiner* (May 1856) quoted in *Clerical Journal*, 8 July 1856, pp. 328-9.

[40] James Martineau, 'St Paul', *National Review* 1 (October 1855), p. 438.

Likewise Francis Newman, once a friend of Golightly but now a Unitarian freethinker, thought Jowett's commentary was calculated 'to cause a panic in High and Low Church alike.'[41] Indeed, as Hinchliff observes, Jowett's essay on the atonement criticised the conventional belief of the day 'in terms which not only attacked the penal substitutionary theology of the Evangelicals but also the satisfaction language of the medieval theologians beloved by High Churchmen.'[42] As a result people from a broad spectrum of theological opinion censured Jowett. For example, the evangelical *Christian Observer* chastised the Professor: 'to deny or set aside a doctrine which is the fundamental principle of the Gospel ... may be called latitudinarianism, may be called rationalism, may be called neology; but it *is* really, and in fact, absolute unbelief.'[43] Meanwhile the *Ecclesiastic and Theologian* (known as a 'high church' journal) described Jowett's commentary as 'saddening and sickening' and lamented: 'We can only ask in dismay, – how much of religion is left?'[44]

Opposition to Jowett's publication within Oxford itself did not begin to gather momentum until early November 1855. Golightly was already active behind the scenes, planning a protest, and his old friend John Tucker (once of CMS, now of West Hendred in Berkshire) wrote in support:

> I was very glad to receive your 'report of progress' in this important business, though I was disappointed somewhat to find – owing to the vis inertiae [power of inertia] which is yet far from extinct in Regius Professorships & Doctorates of Divinity – the progress so slow.[45]

Tucker later remarked on Jowett: 'I can pity his unsettled mind; – but his publishing his evil thoughts, there can be nothing to justify.'[46] Likewise W.S. Dear encouraged Golightly: 'I suppose quarrels, partizanship, unsettling of the minds of the Undergraduates are dreaded: but what if *a nomination to a Bishoprick* shd follow not long after the nomination to the Professorship?'[47] The first salvo was fired on 11 November, when Edward Pusey entered the University pulpit to preach on *All Faith the Gift of God*, in which Jowett's rationalist theology was clearly in sight. He proclaimed: 'Reason, unaided, cannot even penetrate into the sphere of the objects of Faith ... intellect, unenlightened by Divine light, intuitive as it may be in human things, is blind

---

[41] Francis W. Newman, 'Jowett and the Broad Church', *Westminster Review* 16 (July 1859), p. 53.
[42] Hinchliff, *Jowett*, p. 62.
[43] *Christian Observer* (October 1855), p. 653.
[44] 'Jowett on the Epistles of S. Paul', *Ecclesiastic and Theologian* 17 (November 1855), pp. 489, 514.
[45] Tucker to Golightly, 6 November 1855, LPL MS 1811, fo. 3.
[46] Tucker to Golightly, 31 January 1856, LPL MS 1811, fo. 15.
[47] Dear to Golightly, 6 November 1855, LPL MS 1805, fos 78-9.

in Divine'.[48] The following Sunday he declared that if faith in God 'is not absolute or perfect, it is not faith'.[49] Pusey maintained against Jowett: 'No consistent minds will ever occupy such ground as this. They must go on to full unbelief, or they must return to definite faith'.[50] Soon members of the Oxford Union for Private Prayer (founded in 1850 in Golightly's home[51]) were being asked to intercede against 'the evils that must arise from the unchecked propagation of [Jowett's] doctrines, against which we feel it to be the duty of every disciple of the Lord Jesus Christ to protest.'[52]

Various forms of public campaign were considered. The commentary might be brought before the Visitor of Balliol College (Bishop Jackson of Lincoln) or condemned by the University's Convocation, just as William Ward's *Ideal of a Christian Church* had been a decade earlier. Alternatively the Archbishop of Canterbury might be requested to summon Jowett before the Court of Arches on a charge of heresy; or, because his work was published in London, the Bishop of London might take it up.[53] Instead, on 10 December, Golightly and Professor J.D. Macbride (Principal of Magdalen Hall) wrote publicly to their friend Richard Cotton, the Vice-Chancellor, asking him to summon Jowett to sign the Thirty-Nine Articles. Despite the University Reform Act of 1854, subscription was still required by tutors and professors, as well as, of course, by all Anglican clergymen. Golightly and Macbride claimed that Jowett's understanding of the atonement was 'plainly contrary to that of the Church of England'.[54] Two days earlier another correspondent, probably Charles Heurtley (Lady Margaret Professor of Divinity and another of Golightly's old friends), gave Cotton his verdict on Jowett's work:

> Of the book at large I am not prepared to speak, as I have not had leisure to read more than detailed portions of it: but of the Essay which you specified I have no hesitation in saying that it either *denies* or *explains away* the doctrine of Scripture on the subject of the Atonement, as that doctrine is received & taught by the Church of England.[55]

---

[48] Edward B. Pusey, *All Faith the Gift of God. Real Faith Entire* (Oxford, 1855), pp. 16, 24.
[49] Ibid., p. 44.
[50] Ibid., p. 93.
[51] Hill Diary, 25 November and 2 December 1850, Bodleian MS St Edmund Hall 67/18. See rules and membership lists for the Oxford Prayer Union at Bodleian 1265 d.41.
[52] Circular, 1 December 1855, LPL MS 1810, fos 18-9. Golightly drafted this circular: Tucker to Golightly, 10 November 1855, MS 1811, fos 5-6.
[53] Tucker to Golightly, 7 December 1855, LPL MS 1811, fos 7-8.
[54] *Oxford Herald*, 15 December 1855. Draft at LPL MS 1810, fos 39-41.
[55] [Heurtley?] to Cotton, 8 December 1855, BCL IIE3/2. This indicates that Cotton was active in the matter before public pressure from Golightly and Macbride; *pace* Abbott and Campbell, *Life of Jowett*, i. p. 238.

Jowett was duly summoned.[56] He consulted Mark Pattison who advised him to sign immediately, and Henry Liddell who said it was a matter for his conscience.[57] Jowett claimed to be 'very much affected' by a critical note from Pusey,[58] but was reported to have signed the Articles 'without hesitation', with the words 'O yes, just give me a pen'.[59] His motives for subscribing, and apparent nonchalance in the act, provoked much debate at the time, and continue to do so.

Writing forty years after the event, Abbott and Campbell portray the tension between Jowett's outward confidence and his private concern. They remark that the anecdote about 'just give me a pen', 'has been treasured as indicating his perfect coolness on the occasion. And such truly was his demeanour outwardly. But in reality he was much perturbed, and on returning to his room, where a friend awaited him, his first words were, "They have done me harm; but I shall live it down".'[60] Jowett's own description to Stanley of his meeting with Vice-Chancellor Cotton, despite its self-assurance, also reveals this tension:

> Since I made up my mind what to do I have been quite at rest about the whole subject. You will perhaps have seen in the newspapers that I have taken the meaner part & signed. It seemed to me that I could not do otherwise without virtually giving up my position as a Clergyman.
>
> Scene. V.C.s study
>
> A domestic picture of Dr & Mrs C. – Enter hereticus – 'I am come to comply with your request'. 'Will you write your name on this sheet of paper & on that?' Done. V.C. turns over letters from Golightly & Heurtley mumbling something in an under tone of voice. But before the words are out hereticus says 'good morning' & escapes.
>
> It grieves me to have been put to this sort of schoolboy degradation and also to think that such things are possible nowadays. I don't intend to write a single word in reply to the attacks on me. Without taking any notice of them I shall enlarge the Essay on the Atonement in a Second Edition ... Liddell has been most kind. I often think of a sentence in a sermon of his which you repeated to me: 'No man ever entered into controversy without being sorry for it'.[61]

---

[56] There is no evidence that Cotton 'exceeded his authority'; *pace* Hinchliff, *God and History*, p. 56.
[57] V.H.H. Green, *Oxford Common Room: A Study of Lincoln College and Mark Pattison* (London, 1957), p. 219.
[58] Jowett to Stanley, 14 December 1855, BCL IIIS/76.
[59] Cox, *Recollections of Oxford* (second edition, 1870), p. 414.
[60] Abbott and Campbell, *Life of Jowett*, i. p. 239.
[61] Jowett to Stanley, 14 December 1855, BCL IIIS/76. For Liddell's aphorism, see Arthur P. Stanley, *Essays Chiefly on Questions of Church and State from 1850 to 1870*

In a jocular note to an infant correspondent, Jowett remarked: 'A little monkey of an old gentleman who dresses himself in black and has three pokers walk before him has been teazing me lately'.[62] To Stanley he lamented: 'I earnestly hope that this matter which my book has stirred up may go no further. ... It is a great misfortune to be even unintentionally the cause of stirring up a row in a place of education.'[63] Stanley advised his friend to return the challenge to his Oxford opponents:

> I think you were perfectly right in signing. You could sign with as much truth as Macbride & Golightly who differ far more from the Liturgical Statements of the doctrine [of the Church of England], than you from the Articular Statements – you could sign with far more truth than Pusey against whose express opinions the 31st Article [on the offering of Christ on the cross and 'mass sacrifice'] is directly aimed, whilst at the most it touches yours only indirectly & by the way.

A long-time opponent of subscription, Stanley suggested seriously that Jowett approach the Vice-Chancellor with quotes from Pusey's publications on eucharistic sacrifice and Macbride's on baptismal regeneration, and request that Cotton likewise call them to sign the Articles. He concluded: 'It is the only process which would both nullify the proceeding in your case, & from the absurdity of it in all cases.'[64]

Having signed the Articles, Jowett was next criticised for doing so. By subscribing he was said to lack 'moral courage'[65] and to oppose 'common truth and integrity'.[66] Macbride reported that Jowett had faltered when summoned by the Vice-Chancellor, which the *Record* thought 'shows that he has still some sense of shame'.[67] The *Christian Times* observed: 'The Church of England is falling into moral chaos. In a short time her creed will become as uncertain as her ritual – her doctrines as powerless as her discipline'.[68] Likewise the Unitarian *Christian Reformer* gleefully asked: 'Was there ever a more complete reductio ad absurdum of the supposed efficacy of a test in excluding error from a religious community? ... The demon of heresy mocks at the exorcisers, and will not be cast out.'[69]

Recent debate has centred on Jowett's words 'just give me a pen' and 'I could not do otherwise without virtually giving up my position as a

---

(London, 1870), p. v; Henry L. Thompson, *Henry George Liddell, DD, Dean of Christ Church, Oxford: A Memoir* (London, 1899), pp. 188-9.

[62] Jowett to Frank Sellar, 26 December 1855, BCL IF13/43.
[63] Jowett to Stanley, [15 December 1855], BCL IIIS/77.
[64] Stanley to Jowett, 15 December 1855, BCL MS 410.
[65] Quoted in *Leeds Mercury*, 18 December 1855.
[66] *Christian Observer* (January 1856), p. 71.
[67] *Record*, 31 December 1855.
[68] *Christian Times*, 14 December 1855, p. 789.
[69] 'Jowett on the Epistles of St Paul', *Christian Reformer* 12 (July 1856), p. 431.

Clergyman.'⁷⁰ These remarks might indicate that Jowett signed dishonestly, as some of his opponents thought, merely to retain his position at Balliol. However, Hinchliff argues that Jowett's action was in fact 'difficult to fault' and 'wholly justified',⁷¹ since 'he always stressed the impossibility of treating theological statements as if they were precise and exhaustive definitions' and 'as a good Arnoldite he would think it absurd to assume that everyone could agree on the precise meaning of a theological statement.'⁷² There is a revealing account of Jowett's interview with Bishop Wilberforce of Oxford ten years earlier, as a candidate for ordination, which supports this view:

B[ishop]	One more question I wish to ask – in what sense do you sign the Articles – certain modes I consider dishonest, without at all wishing to narrow their limits
Can[didate]	– a pause – In Paley's Sense
B.	What does Paley say?
Can.	That it is an absurdity if the legislature meant to say you assented to four or five hundred disputed propositions. It only meant that you were an attached member of the Ch. of England.
B.	No I don't mean that I require assent to four or five hundred disputed propositions &c &c
Can.	One question I should like to ask. Do you think Dr Arnold was justified in signing them?
B.	Yes.⁷³

It is not clear whether Golightly and Macbride anticipated that Jowett would sign the Articles. His compliance momentarily took the wind out of their sails, but Tucker was soon encouraging Golightly: 'I fear if things are left as they are, it will be established that men may sign the Articles, holding any thing, every thing & nothing'.⁷⁴ Therefore, in the new year Golightly tried another avenue of attack, publicly challenging Robert Scott (the new Master of Balliol): 'are you doing right before God and man in upholding Mr Jowett in the position of a Tutor of Balliol College?'⁷⁵ Behind the scenes, he attempted to rally former members of Balliol into applying further pressure to Scott, although one asked privately: 'why must we single out Jowett individually, he is one out of many more both at Oxford and elsewhere who are introducing a new Series of Vols.

---

⁷⁰ The important word 'virtually' was missed by Abbott and Campbell, *Life of Jowett*, i. p. 240, followed by Faber and Hinchliff.
⁷¹ Hinchliff, *God and History*, pp. 56-7.
⁷² Hinchliff, *Jowett*, pp. 63-4.
⁷³ Jowett to Stanley, nd [1845], BCL IIIS/6.
⁷⁴ Tucker to Golightly, 27 December 1855, LPL MS 1811, fo. 12.
⁷⁵ Golightly to Scott, 24 January 1856, PHL SCO 1/12/1.

of Theology – if that can be called Theological science at all, wh is based upon no fixed principles.'[76] Despite the well-known antipathy between Scott and Jowett, the Master resisted this opportunity to dismiss his Balliol rival, only admitting that the subject had been 'one of much thought and painful anxiety'.[77]

The ongoing controversy provoked a deluge of sermons and tracts in Oxford and nationwide, in response to Jowett's teaching.[78] During 1856 the University pulpit 'resounded with frequent vindications' of the doctrine of the atonement, and Vice-Chancellor Cotton organised a special series of sermons in the two months before Easter.[79] The series was begun by Professor Heurtley, with an address entitled simply *The Doctrine of the Atonement,* in which he argued for the traditional interpretation.[80] The next week, Thomas Bernard (a select preacher) spoke on *The Exclusion of Wisdom,* about God making foolish the wisdom of the world.[81] He was followed by E.M. Goulburn (a Balliol graduate and headmaster of Rugby School, but out of step with the 'broad church' movement) on *The Goodness and Severity of God.* Goulburn maintained that 'the holiness, justice, and truth of God, (attributes which wear an awful aspect to the sinner), are an element of His Nature as essential to its perfectness as mercy, love, and goodness'.[82] He warned that to reject the doctrine of the vicarious sacrifice of Christ, 'against the simple statements of Scripture', because it violates one's moral sense, 'is not wisdom, is not independence of thought, is not a high reach of mind, – it is simply folly'.[83] Next in turn was Charles Baring who spoke on *Christ's Death a Propitiatory Sacrifice,*[84]

---

[76] J.M. Chapman to Golightly, 18 February 1856, LPL MS 1805, fo.15. See also Chapman to Scott, 12 January 1856, PHL SCO 1/6/1; W.J. Trower to Scott, 22 February 1856, PHL SCO 1/40/1.

[77] Scott to Trower, 26 February 1856, LPL MS 1810, fo. 47.

[78] For example, Charles R. Alford, *First Principles of the Oracles of God: Vindicated from the Aspersions of Professor Jowett and Authors of the Rationalistic School* (London, 1856); Robert W. Browne, *Justification by Faith in the Atonement* (London, 1856); Andrew R. Campbell, *The Satisfaction and Sacrifice of the Death of Christ, considered in reference to recent objections* (London, 1856); Benjamin M. Cowie, *On Sacrifice; the Atonement, Vicarious Oblation, and Example of Christ; and the Punishment of Sin* (Cambridge, 1856); Henry Melvill, 'The Day of Atonement', *Pulpit* 69 (1856), pp. 342-8; Hugh Stowell, 'The Atonement', *Pulpit* 69 (1856), pp. 221-5. See also Trower to Golightly, 13 December 1855, LPL MS 1810, fo. 27

[79] Cox, *Recollections of Oxford,* pp. 395-6. Scott declined to take part: Cotton – Scott, 18 January 1856, PHL SCO 1/7/1-2. Archbishop Whately thought the sermon series a bad idea: Whately to Hawkins, 9 March 1856, OCL Miscellaneous Letters, vol. 4, no. 316.

[80] Charles A. Heurtley, *The Doctrine of the Atonement* (Oxford, 1856).

[81] Thomas D. Bernard, *The Exclusion of Wisdom. Offences in Christ* (London, 1856).

[82] E.M. Goulburn, *The Goodness and Severity of God as Manifested in the Atonement* (Oxford, 1856), p. 5.

[83] Ibid., p. 9.

[84] Charles Baring, *Christ's Death a Propitiatory Sacrifice* (Oxford, 1856).

described by Maurice (in jest?) as 'one of the most Lential works he ever read'.[85] When Baring was elevated to the see of Gloucester and Bristol in June 1856, Jowett remarked: 'A worse appointment could not have been made. No other qualification but that which ought to be a disqualification – strong evangelicalism'.[86]

Continuing the sermon series, Bishop Wilberforce and Frederick Meyrick (a select preacher) both challenged Jowett's thesis that atonement through sacrifice was morally repulsive and therefore not the way in which God would act. Meyrick spoke on *God's Revelation and Man's Moral Sense*,[87] and Wilberforce on *Our Reception of the Truth of Christ's Message, a Part of Our Moral Probation*, in which he exhorted the congregation: 'when the sophist whispers to thee his objections to the simple truths of Christ's Atonement, remember that it is *God's* message to thee; and that to strive to mend it, is to disbelieve its truth, – and that to disbelieve its truth, is to throw away thy soul.'[88] Finally, on the Sunday before Easter, the sermon to the University was given by Stephen Rigaud (with whom Golightly had once clashed in the 1840s over the *Oxford and Cambridge Review*), now headmaster of Ipswich School and soon to be Bishop of Antigua. He took as his title, *The Inspiration of Holy Scripture*, attacking Jowett's misuse of the Bible as the root cause of his doctrinal error. He proclaimed: 'I see no alternative between a general rejection of the Inspiration of Scripture and the gloomy abyss of Infidelity; or between a half-rejection of it and the cold, negative, heartless creed of the Socinian', a view Rigaud saw sadly confirmed in Jowett's essay on the atonement.[89]

In the face of such authoritative pronouncements, few were willing to speak up publicly in Jowett's defence. When J.B. Lightfoot (New Testament scholar and future Bishop of Durham) published a rare complimentary review,[90] Stanley applauded his courage, saying it was 'specially creditable not to have been deterred from saying this much by the popular clamour which has hounded on the Conybeares, Goulburns, or Wilberforces, and has muzzled the

---

[85] Stanley to Jowett, 29 December 1856, BCL MS 410.
[86] Jowett to Stanley, nd, BCL IIIS/73.
[87] Frederick Meyrick, *God's Revelation and Man's Moral Sense Considered in Reference to the Sacrifice of the Cross* (Oxford, 1856).
[88] Samuel Wilberforce, *Our Reception of the Truth of Christ's Message, a Part of Our Moral Probation* (Oxford, 1856), p. 22.
[89] Stephen J. Rigaud, *The Inspiration of Holy Scripture, with reference to the Epistles of St Paul. Oppositions of Science* (Oxford, 1856), p. 40. These Lent sermons were printed individually and in a rare combined volume, *Christian Faith and the Atonement. Sermons preached before the University of Oxford, in Reference to the Views Published by Mr Jowett and Others* (Oxford, 1856) (copy at Heythrop College Library, London), with a preface by Cotton, and a catena against Jowett probably by J.M. Chapman. See Chapman to Golightly, 18 February 1856, LPL MS 1805, fo. 14.
[90] Joseph B. Lightfoot, 'Recent Editions of St Paul's Epistles', *Journal of Classical and Sacred Philology* 3 (March 1856), pp. 81-121.

"North British", the "Edinburgh", and the "Times".[91] Resistance to Jowett continued unabated in a variety of forms. At a scholarly level, E.A. Litton's Bampton Lectures of 1856 addressed the problems of Jewish sacrificial imagery raised by Jowett, and Henry Mansel's Bamptons two years later are described by Boyd Hilton as 'a sophisticated climax' of reaction to the commentary.[92] At a more popular level, a new evening sermon series was begun at St Mary-the-Virgin, Oxford in Lent 1857, proposed by Meyrick and supported by Pusey and Wilberforce, which continued annually for many years.[93] Meanwhile the University looked for further ways to promote traditional Christian orthodoxy amongst its junior members. One of the Mrs Denyer Theological Prizes for 1857 was offered for the best essay on the subject, 'The manifestation of the union of Divine Justice and Mercy in the Atonement', awarded to Henry Boyd (future Principal of Hertford College). It was probably for this prize that William H. Fremantle (future Dean of Ripon), who had been tutored by Jowett at Balliol, wrote an essay in defence of his former teacher – but it was never submitted due to the disapproval of his uncle, William R. Fremantle, a friend of Golightly.[94] Likewise at Cambridge University, the Norrisian Prize for 1857 was awarded to Frederic Farrar (future Dean of Canterbury) for an essay entitled *The Christian Doctrine of the Atonement not Inconsistent with the Justice and Goodness of God*. Farrar is a surprising winner, having been strongly influenced by Maurice.[95] Although at pains to maintain the traditional interpretation of the atonement, Farrar chastised the 'violent bigots' who 'take refuge from their argumentative weakness in dogmatic acrimony, and fiercely attribute the often honest inquiries of the objector to some root of bitterness springing up from an evil life'. He quoted approvingly Coleridge's dictum, 'He who begins by preferring Christianity to truth, will soon learn to love his own sect better than

---

[91] Stanley to Jowett, March 1856, in R.E. Prothero and G.G. Bradley, *The Life and Correspondence of Arthur Penrhyn Stanley* (2 vols, London, 1893), i. p. 476. Stanley himself reviewed the second edition of Jowett's commentary in the *Times*, 15 October 1859. See Abbott and Campbell, *Life of Jowett*, i. p. 235.

[92] Hilton, *Age of Atonement*, p. 290.

[93] Frederick Meyrick, *Memories of Life at Oxford, and Experiences in Italy, Greece, Turkey, Germany, Spain, and Elsewhere* (London, 1905), pp. 103-4; Meyrick to [A.R. Ashwell?], 30 May 1876, Bodleian MS Wilberforce c.26, fos 61-5.

[94] *Recollections of Dean Fremantle, Chiefly by Himself* edited by the Master of the Temple (London, 1921), pp. 51-3. For W.R. Fremantle's views of the atonement, explicitly rejecting Jowett's teaching, see 'Atonement' in Edward Garbett (ed.), *Evangelical Principles: A Series of Doctrinal Papers Explanatory of the Positive Principles of Evangelical Churchmanship* (London, 1875), ch 3.

[95] Reginald Farrar, *The Life of Frederic William Farrar* (new and revised edition, London, 1905), pp. 22-5, 136.

Christianity, and end by loving his own self better than all'.[96]

In October 1859 Jowett published a second edition of his commentary, with his essay on the doctrine of the atonement increased to four times its original length and just as controversial. Six months later, however, he was embroiled in the furore over *Essays and Reviews*, a provocative volume by seven 'broad churchmen' with Oxford connections, including Jowett and his friends Mark Pattison and Frederick Temple.[97] One of the most inflammatory and influential pieces in the collection was Jowett's essay 'On the Interpretation of Scripture'. Within the broader context revealed here, this famous essay can be understood as a direct riposte to opponents of his New Testament commentary in Oxford and beyond. It had initially been intended for publication in the second edition of his commentary in 1859, and would have made a fitting partner to his essay on 'The Doctrine of the Atonement', but was not completed in time. Its radical challenge to interpret Scripture 'like any other book' was a response to criticisms levelled at the first edition.[98] For instance, in 1856 Benjamin Newton had chastised Jowett for not 'bowing' to Scripture but sitting in judgment upon it, and treating the Bible merely like 'a valued human book'.[99] Likewise another critic asked: 'Shall we sit in judgment upon the contents of Holy Scripture, and study it in the same spirit, as we would read a play of Sophocles, or peruse a book of Thucydides?'[100] As has been seen, many reviewers and those who preached against Jowett in the University pulpit at Oxford throughout 1856, accused him of having a wrong view of Scripture, and not valuing revelation highly enough.[101] The *Literary Churchman* saw the real question as 'the submission of man's moral intuitions to revealed truth'.[102] The need to acknowledge some matters as a 'mystery',[103] and to accept God's teaching as

---

[96] Frederic W. Farrar, *The Christian Doctrine of the Atonement not Inconsistent with the Justice and Goodness of God* (Cambridge, 1858), pp. 12-3.

[97] Ieuan Ellis, *Seven Against Christ: A Study of 'Essays and Reviews'* (Leiden, Netherlands, 1980); Josef L. Altholz, *Anatomy of a Controversy: The Debate over Essays and Reviews 1860-1864* (Aldershot, 1994).

[98] *Essays and Reviews* (London, 1860), pp. 377, 404.

[99] Benjamin W. Newton, *The First and Second Chapters of the Epistle to the Romans Considered. With Remarks on Certain Doctrines Recently Promulgated by the Savilian Professor of Geometry, and the Regius Professor of Greek, in the University of Oxford* (London, 1856), pp. 63, 89.

[100] Alford, *First Principles*, pp. 32-3.

[101] Rigaud, *Inspiration of Holy Scripture*, passim; Heurtley, *Doctrine of Atonement*, pp. 8, 11; Pusey, *All Faith the Gift of God*, p. 75; *Christian Observer* (October 1855), p. 657; *Record*, 25 January 1856; 'Biblical Theology and Modern Thought; or, Reason and Faith', *Journal of Sacred Literature and Biblical Record* 3 (July 1856), p. 277.

[102] *Literary Churchman*, 19 April 1856, p. 148.

[103] Meyrick, *God's Revelation*, p. 15; Pusey, *All Faith the Gift of God*, pp. 79-82.

'little children',[104] were recurrent themes. In this context Jowett's assertions in *Essays and Reviews* were a stern rebuttal to his Oxford detractors.

Although Jowett ceased to write theological works, his New Testament commentary with its essay on the atonement was groundbreaking. Looking back thirty years later, John Tulloch could reasonably claim that its publication saw the beginning of a 'new historical epoch in theology'.[105] Golightly had spoken too soon when he told Archbishop Sumner he was satisfied his protest had been 'calculated to deter other parties coming forward in the same line.'[106] As early as 1856, John McLeod Campbell was propagating similar views in Scotland with his *The Nature of the Atonement*. Despite, or perhaps because of, the extensive opposition to Jowett's commentary, his ideas continued to gain ground. As Ieuan Ellis concludes, 'In Jowett, more than anyone else, occurred that momentous change from Easter to Christmas, from Christ as Atoner to the preacher of reconciliation who appealed to the spiritual faculty inherent in man.'[107] From the late 1850s a shift in emphasis steadily took place from *Christus Redemptor* to *Christus Consummator*, from 'lamb' to 'man', symbolised by a spate of Lives of Christ and the appearance of *Lux Mundi* in 1889, subtitled 'Studies in the Religion of the Incarnation'.[108] Jowett was a radical pioneer in this process and there was nothing Golightly and his allies could do to stop him.

---

[104] Bernard, *Exclusion of Wisdom*, pp. 20, 24; Goulburn, *Goodness and Severity*, p. 7; Pusey, *All Faith the Gift of God*, p. 86; Wilberforce, *Our Reception of the Truth*, p. 20.
[105] John Tulloch, *Movements of Religious Thought in Britain During the Nineteenth Century* (London, 1885), p. 331.
[106] Golightly to J.B. Sumner, 14 August 1856, LPL MS 1809, fo. 101.
[107] Ellis, *Seven Against Christ*, p. 97.
[108] Daniel L. Pals, *The Victorian 'Lives' of Jesus* (San Antonio, Texas, 1982).

CHAPTER 5

Bishop Wilberforce and the Spread of Ritualism

Although the influence of the Tractarians within the University of Oxford was at a low ebb in the 1850s, their theological principles had been flung far and wide, disseminated through numerous parishes across Britain and beyond. Their controversial doctrinal views on the church, its ministry and its sacraments, helped to lay the foundations for a radical change in Anglican ritual over subsequent decades. Just as Oxford's Tractarians sought to distance themselves from traditional Protestant doctrine, so the next generation began to reject traditional Protestant practices – a shift seen most vividly in the service of holy communion. Innovations like incense, wafer bread and medieval vestments, commonly identified with Roman Catholicism, were introduced into Anglican churches around the country.[1] Meanwhile the ecclesiological movement began to change public perceptions about church buildings and church furnishings. The Cambridge Camden Society led the way with a bold initiative to build new churches and 'restore' old ones, on the medieval gothic pattern.[2] There was considerable cross-fertilization between Tractarianism, ecclesiology and ritualism, which irrevocably transformed the face of the Church of England.

Charles Golightly was embroiled in these debates in Oxford diocese (and to an extent Chichester diocese) during the 1850s and 60s. For the first time, his focus moved away from the University to wider issues within the diocese. In a previous decade his *bête noire* had been the Tractarians and their figurehead, John Henry Newman. Now the ritualists and their episcopal sympathiser, Bishop Samuel Wilberforce, were the focus of Golightly's Protestant energies. Instead of lecture rooms, periodicals and the University pulpit, his agitation reached into normal parish churches. Theological colleges and public schools were not beyond his scrutiny. In his first anti-Tractarian pamphlet in 1840, Golightly had appealed to the Bishop of Oxford to put an end to Newman's habit of mixing water with the wine at holy communion. Yet such a practice now seemed minor in the face of the ritualist pandemic. A whole raft of ritualist

---

[1] On ritualism, see especially Nigel Yates, *Anglican Ritualism in Victorian Britain, 1830-1910* (Oxford, 1999).

[2] Nigel Yates, *Buildings, Faith, and Worship: The Liturgical Arrangement of Anglican Churches 1600-1900* (revised edition, Oxford, 2000); James F. White, *The Cambridge Movement: The Ecclesiologists and the Gothic Revival* (Cambridge, 1962; reissued 1979).

practices became Golightly's target – from auricular confession to stone altars to sisterhoods. Once again he was battling against the tide to preserve the Protestant Reformed heritage of the Church of England.

During these intense campaigns, Golightly's reputation as an ecclesiastical agitator reached new heights. His most effective ploys against the Tractarians, such as anonymous pamphlets and unsolicited letters to bishops, were put into action again. It was during the 1850s that the famous riddle about 'the Oxford spy' reached widest circulation around the local diocese. Golightly's notoriety for dishonourable methods soon took on legendary proportions and sometimes outstripped reality. It was said, for example, that he was 'found in men's rooms, examining their books in their absence, and making a catalogue of suspicious prints or pieces of furniture for the edification of provosts and principals.'[3] His enemies found it easy to deride and denounce him as a gossip and a busybody. One critic, remembering Golightly's lack of parochial responsibilities and perhaps intending a contrast with the ritualist 'slum priests', complained:

> With all his zeal for the Church, how odd it is that he takes no work in it! As he is a man of means, as well as orthodoxy, why should he not spend himself as a missionary in Shoreditch or Whitechapel. There is plenty of work for him to do; and he might just as well convert the heathen as convert his brethren. But this is not his line. His line is that of Hood's Trumpet, to collect all –
>
> > The tales of shame,
> > The constant runnings of evil fame,
> > Foul and dirty, and black as ink,
> > That the ancient gossips with nod and wink,
> > Pour in his ears like slops in a sink.[4]

However, Golightly was not without a significant number of Protestant supporters. Hundreds of clergymen and thousands of laymen were persuaded to sign anti-ritualist petitions addressed to Bishop Wilberforce. Others made their feelings felt through the local press. As a result the ritualist cause in Oxford diocese suffered serious setbacks. For almost a decade Golightly kept up the Protestant agitation with hardly a lull.

Cuddesdon College

Almost as soon as he had been consecrated Bishop of Oxford in 1845, Samuel Wilberforce was making plans to establish a diocesan theological college near his episcopal palace at Cuddesdon.[5] He proclaimed to his clergy that such an

---

[3] Richard Simpson, 'Cuddesdon Casuistry', *Rambler* 9 (April 1858), p. 282.
[4] *Saturday Review*, 9 July 1859, p. 46.
[5] Ashwell and Wilberforce, *Life of Samuel Wilberforce*, i. p. 349.

institution was in fact 'essential' for the welfare of the diocese.[6] Funds were rapidly raised and buildings designed by the diocesan architect, George E. Street (later famous for his work on London's law courts and numerous ecclesiastical buildings). The foundation stone was laid in April 1853 and Cuddesdon College formally opened in June 1854 amidst great celebrations.[7]

One of the concerns raised frequently about small theological colleges was that, isolated from the diverse opinions taught at the Universities, they would breed 'party spirit'. Indeed those founded at Chichester (1839) and Wells (1840) had quickly gained a Tractarian reputation.[8] When a theological college was proposed for Lichfield in 1852, the local opposition was so vociferous that the scheme was delayed for five years.[9] Similar suspicions surrounded the establishment of Cuddesdon. Before building had even begun, it was said the college would be 'more or less under Tractarian influence'.[10] Golightly's friend, William R. Fremantle (the influential incumbent of Claydon and later Dean of Ripon) wanted publicly to oppose the plan, but kept quiet for the sake of the peace of the diocese.[11] However, the *Record* was not so considerate. It derided the celebrations at the opening of the college as the 'monster show of the month', an 'Episcopal gala' which boded much 'future evil' for the Church of England. An appeal was made that 'lovers of Gospel truth and Protestant simplicity' should combine to establish their own colleges 'where something better may be taught that posture, prostrations, and sing song'.[12] Another observer rebuked Chichester, Wells and Cuddesdon as 'nurseries of Anglican Popery' which would 'bring forth the deadly fruits of Romish teaching and Romish superstitions under the pretence of Anglicanism ... Let us be quiescent no longer. Peace with these betrayers of our Protestant Christianity is impossible.'[13] Suspicion of Wilberforce's motives was fuelled by his family

---

[6] Samuel Wilberforce, *A Charge to the Clergy of the Diocese of Oxford, at his Second Visitation* (London, 1851), p. 17.
[7] For details of these events, see Owen Chadwick, *The Founding of Cuddesdon* (Oxford, 1954).
[8] William M. Jacob, 'The Diffusion of Tractarianism: Wells Theological College, 1840-49', *Southern History* 5 (1983), pp. 189-209; Arthur Burns, *The Diocesan Revival in the Church of England c.1800-1870* (Oxford, 1999), pp. 151-6.
[9] James Bateman, *The Tractarian Tendency of Diocesan Theological Colleges* (London, 1853); Charles Hebert, *Theological Colleges and the Universities; or, What Special Training Should be Given to the Future Clergy?* (Burslem, 1853); *Statement of Facts Connected with the Movement in Opposition to the Establishment of a Diocesan Theological College at Lichfield* (London, 1856).
[10] Bateman, *Tractarian Tendency*, p. 25.
[11] Wilberforce to William R. Fremantle, 28 November 1853, in Ronald K. Pugh (ed.), *The Letter-Books of Samuel Wilberforce, 1843-68*, Oxfordshire Record Society 47 (Leeds, 1970), pp. 285-6.
[12] *Record*, 6 July 1854.
[13] *Record*, 18 September 1854.

connections. His brothers, Henry and Robert, and his brother-in-law, Henry Manning, had all converted to Roman Catholicism in the early 1850s.[14] As one evangelical forcibly put it, they had fallen 'into that frightful abyss of spiritual darkness' and all eyes were on the bishop to see if he would follow suit.[15]

From the start Wilberforce was determined to head of such allegations. Again and again he emphasised that Cuddesdon College would represent the mainstream of the Church of England, without bias to any particular theological party. At the laying of the foundation stone he asked for prayers that the institution would be 'ever free from party and sectarian disputes; that we may rear therein ripened clergymen with the spirit of Richard Hooker and the temper of Lancelot Andrewes.'[16] At the opening of the college Wilberforce proclaimed: 'what we are doing here is for the Church of our fathers; for no section of it, for nothing narrower than that true Church of England as God in His providence has planted it in this land.'[17] He maintained that theological study, such as that offered by Cuddesdon, would help students to avoid 'extreme opinion on any side' and to rid themselves of 'Private imaginations, the conceits which are bred of the fancy, narrow mindedness, a set of shallow opinions, self-willed rashness, ignorant obstinacy, party spirit, with its shibboleths and its unchristian judgments, and its uncharitable speeches and all its injuries to souls'.[18]

As the first principal of his new institution, Wilberforce chose Alfred Pott, one of his chaplains, his chief clerical secretary and the vicar of Cuddesdon. However, the appointment of a vice-principal presented more of a dilemma. In December 1853 the bishop had offered the post to the young H.P. Liddon, recently ordained to a curacy under William Butler at Wantage.[19] Yet the invitation was soon withdrawn when Wilberforce discovered the extent of Liddon's views on auricular confession and his close relationship with Edward Pusey. He could not afford to have his college so easily identified in the public mind with Tractarian extremism. He was worried lest students also go to Pusey for counsel and thus the college become 'a mere collection of young men under his direction'.[20] Nine months of tortured negotiation followed in which Liddon

---

[14] Newsome, *Parting of Friends*.
[15] *Record*, 9 November 1854.
[16] *Guardian*, 13 April 1853, p. 245.
[17] George A. Selwyn, *'A Little One Shall Become a Thousand'. A Sermon preached at the opening of the Cuddesdon Theological Institution ... to which is added, an Appendix, containing an account of the proceedings, and the speeches delivered by the bishops present* (Oxford, 1854), p. 19.
[18] Samuel Wilberforce, *A Charge to the Diocese of Oxford, at his Third Visitation* (London, 1854), p. 11.
[19] John O. Johnston, *Life and Letters of Henry Parry Liddon* (London, 1904); Michael J. Chandler, *The Life and Work of Henry Parry Liddon* (Leominster, 2000).
[20] Wilberforce to Liddon, 7 June 1854, Bodleian MS Wilberforce d.40, fo. 149.

was eventually persuaded to go to John Keble instead for spiritual advice.[21] When his appointment as vice-principal was confirmed, a well-wisher gleefully predicted that Cuddesdon would now fulfil 'the worst expectations of its Recordite enemies, & I trust the best anticipations of its friends'.[22]

It was not long before Cuddesdon attracted attention for its ritualist practices. Supporters of the institution began to complain against the ornate decoration of the chapel, the Gregorian chants, and singing of the Nicene creed.[23] One said the altar was 'very like another part of the Vineyard', while less friendly observers called the college 'dangerous'.[24] At the first annual festival in June 1855 visitors were shocked to see vergers carrying poles surmounted by gilt crosses during a procession through the village.[25] This procession had been organised by a student, Frederick Lee, who was soon appointed curate at Kennington, near Oxford, where he won early notoriety for introducing incense, reredos, cross, candles, stole and a choir in surplices and red cassocks (donated by Sir George Bowyer of Radley Park, a convert to Roman Catholicism). Lee was dismissed from his curacy by Wilberforce after only a year, due to complaints by Golightly and others.[26]

In January 1856 a small group of bishops were staying with Wilberforce at Cuddesdon Palace and had a tour of his new theological institution. Liddon noted in his diary that they objected to nothing, although the cross may have caused 'some secret dissatisfaction.'[27] During the following summer vacation Wilberforce asked for changes to be made in the style of music, ritual washing and content of the service-book.[28] Nevertheless, visitors to the chapel a few months later were shocked at its decoration and made 'a series of very vulgar

---

[21] Liddon – Wilberforce, 28 December 1853 – 19 June 1854, Bodleian MS Wilberforce d.40, fos 139-51; Butler to Wilberforce, 1 February and 26 March 1854, MS Wilberforce c.20, fos 151-4; Keble to Wilberforce, 24 June and 7 July 1854, MS Wilberforce d.39, fos 151-6; Wilberforce to Liddon, 24 July 1854, PHL Liddon House Papers; Pusey to Liddon, 19 June and 26 July 1854, PHL LBV 67/29 and 67/32; Wilberforce to Keble, 3 July 1854, in *Letter-Books of Samuel Wilberforce*, p. 305.
[22] A. Newdigate to Liddon, 15 August 1854, PHL Liddon Papers, box 2/13.
[23] Liddon Diary, 21 January, 7, 22 and 30 March, 6 August 1856, CCA VP1/2.
[24] Liddon Diary, 30 May and 4 June 1855, CCA VP1/2.
[25] Liddon Diary, 5 June 1855, CCA VP1/2; *Guardian*, 13 June 1855, p. 459; *Bucks Herald*, 5 February 1859; T.W. Perry – Liddon, 16-17 February 1859, KCL Liddon Papers. There is no evidence that Golightly attended this festival; *pace* Chadwick, *Founding of Cuddesdon*, p. 67.
[26] Henry R.T. Brandreth, *Dr Lee of Lambeth: A Chapter in Parenthesis in the History of the Oxford Movement* (London, 1951), pp. 13-5; Peter Maurice, *The Ritualism of Oxford Popery, a Letter to Dr Macbride* (London, 1867), pp. 24-5.
[27] Liddon Diary, 30 January 1856, CCA VP1/2.
[28] Liddon Diary, 27 July 1856, CCA VP1/2.

remarks about Popery'.[29] During another episcopal party at Cuddesdon Palace in early 1857, A.C. Tait (now Bishop of London) and W.J. Trower (Bishop of Glasgow and Galloway) remonstrated with Wilberforce and advised that the college chapel be made less 'gaudy'. So the cross was removed, the white and green altar cloths forbidden, the painted figures on the wall covered over, and use of the eastward position at the eucharist ceased. Walter Hamilton (Bishop of Salisbury) tried to explain to Liddon that it hindered a bishop if he became identified with a distinctive theological party, yet Liddon felt 'aggrieved' at the enforced changes, and saw them as 'lost ground'.[30] A fortnight later he wrote: 'The chapel is beginning to look terribly bare. ... Nor is there the consolation of hoping that these concessions will go any great way towards pacifying the Puritan mind. The chapel will be thought Jesuitical if it is not condemned as Popish.'[31]

In September 1857, further private pressure was put on Wilberforce by Golightly. They had been contemporaries at Oriel College in the mid-1820s and enjoyed an early friendship, an acquaintance renewed when Wilberforce returned to Oxford as bishop twenty years later, but now their relationship began to deteriorate badly. Having been informed by his friend Trower about the nature of training at Cuddesdon,[32] Golightly wrote to Wilberforce to express his concerns about Liddon's influence. Immediately the bishop tried to play down the issue:

> Oh how I value people for speaking out to me with love & plainness instead of growling behind my back. ... There are it is true *little* things I should myself wish otherwise; but men must work by instruments & when you have instruments of the greatest possible excellence in fundamentals it would in my judgement be very wrong to cast them away for non essentials. I think my Vice Principal eminently endued with the power of leading men to earnest devoted piety: with such a man I do not think I ought to interfere except as to any thing substantially important. Hence in trifles I do not meddle. I have a strong conviction that Cuddesdon college *is* doing God's works for men's souls mightily.[33]

Later Wilberforce reiterated his confidence in Liddon:

---

[29] Liddon Diary, 23 October 1856, CCA VP1/2. See Liddon – Henry A. Tyndale, 24-28 October 1856, CCA VP1/12-14.

[30] Liddon Diary, 2-3 February 1857, CCA VP1/2; Liddon to Wilberforce, 8 February 1858, Bodleian MS Wilberforce d.40, fo. 155. See Keble to Wilberforce, 6 February 1857, MS Wilberforce d.39, fos 186-7. Trower was put up to visiting the chapel by Tait: Trower to Golightly, 5 March 1858, LPL MS 1811, fo. 59.

[31] Liddon Diary, 17 February 1857, CCA VP1/2.

[32] See Trower to Golightly, 27 February, 4 and 5 March 1858; Trower to Wilberforce, 27 February 1858; LPL MS 1810, fos 52-9, 67-9. Golightly later planned to publish *A Letter to the Bishop of Glasgow and Galloway*: Golightly to Tait, 9 February 1858, LPL Tait Papers, vol. 79, fo. 162.

[33] Wilberforce to Golightly, 23 September 1857, LPL MS 1811, fos 211-2.

There may be shades of difference as to things on which members of the Church of England may lawfully differ between us. But I have ever found him most loyally ready to act in such matters on my judgement when he knew it: & I have rarely met with any man living who had equal gifts for stirring up the spark of good in a young man's heart into a flame. Now my *first* & greatest object in founding the college was to get under God's blessing a more earnestly religious *young* clergy – & I thought it *far* better to get such a real man than one who might agree with me in every thing & be less real.[34]

Nonetheless, Wilberforce agreed to change anything at the college which Golightly thought tended to Roman doctrine or ritual.[35] Liddon reflected to Pott: 'Probably the Bishop thinks it right to silence an eccentric controversialist at the outset. ... Golightly does not require much of a stimulant to write a pamphlet on any subject which he had better leave alone.'[36]

Further private complaints came from Wilberforce's friend, Charles Anderson, who warned against the music of Thomas Helmore and flower decorations which 'have the look of effeminacy'.[37] He advised the bishop to 'hold them in at Cuddesdon, for I think it a pity that young Clergy shd be encouraged in what might if injudiciously begun, destroy all their usefulness in a new Parish. ... Extreme ritualism & frippery ornament are most repugnant to the English mind.'[38] Perhaps with these tendencies in mind, John Sandford (Archdeacon of Coventry) exhorted ordinands at the college festival of June 1857 to 'drink deep at the fountain-head, instead of borrowing your views from ephemeral and party writings, which are the bane of our age and country.'[39] Meanwhile Wilberforce reassured the diocese via his triennial charge that he had noticed in students at Cuddesdon 'an increased quietness and moderation of tone on things doubtful', and he invited any local clergy to visit the college and observe its practice.[40]

The Public Outcry

In January 1858 the dispute went public. The *Quarterly Review*, in an article on 'Church Extension', criticised the establishment of theological colleges, and their tendency to breed 'party spirit':

---

[34] Wilberforce to Golightly, 4 October 1857, ibid., fo. 217.
[35] Wilberforce to Golightly, 26 September 1857, ibid., fos 213-4.
[36] Liddon to Pott, 3 October 1857, in Chadwick, *Founding of Cuddesdon*, p. 69.
[37] Anderson to Wilberforce, nd, Bodleian MS Wilberforce d.28, fo. 41.
[38] Anderson to Wilberforce, 8 November 1857, ibid., fo. 69.
[39] John Sandford, *Clerical Training. A Sermon, preached on the anniversary of the Theological College for the Diocese of Oxford* (Oxford, 1857), p. 20.
[40] Samuel Wilberforce, *A Charge Delivered at the Triennial Visitation of the Diocese* (Oxford, 1857), p. 29.

> It is the nature of all such institutions to go further than was intended in the line of the impulse first given, whatever that may be; and there is nothing that we should deprecate more than the foundation of rival colleges by hostile parties in the Church to vie with each other in sectarian bigotry and perpetuate our unhappy divisions. ... the utmost vigilance on the part of their superiors is necessary to correct their inherent tendency to extravagance, and to obtain the confidence of the public by the most rigid forbearance from all sectarian teaching, and all external badges of party.[41]

Cuddesdon College was specifically named. According to the *Quarterly* it had lost its 'indispensable neutrality of character' and instead showed signs of an 'exclusive, partisan spirit'. The college chapel was described as 'fitted up with every fantastic decoration to which a party-meaning has been assigned'; the altar as 'adorned with flowers, surmounted with lights, covered with a lace-bordered napkin, and in every particular affecting the closest approximation to a Popish model'; the eucharist as conducted 'with rinsings of cups in the newly-revived piscina, with genuflexions, and other ceremonial acts which are foreign to our ritual and usages'; and the service-book as 'concocted from the "seven canonical hours" of the Romish Church'. The reviewer asked: 'what effect must this ostentatious playing at Romanism have on the Protestant public?'[42]

Golightly saw his opportunity. He circulated excerpts from the *Quarterly* throughout Oxford diocese, adding that according to one Cuddesdon student 'nobody can pass through the Institution, and continue a Protestant'. The tendency of the college, Golightly claimed, was 'to sow broad cast the seeds of Romish perversion in the counties of Oxfordshire, Berkshire, and Buckinghamshire.'[43] At a meeting of the Church Pastoral Aid Society in Manchester, Hugh Stowell (a leading evangelical) took up the cry, declaring that

> a large number of the younger clergy were preparing to be the voices of the Church of Rome in the Church of England, and some of our Bishops were caught in the snare, and were either dupes or designers in the matter. ... It was high time these things were exposed, for we had been asleep too long.[44]

Some believed Golightly and the *Quarterly Review* were allies in 'a prearranged scheme';[45] others reckoned he was acting under the direction of leading churchmen in Oxford such as Benjamin Symons (now in his 70s and still Warden of Wadham College) and E.A. Litton (evangelical rector of St

---

[41] R.H. Cheney, 'Church Extension', *Quarterly Review* 103 (January 1858), p. 162.
[42] Ibid., pp. 162-3.
[43] Alfred Pott, *Correspondence Relating to Cuddesdon Theological College, in Answer to the Charges of the Rev. C.P. Golightly, and the Report of the Commissioners Thereon* (Oxford, 1858), p. 3.
[44] *Manchester Examiner* quoted in *Record*, 5 February 1858.
[45] Robert Milman to Liddon, 1 February 1858, PHL Liddon Papers, box 1/10.

Clement's, Oxford).[46] However, there is no evidence to support either claim. Although Golightly no doubt sought advice from friends (as he usually did when engaged in public controversy), he was probably both the initiator and the main strategist of this campaign.

The charges against Cuddesdon were promptly rejected as 'a barefaced lie', 'utterly false and ungrounded', and 'malicious and wicked'.[47] The *Quarterly*'s article was called 'slipshod stuff' which 'savours not a little of malice aforethought' and it was chastised for 'the vulgar intemperance of personal animosity and moral guilt'.[48] Yet the sternest criticism was reserved for Golightly himself. He was rebuked for 'uncharitable meddling', 'illiberal zeal' and 'pertinacious bigotry'.[49] He was called 'a great busybody and mischief-maker', and 'a Recordite leader and anti-Tractarian martyr' with 'exuberant zeal which appears to consume him'.[50] The *Clerical Journal* pronounced:

> Mr Golightly's cowardice was quite equal to his ignorant and mischievous prejudices, for he seized the moment when he thought Cuddesdon was fallen to give it a kick and sink it still lower. The *Quarterly Review* had spoken – an undoubted oracle had pronounced the sentence – and it only remained that the pious and evangelic Mr Golightly should hasten on its execution.[51]

Trower reminded Wilberforce that Golightly had 'never shrunk from defending the doctrines of the Ch. of E. when he has believed them to be endangered on either side'.[52] Yet this did not stop Wilberforce speaking of 'evil surmises' and 'malicious misrepresentation'.[53] He called Golightly his 'gossipping friend' and his 'excellent, but not very judicious friend', and condemned him for attempting to 'excite a storm by appealing to the prevalent suspicions of the hour'. The bishop reassured Pott: 'the habits of his mind make him unable to form an unbiased judgment on any matter which appeals to his inveterate prejudices – I doubt whether any Diocesan College could satisfy him'.[54] Meanwhile Golightly received a direct episcopal rebuke, although Wilberforce continued to hold out the hand of friendship:

> I think you were blinded by party spirit: or you must have felt that the charge of spreading Romanism &c, a charge as poisonous to their character as if you had

---

[46] Manuel Johnson of the Radcliffe Observatory, quoted in Liddon Diary, 10 February 1858, PHL.
[47] Pott, *Correspondence*, pp. 13, 15, 18.
[48] *Guardian*, 3 March 1858, p. 182; Pott, *Correspondence*, p. 13.
[49] *Clerical Journal*, 8 March 1858, p. 99.
[50] *English Churchman*, 4 February and 11 March 1858, pp. 105, 227.
[51] *Clerical Journal*, 8 March 1858, p. 99.
[52] Trower to Wilberforce, 27 February 1858, LPL MS 1810, fo. 55.
[53] *Guardian*, 3 March 1858, p. 183.
[54] Wilberforce to Pott, 1 and 15 February 1858 in Pott, *Correspondence*, pp. 4, 9.

charged them with adultery ... with not a particle of sifted evidence to support it ... as gross a violation of the ninth commandment & of St Paul's law of Christian charity as could easily be committed. Nothing in the administration of my Diocese has ever wounded my heart so deeply. But I freely forgive you as I hope to be forgiven. I have not a particle of ill feeling to you nor have ever had. I earnestly pray for you; alas! that I should have to do so my dear friend amongst 'persecutors & slanderers' & am ready to meet you as I have ever met you as your sincere friend.[55]

William Butler expressed his 'deep regret, that Mr GOLIGHTLY in his old age has not learnt wisdom, and that, as in days of old, he should still spend his time in the possibly exciting, but assuredly profitless and unedifying occupation of hunting for mare's nests.'[56] Anderson, though, saw Golightly being used as a tool for more sinister purposes:

The Devil is ready enough to enter into any one even Churchmen in the guise of an Angel of Light, and the more the Church of England lifts her truthful head the more the Papist & the Puritan will fight their several ways against her: and I have no doubt that they combine at Oxford through the medium of the rationalistic people, who are liberal and farsighted enough to be friends with both in order to undermine the Christian Faith, and that if poor Portcullis [Golightly] knew how he was made a tool of by others he would be ready to rush like the herd of swine and drown himself in the Cherwell.[57]

Similarly the *Union* viewed Golightly as just a pawn in the game:

Poor Mr Golightly is known to have been the cats paw of a clever and narrow-minded clique at Oxford, headed by a Germanising Evangelical; and, therefore, his false and badly patched-up gossip may be forgiven. If this 'not very judicious' parson would attend to the poor people of Headington, and not rake up groundless charges against those of his brother-clergymen who are doing a more effectual and successful work than himself, he would gain more respect from straightforward people generally, if he lost the praises of the low-minded Puritans at Oxford.[58]

Despite this caustic abuse, Golightly's friends came to his defence. One declared: 'The Public does not want a railing accusation against the person who

---

[55] Wilberforce to Golightly, 24 April 1858, LPL MS 1811, fo. 223. For Golightly's response, see Golightly, *Letter to the Dean of Ripon*, p. 17.
[56] Handbill, 2 February 1858, Bodleian MS Wilberforce c.20, fo. 158. For Butler's authorship, see Liddon Diary, 1 February 1858, PHL.
[57] Anderson to Wilberforce, 3 February 1858, Bodleian MS Wilberforce d.28, fos 76-7. 'Portcullis' is probably a play on Golightly's middle-name, Portalès.
[58] *Union*, 26 February 1858, p. 136.

makes a charge; but proof that the charge is unfounded.'[59] The *National Standard* called Golightly 'true-hearted, honest, and resolute', a man whose 'zeal as a faithful minister of the Gospel never slumbers' and who had 'done nothing but what it was his duty to do ... the whole community owes him a debt of gratitude'.[60] Likewise Bishop Trower encouraged him to persevere: 'after the experiences of the last 20 years, I see not how it is possible with a safe conscience to stand aloof, while the principles of the Church of England and the Reformation are undermined, & a totally different ἦθος is being insidiously wrought into the Clergy.'[61]

Those inclined to view the affair as altogether less serious poked fun at both Cuddesdon and its critics. The following ditty by some local wag circulated Oxford:

> GO LIGHTLY when you make a charge
> Against a Christian brother,
> Nor with the bigot's pen enlarge
> The failings of another.
>
> 'Tis true, in Cuddesdon's priestly home
> Hard is the student's lot;
> But still, he is not sent to *Rome* –
> He simply 'goes to POTT'.[62]

The Archdeacons' Inquiry

Liddon was confident that increased interest in Cuddesdon College could only be beneficial:

> All that I hear in Oxford makes me think that this Golightly explosion will in the end, by God's mercy, do us great good. It will dissipate reports which may have been prevalent, or anyhow it will relegate them to those strongholds of Ultra-Low Church prejudice, where belief in these matters in no way depends on fact.[63]

At Pott's request, and with what Golightly termed 'Napoleonic rapidity', Wilberforce appointed his three archdeacons to hold a commission of inquiry.[64] Liddon later complained that this 'gave a fictitious importance to charges

---

[59] Richard Twopeny, *Some Remarks upon the Visitation of Cuddesdon College, and the State of the Church in the Diocese of Oxford* (London, 1858), p. 16.
[60] *National Standard*, 13 and 27 March 1858, pp. 41, 89.
[61] Trower to Golightly, 10 February 1858, LPL MS 1810, fo. 51.
[62] *Jackson's Oxford Journal*, 27 March 1858, p. 5.
[63] Liddon to Wilberforce, 8 February 1858, Bodleian MS Wilberforce d.40, fo. 154.
[64] Golightly to Tait, 9 February 1858, LPL Tait Papers, vol. 79, fo. 161. For rumours of Golightly's close contact with Bishop Tait during the crisis, see *Union*, 12 February 1858, p. 105; 15 July 1859, p. 433. But compare Liddon Diary, 29 January 1858, PHL.

against the college which were either groundless or absurd; – unless indeed the opinions of the Puritanical party were to be made the rule of faith and practice in the diocese.'[65] Yet the *Record* put all the authorities in the dock: 'It is not so much the Principal and Vice-Principal who are on their defence before the Bishop and the three Archdeacons. It is all these parties who are collectively on their trial in the face of the Church of England.'[66]

The commissioners met at Cuddesdon on 6 February 1858 with Golightly in attendance.[67] Liddon thought Golightly's contributions 'exceedingly amusing' and reminiscent of Fusby, a character in Newman's novel *Loss and Gain* who took sensual pleasure in hunting Tractarians.[68] It was agreed by the archdeacons that the chapel had 'too lavish a display of ornaments' which encouraged 'a disproportionate regard for the accessories of Public Worship'. However, the candles near the altar were said never to be lit unless the whole chapel was lit, and use of a lace cloth had been discontinued as a result of the recent 'Westerton Judgment' (concerning the ritualistic practices of Robert Liddell at St Paul's, Knightsbridge). 'Genuflexions' were hard to define but Pott and Liddon denied they were practised, and rinsing of the sacramental vessels in the piscina had been abandoned. Furthermore, the archdeacons concluded there was 'no reason for imputing a party meaning to any of these decorations'.[69] Richard Twopeny (vicar of North Stoke, between Oxford and Reading) strongly disagreed. He rejected such 'excessive ornamentation' as 'a badge of party, a display of colours', belonging to those who wished the Church of England to resemble the Church of Rome. Even the cross, he thought, which ought to be a symbol 'of peace and unity, has been perverted to become the badge of a party'.[70] Likewise Joseph Wilson (a local magistrate) declared:

> There is not much, probably, in a lace cloth and a metal cross; no indication of party was intended; but this is a poor reason for the use of toys and fripperies to satisfy morbid tastes at the risk of creating prejudice in many minds, of causing serious offence, and by a continued series of such trifling practices, unavoidably creating a party, and affixing to it its own characteristics.[71]

Upon investigation, the three archdeacons found the Cuddesdon service-book to be 'not only unexceptionable, but highly valuable', although they

---

[65] Liddon to Golightly, 24 November 1875, LPL MS 1808, fo. 55.
[66] *Record*, 26 February 1858.
[67] For Golightly's account of the Commission, see Golightly to Tait, 9 February 1858, LPL Tait Papers, vol. 79, fos 161-2; Golightly, *Letter to the Dean of Ripon*, pp. 34-5.
[68] Liddon Diary, 6 February 1858, PHL. For Fusby, see Newman, *Loss and Gain*, pp. 321-3.
[69] Pott, *Correspondence*, pp. 7-8
[70] Twopeny, *Some Remarks*, pp. 6, 8.
[71] Joseph H. Wilson, *Thoughts on Church Matters in the Diocese of Oxford. By a Layman and Magistrate for that County* (London, 1858), p. 27.

recommended it be remodelled because of its 'unfortunate resemblance' to the Roman Breviary.[72] The prayers were said to be taken from the same source as those in the Book of Common Prayer, to which the *Christian Observer* retorted: 'So the slime and mud in which worms crawl and insects are engendered, are taken from the same source as the purest spring water; – one rivulet supplies them both!'[73] A defender of the college, however, thought such abuse of the service-book merely prejudiced:

> Truly 'unfortunate' it is that it was not so disguised and wrapped up as to suit the Protestant palate; the contents may be the same – that is not the question. Call your Antiphons 'The Golden Treasury', and your book itself, 'Gospel Manna, or Crumbs of Comfort for Starving Souls'; date it Clapham instead of Cuddesdon, and let Seeley publish it, and in the 'portfolio' of the 'Record' you may hope for a Protestant canonization.[74]

When the archdeacons' inquiry was complete, Wilberforce boldly declared (with what the *Record* thought 'complacency' and 'quiet arrogance'[75]) that their report completely refuted every charge brought against Cuddesdon. He reaffirmed his belief that the college intended 'to foster no party spirit, but to nourish in young men going into Orders habits of self-denial and true earnest piety on the simplest Church of England model'.[76] The *Guardian* too was satisfied: 'We had very little doubt at the time, judging from the well-known antecedents of the personage who appeared as the accuser of his brother clergy and of his Bishop, that on inquiry it would turn out that he had found what is popularly called a mare's nest.'[77] Likewise the *English Churchman* proclaimed: 'the report of the Commissioners proves that upon this, as upon former occasions, Mr Golightly's party-zeal has led him to commit a manifest breach of the ninth Commandment.'[78]

By no means all were pacified, however. Even the Roman Catholic *Rambler* sarcastically congratulated the authorities for their 'equivocation and suppression of truth'.[79] Arthur Isham (a rural dean) thought that far from disproving the charges, the archdeacons' report 'exhibits a complete justification for the attack'. To the principal he protested:

---

[72] Pott, *Correspondence*, p. 8.
[73] 'State of the Diocese of Oxford', *Christian Observer* (July 1859), p. 467.
[74] *Counter-Thoughts on Church Matters in the Diocese of Oxford. A Letter, addressed by a Clergyman of that Diocese to a Layman & Magistrate of that County* (London, 1858), p. 40.
[75] *Record*, 17 March 1858.
[76] Wilberforce to Pott, 15 February 1858, in Pott, *Correspondence*, p. 9.
[77] *Guardian*, 3 March 1858, p. 181.
[78] *English Churchman*, 25 February 1858, p. 179.
[79] Simpson, 'Cuddesdon Casuistry', p. 285.

You make ceremonialism an important adjunct. This I consider to be full of danger, as likely to alloy the very doctrine of Christ. Gorgeousness in ritualism, and simplicity of faith, cannot stand together. ... Mr Golightly is not the only objector. There is a deep uneasiness in many minds about the College, which will not be allayed by the Report of the Commissioners.[80]

In reply, Pott lamented: 'The Church of England must be indeed given over to a spirit of schism, when a shelf behind the Communion Table, or a fringe on Communion linen, are alleged as reasons for suspicion and separation.'[81]

Golightly, of course, thought his charges confirmed rather than contradicted by the archdeacons and circulated excerpts from their report, announcing his intention 'to leave the diocese to judge'.[82] The *Guardian* was surprised that he had not 'at once frankly acknowledged his mistake and apologised for spreading the slander'.[83] Yet the *English Churchman* thought this typical of Golightly's character:

His zeal is a virtue of a most uneasy and restless kind, and he seems to possess some of the tastes and instincts of the fabled salamander which lives in the fire. He has returned to the charge in a document of which we will only say that, if he had any sense of decency, or any power of reasoning, he should never have allowed it to see the light, and the circulation of which in the very teeth of his Diocesan is alone a breach of etiquette and a reckless imputation on the good faith of his Clerical brethren. We cannot conceive what pleasure any Christian man can feel in this perpetual hunt after the presumed faults and transgressions of his neighbours. The gusto with which such a discovery of a 'leaning to Tractarianism' is eagerly ferretted out by Mr Golightly's confederates is a painful exhibition, to our minds, and we think both he and his Recordite friends might employ their time and pens to much better effect by concentrating their attention and their powers on some other subjects to which they are solicited both by duty and by the law of charity.[84]

In the light of the archdeacons' report, the *Quarterly Review* came under pressure to withdraw its charges against Cuddesdon. The author of the article remained silent, but Whitwell Elwin (the *Quarterly*'s editor) was prepared to defend its remarks. He wrote to John Murray (the review's publisher): 'I am sure I can make good our position, and show the danger of the Cuddesdon system. ... There is no doubt it is a semi Roman Catholic College. ... I think we can crush the Bishop of Oxford.'[85] Nevertheless with private pressure brought

---

[80] *Jackson's Oxford Journal*, 6 March 1858.
[81] *Jackson's Oxford Journal*, 13 March 1858.
[82] Handbill, 20 February 1858, Bodleian MS Wilberforce c.20, fo. 160.
[83] *Guardian*, 3 March 1858, p. 181.
[84] *English Churchman*, 11 March 1858, p. 226.
[85] Whitwell Elwin to John Murray, 27 February 1858, in *Some XVIII Century Men of Letters: Biographical Essays by the Rev. Whitwell Elwin, some time editor of the*

to bear by Bishop Phillpotts of Exeter and by William Gladstone (on Wilberforce's behalf), the *Quarterly* eventually issued a grudging statement that it had not meant to imply Roman Catholic doctrine was believed at Cuddesdon College:

> The questions were purely questions of ritual, upon which there is, and always has been, great difference of opinion within the English Church; and though we retain the same sentiments that we expressed in the Article, we entirely acquit the authorities of entertaining any ulterior or covert designs.[86]

Ironically, Elwin later sent two of his sons to Cuddesdon.

In early April 1858 a private meeting of rural deans took place at Cuddesdon Palace, when all but five assented to a vote of confidence in favour of Principal Pott and the innocence of his theological college. Yet when someone proposed that this vote be made public, they quickly back-peddled, illustrating to Richard Twopeny (who was present at the meeting) that 'their vote was contrary to their conviction'.[87] Wilberforce continued his policy, when speaking about Golightly, of mingling praise and reproof. He told the rural deans of Golightly's 'simplicity and transparency of character' and his steadfastness in previous years 'bearing the reproach of his contemporaries'. He 'did not believe a more single-hearted man lived'.[88] Nevertheless he charged Golightly with 'disingenuousness' for ignoring his offer to talk in private about Cuddesdon College and for pretending, when asked to substantiate his public charges, that they were not his own but those of the *Quarterly Review*. When Golightly heard about Wilberforce's comments, in self-defence he circulated to the rural deans part of his private correspondence with the bishop.[89] This dissemination of private letters only widened the breach between the two men and Wilberforce noted: 'it will make me very cautious in any future communication with Mr G.'.[90]

Quarterly Review, with a Memoir edited by Warwick Elwin (2 vols, London, 1902), i. p. 190.

[86] *Quarterly Review* 103 (April 1858), p. 574. See Gladstone to Wilberforce, 2 March – 16 April 1858, Bodleian MS Wilberforce d.36, fos 149-58; Golightly, *Letter to the Dean of Ripon*, pp. 38-45.

[87] Twopeny, *Some Remarks*, p. 18. See Henry Bull, *Some Remarks upon the Remonstrance lately addressed to the Archdeacons and Rural Deans of the Diocese of Oxford. A Letter addressed to the Rev. W.R. Fremantle* (Oxford, 1859), pp. 13-4.

[88] Golightly, *Letter to the Dean of Ripon*, p. 46.

[89] Bodleian MS Wilberforce c.20 fos 176-85; Wilberforce to Golightly, 24 April, 3 and 20 May 1858, LPL MS 1811, fos 221-7; W.B. Lee to Golightly, 3 May 1858, MS 1808, fos 46-7.

[90] Wilberforce to Archdeacon Clerke, 17 May 1858 (draft), Bodleian MS Wilberforce c.20, fo. 182.

College Concessions

Although his college had been publicly vindicated, when the furore died down Wilberforce urged quiet alteration in the nature of chapel worship. Bishop Trower was not alone in viewing Cuddesdon as evidence that its founder had thrown his weight 'into the side of a new, ornate, symbolical, Ritual'.[91] John W. Burgon (fellow of Oriel College) also cautioned Wilberforce: 'Like Caesar's wife, Cuddesdon must be *unsuspected*. There must be a *studied* inoffensiveness. What is tolerable elsewhere, is intolerable there.'[92] Some, like Hardwick Shute (who had lectured at Cuddesdon), warned that to concede any ground would be seized on by Protestant critics 'as a confession of weakness or worse', but Wilberforce went ahead with his changes.[93]

At the start of the crisis Liddon had agreed to any necessary alterations:

> I shall joyfully acquiesce. ... I fear that you may, from time to time have sacrificed your better judgment to your kind consideration for my individual prejudices. Of course I *do* rejoice in the external expression of religious worship; and believe it to be abstractedly right and desirable. But under the circumstances I would gladly prefer to reduce everything to the minimum of the τὸ πρέπον [what is fitting] rather than again hazard the greater – infinitely greater – interests at stake.[94]

Therefore, following the advice of the archdeacons' report, the silk hangings from the walls of the chapel were replaced by plain oak panelling and the service-book was remodelled,[95] although if it had been Liddon's decision he would rather have met this 'outbreak of silly fanaticism by civil but unyielding resistance'.[96] He acknowledged that these changes dealt only with surface issues:

> That we shall be exposed to such onslaughts hereafter – I can hardly doubt. Golightly's objection lay against a moral & intellectual atmosphere: his attack was directed against the accidental tokens of that atmosphere, because from want of address & penetration, he was unable to analize its characteristic life. ... But he & those who think with him must understand as well as we do, that a religious tone though it may express itself in this or that phrase or ornamentation does not (God forbid) depend upon it; and he will not be satisfied with a Panelled Chapel,

---

[91] Trower to Golightly, 1 February 1858, LPL MS 1810, fo. 48.
[92] Burgon to Wilberforce, 20 March 1858, Bodleian MS Wilberforce d.47, fo. 193.
[93] Hardwick Shute, *Cuddesdon College. By One Who Knows It* (Oxford, 1858), p. 17.
[94] Liddon to Wilberforce, 8 February 1858, Bodleian MS Wilberforce d.40, fos 155-6.
[95] Pott to Wilberforce, 5 April 1858, Bodleian MS Wilberforce c.20, fo. 175. See correspondence on 'Litany of Our Blessed Saviour', May 1858, PHL Liddon House Papers and Bodleian MS Wilberforce d.40, fos 158-63.
[96] *Spectator*, 13 November 1875, pp. 1421-2.

and our revised Service Book.[97]

Naturally, such concessions to Protestants in the diocese only infuriated those in the ritualist vanguard. The *Union* sarcastically jibed:

> One half gallon of whitewash judiciously applied, and the sanctuary might, perhaps, present an appearance even still more in accordance with the 'customary simplicity of our beloved Church'. ... Sad, indeed, was the hour when compromise gained the day at Cuddesdon ... If Cuddesdon College is to be moulded after the type of the ancient Church of Laodicea, the sooner it is shut up the better; or turned into a home for decayed needlewomen; or made a storehouse for apostate priests.[98]

Later in the month it continued to round on what it saw as the weak compromising of the college authorities:

> such pitiable subterfuges as these will only lower the place in the estimation of all people who profess Catholic principles, and never be the means of satisfying the carping Protestants who make Mr Golightly their cats-paw, and who are now glorying over their present success. ... Such an onslaught was to have been looked for; and would that it had been met manfully, resolutely, uncompromisingly, and without any equivocation! ... Compromises in cases of this character are nothing less than deliberate sins – the old story of 'Pilate satisfying the people'.[99]

The annual festival of June 1858 was shorn of its usual ceremony, without cross, flowers, banners, Gregorian music or procession through the village.[100] Again the *Union* lamented: 'Upon the whole there was a visible lack of heartiness and spirit; and the most earnest supporters of the College are distressed at the spirit of compromise which broods over the place'.[101]

Student Idiosyncrasies and Secessions

One supporter of Cuddesdon argued that its distinctive theological position was an asset: 'Individuality of character is indispensable to living success. ... There is plenty of room in the Church of England for many Colleges of every shade of opinion.'[102] Nevertheless the authorities tried to show that the institution lay firmly within the Anglican mainstream. Throughout the troubles, Wilberforce

---

[97] Liddon to Wilberforce, 19 June 1858, Bodleian MS Wilberforce d.40, fos 165-6.
[98] *Union*, 8 April 1859, p. 210.
[99] *Union*, 23 April 1858, p. 258.
[100] Liddon Diary, 1 June 1858, PHL; *Guardian*, 2 June 1858, p. 446.
[101] *Union*, 4 June 1858, p. 362.
[102] *Further Thoughts upon the Diocese of Oxford, with especial reference to Cuddesdon College, in reply to Mr Twopeny. Pamphlet, No.II by an Oxfordshire Idler* (London, 1858), p. 14.

insisted there was 'no party bias' at Cuddesdon.[103] In September 1858 he rejoiced that he could say of his ordinands: 'No party, no pamphlets, no Roman postures or imitations rule my Candidates'.[104]

There was certainly a breadth of opinion amongst the early Cuddesdon students. Some had an abhorrence of the ritualism they found there. Amongst Liddon's private notes on ordinands are verdicts such as: 'Puritan tendencies – great aversion to aesthetics – corrected during his residence here'; 'joined in taking in the Record, and in active opposition to the Spirit of the place'; 'gave greater trouble than any man we have yet had. Organised opposition (i) to choral services (ii) to doctr[ine] of sacraments (iii) to fasting.' On the other hand, some did not think the ritualism at Cuddesdon went far enough. For instance, Liddon noted that one student had '*twice* spoken of the college as a "Protestant" affair' and another was 'Disappointed in Cuddesdon: was looking out for a mediaeval ideal'.[105] This second group did the college most damage with unhelpful publicity.

When the controversy first broke over Cuddesdon in February 1858, Charles Anderson wrote to Wilberforce:

> it is some of those silly aesthetical people that have raised this dust by what may be called trifles in themselves but which become serious evils in times of suspicion, distrust, and malignity – and common sense which is so scarce an article, becomes invaluable in managing an Institution like Cuddesdon, and which has been somewhat wanting in your subordinates, or at least in some of the Students ... I am very sorry that aesthetics were not checked at the outset because I think they have got into too full swing.[106]

Some months later he again warned: 'Depend on it, ritualism after having been greatly neglected is beginning to want a pruning knife'. Curates, Anderson wrote, needed to be taught that helping people in their 'everyday struggles' was of 'tenfold more importance than the cut of a surplice, or bow at the altar or even the medieval inch'.[107] The students' distinctive dress was raising eyebrows in the neighbourhood and even supporters of the college had to encourage the public to look beyond appearances: 'if they wear long coats and eschew shirt-collars, I, who have more collar and less coat, should no more judge a man by

---

[103] Wilberforce to Pott, 1 February 1858, in Pott, *Correspondence*, p. 4.
[104] Wilberforce to Anderson, 18 September 1858, Bodleian MS Wilberforce d.28, fos 155-6. Preaching at the ordination on 19 September, Arthur Purey-Cust exhorted the congregation to be 'free from bitterness and party spirit', and warned of the temptation 'to become men of faction and of party, and to mistake persecution for zeal': A.P. Purey-Cust, *The One True Motive of the Minister of Christ* (Oxford, 1858), pp. 19, 22.
[105] CCA VP1/1, fos 315, 319-21, 327.
[106] Anderson to Wilberforce, 3 February 1858, Bodleian MS Wilberforce d.28, fos 75-6
[107] Anderson to Wilberforce, 28 November 1858, ibid., fos 168-9.

his dress, than a book by its binding, or title'.[108] One ordinand, Francis Burnand (future editor of *Punch*), was surprised by Liddon's unusual appearance. At Cambridge he had been used to clerical dons 'attired in the ordinary black suit and white tie, with college cap and MA gown, and, as a rule, with a fine head of hair and full whiskers', but at Cuddesdon he was greeted by 'an Italian-looking ecclesiastic, glittering-eyed, clean-shaved, and closely-cropped, wearing a white band for a collar, and a black cassock with a broad belt'.[109] To his vice-principal, Wilberforce complained at length about such idiosyncrasies:

> Our men are too *peculiar*, especially some at least of our best men. I shall never consider that we have succeeded until a Cuddesdon man can be known from a non-Cuddesdon man only by his loving more, working more & praying more. I consider it a heavy affliction that they should wear neckclothes of peculiar construction, coats of peculiar cut, whiskers of peculiar dimensions: that they should walk with a peculiar step; carry their heads at a peculiar angle to the body, & read in a peculiar tone. I consider all this as a heavy affliction, first because it implies to me a want of vigour, virility & self-expressing vitality of the religious life in the young men. It shews that they come out too much cut out by a machine & not enough indued with living influences, & secondly because it greatly limits their usefulness, & ours, by the natural prejudice it excites. Then there are things in our actual life I wish changed. 1. The tendency to crowd their walls with pictures of the mater dolorosa &c, their chimney piece with crosses, their studies with saints – all offend me, & all do incalculable injury to the college in the eye of chance visitors. 2. The habit of some of our men of kneeling in a sort of rapt prayer on the steps of the communion table when they cannot be *alone* there: when visitors are coming in & going out & talking around them: such prayers should be 'in the closet' with 'the door shut' – and setting apart their grave danger as I apprehend them to the young men they really force on visitors the feeling of the strict resemblance to what they see in Belgium &c, & never in Church of England churches. ... Pinder has not at Wells; Curt[e]is has not at Lichfield this effect on the pupils. Why should Cuddesdon have it?[110]

Several of these idiosyncrasies could be traced directly back to Liddon. For instance, the bishop lamented, one student 'walks, holds his head, speaks as if he had just practised your modes before a glass. He has not a manly individuality.'[111]

It had never been intended that Liddon should have such a dominant role in determining the direction of the college. Wilberforce had originally hoped to

---

[108] *Counter-Thoughts*, p. 48.

[109] Francis C. Burnand, *Records and Reminiscences Personal and General* (fourth revised edition, London, 1905), p. 184. Wilberforce encouraged Liddon to cut his whiskers: Liddon Diary, 28 March 1858, PHL.

[110] Wilberforce to Liddon, 20 November 1858, Bodleian MS Wilberforce d.40, fos 196-9.

[111] Ibid., fo. 203.

offer close supervision, aiming to see and pray with his ordinands 'day by day'.[112] Yet in the midst of an episcopate of legendary activity this proved impossible to sustain. In 1857, for instance, he spent only 85 days of the year at Cuddesdon Palace.[113] Nor was Pott able to work closely with the students. He lived off site and his attention was absorbed by his responsibilities as vicar of the parish, as a husband with a growing family and as the one in charge of the college's financial and administrative affairs. Pott was absent through illness for Lent and Trinity terms 1857, so Liddon in effect became acting-principal.

Liddon was prepared to admit that to a certain extent Cuddesdon 'reflects the idiosyncrasies of my personal character', but he nonetheless insisted that 'the outline and structure of our system is emphatically that of the Church'.[114] Several were concerned by his heavy influence. Edward King (who began as chaplain in November 1858) warned that the college's problems stemmed from the vice-principal's 'determination, *on principle*, to fit the Cuddesdon shoe on every foot'. Liddon's strong will, he wrote, was a 'prominent evil'.[115] Similarly Burgon remonstrated: 'If he likes to file a notch in a sovereign which belongs to *him, that* is *his* affair: but if he makes a notch in *the die,* & so *coins my* sovereigns with a flaw in them, – then I grow savage.'[116]

The isolated nature of Cuddesdon was partly blamed for creating an environment in which Liddon was able to hold sway. With his eye clearly on the college, Bishop Sumner of Winchester explained why he was opposed to theological education detached from the Universities:

> It is the characteristic merit of an University that its teaching is affected by the peculiarities of no particular school. If the individual colleges have their idiosyncrasies, the harm is counteracted by their mutual relation to the general body, – the common centre round which all revolve, and where they lose their shibboleths, if they have any. The eclectic institution, on the contrary, wears the colours of its single presiding head, sees with his eye, listens with his ear, speaks with his voice, walks with his gait, and in the very path in which he himself has trodden. Under such exclusive influence independent opinion has scarcely power to act, the character is moulded after one uniform type, and the mind of the student, like the habit he wears, is shaped into a distinctive cut and fashion.[117]

Likewise Bishop Tait proclaimed that at the Universities, unlike at theological colleges, 'the very number of teachers must be the best safeguard against the

---

[112] Selwyn, *A Little One*, p. 17.
[113] Ashwell and Wilberforce, *Life of Samuel Wilberforce*, ii. p. 358.
[114] Liddon to Laurence C. Cure, 22 May 1858, CCA VP1/25.
[115] King to Wilberforce, 27 November 1858, Bodleian MS Wilberforce d.40, fo. 78.
[116] Burgon to Wilberforce, 20 March 1858, Bodleian MS Wilberforce d.47, fo. 193.
[117] Charles R. Sumner, *Church Progress. A Charge Delivered to the Clergy of the Diocese of Winchester* (London, 1858), p. 18.

exclusiveness of narrow sects'.[118] In June 1859 Bishop Jackson of Lincoln again warned Cuddesdon students that without the diversity natural in a large University, a small and isolated college had 'a tendency to narrow and exclusive views', particularly if under 'a single presiding mind'. They were thus in danger of suffering from 'that curse of our time, under which Christian charity seems withering away, – party spirit, with its jealousies, and miserable suspicions, and lying accusations, – Satan's triumphant substitute for godly zeal'.[119]

Reflecting on the ritualism promoted at Cuddesdon by Liddon, the *Record* asked:

> What must be the effect on the students but to teach them that God is best honoured by a full amount of hangings, pictures, gilding, and Church ornaments; that the Church of England, even where her liberty on this side is strained to the utmost, is a harsh stepmother, who grudges them these innocent helps to devotion, and that they must step over to the Mother Church, if ever their devotional instincts are to have their full play, and find their natural home?[120]

Although the vice-principal himself was said to be 'as likely to become a "Romanist" as to become a "Mormon"',[121] conversions to the Church of Rome from amongst his students dogged the college. When Pott reassured the archdeacons' commission in February 1858 that no student had seceded to Rome, Golightly retorted: 'Early days yet, Mr Principal. ... You are now sowing; hereafter you will reap.'[122] In fact one student, John Flesher, had already become a Roman Catholic the previous November, a step viewed by Liddon as 'a disaster'.[123] At the same time Arthur Alleyne was in need of counsel, suffering from similar doubts and ready to pull out of his ordination.[124]

In September 1858, J.A. Maude (whose father was a prominent anti-ritualist) became the second Cuddesdon student to secede.[125] Ironically, Maude attributed

---

[118] A.C. Tait, *A Charge Delivered in November, MDCCCLVIII to the Clergy of the Diocese of London, at his Primary Visitation* (London, 1858), p. 28.

[119] John Jackson, *Rest before Labour: The Advantages and Dangers of Theological Colleges* (London, 1859), pp. 13-4.

[120] *Record*, 26 February 1858.

[121] Shute, *Cuddesdon College*, p. 11.

[122] *Record*, 24 December 1858.

[123] CCA VP1/1, fo. 327. See John H. Flesher to Liddon, 21 January – 20 February 1857; Susan Foster to Liddon, 2 January 1857, KCL Liddon Papers; Wilberforce to Liddon, 8 January 1857, PHL Liddon House Papers.

[124] Arthur O. Alleyne – Liddon, 12 October – 19 November 1857, KCL Liddon Papers; Alleyne – Liddon, 30 July 1857 – 11 April 1858, PHL Liddon Papers, box 1/10.

[125] *Record*, 24 and 27 September, 1 and 6 October 1858; Liddon to J. Arthur Maude, 26 September and 9 November 1858, CCA VP1/2, fos 168-71; Maude to Liddon, 7 November 1858, VP1/27; Maude – Liddon, 24 September – 26 December 1858, KCL Liddon Papers; Wilberforce to Francis Maude, nd, Bodleian MS Wilberforce c.20, fo.

his conversion partly to the concessions over ritual made by the college the previous spring: 'I was considerably shaken in my respect for High-Church principles by the mode in which Mr Pott replied to the accusations of Mr Golightly; I felt that his reply was wanting in firmness and clearness, and that it was certainly not calculated to strengthen or restore an already weakened confidence.'[126] At the Brompton Oratory he prayed 'daily for many old Cuddesden [sic] friends, whom I know to have *no sort of business* to be in Anglican orders.'[127]

Pott insisted the secessions of Flesher and Maude had nothing to do with their stay at Cuddesdon, since both were at the college for only a few weeks and had arrived with doubts.[128] However, more students were to follow suit. In December 1858 Francis Burnand was caught with a book entitled *Mariologia* in his room and was asked to leave the next day.[129] He became the third to secede, upon which Liddon reflected: 'How utterly humbled before GOD I feel at this miserable fruit of my ministry!'[130] Arthur Cumberlege was the fourth ordinand to secede in November 1859.[131]

A Change of Staff

In December 1858 the *Record* asked: 'Ought not the College to be closed, or, at all events, the College officers dismissed, and the Institution put upon another footing?'[132] By then this process had already quietly begun. The previous March the chaplain, Albert Barff, had been an early casualty of Golightly's attack upon the college.[133] In October Pott had resigned as principal due to continued ill-health, though he was to remain in post until Easter 1859.[134] A variety of men were considered to replace him, such as E.H. Plumptre (Professor of Pastoral Theology at King's College, London), R.W. Church (Newman's former ally in Oxford, who had recently left Oriel College to be

---

186; Liddon to Wilberforce, 24 June and 29 December 1858, MS Wilberforce d.40, fos 168-9, 220-5.

[126] *Record*, 6 October 1858.

[127] Maude to Liddon, 16 December 1858, KCL Liddon Papers.

[128] *Record*, 27 September and 1 October 1858.

[129] Burnand, *Records and Reminiscences*, pp. 188-93. Liddon Diary, 3-18 December 1858, PHL; Liddon to Wilberforce, 4 December 1858, Bodleian MS Wilberforce d.40, fos 209-10.

[130] CCA VP1/1, fo. 335.

[131] Liddon to Wilberforce, 12 November 1859, Bodleian MS Wilberforce d.40, fos 248-55. Arthur Cumberlege to Liddon, 12 November 1859; Alleyne to Liddon, 11 November 1859; Charles Cumberlege to Liddon, 15 November 1859, KCL Liddon Papers; Charles Cumberlege to Liddon, 21 November 1859, PHL Liddon House Papers.

[132] *Record*, 24 December 1858.

[133] Liddon Diary, 18 February – 10 March 1858, PHL.

[134] Liddon Diary, 23 October and 2 November 1858, PHL.

rector of Whatley in Somerset), Frederick Meyrick (fellow of Trinity College, Oxford), Arthur Purey-Cust (a rural dean) and Burgon.[135] Liddon wanted Robert Milman (vicar of Lambourn and a future Bishop of Calcutta) as someone with similar views to his own, but Wilberforce felt strongly that the new principal needed to counter-balance his vice-principal. He explained:

> I do not feel that our Theological standing place is *identical*. ... You have not *intended* to teach beyond our standing point and I have always felt that *un*intentional deviations whether in lecture, conversation, example or ritual were modified & as I should of course say corrected by Pott's connection with the College as Principal. ... if I now appoint a Principal who exactly represents *your* standing point the colour & character of the College must be altered and the alteration will be a removing of it further from what appears to me to be the most exact line of Church of England life.[136]

King advised Wilberforce: 'there should be a Principal whom the students would regard as their head – one who would clearly put the Vice Principal in his right place – which is the *second*.'[137] The bishop hoped that the new man would be able 'to correct our evils, to counter act our peculiarities, & to widen our sympathies',[138] but Liddon wanted as little change as possible:

> We cannot afford, my dear Lord, to make any changes in our System however trivial, for a long time to come. Our past concessions have been invariably interpreted, not as a charitable deference to prejudice, but as a confession of weakness or as a confession of error. ... There is in fact no choice *now* between a complete Revolution and the most Rigid Conservatism.[139]

As Pott later reflected: 'Liddon was not a man ready in any way to compromise his own judgment, or to give way to clamour. His error lay rather in the other direction.'[140]

First Burgon was offered the principalship, as someone who might satisfy both Liddon and old-fashioned Protestants like Golightly. Yet Liddon was far from confident that they could work together:

> I cannot doubt that if he came here he would turn things upside down. Perhaps such a change may be thought well. But I could not be a party to it. I could not bear to be in a state of chronic visitation & ill-concealed opposition of thought and

---

[135] For discussion between Liddon and Wilberforce of various candidates, see Bodleian MS Wilberforce d.40, fos 176-219.
[136] Wilberforce to Liddon, 20 November 1858, ibid., fos 194-5.
[137] King to Wilberforce, 27 November 1858, ibid., fos 78-9.
[138] Wilberforce to Liddon, 20 November 1858, ibid., fo. 199.
[139] Liddon to Wilberforce, 24 November 1858, ibid., fos 192-3.
[140] Johnston, *Life of Liddon*, p. 33.

action towards the man whom I ought to try by God's grace to second and obey.[141]

Burgon for his part refused to take the post unless Liddon was removed, and he would insist on radically transforming Cuddesdon: 'I should have, singlehanded, to revolutionize, – calmly and gently, but with the whole determination of my nature to revolutionize – *the entire system of the College*, as well as *to create a fresh atmosphere within it*'.[142] In the end Burgon turned down the offer, primarily because of financial considerations.[143] Instead, in late December 1858, Henry H. Swinny (vicar of Wargrave) was appointed principal. Golightly thought him 'a Protestant, and a good and pious man',[144] while Wilberforce hoped his influence would 'prevent idiosyncrasies of manner &c being acquired by our men'.[145] Not surprisingly, Swinny acknowledged that he and Liddon 'would never be in harmony'.[146]

The change of principal brought into question Liddon's own position at the college. On several occasions during 1858 he had offered his resignation and now Wilberforce began to take the suggestion more seriously.[147] The bishop became increasingly aware of the extent of their disagreement and realised that they were working to opposing agendas:

> I want to turn out the Established English clergyman with a more awakened heart, quickened self-devotion & better furnished Theology: you want to get *more* of a reformed Seminary Priest. I believe that resemblance to that type will spoil our men's usefulness & ruin us.[148]

According to Burgon, it was 'as reasonable to expect that a chronometer could keep time while half the mechanism was defective' as to hope Cuddesdon College could function effectively with Liddon on the staff. He advised Wilberforce:

> if you wish to restore health in that quarter, you must employ, *not* healing plaster, but the knife: & you must cut deep: & you must cut *now*; – or the mischief will go too far. It will indeed! You are chivalrous, & unwilling to part with Liddon. ... But he has had his trial. He has proved his method, & it has failed *egregiously*. Amiable, & excellent, learned as he is, he has been the ruin of the College. Is *he*

---

[141] Liddon to Wilberforce, 19 November 1858, Bodleian MS Wilberforce d.40, fo. 180.
[142] Burgon to Wilberforce, 9 December 1858, Bodleian MS Wilberforce d.47, fo. 197.
[143] Liddon Diary, 10-11 December 1858, PHL.
[144] Golightly, *Position of Samuel Wilberforce*, p. 19.
[145] Wilberforce to Liddon, 20 November 1858, Bodleian MS Wilberforce d.40, fo. 200.
[146] Swinny to Liddon, 11 February 1859, KCL Liddon Papers.
[147] Liddon to Wilberforce, 8 February, 18-19 November, 29 December 1858, Bodleian MS Wilberforce d.40, fos 156, 179, 183, 224. Liddon Diary, 6 November 1858, PHL.
[148] Wilberforce to Liddon, 20 November 1858, Bodleian MS Wilberforce d.40, fo. 203.

then to be alone considered? – to the disadvantage of yourself – the men – the neighbourhood – the diocese – the Church!¹⁴⁹

Matters came to a head at Christmas 1858 when Edward Elton (vicar of neighbouring Wheatley) warned Wilberforce that he had heard it said at the Brompton Oratory 'that if any one went to Cuddesdon with the *slightest* Roman tendency, under the V.P. he would be sure to go to Rome'.¹⁵⁰ As a result the bishop laid down new rules concerning celebration of holy communion, books of devotion and auricular confession.¹⁵¹ He asked Liddon not to teach his personal views on eucharistic consecration, which put the vice-principal in 'a most painful dilemma – I must be either insincere or disobedient.'¹⁵² These scruples came as a revelation to Wilberforce who had assumed Liddon never publicly went beyond his own teaching.¹⁵³ He further discovered that Liddon had been giving Pusey's adaptations of Roman Catholic books of devotion to students, despite his express disapproval.¹⁵⁴

Liddon was depressed: 'The Bishop is yielding everything to its enemies. He clearly *suspects* me: and Pott who is weak sides with the assailants – or almost so.'¹⁵⁵ Yet Butler encouraged him that Wilberforce must be taught 'that some of us believe certain things too deeply ... to give them up for the sake of ἀρέσκεια [gaining favour].'¹⁵⁶ He lamented that there seemed to be 'a resolute determination to prevent a higher life than "the parsonage & pony-carriage" from taking root in the Church of England.'¹⁵⁷ Meanwhile Wilberforce was also using Butler as a confidant:

> *You* at Wantage have as much right to teach your *shade* of the common teaching & be considered a loyal son of the Church as I have mine here: & I with no compromise can *as Bishop* wholly support & maintain you – maintaining my own proper claims to *my own* views ... But when I come to the College here the case is different – *I* am judged of in my secret intention for the Diocese by the *exact* Shade imparted here to the men sent out. ... if from Cuddesdon go out as the *best* men, men of the *most* sacerdotal type it cannot it seems to me but happen that I am counted for a deceiver, professing one thing in my own words & conduct to the Diocese & then sending out from my own training College men of a different Shade ...¹⁵⁸

---

¹⁴⁹ Burgon to Wilberforce, 9 December 1858, Bodleian MS Wilberforce d.47, fo. 202.
¹⁵⁰ Elton to Wilberforce, 25 December 1858, PHL Liddon Papers, box 2/13.
¹⁵¹ 'Rules for next Term', 27 December 1858, ibid..
¹⁵² Liddon to Wilberforce, 7 January 1859, Bodleian MS Wilberforce d.40, fo. 230.
¹⁵³ Wilberforce to Liddon, 15 January 1859, PHL Liddon Papers, box 2/13.
¹⁵⁴ Wilberforce to Butler, 5 February 1859, Bodleian MS Wilberforce d.33, fo. 81.
¹⁵⁵ Liddon Diary, 1 January 1859, PHL.
¹⁵⁶ Butler to Liddon, 8 January 1859, PHL Liddon Papers, box 2/13.
¹⁵⁷ Butler to Liddon, 10 January 1859, KCL Liddon Papers.
¹⁵⁸ Wilberforce to Butler, 22 January 1859, Bodleian MS Wilberforce d.33, fos 75-6.

Since Liddon would not change, Wilberforce gradually realised that the only way to save his college and his own reputation was to sacrifice his young associate:

> there is in him a strength of Will – an ardour – a restlessness a dominant imagination which makes him unable to give to the young men any tone save exactly his own tone. Under this conviction I have from my hearing of this diversity of ritual been drifting with a really heart tearing pain to the conviction that I *must* accept *his* tendered resignation to act myself with honesty to the Diocese.[159]

He wrote again to Butler a few days later:

> Doctrinally L. might hold all he holds & work happily with me. It is that He is fit only to be absolute, great as is his love & tenderness & forbearance, he *must* re-impress his *exact* self ... I always hoped that I could have influenced L. enough to keep down the 'tinting' process to such a pitch that I could quite honestly retain him & that a few years hence the difficulty would be mellowed out – I come to the opposite conclusion with a torn heart.[160]

At the end of January 1859, almost a year to the day since Golightly's first letter concerning the charges in the *Quarterly Review*, Wilberforce finally accepted his vice-principal's resignation.[161] He lamented to Liddon: 'nothing can more grieve me than that we should part at this time when it will seem like a triumph to Golightly & Co., & yet what can I do?'[162] Meanwhile Burgon encouraged him: 'Liddon's resignation, believe me, *was inevitable*. I mean, the days of your College were numbered else.'[163] Liddon continued in post until Easter and was replaced by W.H. Davey, previously vice-principal of Chichester Theological College. Liddon's friends saw his departure as a major set back for the college:

> the Bishop has made a false move ... under its new trammels the College will take the position of a High Church Seminary of a very low standard, and what can well be worse than that.[164]

> Perhaps England is not yet ripe for the old Cuddesdon teaching and practice.[165]

> Cuddesdon College can never prosper now![166]

---

[159] Ibid., fo. 77.
[160] Wilberforce to Butler, 26 January 1859, ibid., fos 79-80.
[161] Liddon to Wilberforce, 29 January 1859, Bodleian MS Wilberforce d.40, fos 244-5.
[162] Wilberforce to Liddon, 26 January 1859, PHL Liddon Papers, box 2/13.
[163] Burgon to Wilberforce, 11 February 1859, Bodleian MS Wilberforce d.47, fo. 204.
[164] Henry Lanphier to Liddon, 19 February 1859, KCL Liddon Papers.
[165] Albert Barff to Liddon, 10 February 1859, KCL Liddon Papers.

[Cuddesdon] will sink to the same level as Wells or Chichester ...[167]

Looking at the quarter from whence the pressure has come which has produced this change, the prospect of Religion in England looks gloomy indeed.[168]

Liddon concluded: 'My first great attempt at work in life has failed. This no doubt is good for my character.'[169]

In November 1858, due to the constant negative publicity surrounding Cuddesdon, Wilberforce had feared 'the falling off of all save *extreme* men'.[170] In a vain attempt to prevent this, Liddon had been sacrificed. Yet by May 1860 the *Union* was lamenting that the staff changes had 'utterly ruined' the college:

Of old, there were always more than *twenty students*: now (after every attempt to hook them in has been made and failed) there are but *seven*! And the very truth is that the polite dismissal of the very man, Mr Liddon, who stamped an impress upon Cuddesdon College, and made it a success, has turned out a more fatal mistake and a greater loss than was ever anticipated. Many enrolled themselves as *alumni* for the single and simple privilege of sitting at his feet; for he is verily a Tractarian 'Gamaliel'. ... When, as we are credibly informed, fourteen sets of chambers are vacant and dusty in his lordship's pet institution, and no fresh names are on the books for next term, the simple and very practical consideration of £.s.d. may effectually prove to him that the reformation at Cuddesdon College – intended to hoodwink the High and Dry Anglicans and keep quiet the troublesome Puritans – was a great and grievous mistake, and that the only people who really gained by the alteration were Messrs. Litton and Golightly, who did so well and effectively the dirty work of their party – the lowest type of miscalled Evangelicals.[171]

With Liddon at the helm, Wilberforce's institution would probably have sunk without trace, a brief but failed experiment in theological education. Without Liddon it managed to stay afloat, though only just. Despite the noisy campaign of the college's Protestant critics it had kept its doors open and, once out of the spotlight, slowly but surely began to attract students again. Cuddesdon College had survived its first and sternest test. Yet Golightly was not finished, and twenty years later he was to return for a second damaging assault upon the institution.

---

[166] Maria E. Austis, 11 February 1859, KCL Liddon Papers.
[167] Verney C.B. Cave to Liddon, 10 February 1859, KCL Liddon Papers.
[168] John H. Burgess to Liddon, 9 February 1859, KCL Liddon Papers.
[169] Liddon Diary, 9 February 1859, PHL.
[170] Wilberforce to Liddon, 20 November 1858, Bodleian MS Wilberforce d.40, fo. 202.
[171] *Union*, 25 May 1860, pp. 321-2.

The Lavington Case

Samuel Wilberforce was ruler of the Oxford diocese, but he also had some responsibility for the small parish of Lavington, a village in Sussex, in the diocese of Chichester. It was a responsibility not due to his ecclesiastical office but to his familial ties, a connection which began in 1828 when he married one of the daughters of John Sargent, the well-known rector of Lavington.[172] Sargent was a leading evangelical minister, friend of Charles Simeon in Cambridge, biographer of the missionary hero Henry Martyn, and viewed by some as a model country parson (a sort of evangelical equivalent to John Keble).[173] Sargent himself had married a cousin of William Wilberforce and the link between the two families was further strengthened in 1834 when Henry Wilberforce married another of the Sargent sisters. Via his wife, Samuel Wilberforce inherited the advowson of Lavington – the legal right to present a minister to the vacant benefice.

A third Sargent sister married Henry Manning, who had gone to Lavington in January 1833 as curate to her father. Only a few months after arriving in the village, he was promoted to rector upon John Sargent's sudden death. Soon Manning's influence was felt far beyond the confines of his parish, as he rose to prominence in the diocese of Chichester and began to attract national attention. Manning's sympathy with the Tractarian movement became increasingly obvious, which provoked hostility in Sussex and led Charles Golightly to fire a few pot-shots at him from Oxford, in the press and in private. For example, when Manning was surprisingly appointed Archdeacon of Chichester in December 1840, Golightly wrote to warn the Bishop of Chichester that his teaching was 'most injurious to true religion'.[174] On another occasion he called Manning 'one of the most subtle and dangerous characters of the day',[175] and in return the archdeacon compared Golightly to the devil.[176] When Manning finally seceded to the Church of Rome in April 1851, Bishop Wilberforce had his first opportunity to make an appointment to the family living at Lavington. To replace his brother-in-law he chose Richard Randall, son of James Randall (Wilberforce's Archdeacon of Berkshire from 1855). Yet Golightly's interest in affairs at this small Sussex parish did not end with Manning's departure and he was soon on the tail of the new rector. It also gave him another chance to strike a blow at Bishop Wilberforce.

A fresh wave of trouble began in November 1856 when Richard Randall appointed a young graduate of Oriel College, Edward Randall (no relation), as

---

[172] On the Sargent-Wilberforce connection with Lavington, see Anna M. Wilberforce, *Lavington: The History of a Sussex Family* (np, 1919).

[173] For Wilberforce's memoir of his father-in-law, see Samuel Wilberforce (ed.), *Journals and Letters of the Rev. Henry Martyn* (2 vols, London, 1837), i. pp. 1-24.

[174] Golightly to Shuttleworth, 29 December 1840, LPL MS 1809, fos 49-50.

[175] Golightly to Kaye, 24 May 1844, LRO Cor. B5/1/22.

[176] Golightly, *Letter to the Dean of Ripon*, p. 18.

his curate. Almost immediately disagreements over ritual became apparent between the two men. For instance, on one occasion when the curate was presiding at holy communion, the rector interrupted the service to move him bodily from the table's north end to face east. Richard Randall used the mixed chalice, bowed before the consecrated elements, elevated the chalice, crossed himself, and made the sign of the cross on the water at baptism. He recommended his curate read devotional manuals which advocated the doctrine of the real presence, and was said to have taught the beatitude, 'Blessed is the child that believes that the body and blood of Christ is upon the altar, though he does not see it.' A hymn book used in Lavington church contained a suspect verse translated from Thomas Aquinas' *Pangue lingua*:

> Word made flesh! Thy own word maketh
> Very bread thy flesh to be;
> Wine the blood of Christ becometh,
> What no human eye can see;
> Yet, to every guileless spirit,
> Faith will teach the mystery.

Matters came to a head in December 1857 when Edward Randall claimed to have discovered on catechising the children of the local school that they had been taught by the rector that there were seven sacraments and that 'the Mass' was another name for holy communion. He got hold of an incriminating paper which Richard Randall had given to the school-master, bearing a close resemblance to the teaching on the seven sacraments of the medieval theologian, Peter Dens.[177]

In February 1858, Edward Randall finally complained about the practices in Lavington to Bishop Gilbert of Chichester. In earlier days, Gilbert had been a severe critic of the Tractarians in Oxford, during his time as Principal of Brasenose College and Vice-Chancellor of the University. In the early 1840s he had been a keen encourager of Golightly's anti-Tractarian campaigns. Yet now, almost twenty years later, the situation had changed and Gilbert was desperate to ensure that ritualist controversies in his diocese did not escalate out of control. Edward Randall had informed not just his bishop but also Lord

---

[177] *The Lavington Case. Affidavits, (Sworn, and filed in the Court of Queen's Bench), of the Rev. Edward Randall, MA, late Curate of Lavington, of Mr H.B. Harding, Late Choir Master, and of Mr H.L. Buck, with comments thereon* (Brighton, 1859). Coverage in the *National Standard* was published as *A Statement Submitted to the Clergy and Laity of the Diocese of Chichester, respecting Romish Doctrines and Practices in the Parish of Lavington, Sussex. By an English Churchman* (London, 1858). See also Edward Randall in *Brighton Gazette*, 11 August 1859; Charles P. Golightly, *Facts and Documents shewing the Alarming State of the Diocese of Oxford. By a Senior Clergyman of the Diocese* (London, 1859), pp. 25-8. On devotional reading, see R.W. Randall to Liddon, 21 December 1857, KCL Liddon Papers.

Shaftesbury, William Selwyn (Lady Margaret Professor of Divinity at Cambridge and an old friend of Golightly from Eton days[178]) and the *Times*, so Gilbert was horrified that Lavington parish might suddenly be splashed over the newspapers, as was then happening to Cuddesdon College. He rebuked the curate for behaving in a 'precipitate and unjustifiable, as well as unecclesiastical and insubordinate way' and insisted that the *Times* be muzzled. Instead he investigated the charges privately, declaring himself satisfied that Richard Randall was not guilty of 'the least inclination on his part towards Rome, and of a design to insinuate her teaching among the children.'[179] He advised the curate to leave Lavington as soon as possible, threatening to revoke his licence, and went so far as to suggest he was 'insane'.[180] Richard Randall was dismayed to hear about the accusations his curate was making and reprimanded him for 'these slanderous words which you are recklessly throwing about'.[181] Meanwhile, Bishop Wilberforce and Archdeacon Randall both cancelled their testimonials for Edward Randall, chastising him for his 'disgraceful conduct' and 'most unhandsome behaviour'.[182]

In March, Edward Randall happened to be in Oxford to receive his MA degree, and it was the turn of his college superiors to apply the pressure. At Wilberforce's prompting, he was summoned by John Burgon (fellow of Oriel) who read him the riot act. Burgon reported the remarkable interview to the rector of Lavington:

> In the course of a very long conversation, I took occasion to apply to his conduct the epithets 'treacherous', 'base', and 'ungrateful'. I showed him that he had played the part of a viper towards those who had cherished him, that unbounded impudence and inordinate conceit had characterized his conduct, and much beside. Far, far more did I tell him than I can repeat. He has never, I think, been so spoken to before. My object was to get him to resign his curacy, and write a letter of apology to you and the Bishop of Oxford. ... I did not fail to point out to him the great wickedness of thus going about casting fire-brands in every direction. A man with a spark of modesty would have been crushed with the bitter taunts I flung in his teeth – armed as I was with his college antecedents, and many other awkward reminiscences. I taunted him too with his ignorance, and unfitness to play the censor of anybody.

When Burgon heard that the young man intended to consult a lawyer, he sent for him again:

---

[178] Golightly's Eton Journal (1822-23), Stack MS 6a.
[179] Gilbert to Edward Randall, 24 February 1858, in *Lavington Case*, pp. 17-8.
[180] Gilbert to Edward Randall, 19, 22, 30 and 31 March 1858, in *Lavington Case*, pp. 19-22; Gilbert to R.W. Randall, 7 May 1858, in J.F. Briscoe and H.F.B. Mackay, *A Tractarian at Work: A Memoir of Dean Randall* (London, 1932), p. 107.
[181] Quoted in Briscoe and Mackay, *Tractarian at Work*, p. 99.
[182] Wilberforce to Edward Randall and James Randall to Edward Randall, 10 March 1858, in *Lavington Case*, pp. 18-9.

> His conduct, I explained to him, was worse and worse. Some evil spirit, I said, is surely urging you on. You labour under some horrid delusion, and display yourself in the light of a vindictive mischief-maker. ... you are setting yourself up like one possessed, and pursuing a course which can be productive of good to no one, of mischief to many, and of ruin to yourself.[183]

Burgon added, according to one report, that if Randall attempted to take the affair to court 'the Bishop of OXFORD would cut him up root and branch, and that he himself would leave him no rest for the sole of his foot in England!'[184] It was rumoured that the authorities offered him work in Australia to get him out of the way. As was later pointed out, there was an impression of ranks being closed by the influential powers in league against the young curate:

> He has subtle and influential enemies to deal with. The party whose proceedings he has exposed are unscrupulous and malignant. To blacken character, to impugn the veracity of brethren, to tamper with witnesses, to conceal and garble facts, to dissemble, and to trifle with truth, are arts with which Tractarianism is, unhappily, too familiar; and we do not wonder that a young man, whose ministerial prospects are at stake, should shrink from being exposed to them.[185]

Nevertheless, Edward Randall was not to be intimidated. While in Oxford he sought help from Charles Golightly, whom he certainly knew by reputation if not personally. With Golightly as an ally he might do real damage to the Bishops of Oxford and Chichester. Burgon informed Richard Randall:

> It is quite plain that G., smarting under the result of the Cuddesdon business, and always on the look-out for troubled water, is the instigating person here. ... I do not think it will come to anything, for E.R. certainly has no legal case. But there can be no doubt whatever that a great deal of mischief will be done by the gossip of that inveterate mischief-maker, Golightly. I would gladly call on him, for we are on very amicable terms – and I really believe him to be, in his peculiar way, a good man – but I should not be able to do you any good, in the present state of my information.[186]

Golightly accompanied Edward Randall to London to present the affairs at Lavington to the committee of the Church Protestant Defence Society, which had been established in 1853 under the presidency of Lord Shaftesbury to fight against ritualism in the Church of England. The Society, however, declined to

---

[183] Burgon to R.W. Randall, 16 March 1858, in Briscoe and Mackay, *Tractarian at Work*, pp. 101-2.

[184] *National Standard*, 9 October 1858, p. 133. Golightly hinted at this interview in *Facts and Documents*, p. 30. For Burgon's denials, see *Guardian*, 23 February 1859, p. 166.

[185] *National Standard*, 28 August 1858, p. 634.

[186] Burgon to R.W. Randall, 16 March 1858, in Briscoe and Mackay, *Tractarian at Work*, pp. 102-3.

take the case further without corroboration of the curate's version of events.[187]

Only in August 1858 did the affair become public when (possibly at Golightly's prompting) the newly-founded *National Standard* first broke the story. Just as Bishop Wilberforce had set up a commission to investigate the charges against Cuddesdon College, the newspaper appealed for Bishop Gilbert to set up a formal commission to investigate the charges surrounding Lavington.[188] It thought Richard Randall should be immediately dismissed from the Church of England, since 'It is perfectly evident that the present Rector of Lavington has no more business in the English Church than the late one.'[189] The affair attracted the attention of the Brighton Protestant Association, where Wilberforce was described as 'the most mischievous man in England.'[190] Henry Harding (late choir-master at Lavington) and William Marigold (school-master at Lavington), who both resigned due to ritualism in the parish, wrote to the newspapers in support of the version of events given by Edward Randall.[191] It was said that, in retribution, Bishops Gilbert and Wilberforce then tried to have Harding dismissed from his new post as organist and choir-master in nearby Midhurst.[192]

The most persuasive piece of evidence against Richard Randall was his written paper on the seven sacraments for the children of Lavington school. The rector claimed it was intended only to warn them against error, to show the distinction between the doctrine of the Church of England and the Church of Rome.[193] Marigold insisted, however, that Randall had meant it to be taught as it stood.[194] In reproof of the rector's naivety, assuming he had merely been misconstrued, Gilbert warned:

> You cannot make skilful controversialists of plain English labourers, nor of their

---

[187] For correspondence between the Church Protestant Defence Society and Bishop Gilbert, see *Record*, 7 March 1859. See also 'MA Oxon' (Golightly) in *National Standard*, 18 September 1858, p. 65; Wilbraham Taylor (secretary of the CPDS) in *National Standard*, 18 June 1859, pp. 592-3.

[188] *National Standard*, 28 August 1858, p. 634; 18 September 1858, p. 61.

[189] *National Standard*, 9 October 1858, p. 133. For similar views, see *Brighton Gazette*, 4 November 1858.

[190] *Brighton Gazette*, 30 September 1858.

[191] *Brighton Gazette*, 23 September 1858; *National Standard*, 23 October 1858, pp. 184-5.

[192] *Brighton Gazette*, 25 November, 2, 9, 16 and 23 December 1858. For defence of the evangelical credentials of W.G. Bayley, rector of Midhurst, see *Record*, 17 and 22 December 1858. For more letters by Harding, see *National Standard*, 21 May 1859, pp. 497-8; 9 July 1859, p. 41.

[193] *Brighton Gazette*, 16 September 1858; R.W. Randall to Gilbert, 8 December 1858 in *Teaching and Practices in the Parish of Lavington. A Correspondence between the Rector and the Lord Bishop of Chichester* (Oxford, 1859), p. 4.

[194] *National Standard*, 23 October 1858, pp. 184-5.

children. They do not understand what you are about. You puzzle them, and however reluctant you may be to admit the fact, you excite suspicions where you intended only to benefit, and at the cost of much labour you impede your own usefulness.[195]

The *Record*, however, thought Randall and his episcopal allies guilty of misrepresentation, and declared: 'a charge of open, unscrupulous, and unblushing falsehood, must lie at the door of Mr R. RANDALL ... a tissue of falsehood, deliberate and prepared.'[196] It maintained:

the most melancholy feature of this English semi-Romanism is not so much the perversion of its doctrinal views as the moral obliquity which invariably attends its practices. We look for common truth and honesty – a decent regard to the moral virtues – in Jew, Turk, or infidel; but it is in vain to look for them in the disciples of Tractarianism. The grand doctrine of that apostate Church to which in spirit they are joined – that the foulest lie may be resorted to for the advancement of truth – seems to have sunk already into their very bone and marrow.[197]

In the midst of such accusations, Bishop Wilberforce encouraged his protégé in Lavington: 'You must bear up. You are true to the church of England and truth must prevail. Lying lips are but for a moment.' As with Liddon's difficulties at Cuddesdon College, the bishop concluded that it was partly Randall's idiosyncrasies in dress and manner which attracted unhelpful attention: 'You will soon live this down, if you will not (1) dress peculiarly, (2) read nothing but Romish books, (3) try in preaching, manner, etc., to be less priestly and more like others'.[198] Though Wilberforce publicly defended Randall, he was privately concerned by some of his practices, as he later wrote:

Remember how down to the least things (the *Glorias*) you have always maintained your view against mine, and then remember that when the storm broke on you, I gave no hint of all this, but defended you and mainly got your own bishop to defend you, and have borne all the brunt really of 'the Lavington case'. ... I could not justify your acts. I had publicly stated over and over that the acts did not mean Romanizing in you ... all I could do was either (1) to justify your acts or (2) say (the truth) that I had always disapproved them and had no jurisdiction over you ...[199]

---

[195] Gilbert to R.W. Randall, 23 December 1858, in *Teaching and Practices*, p. 8.
[196] *Record*, 10 November 1858.
[197] *Record*, 29 October 1858.
[198] Wilberforce to R.W. Randall, 6 November 1858, in Briscoe and Mackay, *Tractarian at Work*, p. 110.
[199] Ibid., p. 118. For Wilberforce's denial that Randall was under his control, see *An Impartial Account of the Recent Agitation in the Diocese of Oxford with the Addresses to the Bishop, and His Lordship's Replies* (London, 1859), p. 8.

Although Lavington was formally under the jurisdiction of Bishop Gilbert, he was seen by some as merely a puppet of Bishop Wilberforce. The Cuddesdon crisis had done considerable damage to Wilberforce's reputation and the troubles at Lavington added fuel to the fire. His personal connection with the parish and his patronage of Richard Randall was well known, so he was tarred with the same brush. Indeed, he was forced to deny that he believed there were seven sacraments.[200] Burgon insisted that Randall therefore be especially careful:

> Can it be wise or right, in these days of rebuke and suspicion, at Lavington of all places, and connected with the Bishop of Oxford as you are, of all persons, Can it be wise or right to do or say anything which shall at all appear like coquetting with the impurities of Romish Doctrine? ... Then pray consider further, how great an injury you may do to the Bishop of Oxford, your friend and patron, by an act of indiscretion which in any of your neighbours might be unproductive of evil. If this scandal spreads, it is he, not you, whose name gives zest to the accusation. ... Now the very good he is doing to the whole Church may be marred or retarded by the indiscretions and errors of his known friends. Such considerations alone should make you doubly watchful.[201]

Prosecution

When the Lavington choir-master and school-master came forward to support the charges of their curate against their rector, the Church Protestant Defence Society decided it was time to act. They petitioned Gilbert to order a public inquiry, declaring that this was not just a matter of local concern, but one 'in which the interests of the whole Church of England are bound up'.[202] The bishop, however, continued to resist all such requests, thus betraying according to the *Record* 'a spirit of partisanship wholly inconsistent with the right exercise of Episcopal functions.'[203] The *Christian Observer* saw the influence of Wilberforce in this shunning of publicity: 'there was another party behind the scenes, by whom the bishop [Gilbert] suffered himself to be guided, who was well aware that the laws ecclesiastical had been violated by the rector, and had his own reasons for dreading the exposure of the fact.'[204] Likewise the *National Standard* wrote of Gilbert:

> This feeble prelate will not ... act without the counsel and advice of his more expert and subtle brother the Bishop of OXFORD and Squire of LAVINGTON.

---

[200] *Record*, 7, 10, 14, 19 and 21 January 1859.
[201] Burgon to R.W. Randall, 16 March 1858, in Briscoe and Mackay, *Tractarian at Work*, pp. 103-4.
[202] *Record*, 7 March 1859.
[203] *Record*, 8 June 1859.
[204] 'The Lavington Case', *Christian Observer* (September 1859), p. 612.

They have gone together hitherto in this disgraceful business, and done all that was in their power to screen the offender. Doubtless, they will yet strain every nerve to stifle a judicial investigation if they can.[205]

At Gilbert's persistent refusal to issue a commission, Golightly decided to take the matter to court, declining the offer of the Church Protestant Defence Society to pay his legal expenses.[206] In February 1859 he announced his intention to seek a *mandamus*, compelling the bishop to issue a commission of inquiry under the 1840 Church Discipline Act. He was backed by sixty-five of the local inhabitants of Lavington and nearby Graffham who in April petitioned Gilbert to investigate the charges.[207] However, Golightly was disappointed by the lack of support he received from the Sussex clergy, none of whom publicly stood alongside him.[208]

The local rural deans and the Archdeacon of Chichester (Gilbert's old friend from Brasenose College days, James Garbett, formerly Oxford's Professor of Poetry) rallied around their bishop. They issued a vote of confidence, affirming their 'profound conviction that the principles of our Reformed Church are safe in your hands' and observing that if a member of one diocese (such as Golightly) had the right to interfere in another diocese it would lead to 'capricious tyranny, subversive of all ecclesiastical order, and threatening endless confusion in the Church.'[209] Gilbert insisted that he had already investigated the charges against Randall back in February 1858, so there was no point in a commission of inquiry. As a sop to his Protestant critics he now commanded that Lavington's suspect hymnal be given up, which Randall resisted, but Wilberforce advised that submission was the wisest course:

> My dear friend, you are still too fond of sticking to your own liking. You ought to remember that a Commission will mean infinite triumph for Golightly, a deep blow to the Church, a wound to me, and that only by enabling your Bishop to say, 'he has yielded to my Godly Judgement', can he meet the *Mandamus*. Yet it is not too late. You have been obstinate. Go straight over to that really kind old man and put all in his hands by a son's submission.[210]

The *Examiner* proclaimed: 'We shall see whether the English public will be content with a bishop's parlour for a court of justice, and consider a chat over the fender, or perhaps over the bottle, a decent and effective substitute for

---

[205] *National Standard*, 12 February 1859, p. 158.
[206] *National Standard*, 18 June 1859, pp. 592-3.
[207] For the petition and the bishop's reply, see *National Standard*, 23 April and 21 May 1859, pp. 398, 497. See Briscoe and Mackay, *Tractarian at Work*, pp. 115-6; R.W. Randall to W. Randall, 15 April 1859, PHL RAN 3/414.
[208] T.A. Holland to Golightly, 25 November 1861, LPL MS 1807, fos 101-4.
[209] *English Churchman*, 7 July 1859, p. 646. See *Record*, 13 July 1859.
[210] Briscoe and Mackay, *Tractarian at Work*, p. 115.

judicial investigation.'[211]

By taking the matter to court, Golightly was seen by some as transforming the Lavington case from a dispute amongst individuals into a party affair, although perhaps his refusal of the financial support of the Church Protestant Defence Society was an attempt to maintain his non-party credentials. He was described as the representative of 'that restless party who claim to monopolise the orthodoxy of the Church and see nothing tolerable except their own shibboleth',[212] and as promoting the case 'in the name of the Evangelical party'.[213] The *Morning Post* stated:

> the proceedings initiated by Mr GOLIGHTLY are obviously for no earthly purpose but that of carrying into the diocese of Chichester an agitation similar to that which has so signally failed in the diocese of Oxford. ... whether we consider the trumpery nature of the suit, the insufficient legal grounds on which it proceeds, or the probable effect of a continual resort to the civil courts to compel ecclesiastical processes in aid of party movements – we see enough to pronounce this second movement of Mr GOLIGHTLY as a great scandal to him and his profession.[214]

The *Clerical Journal* thought that Golightly 'far exceeds his province, and that the *odium theologicum* in his heart makes him forget both his duty to his superiors and to the Church of which he is a priest ... there appears to be egregious conceit and arrogant presumption in his pertinacious pugnacity.'[215] He was called a 'fussy' man of 'restless spirit' who was 'determined to pursue the vocation of ecclesiastical agitator'.[216]

The Lavington case went to court, before the Queen's Bench, in June 1859. Judge Wightman (a member of Robert Liddell's 'Tractarian' congregation at St Paul's, Knightsbridge[217]) concluded that under the Church Discipline Act a bishop had discretion whether or not to issue a commission of inquiry and was not bound to do so. Judge Hill (a member of J.W. Reeve's 'evangelical' congregation at Portman Chapel, Marylebone) was not convinced a bishop had discretion under the Act, but concluded that since Golightly had no connection with Lavington parish or Chichester diocese he was not an aggrieved party and so could not bring the suit. The case was therefore dismissed, with costs. Judges Campbell and Erle, who had heard the case but been promoted to other spheres before judgment was given, were said to concur in the result; but complaint was made that neither Wightman nor Hill had remained in court to

---

[211] *Examiner*, 18 June 1859, p. 387.
[212] *Morning Post*, 15 June 1859.
[213] *Morning Post*, 4 July 1859.
[214] *Morning Post*, 15 June 1859.
[215] *Clerical Journal*, 22 June 1859, p. 267.
[216] *Morning Post*, 15 June 1859.
[217] *Record*, 11 July 1859.

hear the case argued in full.[218] There were calls for a new Church Discipline Bill to clarify the law.[219]

The *Morning Post* greeted the judgment as 'a great gain to the peace of the Church' because it would 'check the haste which violent party men have too often shown to trump up accusations against clergymen who do not think and act as they do.' It continued:

> the recent decision will seriously check the fierce zeal of the puritanical party, not, unhappily, by teaching them more charity and moderation, but by protecting the Bishops from their unfortunate interference. We cannot conceive anything much worse for the Church than a readiness to put the law courts in motion against the bishops and clergy at every opportunity. Continual litigation foments continual bitterness and party feeling, and it widens rather than heals the breaches and divisions that are so deplorably abundant at this time. Mr GOLIGHTLY has chosen to come forward as the disturber of the Church and accuser of the brethren; but by this decision he gets his quietus, and we trust that he will now retire to the rural delights of Headington and devote his declining years to a more quiet exhibition of Christian zeal, and more demonstrative manifestations of the charity that thinketh no evil.[220]

The *Times* thought that to give bishops discretion was a risky policy: 'A Bishop may be timid, partial, or obstinate, and he may be actuated by many motives ... in shrinking from the duty of publicly calling a priest to order.' On the whole, though, it saw the judgment as common sense:

> In every diocese of the kingdom there are clergymen whose views of Church doctrine or ritual are abominable in the eyes of others, and if a public inquiry could be demanded in all such cases Commissions might as well sit in permanence. ... The scandal to the Church would be incessant, and the disturbance of society beyond endurance. ... Would plaintiffs ever be wanting, or defendants either?[221]

Even the *Record*, though not content with the decision, recognised that the action of bishops was 'a two-edged weapon that may be used on either side with equal advantage', and that the absence of episcopal discretion 'might open the way to vexatious complaints on the part of Tractarians against Evangelicals, as well as on the part of Evangelicals against Tractarians'.[222] However, the *Brighton Gazette* lamented: 'The decision in the Lavington case converts

---

[218] For reports of the trial, see *English Reports* 121, pp. 80-7; *Law Journal Reports* 38 (Queen's Bench), pp. 23-31; *Weekly Reporter*, 23 July 1859, pp. 629-31; *Jurist*, 11 February 1860, pp. 120-4; *Times*, 7 and 17 June 1859, 4 July 1859.
[219] *National Standard*, 9 July 1859, p. 37.
[220] *Morning Post*, 4 July 1859.
[221] *Times*, 5 July 1859.
[222] *Record*, 6 July 1859.

Bishops into despots and Churchmen into serfs. However much they may dislike the fantastic tricks of fanciful Tractarians the people can move neither hand nor foot if their Bishop is also favorable to the growth of ill-weeds.'[223] Meanwhile choir-master Henry Harding asked: 'Mr Randall and his friends may rub their hands in ecstasy at the escape which the defects of the law have made for him; but how does he and how do they stand *in the sight of God?*'[224]

For his part in the affair, Golightly received yet more personal abuse. It was said that even anti-ritualists in the Lavington neighbourhood thought him 'an officious humbug',[225] and the Queen's Bench was praised for giving this 'meddling busy-body a salutary lesson'.[226] The *Union* rejoiced 'in the failure of tactics which were as insolent as they were petti-fogging and discreditable'. It rebuked Golightly for spending his energies in ecclesiastical warfare instead of parochial ministry:

> may we not hope that Mr Golightly will thenceforth confine his attention to his own parish? If all we hear be true, there is ample scope for the exercise, in a better and more legitimate direction, of that restless energy which has been employed so abortively in the Lavington case. We scarcely dare to hope that it would be exerted for good; but it would be something gained if his mischievous activity were restrained within a more contracted sphere.[227]

> He wanted, it appears, to be the clerical Stowell – the regular Accuser of the brethren – no enviable office. The diocese of Oxford, one would have thought, would have afforded Mr Golightly occupation enough if he had been any ordinarily malicious character. But it seems he is not satisfied with so moderate a charge. He calls for the moon. The realm of England and all its dioceses will not satisfy the rapacious maw of this Universal Busy-body. ... Mr Golightly rejoices to be free from clerical engagements that, like the French Abbé, he may roam the world at large in search of news and scandal, and return home at a decent hour at night to read a chapter and some Calvinistic prayers to his happy Protestant household.[228]

Golightly was again colourfully portrayed as 'the modern Titus Oates':

> no clergyman of ordinary learning would be safe if Golightlies were multiplied. ... Ordinary Christians would fail; but a master of inuendo [*sic*] and exaggeration could turn even virtues into vices. Heaven save us from imaginative Golightlies! ... The fact is, that nothing is so difficult as to explain fairly the doctrines of the Church of England, without conveying the impression that there is little difference

---

[223] *Brighton Gazette*, 7 July 1859.
[224] *National Standard*, 9 July 1859, p. 41.
[225] *Union*, 5 August 1859, p. 485.
[226] *Clerical Journal*, 8 August 1859, p. 351.
[227] *Union*, 8 July 1859, p. 424.
[228] *Union*, 15 July 1859, p. 433.

between them and those of the Church of Rome. Unless people have a peculiarly controversial tone of mind, or one perfectly heretical, a Golightly could always pick up enough mud to circulate through the *Times* newspaper at the expense of a Catholic priest in our communion. What could be more dangerous ground with a Golightly at your elbow than the origin of the Prayer Book? ... What would Golightly make of a fellow-priest who explained that nearly all the Collects, Epistles, and Gospels, in the Prayer Book were used in the Roman chapel close by? And, if he heard mention of Θεοτόκος, he would certainly expect to have the satisfaction of burning the utterer. It is to be hoped that Mr Golightly will retire into private, henceforth, a sadder and wiser man. Loss of time, of course, is to him of little account; but loss of pence will trouble him, we suspect, like his worthy prototype [Titus Oates], much more.[229]

In similar vein, the *Saturday Review* described Golightly as part of the 'historical succession of blockheads and busybodies who have felt the mighty constraint laid upon them to act as Attorney-General for all mankind.' It continued:

We sincerely trust that this very wholesome result will have the advantage of scotching the Golightly brood. Informers may have a high and lofty vocation ... but, after all, everybody rejoices when they get this sort of reward. Mr Golightly has done his duty – it is a costly duty – he has his reward in his lawyer's bill. ... There is always some aggrieved school-master, or curate, or pew-opener, or gossip, ready with his or her tale against the parson. We should do the clergy of England perhaps injustice in saying that their ranks contain more than one Golightly. But while he survives, the whole Church is at his mercy – or rather would have been at his mercy, had not the Queen's Bench interfered in behalf of outraged common sense and common decency. But what a loss to Mr Golightly to have his promising career of usefulness thus cut short by the unsympathizing Queen's Bench! What *Chroniques Scandaleuses* would have poured into Holywell-street, Oxford! What tales of immorality, false doctrine and heresy, loose living and salmon-fishing, have Mr Golightly, Mrs Grundy, and the *Record* lost! ... Of all the tyrannies which disgrace and debase the human mind – of all the insolent interferences with the duties and responsibilities of others – that outrageous system which Mr Golightly so faithfully represents is the worst; and we are thankful that this authoritative check has been imposed upon it.[230]

In the midst of this fierce chastisement, the *Record* gave Golightly rare praise 'for the high principle and disinterested manner in which he has so nobly thrown himself into the breach, and, regardless of personal obloquy and expense, tried to save the honour of the Church of England'.[231] Likewise the *National Standard* applauded him

---

[229] Ibid., p. 434.
[230] *Saturday Review*, 9 July 1859, p. 46.
[231] *Record*, 11 July 1859.

for his fidelity to the cause of Protestantism, and his spirited and disinterested conduct. He deserves the highest praise, and we hope that he will have his reward in the approbation and sympathy of all the true sons of the Church at this crisis of her peril and trial. When so many of her Bishops seem to have agreed together to betray the best interests of our Protestant Zion, it is a matter of pride and thankfulness that there are some amongst her Presbyters who are faithful found amongst the faithless, and who do not shrink from incurring Episcopal displeasure in the defence of the truth.[232]

Because Judge Hill might have granted a *mandamus* if Golightly had been local to Chichester diocese, it was suggested that someone from Sussex should pursue the court case. Rumours spread that a local incumbent would take it up,[233] and that a local farmer had been offered all his expenses plus a farm if he would do so.[234] No such action was taken, possibly because of the harsh treatment dealt out to Golightly, or because under the Church Discipline Act legal proceedings had to be initiated within two years of the offence, which had almost passed. The *National Standard* insisted, however, that continued agitation would bring fruit in the end:

> The law can do nothing – the Bishops either cannot or will not do anything – but there is a power stronger than law, there is a voice louder than that of Bishops – let that power be exerted – let that voice be heard. Public opinion, unanimously expressed and morally brought to bear, is omnipotent. There need be no violence, no illegality, no virulence; let there be the calm but decided expression of the Laity's decision – and the matter is at an end. Incumbents and curates must submit, and even archbishops and bishops will be powerless to resist.[235]

Edward Randall moved far away from Sussex, to an incumbency at Castle Douglas in Scotland, followed by chaplaincies at Aegina and Patras in Greece. Richard Randall remained at Lavington until 1867 when he went to All Saints, Clifton, a newly-built flagship for ritualism. He ultimately succeeded John Burgon as Dean of Chichester.

Facts and Documents

Cuddesdon and Lavington were not the only two places which brought Bishop Wilberforce trouble because of their 'advanced' ceremonial practices. Throughout 1858 and 1859 a wider agitation against ritualism took place across the whole Oxford diocese, involving thousands of people and hundreds of pamphlets and letters to the press. Wilberforce's own attitude to ritualism came under close scrutiny for a sustained period and once again Golightly assumed a

---

[232] *National Standard*, 11 June 1859, pp. 565-6.
[233] *Jackson's Oxford Journal*, 9 July 1859.
[234] *Union*, 5 August 1859, p. 485.
[235] *National Standard*, 6 August 1859, p. 133.

central role in stirring up the debate.

Within the space of a few months, a number of isolated but well-publicised disputes concerning ritualism took place in various parishes across the diocese. During the summer of 1858 John Shaw (vicar of Stoke Poges near Slough) headed a campaign against R.T. West, curate under William Gresley at Boyne Hill. West was accused of compelling a pregnant woman to confess her sins and asking her 'most improper questions, especially with regard to the seventh Commandment'. Wilberforce was berated for defending the curate, although a commission of inquiry found the woman's allegations to be unsubstantiated.[236] At a meeting of the Oxfordshire and Banbury Agricultural Society in September, the usual toast to 'The bishop and clergy of the diocese' was dropped for fear it would be rejected, while at the Royal South Bucks Agricultural Association there was uproar when this toast was proposed and many drank instead to 'Mr Shaw and the clergy'.[237] One observer wrote: 'the British farmer gave a silent but convincing proof that he is not yet prepared to subject his wife and daughters to the filthy questions and insinuations of Cuddesdon neophytes or Anglican divines.'[238]

That autumn, parishioners at St Giles', Reading reported their clergy for circulating a tract on holy communion which taught 'doctrines very near akin to transubstantiation'.[239] Meanwhile, in Oxford members of Holywell parish signed a petition against their vicar for introducing various ritualistic innovations 'contrary to the spirit of the Reformation', such as lighted candles in broad daylight, coloured stoles, intoning, a piscina and super-altar, 'extreme ornaments' in the decoration of the chancel, and a stone altar.[240] It was rumoured, of course, that Golightly (who lived in Holywell parish) had instigated this petition.[241] Wilberforce ordered that the stone altar be replaced by a wooden table, but Golightly cited ten more churches or chapels in the diocese with stone altars.[242] Other critics counted as many as twenty-four.[243]

---

[236] *Times*, 18 August and 25 September 1858, *et passim*; Ashwell and Wilberforce, *Life of Samuel Wilberforce*, ii. pp. 386-405. For Gresley's previous clash over auricular confession with Bishop Gilbert of Chichester, see Gresley – Gilbert, February – June 1852, PHL GRES 1/4/1-9.

[237] *Times*, 18 September 1858; *Jackson's Oxford Journal*, 25 September, 2 and 16 October, 18 December 1858.

[238] *Times*, 18 September 1858.

[239] *Jackson's Oxford Journal*, 13 November 1858; William H. Ridley, *The Holy Communion* (London, 1857).

[240] *English Churchman*, 30 December 1858, pp. 1234-5.

[241] *Union*, 18 March 1859, p. 162.

[242] Golightly, *Facts and Documents*, p. 15.

[243] John Tucker, *A Letter to the Lord Bishop of Oxford; being a rejoinder to his Reply to the Address of the Rev. E.A. Litton and other Clergymen of the Diocese* (London, 1859), pp. 6-7. For Wilberforce's justification, see *Impartial Account*, p. 30. Cf. Peter Maurice,

Similar trouble occurred in the village of Addington, near Buckingham, where Wilberforce reconsecrated the church which had been rebuilt by the local landowner, John Hubbard (later first Baron Addington). During the ceremony the bishop took part in a surpliced procession from the lych gate to the church, via the boundary of the new churchyard, headed by the curate, T.W. Perry (carrying a processional cross) and the churchwardens with banners. In the midst of the holy communion service Wilberforce prevented Perry's attempt to mix water with the wine, but at the subsequent luncheon he publicly defended the use of crosses, as distinct from crucifixes.[244] The *Christian Observer* advised that because processions had become 'the signals of party warfare, it is high time they were put down by authority'.[245]

In late January 1859 (a year after he first drew public attention to ritualism at Cuddesdon College), Golightly published an anonymous pamphlet entitled *Facts and Documents shewing the Alarming State of the Diocese of Oxford*. He warned:

> Of late years the Romanizing movement has assumed another phase. The same end is sought for, but by a different route. Attempts are being made to bring the Church of England to Rome by the furtive introduction not, as was Mr Newman's method, of Romish doctrine, so much as Romish practices and observances; and so the gradual accustoming of the public mind, especially in the case of the young, to the externals of the Romish system, in the hope that the doctrine would then follow of itself. And of this movement the Diocese of Oxford is the centre ...[246]

The 'documents' were a couple of ritualistic works which Golightly attempted to link, somewhat dubiously, with Oxford diocese. The first was John Purchas' *Directorium Anglicanum* (1858), a detailed instruction manual on all matters of ritual. Although Purchas had no link with Oxford University or Oxford diocese, he acknowledged in the preface that F.G. Lee (sacked as curate of Kennington near Oxford) was his 'fellow-labourer and joint-compiler' and that he had received help from T.W. Perry and Thomas Chamberlain (vicar of St Thomas', Oxford).[247] The second document was *The Churchman's Diary*, a short almanac

---

Postscript to the Popery of Oxford: The Number of the Name of the Beast (London, 1851), pp. 8-12.
[244] *Guardian*, 12 January and 2 March 1859, pp. 24-5, 191; *Record*, 14 and 26 January, 23 February 1859; William R. Fremantle, *Reasons for Signing the Remonstrance lately addressed to the Archdeacons and Rural Deans of the Diocese of Oxford. A Reply to the Rev. Henry Bull* (Oxford, 1859), pp. 9-13; T.W. Perry – Liddon, 16-17 February 1859, KCL Liddon Papers.
[245] 'State of the Diocese of Oxford', *Christian Observer* (August 1859), p. 539.
[246] Golightly, *Facts and Documents*, p. 8.
[247] John Purchas (ed.), *Directorium Anglicanum; being a Manual of Directions for the Right Celebration of the Holy Communion, for the Saying of Matins and Evensong, and for the performance of Other Rites and Ceremonies of the Church, according to Ancient*

issued annually to guide ritualistic clergy in the leading of church services. It was published by Parker of Oxford and reputedly edited by Chamberlain. From these documents Golightly quoted the ritualistic ideal concerning subjects such as auricular confession, crosses, processions, wafer bread, the mixed chalice, elevation of the eucharistic elements, the sign of the cross, anointing with oil, masses for the dead and eucharistic vestments. He then attempted to show that many of these rituals were already being practised in Oxford diocese, by quoting 'facts' concerning the recent events at Addington, Boyne Hill, Cuddesdon and Holywell. Furthermore Golightly accused Bishop Wilberforce of ignoring, or even condoning, this ritualism. The bishop's frequent denunciations of Roman Catholicism were irreconcilable with his oversight of affairs at Cuddesdon and Lavington: 'alas! how grievously are his Lordship's professions contradicted by his acts!'[248] In a shrewd attempt to galvanize support for this protest from a broad theological spectrum, Golightly proclaimed that he came forward as 'neither a High Churchman, nor a Low Churchman', but 'simply a Protestant, and a true son of the Church of England'.[249]

Facts and Documents quickly raised a fresh storm. Although Golightly signed himself 'A Senior Clergyman of the Diocese', his name was soon known. As one commentator remarked:

> The Pamphlet is anonymous, but its authorship is sufficiently transparent. There are not, it is to be hoped, *two* Senior Clergymen in the Diocese so utterly abandoned to the love of ecclesiastical gossip, as to lose in its pursuit all respect for decency, good feeling, and truth.[250]

Golightly was accused of 'stirring up, in every direction, strife and suspicion, mistrust and unkindly surmise.'[251] He had allowed, it was said, 'the interest of party strife ... to distort his judgment, his feeling, and his truth'.[252] Like many observers, the *Morning Post* was distressed that peace within the Church of England seemed impossible:

> there are persons whom nothing will satisfy – unquiet men, who love something

---

Uses of the Church of England (London, 1858), pp. xxii-xxiii. See *Record*, 4 March 1859.

[248] Golightly, *Facts and Documents*, p. 33. One historian in the 1930s colourfully wrote: 'The tireless Golightly, hovering aloft in search of prey, scented a lordly victim and swooped down on him like a vulture': J. Lewis May, *The Oxford Movement: Its History and its Future. A Layman's Estimate* (London, 1933), p. 231.

[249] Golightly, *Facts and Documents*, p. [3].

[250] *An Examination of 'Facts and Documents, Shewing the Alarming State of the Diocese of Oxford'. By One who has a Regard for Truth* (Oxford, 1859), p. 3.

[251] *Impartial Account*, p. 5.

[252] *Examination of 'Facts and Documents'*, pp. 9-10.

to rail at, who have an inborn love of controversy, and are as lively in hot water as salamanders in a furnace. These men will not let the Church rest. They are afflicted with a morbid fear of what is dreadful, and a perverse love of what is troublesome. Their monomania takes chiefly the form known in the medical profession as the *lues anti-Puseiana* [anti-Puseyism plague], and under it their sufferings are really awful. ... One of the most troublesome men of this class is a Mr GOLIGHTLY, better known in Oxford as AGAG ...[253]

Golightly's pamphlet was called 'absurd',[254] 'palpably inconsequential and illogical',[255] and 'rabid Protestantism-run-mad'.[256] His charges were proclaimed to be 'wholly without foundation',[257] 'rash and ill-considered',[258] 'wilful and gratuitous falsehood',[259] and written under 'malus animus'.[260] Others resorted to simple mockery. *Facts and Documents* expressed alarm at the spread of sisterhoods in the Oxford diocese, so one reader responded:

We have heard of sensitive Protestants in Oxford who at every turn of the street on a dark night expect to come across a Tractarian assassin lying in wait with a stiletto. Our writer may be one of this class; and as he passes the corner of Holywell, may be nervously on the look out for a malignant Sister of Mercy ready to work her wicked will upon the champion of Protestantism.[261]

Burgon thought *Facts and Documents* a 'miserable pamphlet', and spoke of 'the base calumnies, the practical falsehood, which has festered into so considerable a sore'. He lamented:

few things are more *drying* than Theological controversy. Upon the whole district where the strife prevails, a chill shade descends. Neighbours are made suspicious one of another. The spirit of party gets abroad, and severs man from man, – estranging very friends, and destroying the unity that should be the sign of true discipleship.[262]

Elsewhere Burgon protested that to link the *Directorium Anglicanum* and the *Churchman's Diary* with the Oxford diocese was exceedingly tenuous: 'Why, by such a process, almost anything might be proved, at any time, of any diocese

---

[253] *Morning Post*, 10 March 1859.
[254] *Guardian*, 9 March 1859, p. 209.
[255] Bull, *Some Remarks*, p. 5.
[256] *Union*, 11 March 1859, p. 153.
[257] *Impartial Account*, p. 3.
[258] Bull, *Some Remarks*, p. 6.
[259] *Examination of 'Facts and Documents'*, p. 4.
[260] *Literary Churchman*, 1 March 1859, p. 79.
[261] *Examination of 'Facts and Documents'*, p. 5.
[262] *Literary Churchman*, 1 June 1859, p. 193. For Burgon's authorship, see Burgon to Wilberforce, 6 June 1859, Bodleian MS Wilberforce d.47, fos 209-10.

in England!'[263] Likewise the *English Churchman* asserted: 'the smoke bears an unusual proportion to the fire',[264] and the *Morning Post* proclaimed the pamphlet's argument 'a glaring piece of false reasoning, which ought to send Mr GOLIGHTLY back to his first lessons in ALDRICH by way of correction to his logic, and to the ten commandments by way of refresher as to his duty towards his neighbour.'[265] The *Clerical Journal* concluded: 'The thing is certainly a literary phenomenon, and if a copy should survive a century or two it may become valuable as a curious specimen of a syllogism by which nothing is really inferred or concluded.'[266] Nevertheless, the pamphlet could not be ignored and the controversy soon began to escalate.

One result of Golightly's continued agitation was that it put a final end to whatever shreds of his friendship with Samuel Wilberforce still remained. In *Facts and Documents* he alluded to the large number of Wilberforce's relatives who had seceded Roman Catholicism.[267] This personal remark was reviled as 'cowardly', 'contemptible',[268] and 'low-minded, dishonourable, and atrocious conduct',[269] while Wilberforce himself called it 'heartless'.[270] One pamphleteer challenged Golightly: 'How grievously, Rev. Sir, do your own professions of sympathy for the Bishop seem to be contradicted by your acts!'[271] Likewise, Burgon thought Golightly guilty of an 'act of insubordination' and 'grievous breaches of canonical obedience'.[272] However, he was applauded by his supporters for sounding 'the trumpet of alarm',[273] and for convicting Wilberforce of 'the most lamentable faithlessness and duplicity. ... Archbishop LAUD did scarcely more, in his day and generation, for the extinction of the Reformation than this subtle Prelate is now doing.'[274]

Bishop Wilberforce summoned Golightly to Cuddesdon Palace to discuss the pamphlet. Yet Golightly refused, still smarting at the bishop's charge of his 'disingenuousness' before the rural deans the previous April.[275] The personal

---

[263] *Guardian*, 23 February 1859, p. 166.
[264] *English Churchman*, 10 March 1859, p. 234.
[265] *Morning Post*, 10 March 1859.
[266] *Clerical Journal*, 8 March 1859, p. 105.
[267] Golightly, *Facts and Documents*, p. 32. For details of Wilberforce's many relatives who seceded to Rome, see *Record*, 22 October 1858; *Jackson's Oxford Journal*, 27 November 1858.
[268] *Examination of 'Facts and Documents'*, pp. 9-10.
[269] *Union*, 18 March 1859, p. 162.
[270] *Impartial Account*, p. 9.
[271] *A Letter to 'A Senior Clergyman' in reply to 'Facts and Documents' bearing upon the State of the Diocese of Oxford. By a Clergyman of the Diocese* (Oxford, 1859), p. 12.
[272] *Literary Churchman*, 1 June 1859, pp. 193, 195.
[273] Henry Barne, *A Letter Addressed to the Rev. A.P. Cust ... on the State of the Diocese of Oxford* (London, 1859), p. 5.
[274] *National Standard*, 12 February 1859, p. 158.
[275] Wilberforce – Golightly, 5-7 February 1859, LPL MS 1811, fos 228-32.

animosity between the two men was palpable, and in his diary Wilberforce noted: 'Golightly's business. He refusing to come at my bidding!! I ought not to have allowed myself to give him a hit – & have led him into this sinful revenge. Lord pardon him & me.'[276] Golightly later justified himself:

> It was a proposal to put my head into the lion's mouth, and I declined the venture. … my refusal to trust myself alone and without a witness in the presence of one whose imagination was so lively, and his memory so treacherous, and who (to mention no other perils) might not have given a perfectly accurate account of the conversation that passed between us at the next meeting of the Rural Deans, savoured less of 'sinful revenge' than wise and prudent caution.[277]

The bishop wrote to rebuke Golightly for his intransigence and resignedly acknowledged that their old friendship was over:

> I would fain have spoken with you face to face as a brother in Christ & I believe that His glory & the good of His Church might have been promoted by the clearing away of misunderstanding & the healing of differences which our meeting would have accomplished. You refuse the hand of a Friend of many years held out to you, and I can do no more than pray God to shew you, before you render your account to Him, in what a spirit you have been acting.[278]

This was the last known direct contact between the two men. Golightly described this final letter as 'so fearfully denunciatory that …it makes my flesh creep to think of it', although Wilberforce afterwards told a mutual friend: 'You know that I am very placable and willing to be on the old terms of intimacy with him.'[279] Four months later, when the diocesan agitation was still at its height, he noted: 'Golightly *never forgives*.'[280] Recalling Golightly's old nickname, 'Agag', one humorist observed that in the Old Testament King Agag had been 'hewed in pieces' by the prophet Samuel.[281]

Petitions and Protests

John Burgon reassured Wilberforce that Golightly's hostility was not typical: 'you are immensely popular, remember, *with those who say nothing*. One noisy cur will disturb a whole street. The other 99 are asleep in their kennels.'[282] Some months before, when suffering similar attacks, the bishop pined: 'I have no doubt that the silence of the Diocese is contempt of these assassins but

---

[276] Wilberforce Diary, 7 February 1859, Bodleian MS dep. e.326.
[277] Golightly, *Letter to the Dean of Ripon*, pp. 53, 55.
[278] Wilberforce to Golightly, 9 February 1859, LPL MS 1811, fos 233-4.
[279] Golightly, *Letter to the Dean of Ripon*, p. 55.
[280] Wilberforce Diary, 2 June 1859, Bodleian MS dep. e.326.
[281] *Morning Post*, 10 March 1859.
[282] Burgon to Wilberforce, 11 February 1859, Bodleian MS Wilberforce d.47, fos 205-6.

contempt does not turn away the dagger's point.'[283] In the furore surrounding *Facts and Documents*, public support was soon forthcoming in a rash of petitions, signed by hundreds of clergymen – but each one provoked a counter-petition.

First Wilberforce's three archdeacons and twenty-four of his rural deans (who the *Record* thought mere 'satellites of the Bishop'[284]) declared their confidence in him. Although they opposed 'all attempts to alter in any respects the ritual of our Reformed Church', they called Golightly's charges 'unjustifiable misrepresentations' and 'presumptuous and unfounded calumnies'. In reply Wilberforce described ritualistic developments as 'childish frivolities' which distract from 'the all-important work of seeking to save souls for which CHRIST died', and insisted: 'I have a jealous dread of every Romanising tendency'.[285] Just six rural deans refused to support their bishop, one of whom, Arthur Isham, wrote a pamphlet accusing him of 'decided partiality towards an innovating party' and of 'introducing and sanctioning novel pomp and ceremony'.[286] As a result, Isham was threatened with dismissal as rural dean if he did not offer 'a simple, uncompromising, and complete retraction'.[287]

The ritualist *Union* newspaper, however, thought that Oxford's diocesan leaders had played into Golightly's hands. Even Archdeacon Edward Bickersteth and several rural deans who were known to be advanced ritually (such as William Butler, Arthur Purey-Cust, Alfred Pott and James Austen-Leigh) had been persuaded to put their names to an address which eschewed ritualism.[288] The newspaper mourned: 'Mr Golightly has achieved another success, which, like those at Cuddesdon and Holywell, is attributable rather to the weak tactics of those whom he assails than to his own skill and strategy.'[289] It argued that if Wilberforce adopted a bold pro-catholic policy, 'he who is now triumphant – making merry with his friends over their spoils – will again benefit society by slinking away into his once normal state of idleness and obscurity.' Yet if the bishop chose compromise, as he had done during the

---

[283] Wilberforce to Butler, 13 October 1858, Bodleian MS Wilberforce d.33, fo. 73.
[284] *Record*, 6 April 1859.
[285] *Impartial Account*, pp. 5-8.
[286] Arthur Isham, *A Letter to Archdeacon Clerke ... stating his reasons for refusing to sign the Address of Feb. 25th, in reference to the pamphlet, 'Facts and Documents, &c.'* (Oxford, 1859), p. 12. See *A Letter to the Rev. A. Isham, in reply to his Letter to Archdeacon Clerke in reference to the Rural Deans' Address to the Bishop of Oxford* (Oxford, 1859).
[287] *Jackson's Oxford Journal*, 9 April 1859. See Golightly, *Letter to the Dean of Ripon*, p. 45; Isham to Golightly, 28 September 1881, LPL MS 1807, fos 257-60. Richard Gordon (rural dean of Elsfield) also refused to sign the address and offered his resignation: Wilberforce's Notes on Parishes 1854-64, ORO ODP d.178, fo. 202.
[288] *Union*, 8 April 1859, p. 210.
[289] *Union*, 11 March 1859, p. 153.

Cuddesdon affair, Golightly would continue

> on all occasions and under all circumstances harassing the Catholic party, reviving bitter animosities, growing more vulgarly personal; and at last – through the supineness and wrong policy of his enemies – winning more and more battles. Depend upon it, no conciliatory compromise can satisfy the dregs of a once respectable party, whose present idleness is only equalled by their profound bigotry and unparalleled ignorance, and who have chosen 'Agag' for their champion. They have a principle, sharp in its outline, clearly defined, but radically false and mischievous in its results – viz., a cordial and intense detestation of everything and everybody Catholic ... Between the one side and the other an impassable chasm, a great gulph [sic] exists – even the line of demarcation separating Protestantism from Catholicism – error from truth; and the more frequently attempts are made to forget the existence of such a division, the more bitterly will the Catholics have to lament their losses.[290]

Nevertheless, the *Illustrated News of the World* thought Golightly had been 'most shamefully maltreated', and that Oxford's ecclesiastical dignitaries had 'only thought of pleasing the Bishop and not of telling the truth, of representing the most slippery and Puseyistic of the Bishops as a model prelate of the Church'. It declared: 'According to the Archdeacons and Rural Deans the Bishop was snow white without a *nuance* of scarlet – the "senior clergyman", black as Erebus, is beyond the farthest shooting ray from the realms of light.'[291] One hundred clergymen (out of approximately 900 in the diocese) issued a remonstrance to the archdeacons and rural deans protesting that the claims in *Facts and Documents* had simply been ignored. The signatories included a number of Golightly's friends who were serving in local parishes, such as Arthur Isham, E.A. Litton, Richard Twopeny, William R. Fremantle and John Tucker. They thought there was 'good cause for alarm and anxiety', reiterated the charges about stone altars and processions in various rural deaneries, and appealed for their leaders to use their influence so that everything 'which in any measure savours of Romanism, and is a departure from the spirit of the Reformed and Protestant Church of England, may be abandoned, that so all the causes of distrust may cease, and peace be restored.'[292] Likewise, ten laymen from Reading warned the archdeacons and rural deans of 'the danger which now threatens our Protestant Evangelical Christianity', and asked them to act upon the concerns raised by Golightly and his allies: 'any attempt to ignore or palliate the Romanizing tendencies they have exposed ... will only tend to spread still further a feeling of dissatisfaction and distrust of the ministers and

---

[290] *Union*, 18 March 1859, p. 162.
[291] *Illustrated News of the World*, 9 April 1859, p. 215.
[292] *Impartial Account*, p. 12; *Jackson's Oxford Journal*, 4 June 1859.

office-bearers of our Reformed and truly Scriptural Church.'[293]

A second major address in support of Bishop Wilberforce was drawn up in March 1859 by the elderly and respected William Wilson, the evangelical rector of Over Worton and brother of Daniel Wilson (late Bishop of Calcutta). As an undergraduate in the Long Vacation of 1826, Golightly had read with Francis Newman at Over Worton, where Wilson showed him 'much kindness and hospitality'.[294] Yet now Wilson's address described *Facts and Documents* as 'wholly unworthy the attention of any reasoning mind ... calculated to encourage the heart-burnings of those who are ignorant, and under the power of their prejudices.' It affirmed that Wilberforce always aimed 'to encourage true Protestantism, and the religion of the Bible, as set forth and explained in the formularies of our Church.'[295] Nearly 500 clergy, more than half the diocese, signed the address, though some were nervous of the reference to 'true Protestantism'. The *Guardian*, for example, saw it as a devious attempt to claim Wilberforce for the Protestant 'party':

> As the Bishop cannot be proved to be a Papist, he is made out to be a 'Protestant'; and the unhappy pamphleteer [Golightly] is tossed overboard with the greater good-will that the memorialists may in this ingenious manner indemnify themselves at his expense. But was there ever such a piece of odd and simple machiavelism?[296]

Wilson, who had known Oxford diocese during the administrations of five of Wilberforce's predecessors, stated that none had so effectually encouraged 'the Scriptural principles and instructions of our Reformed Church'. In similar tone, Wilberforce replied to his supporters by applauding 'evangelical truth' and 'apostolical order' against 'Popery, Latitudinarianism, and Infidelity.'[297] However, almost half the clergy in the diocese still refused to join Wilson's endorsement of their bishop. It was described by Thomas Curme (vicar of Sandford, near Oxford) as a 'whitewashing Address', whose signatories were guilty of 'blindness and prejudice' and had 'an infatuated love for the harlot of Babylon'.[298] More than this would be needed to restore confidence in the church's leaders, as one layman proclaimed:

---

[293] *Record*, 1 April 1859. For a third address to the archdeacons and rural deans which spoke of the need to preserve 'the orthodox faith of our pious Forefathers', see Herbert Randolph to Pott, 28 March 1859, KCL Liddon Papers. For a draft statement for clergy, proclaiming that they had 'no sympathy whatever with the distinctive peculiarities of the Church of Rome' see Bodleian MS Wilberforce c.20, fos 191-2.

[294] Golightly, *Letter to the Dean of Ripon*, p. 63.

[295] *Impartial Account*, p. 14.

[296] *Guardian*, 16 March 1859, p. 238. For defence of Wilson's non-party credentials, see *Guardian*, 23 and 30 March 1859, pp. 258, 278.

[297] *Impartial Account*, pp. 23-4.

[298] *Jackson's Oxford Journal*, 30 April 1859.

It will not do in these days to think to put aside facts by mere authoritative denials. ... The fact is the Bishop, and a great part of the Clergy in his Diocese, have entirely lost the confidence of every true, sincere, God-taught Protestant in the Church. ... Our ancestors parted with a King sooner than give up their religion, and shall we suffer our religion to be filched from us by a party of unfaithful shepherds in the Church?[299]

With feelings running high, campaigners on all sides of the question continued to issue their pamphlets and protests over the next few months. New petitions were sent to Bishop Wilberforce from clergy and laity across his diocese. In April 1859 an address signed by 76 clergy asked the bishop to suppress processions, crosses, stone altars, super-altars, and 'excessive decoration', so that 'dissatisfaction and distrust' might be replaced by 'peace, unity, charity, and purity of worship'.[300] This address was again headed by men like Litton, Twopeny and Tucker, so the *Union* advised Wilberforce to rebuke 'this motley crew of Calvinistic Protestants ... amongst the idlest and most incompetent of his lordship's clergy'. Returning to one of its favourite themes, the newspaper proclaimed that compromise was unacceptable:

> Quietly, and 'on the sly' (as it were), Catholic practices are not only permitted but approved; but, as soon as public opinion is aroused, principles are flung to the winds: wordy addresses, or Anti-Roman claptrap, are published, and some person or thing is readily sacrificed. ... Depend upon it, he [Wilberforce] will get nothing in the end by flattering the Freemantles [*sic*] and Golightlys, or by attending to their preposterous suggestions. If he gives an inch, they, with faces of brass, promptly demand an ell, untill [*sic*] the utter extermination of everything Catholic is triumphantly achieved.[301]

With attempts like this to portray the anti-ritualist clergymen as theological partisans, Twopeny insisted that 'we are actuated by no private or interested or factious motives ... Our only motive has been to defend the true doctrine and pure worship of our Reformed and Protestant Church'.[302] Another clerical petitioner asserted:

> Now can any one seriously believe that so many men of age, high character, long experience, and abilities, are all alarmed at mere fancies raised by an anonymous writer; or in the quietude of their parishes are so excited by mere party spirit, as to leave their work and rush into a controversy, which is, to most of them, painful in the extreme? Assuredly not; with deep grief, not with zealous party spirit, many

---

[299] *Jackson's Oxford Journal*, 23 April 1859.
[300] *Impartial Account*, p. 25; *Jackson's Oxford Journal*, 4 June 1859.
[301] *Union*, 1 April 1859, pp. 193-4.
[302] Richard Twopeny, *Observations on Our Address to the Bishop of Oxford* (London, 1859), p. 15 (copy at CCA X1/25/13).

signed. We wished peace and quietness, but not at the expense of truth ...'[303]

Wilberforce dismissed each of the petitioners' complaints as 'trifles', lamenting the presence of 'a querulous suspicious temper, leading others to whisper insinuations and stir up strife to the grievous breach of Christian charity.' He likened their objection to processions to the Puritan dislike for the surplice, and appealed for them to unite with others in the church against infidelity, instead of wasting their time with such trivial disputes:

> The greatest truths of GOD's Revelation are daily imperilled amongst us. Let us concentrate our attention, and combine our energies in defending these. ... We need the laying aside of fanciful suspicions, the ceasing to sow strife, and to calumniate one another.[304]

The *Record* was dismayed that the serious concerns of experienced clergymen should be 'quietly pooh-poohed' in this way.[305] Others agreed that Wilberforce's attitude was patronising. For example, the *Daily Telegraph* wrote:

> In form it looks as innocent as what dairywomen call 'sleepy cream'; in spirit it is the very corrosive sublimate of ecclesiastical controversy; in fact, it resembles so nearly the universal solvent of alchemists, that our only wonder is how the ink does not take fire and consume the paper. First, this bland apostle ejaculates to his reverend brethren an insinuation of his love, and then, after sundry elongated quibbles, beseeches them to march through Oxford like saints, each brimming over with affection for the other – all linking hands, tuning their voices to harmony, and believing devoutly that SAMUEL WILBERFORCE is a prophet in the land.[306]

Likewise the *Christian Observer* thought that if Wilberforce had his way, the Oxford diocese would assume 'a gaudy exterior of ritual show and splendour, and an obsequious and servile submissiveness, such as it has never worn beneath any protestant bishop.'[307]

In his reply to the address, Wilberforce had compared ritualistic churches favourably to the many non-ritualistic churches which suffered neglect 'with their green walls, damp stones, and mouldy furniture'.[308] Fremantle was insulted and retorted:

> If we old-fashioned Churchmen, with our wooden tables and whitewashed walls

---

[303] *Record*, 9 May 1859.
[304] *Impartial Account*, pp. 28, 31-2.
[305] *Record*, 6 May 1859.
[306] *Daily Telegraph*, 9 May 1859.
[307] 'State of the Diocese of Oxford', p. 529.
[308] *Impartial Account*, p. 31.

and unadorned chancels, are robbers of churches and blasphemers of holy things, the law is open, and any one may implead us. But if we are found to be quite as earnest and zealous as others in maintaining the decency and spirituality of public worship, and quite as successful in securing the attendance of the people, and in attaching them to the Church of our fathers, and in converting sinners to Christ, then let us not be ridiculed, or stamped with opprobrious names, or branded as Puritans and Dissenters.[309]

Another clerical protester mourned: 'What prospect is there of peace in the Diocese? What remains for the Clergy but either timorous silence and unworthy compromise on the one hand, or ceaseless agitation on the other?'[310] John Tucker was one of those not prepared to 'sit still, and silently witness others leading us on to Rome': 'Vital truth is at stake; and it concerns not this Diocese only, nor the Clergy alone, but the whole Church of England, Clergy and Laity, at home and abroad, to see that the Truth is preserved.'[311]

By far the largest, and the last, petition during the agitation in Oxford diocese was delivered to Bishop Wilberforce in July 1859, signed by 4,000 lay people across the diocese (including three MPs, twenty-three magistrates and 179 churchwardens). The supplicants offered to co-operate with Wilberforce in supporting 'the Scriptural principles of the Reformed Church', and asked him to halt the spread of ritualistic practices. The bishop replied that he was opposed to 'Romanizing errors', but nonetheless considered his 'moderate and temperate course ... to be the most just, the most faithful, and the most prudent.'[312]

A Ritualist Bishop?

Just as Oxford University had once held a reputation as the breeding ground of Tractarianism, so now Oxford diocese became notorious in the Church of England as the great centre *par excellence* of the ritualist experiment. The controversies of 1858-59, begun by Golightly and pursued by others, were seen as an issue of national importance. As one commentator put it, 'The condition of the diocese of Oxford has become the great ecclesiastical question of our times'.[313] Wilberforce's leadership and his personal relationship to ritualism came under sustained scrutiny, and some laid all the woes of the diocese at his

---

[309] Fremantle, *Reasons for Signing*, pp. 15-6. For the petitioners' concern for church restoration, see Tucker, *Letter to the Bishop of Oxford*, p. 15; *Jackson's Oxford Journal*, 14 May 1859.
[310] *Jackson's Oxford Journal*, 14 May 1859.
[311] Tucker, *Letter to the Bishop of Oxford*, pp. 3, 16.
[312] *Jackson's Oxford Journal*, 20 August 1859. For analysis of the petition's widespread support, see *Jackson's Oxford Journal*, 14 May and 4 June 1859. A further petition to the Queen or Archbishop of Canterbury was suggested: *Record*, 11 April 1859.
[313] 'State of the Diocese of Oxford', p. 458.

door. It was said, for example, that he was 'now looked upon as the great leader of the Tractarian Heresy in the Church ... his Diocese may be considered as the hot-bed of the Romanizing Conspiracy.'[314] One observer lamented: 'No Popish Jesuit could more clearly lay down the way to betray Protestants by pretended zeal than the Bishop has done',[315] while another appealed: 'Oh! that Protestant England would awake to a sense of her danger!'[316] Likewise the *Record* exhorted:

> It is to be hoped that the prelatic heel has not quite stamped out the expiring embers of true Protestantism, even in the diocese of Oxford, but that the laity and the sound clergy will arouse themselves, and not be restrained by any feelings of false delicacy in resisting the iron yoke of bondage which has been forged for them. Let them not be cajoled by silvery words, nor lulled to sleep by fair promises; the spirit of superstition is at work in their diocese; let them manfully resist it; – if it has been known to lurk beneath 'the wings of an angel of light', it comes within the limits of possibility that it might hide itself beneath episcopal robes.[317]

One crucial question raised by the furore was the right relationship between a bishop and theological 'parties' within his diocese. The *English Churchman*, for example, identified this as the key issue: 'the real question is, what is the duty of the Bishops – what can they do – what are they sworn to do, without fear or favour to any man, or any party in the Church?'[318] Wilberforce came under particular censure because he was thought to have a bias towards the ritualists. One clergyman accused him of making appointments which evidently favoured the ritualists and of regularly rejecting the curates chosen by evangelical incumbents.[319] Richard Twopeny agreed that disillusionment was growing within the diocese because Wilberforce had lost his necessary neutrality:

> Every friend of the Church, to whatever party or section of it he may belong, must deeply lament the feelings now prevalent in the Diocese. Numbers of the Clergy, filled with apprehension and mistrust. The Laity suspicious, dissatisfied, and alienated. ... attachment to the Church and confidence in its Ministers, are undoubtedly losing ground in this Diocese under his Presidency; nor will the prevalence of any party be an adequate compensation for such a loss.[320]

Yet the ritualists likewise thought he was not clearly enough on their side.

---

[314] *National Standard*, 5 February 1859, p. 139.
[315] *National Standard*, 21 May 1859, p. 498.
[316] *Jackson's Oxford Journal*, 18 June 1859.
[317] *Record*, 6 April 1859.
[318] *English Churchman*, 10 March 1859, p. 235.
[319] *Record*, 9 May 1859.
[320] Twopeny, *Some Remarks*, pp. 20, 22.

Owen Chadwick's conclusion on Wilberforce is an accurate summary of the bishop's dilemma: 'In an age of parties he disliked the partisan: and his belief that the Church of England was comprehensive sometimes led partisans to accuse him of double-facing.'[321]

Early on during his appointment as Bishop of Oxford, Wilberforce affirmed his aim to deal with his clergy even-handedly, 'whether they verge to Tract or low Church errors'.[322] In his Diocesan Charge of 1851 he outlined his intention 'as to all points on which good men within our Church may lawfully differ, to be, as your Bishop, of no party'. He wanted to be 'all things to all men', but acknowledged: 'I am well aware that such a course cannot please party men; and that it must therefore expose a bishop to be assailed by his enemies with that reproach which it is the hardest to endure, the reproach of insincerity.'[323] Almost twenty years later he asserted: 'I could not have endured to have been the bishop of a party when God's providence had called me to be the bishop of a diocese.'[324]

Similar themes are evident in the rhetoric which surrounded the diocesan agitation of 1858-59. For example, to his anti-ritualist petitioners, Wilberforce explained that it was necessary for him to be 'the Bishop, not of a party, but of his Diocese' and to act 'with entire fairness ... to good and holy men on both sides'.[325] His influential advocate, John Burgon, insisted that Wilberforce had 'dealt singularly even-handed justice to *all* parties within his Diocese.'[326] Likewise, another episcopal ally maintained:

> The name of Wilberforce ... has not yet been made the tool of a party. God grant that it never may become so! Those who refuse their co-operation, because they cannot bind the son of William Wilberforce in slavery to their party views ... have yet to learn the fulness [sic] of that inherited vigour which will do and dare everything upon an independent footing, secure in the consciousness of truth. ... Suspicion and crimination and jealous party-spirit, though they are often found festering in the hearts of the children of God, cannot, I am sure, be the work of God.[327]

Wilberforce and his supporters regularly observed that a divided church was a

---

[321] Chadwick, *Founding of Cuddesdon*, p. 10.
[322] Wilberforce to Anderson, 13 November 1845, Bodleian MS Wilberforce d.26, fo. 180.
[323] Wilberforce, *Charge* (1851), pp. 45-6.
[324] Samuel Wilberforce, *A Charge Delivered to the Diocese of Oxford, at his Eighth Visitation* (Oxford, 1869), p. 25.
[325] *Impartial Account*, p. 32.
[326] *Literary Churchman*, 1 June 1859, p. 194.
[327] *Further Thoughts*, pp. 9-10. In 1841 Maurice wrote that Samuel Wilberforce's 'name carries with it a witness that the spirit of party may be defied': Maurice, *Reasons for Not Joining a Party*, p. 22.

weakened church and appealed for unity across his diocese. For instance in *A Letter Addressed to the Author of 'Facts and Documents'*, Arthur Purey-Cust grieved to see clergymen

> rushing into print against their Bishop, attacking him in county papers, reviling him in pamphlets, and seeking to stir up the fires of dissension, rather than to provoke unto love and to good works. ... Well may all earnest-minded men tremble, when the Church is thus rent asunder, when such unhallowed means are resorted to for allaying differences of opinion, and when men, realizing to themselves evil in others, seek to do that which our Lord has pronounced impossible, namely, by Satan to cast out Satan.[328]

Another pamphleteer appealed for greater tolerance: 'Let charges and recriminations be laid aside, while we give ourselves to our Master's work, in a spirit of mutual charity and forbearance, and leave it to Him to judge.'[329] Likewise the bishop told the anti-ritualist protestors 'not to allow these passing waves of discord to destroy the work of union which has proceeded hitherto so happily amongst us.'[330] In his Diocesan Charge of 1860, after relative calm had returned, he exhorted his clergy to learn to live 'in brotherly love, and ... to be quiet and to mind our own business'.[331]

The agitation against ritualism had rocked Oxford diocese for more than a year and a half. With his key involvement in the Cuddesdon and Lavington affairs, and the publication of *Facts and Documents*, Golightly's major impact in the Protestant campaign is beyond doubt. Deep and long-lasting divisions within the Oxford diocese became more obvious as a result of his protests. However, he was only able to stir up this '*odium theologicum*', according to the *Clerical Journal*, by working upon theological suspicions already prevalent:

> BEHOLD, how great a matter a little fire kindleth! That the diocese of Oxford, no inconsiderable ὕλη [forest], should be thrown into a state of conflagration by the very little fire of Mr Golightly's pamphlet is a phenomenon only accounted for by the fact that its sparks fell among very inflammable materials, and so some noticeable effect is produced by a very trifling and almost ludicrous cause. ... There never was a case in which silence would have been more truly effective for defence, or have more confounded an enemy; but the storm of words which has rattled on the heads of the assailants has gained them a real position from whence they can throw verbose missiles in return. The result is that the Clergy of the diocese become severed by a broad line of demarcation, instead of their differences being gradually rounded off ... in the *chiaro-oscuro* of actual clerical

---

[328] A.P. Purey-Cust, *A Letter Addressed to the Author of 'Facts and Documents Shewing the Alarming State of the Diocese of Oxford'* (Oxford, 1859), p. 7.
[329] *Counter-Thoughts*, p. 53.
[330] *Impartial Account*, p. 32.
[331] Samuel Wilberforce, *A Charge Delivered at the Triennial Visitation of the Diocese* (Oxford, 1860), p. 42.

life. ... As is usual with religious polemics, little things become great, motives are attributed, and ill-feelings are excited which a grain a Christian charity would have allayed.[332]

One observer summed up Golightly's influence:

> his calumnious pages have had the effect of marring the ministry of almost every hard-working clergyman in the diocese of Oxford, rousing suspicions in the minds of churchwardens scarcely able to read, and awakening distrust where perfect confidence and peace have hitherto deservedly reigned – let him enjoy that satisfaction by all means. He has fairly earned it. May it make him very happy![333]

Another concluded: 'the part which has been taken by *every person but one* in this deplorable agitation seems to be either justifiable, or at least to admit of excuse; the blame and the guilt of the agitation lying entirely at the door of him with whom it originated.'[334]

The Woodard Schools

'Confession & Absolution' are the two great scarecrows of the day, and answer very well in the hands of enemies or sectarians. (Nathaniel Woodard, 1851)[335]

Charles Golightly's involvement with the diocese of Chichester did not begin or end with the Lavington case. He was also active in the early 1850s, and again in the 1860s, in a campaign against the Woodard Schools. He had failed to force Bishop Gilbert of Chichester to set up a formal commission of inquiry into affairs at Lavington, but he had greater success against the schools. His protests did serious harm to their reputation – particularly when Woodard made the mistake of fund-raising in Oxford.

During the 1840s a number of prominent public schools were founded across England, such as those at Cheltenham, Marlborough, Rossall, Brighton, Radley and Bradfield. However, Nathaniel Woodard, curate of New Shoreham in Sussex, noticed a large gap in the market. There were many public schools for the wealthy, and 17,000 parochial schools for poor children, but little provision for the 'middle classes'. Therefore, in March 1848, Woodard issued *A Plea for the Middle Classes*, setting out his plan for a connection of schools for this stratum of society. Within a few months St Mary's School (day) and St Nicholas' School (boarding) were opened in Shoreham, followed by St John's School, which moved in 1850 to Hurstpierpoint.

Almost immediately Woodard's schools began to arouse suspicion amongst

---

[332] *Clerical Journal*, 8 April 1859, p. 149.
[333] *Guardian*, 23 March 1859, p. 259.
[334] *Impartial Account*, p. 34.
[335] Nathaniel Woodard to John Goring, 21 May 1851, LCA Woodard Papers (Religion).

Protestants in Sussex. Particularly disturbing were allegations that the school chaplain was responsible for hearing confessions from pupils – even that these confessions were compulsory. The role of the chaplain, according to Brian Heeney, 'marked a new departure in public school religion'.[336] The founder described their function as follows:

> The Chaplain in our Society is the spiritual *friend* of the boys, accessible to them at all times to hear any of their troubles, of whatever kind or sort. He is however *expected* to see every boy in private about twice a *Quarter*, i.e., once in *six weeks*. He hears anything the boy may wish to say, – prays with him & for him & if he has shown himself an earnest religious child he gives him a '*blessing*' – if otherwise, he dismisses him without one.[337]

Although this was not an explicit admission that auricular confession was encouraged in his schools, it hinted strongly at the practice, with 'blessing' used as a euphemism for 'absolution'. Golightly, like many other Protestants, had a high view of ministerial absolution, as an authoritative declaration of the pardon of God to those who repent and believe in Christ.[338] Yet pronouncement of absolution was to be reserved for public church services, not offered in private. Auricular confession, where priest and penitent met in secret, was beyond the bounds of orthodoxy.

Private confession was widely considered a corrupt Roman Catholic discipline and its revival within the Church of England provoked intense controversy. It went hand-in-hand with other battles over ritualism. Although the subject was not discussed in the *Tracts for the Times*, Edward Pusey and John Henry Newman began hearing confessions in 1838, and as the practice spread over the next decade it caused increasing alarm.[339] Woodard himself was dismissed in 1843 by the Bishop of London from his post at St Bartholomew's, Bethnal Green for a sermon on confession.[340] Opposition was fierce because auricular confession was understood to promote works-righteousness and to place a human mediator between the sinner and Almighty God, instead of 'the

---

[336] Heeney, *Mission to the Middle Classes*, p. 62.
[337] Woodard to Goring, 21 May 1851, LCA Woodard Papers (Religion). See also *S. Nicolas College. Directions to Chaplains*, Woodard Papers (box 1841-49).
[338] Goulburn, *Reminiscences of Golightly*, pp. 14-6.
[339] Newman, *Autobiographical Writings*, pp. 214-5; Edward B. Pusey, *The Church of England Leaves her Children Free to Whom to Open their Griefs. A Letter to the Rev. W.U. Richards* (Oxford, 1850), p. 134; Keith Denison, 'Dr Pusey as Confessor and Spiritual Director', in Perry Butler (ed.), *Pusey Rediscovered* (London, 1983), pp. 210-30. For early alarm in Oxford, see Baden Powell, *The Protestant's Warning and Safeguard in the Present Times* (Oxford, 1841), pp. 17-8; Charles Seager, *Auricular Confession. Six Letters in Answer to the Attacks of One of the City Lecturers on the Catholic Principle and Practice of Private Confession to a Priest ... By Academicus* (Oxford, 1842).
[340] John L. Otter, *Nathaniel Woodard: A Memoir of his Life* (London, 1925), pp. 10-31.

great high priest', Jesus Christ. It was also viewed as a challenge to Victorian etiquette and morality (with young unmarried curates asking women about their sexual sins), and as an attempt to undermine the authority of husbands and fathers, destroying the patriarchal structure of the Victorian family. Protestant concerns were reinforced by a number of high-profile scandals during the 1850s. For instance, in 1850 two clergymen at St Saviour's, Leeds were accused of compelling a female parishioner to confess and asking her about her sexual history.[341] Similarly G.R. Prynne of St Peter's, Plymouth was brought before Bishop Phillpotts in 1852 on charges that he had compelled orphans in the care of the Devonport Sisters to confess.[342] In 1858 Alfred Poole of St Barnabas', Pimlico was suspended by Bishop Tait after four women made allegations that during confession he had asked 'filthy' and 'grossly indecent' questions about their sexual habits.[343] At the same period, Bishop Wilberforce was embroiled in the Boyne Hill affair in the Oxford diocese. As John Shelton Reed observes, 'it is not surprising that few other Anglo-Catholic innovations elicited as much visceral opposition, even among the movement's supporters and sympathizers'.[344] It 'served as a party badge'.[345] To advocate auricular confession was to be marked out as an extremist.

From the start, Woodard worked hard to silence accusations that his schools were 'extreme' and 'partisan' institutions. For example, he gave the right to nominate the headmaster for his first school to Magdalen College, Oxford (patrons of Shoreham parish), in order 'to remove all suspicions of party purpose'.[346] In a pamphlet letter to the clergy of the diocese, he proclaimed that his scheme was 'no farther a party work, than teaching the three Creeds and the Catechism may be considered so',[347] and argued that large schools for the middle classes would help 'to remove that selfish and narrow party spirit, which is natural to those who live by themselves, or in a narrow circle.'[348] Woodard persuaded Bishop Gilbert to be Visitor to the schools, and gained the support of Julius Hare (Archdeacon of Lewes), Henry Manning and James Garbett (consecutive Archdeacons of Chichester). His denial of partisanship

---

[341] Nigel Yates, *The Oxford Movement and Parish Life: St Saviour's, Leeds, 1839-1929*, Borthwick Papers no.48 (York, 1975), pp. 12-4.

[342] Albert C. Kelway, *George Rundle Prynne: A Chapter in the Early History of the Catholic Revival* (London, 1905), pp. 70-114; G.C.B. Davies, *Henry Phillpotts, Bishop of Exeter, 1778-1869* (London, 1954), ch. 9.

[343] *Times*, 12 June 1858.

[344] John S. Reed, *Glorious Battle: The Cultural Politics of Victorian Anglo-Catholicism* (London, 1996), p. 49.

[345] Ibid., p. 64.

[346] Nathaniel Woodard, *A Plea for the Middle Classes* (London, 1848), p. 16.

[347] Nathaniel Woodard, *Public Schools for the Middle Classes. A Letter to the Clergy of the Diocese of Chichester* (London, 1851), p. 22

[348] Nathaniel Woodard, *Public Schools for the Middle Classes* (London, 1852), pp. 19-20.

was helped by the fact that these dignitaries were known to come from a variety of theological backgrounds (indeed the three archdeacons have been called 'broad church', 'high church' and 'low church' respectively).[349] As Heeney points out, Woodard 'sedulously cultivated support from ecclesiastics who were known to differ widely from his Anglo-Catholic friends.'[350] In 1848 Woodard reassured Hare: 'I have no thought of making this a party matter ... I have no relish for party strife. My own private views have never been disguised ... but no individualism will be introduced into the plan.'[351] For his part, Hare publicly defended Woodard's schools in a charge to the archdeaconry of Lewes: 'the work is not a party-work; nor has it been undertaken with anything of a party-spirit. It is a work in which all parties ought to unite cordially and zealously. It is a work which ought to be precious in the sight of every one who desires the good of the English nation and Church.'[352]

Such protestations did little to halt growing concern about Woodard's schools. Some felt that Chichester's ecclesiastical dignitaries had been intentionally misled about their true nature. For example, the first headmaster of the Shoreham School, Henry Jacobs, resigned within a month over the issue of auricular confession, protesting to Woodard:

> I have conceived a much stronger dread & aversion than I ever entertained before, to the doctrine & system of Rome, with which I fear you hold in too great a degree ... You will perhaps say, that what the Bishop sanctions, may be received by me – but can I believe that our Bishop would ever have sanctioned your plan, if he had known all I know?[353]

Matters came to a head in 1851. Two boys were removed from the schools because of their fathers' concerns over auricular confession,[354] and the practice contributed to the resignation of the second headmaster, C.E. Moberly.[355]

---

[349] For Hare's attitude to church parties, see Julius C. Hare, *Charges to the Clergy of the Archdeaconry of Lewes, Delivered at the Ordinary Visitations from the Year 1840 to 1854. ... With an Introduction* [by F.D. Maurice] *Explanatory of his Position in the Church with Reference to the Parties Which Divide It* (3 vols, Cambridge, 1856); N.M. Distad, *Guessing at Truth: The Life of Julius Charles Hare (1795-1855)* (Shepherdstown, 1979), pp. 157-61.

[350] Heeney, *Mission to the Middle Classes*, p. 61.

[351] Woodard to Hare, 6 December 1848, LCA Woodard Papers (Correspondence with Hare).

[352] Julius C. Hare, *The True Remedy for the Evils of the Age: A Charge to the Clergy of the Archdeaconry of Lewes, Delivered at the Ordinary Visitation in 1849* (London, 1850), p. 47. Cf. Hare to Woodard, 21 April 1849, LCA Woodard Papers (Religion).

[353] Henry Jacobs to Woodard, 31 August 1848, LCA Woodard Papers (Religion). See John W. Hunwicke, 'Beati Mundo Corde', *Lancing College Magazine* 76 (January 1988), pp. 26-32.

[354] Woodard to T.F. Sanger, 27 April 1851, LCA Woodard Papers (Religion).

[355] Gilbert – Woodard, 1 and 3 August 1851 LCA Woodard Papers (box 1851-60)

Bishop Gilbert warned Woodard:

> Now whatever Dr Pusey, or any other person may say, there can be no doubt that our Anglican Church and system repudiate the private Confessional ... no recourse should be had to self-inflicted or Priest-enjoined Penance as an atonement or a means of obtaining pardon for Sin ... I should be very sorry that so noble an undertaking as yours should fail from any cause. But it will, and I must add it ought to fail, if Confession, and Penance, with consequent Absolution, are introduced into it.[356]

Concerned supporters of the schools soon began to halt their subscriptions. One of these was Golightly's friend, Bishop Trower (formerly rector of Wiston in Sussex).[357] He was joined by his brother-in-law, John Goring, part of an influential local family, whose father and brother had both been MPs for Shoreham. Goring withdrew because he felt Woodard's promise 'to avoid all party views in the training' had not been kept.[358] It was perhaps through Trower and Goring that Golightly at Oxford first became familiar with Woodard's scheme, and other clerical contacts in Sussex kept him informed about developments. For example, Henry Venn Elliott (an evangelical minister in Brighton) told Golightly, 'nothing on earth but Mr Woodard's retirement cd whitewash the school',[359] while Henry Hoper (vicar of Portslade near Brighton) observed: 'the Jesuitism of the managers of the new Institution is transparent.'[360] Golightly began to denounce the institutions privately, leading to the dismissal of their first chaplain, John Knott (who later famously converted to evangelicalism and went out to India with the Church Missionary Society).[361]

In June 1851 Woodard invited the Sussex clergy to the laying of the foundation stone of permanent buildings for the school at Hurstpierpoint, hoping for the 'the union of all Churchmen' at the event.[362] It was boycotted, however, by Trower, Goring and Hoper, and Hoper thought Bishop Gilbert

---

[356] Gilbert to Woodard, 10 May 1851, LCA Woodard Papers (Religion).

[357] Trower to Woodard, 24 May 1851, LCA Woodard Papers (Religion); Trower to Golightly, 27 November 1861, LPL MS 1810, fos 131-2. See Trower to Woodard, July 1848, LCA Woodard Papers (box 1841-49).

[358] Goring to Woodard, 24 May 1851, LCA Woodard Papers (Religion). See *Sussex Express*, 17 January 1857, supplement.

[359] Henry Venn Elliott to Golightly, 27 June 1851, LPL MS 1805, fo. 159.

[360] Hoper to Golightly, 7 July 1851, LPL MS 1807, fo. 201.

[361] Hoper to Golightly, 16 June 1851, LPL MS 1807, fos 194-5. See John W. Hunwicke, 'Lancing's Lost Chaplain and the Crisis of 1851', *Lancing College Magazine* 76 (June 1988), pp. 34-9, (January 1989), pp. 28-31, (June 1989), pp. 31-8. On Knott, see also French to Golightly, 15 July 1870, LPL MS 1805, fos 213-7; Edward P. Hathaway, 'John William Knott: A Memoir', *Churchman* 11 (March 1897), pp. 291-9.

[362] *Sussex Express*, 16 August 1851.

would be glad if he too could 'slip the collar'.³⁶³ Seven other local clergymen, headed by Matthew Glubb and T.A. Holland, refused to attend the ceremony. They also were in touch with Golightly at Oxford and he helped them to draft two public protests against Woodard's system, which were published in the *Sussex Express*. Glubb told Golightly: 'If we get into a controversy, I shall look to you for some help to carry us through it, with credit to the Protestant cause'.³⁶⁴ They proclaimed that the schools were against 'the principles of our Reformed Church',³⁶⁵ depriving pupils of 'a sound Protestant education', and that the practice of auricular confession was 'calculated to make a virtuous youth self-righteous, and an immoral one a hypocrite'.³⁶⁶ One of the seven warned that Woodard's 'semi-Popish system' would make pupils 'the easy victims of Romish subtilty [*sic*] and superstition'.³⁶⁷ Woodard retorted that his assailants had been misled by 'personal vanity & a fanatical party spirit',³⁶⁸ and insisted his institutions were 'genuine Church of England schools'.³⁶⁹ When questioned over confession he declared: 'God forbid that the clamor [*sic*] of Puritans should drive me so far as to forget my duty!'³⁷⁰ Glubb admitted to Golightly that a public protest from Trower, Goring or Hoper would have a greater impact, since he and his six friends were seen merely as 'hot-headed Evangelicals'.³⁷¹

At the Hurstpierpoint event Bishop Gilbert called Woodard 'a true son of our Reformed Church', and Woodard termed himself 'a *bona fide* Church of England man'. Archdeacon Garbett claimed that the bishop's support proved the schools were 'secured against any invasion of the doctrines of our Reformed Church by her deadly enemy, the infidel and anti-Christian Church of Rome'.³⁷² Preaching at the celebration, Archdeacon Hare lamented that religion had

> by a strange and monstrous perversion, become the main seat and focus of war, even among the members of our own Church, – so that, while men are combining and cooperating zealously for every imaginable worldly object, the moment a religious work is taken in hand, it becomes a signal for all manner of jealousies

---

[363] Hoper to Golightly, 25 June 1851, LPL MS 1807, fo. 196.
[364] Glubb to Golightly, 18 July 1851, LPL MS 1806, fo. 24.
[365] *Sussex Express*, 19 July 1851. Drafts at LPL MS 1806, fos 13, 23.
[366] *Sussex Express*, 23 August 1851. Drafts at LPL MS 1806, fos 19-20, 25-7.
[367] *Sussex Express*, 2 August 1851.
[368] Woodard to Glubb, 21 July 1851, LCA Woodard Papers (Religion).
[369] *Sussex Express*, 9 August 1851.
[370] Woodard to Goring, 21 May 1851, LCA Woodard Papers (Religion).
[371] Glubb to Golightly, 7 August 1851, LPL MS 1806, fo. 41.
[372] *Sussex Express*, 28 June 1851.

and suspicions, if not for discord and contention ...³⁷³

He added that 'it is almost as easy to break through a hedge of cactuses, as through a hedge of religious prejudices', and pleaded: 'great would be my delight if I could see our brethren casting aside their party animosities, and joining heartily in promoting a work, which is truly of national importance, and worthy that all loyal members of the English Church should unite for its accomplishment.'³⁷⁴ Hare later advised: 'if an Evangelical objected because the work was wearing, as he thought, a Tractarian aspect, let him join heartily in it and so give it a different colouring. ... There was nothing in the design of the Society which required that it should have any particular sectarian features. It was open to all classes of churchmen'.³⁷⁵

Similar troubles surrounded Woodard's schools in succeeding years. In 1852 J.W. Hewett, a former master, claimed that 'systematic confession is zealously encouraged ... it is intended to be a main feature distinguishing our Schools from others',³⁷⁶ but his charges were dismissed by Gilbert after an official visitation.³⁷⁷ When Hurstpierpoint school was opened in June 1853, the preacher was Connop Thirlwall, Bishop of St David's. He lamented that 'Zealous partisans ... view all which do not wear their own colours with incurable jealousy and distrust', and explained his own maxim:

> when we are satisfied with the general spirit and tendency of an institution, we should not take offence at matters of detail which may appear to us questionable, or even clearly injudicious, but should be ready to concede the greatest possible latitude to the judgment and taste of those who are responsible for them, short of a direct violation of principles.³⁷⁸

Controversy resurfaced in December 1856 when a meeting to raise support for the schools ended in mayhem, provoked by the Brighton Protestant Association. Woodard and his speakers, including Robert Cecil (future Marquess of Salisbury and Prime Minister), the Earl of Carnarvon and Bishop Gilbert, were 'received with cheers, hisses, groans, whistling, cat calls, and every other description of discordant noise'. When Cecil tried to explain that

---

³⁷³ Julius C. Hare, *Education the Necessity of Mankind: A Sermon Preacht at Hurstpierpoint on the 25th of June, 1851, at the Laying of the Foundation Stone of the School for the Middles Classes* (London 1851), p. 17.
³⁷⁴ Ibid., pp. iv-v.
³⁷⁵ *Brighton Guardian*, 12 May 1852.
³⁷⁶ J.W. Hewett to J.T. Rawlison, 2 December 1852, LCA Woodard Papers (Hewett Controversy, 1852-53).
³⁷⁷ *Guardian*, 22 June 1853, p. 407.
³⁷⁸ Connop Thirlwall, *English Education for the Middle Classes. A Sermon, Preached at Hurstpierpoint Church, on the 21st June, 1853, on Occasion of the Opening of St John's School* (London, 1853), pp. 7-8.

the schools were conducted with 'impartiality' he was greeted with cries such as 'No Popery', 'We'll resist Puseyism', 'We don't want to go to confession' and 'Where's Archdeacon Manning?'.[379] Gilbert again warned Woodard: 'Nothing ... can prevent your complete success, but the Incubus of suspicions about Confessions and Absolutions – but that weight will drag your Institutions down, unless it be thoroughly shewn that it does not correctly attach to them.'[380] Woodard, however, wrote another pamphlet complaining at the 'organised system of slander' against his schools, and insisted that there would be 'no party distinctions while I remain Provost ... on this point we are immoveable.' He proclaimed: 'there is nothing to prevent Low Church Clergymen from joining us, if they be earnest men'.[381]

The Oxford Meeting

The final great furore concerning Woodard's schools, and the most crucial, occurred in 1861. Golightly now stepped forward to take a public lead, seeking to portray Woodard as a theological extremist. His opportunity arrived when Woodard went to Oxford to appeal for funds.

According to Woodard's grand scheme, the 'middle classes' were divisible into three groups, requiring three types of school: first there were 'gentlemen of limited means, officers, and Clergymen', then 'tradesmen, farmers, bankers' clerks', and then 'mechanics, small shopkeepers, and gentlemen's servants'.[382] By 1858 three such schools had been established: Lancing College (an upper school), St John's, Hurstpierpoint (a middle school), and St Saviour's, Shoreham (a lower school). Woodard purchased 230 acres at Ardingly as a permanent site for St Saviour's, but considerable extra funds were required, so two great meetings in London and Oxford were organised to raise support. The first took place at St James' Hall in London in June 1861, attended by, amongst others, Bishop Gilbert, Archbishop Longley of York, Lord Lyttelton, Lord Redesdale and Lord John Manners. It was chaired by the aged Lord Brougham (Lord Chancellor in the 1830s) who asserted that he was joined on the platform 'by the tried friends of education, without regard to sect or party or distinction of any kind – the friends of the education and improvement of the people. (Cheers.)'[383] The *Brighton Gazette* agreed that 'Education is a matter of too great importance to be left to struggle on through the conflicts of parties; it should occupy a middle position between the extremes of opinion'. T.A.

---

[379] *Sussex Express*, 6 December 1856, supplement.
[380] Gilbert to Woodard, 3 January 1857, LCA Woodard Papers (box 1851-60).
[381] Nathaniel Woodard, *S. Nicolas College, and the Rev. J. Goring and Others. A Letter to the Substantial Tradesmen, Farmers, and Others of the Employing Classes of the County of Sussex* (London, 1857), pp. 10, 22, 30.
[382] Woodard, *Public Schools* (1852), p. 19.
[383] *Guardian*, 12 June 1861, p. 558.

Holland recommended management of the schools be given to a Board 'composed entirely of staunch members of our Church, yet fairly representative of the different shades and colours of opinion among her members'.[384]

A second high-profile event was arranged for 22 November 1861 in Oxford's Sheldonian Theatre, due to be addressed by dignitaries including Francis Jeune (Vice-Chancellor of the University), William Gladstone (Chancellor of the Exchequer), Lord Cecil, Bishop Wilberforce, Bishop Gilbert and Bishop Wigram of Rochester.[385] William Thomson (Provost of the Queen's College and soon Archbishop of York) was invited to speak, but refused because 'whilst the object must be one approved by all, it has hitherto been pursued in a somewhat narrow and "party" spirit.'[386] Bishop Wilberforce had recently been on the receiving end of Golightly's campaigns and he anticipated some form of protest at the meeting. He warned Woodard to be prepared 'to meet Golightly & all the specious arts of lowly suspicion in which he is so great a master', and his prediction proved correct.[387] Before the event Golightly wrote to some of the dignitaries due to attend, warning them away and explaining that Woodard belonged to 'the extreme Tractarian party'.[388] He knew he would not be allowed to address the meeting, so arranged instead for an anonymous handbill to be distributed at the doors of the Sheldonian Theatre as the crowds arrived. The handbill was inflammatory, claiming that confession was encouraged at Woodard's schools, that crucifixes were distributed there and that they lacked the support of the influential Sussex clergy.[389]

Speaker after speaker at the event dismissed the handbill's claims. Vice-Chancellor Jeune insisted such 'insinuations' should be met with 'silent contempt', and innocently announced his disbelief that 'any English Gentlemen, any English Clergymen … would boldly propound to them a scheme, which, under the guise of loyal attachment to the Church of England, was designed to entrap them'. He compared Golightly to the robber Cacus from Virgil's *Aeneid*, in whose cave 'nothing was to be found but rage and smoke, and a monster easily to be slain. (Laughter.)'[390] Gilbert meanwhile pronounced the statements on the handbill 'a myth'.[391] However, Wilberforce's speech (said

---

[384] *Brighton Gazette*, 20 June 1861. For Holland's authorship of the letter on p. 7, see Holland to Golightly, 13 December 1861, LPL MS 1807, fo. 124.
[385] For organisation of this meeting, see LCA Woodard Papers (Oxford Meeting, 1861).
[386] Thomson to Woodard, 18 November 1861, LCA Woodard Papers (Oxford Meeting).
[387] Wilberforce to Woodard, 1 February 1862, LCA Woodard Papers (Religion).
[388] Golightly to ?, 19 November 1861, LPL MS 1806, fos 72-3, 90-1.
[389] Handbill, Bodleian G.A.Oxon c.78 (368).
[390] *Times*, 23 November 1861. On Jeune, see J.H.C. Leach, *Sparks of Reform: The Career of Francis Jeune, 1806-1868* (Oxford, 1994).
[391] Charles P. Golightly, *A Letter to the Rev. Dr Jeune, Vice-Chancellor of the University of Oxford, in Vindication of the Handbill Distributed at the Doors of the Sheldonian Theatre on Nov. 22, 1861* (Oxford, 1861), p. 5.

to display his 'usual duplicity'[392] and 'characteristic scorn and evasion'[393]) was more animated:

> No great effort to do good to man was ever yet started or accomplished without the voice creeping out from under some hidden covert, 'You had better let it alone.' (Cheers.) For the most part, these voices, as they have done here, clothe themselves in sounds which are most distasteful to the ears of generous men. Yes, Sir, there was a serpent in Paradise, and we have found that there is a snake in the grass of Hurstpierpoint. (Laughter and cheers.)

Wilberforce argued that if the allegations were in fact true, then the scheme should be supported all the more:

> How do you prevent one or two ill-conditioned fellows carrying out their own ill-conditioned schemes? Why, by filling the room with honest men. Then let the honest men in Oxford come forward, with their love of truth and their affection for our Protestant Church, and those suspected malignants with their dark practices, will be foiled in their evil designs. (Cheers.)[394]

Two weeks later, Golightly defended his handbill in *A Letter to the Rev. Dr Jeune*, highlighting the past controversies at Woodard's institutions concerning auricular confession. He observed that there was 'general distrust and dissatisfaction' amongst the Sussex clergy, and that a rare supporter was the notorious A.D. Wagner, a ritualist clergyman from Brighton and 'an extreme party man'.[395] Golightly made new allegations of rosary beads being distributed at the schools and of a pupil at Hurstpierpoint who wore a four-inch long silver crucifix around his neck. He concluded that Woodard's silence in the face of such charges was 'unworthy of him as a man and an Englishman'.[396] Had it been known that Golightly himself kept an 'exquisitely sculptured' ivory crucifix in his home, his enemies would have held him up to ridicule for double-standards and even his Protestant friends may have been troubled by such a revelation. Golightly's crucifix was a family heirloom, brought back from Paris in the 1780s by an uncle, and preserved behind a glass frame as an historical curiosity rather than an aid to worship – but had Woodard been told of its existence, he could easily have cut the ground from under his adversary's

---

[392] Twopeny to Golightly, 26 November 1861, LPL MS 1811, fo. 127.
[393] *Record*, 5 February 1862.
[394] *Times*, 23 November 1861.
[395] Golightly, *Letter to Jeune*, pp. 4-5. On Wagner, see Anthony R. Wagner and Antony Dale, *The Wagners of Brighton* (Chichester, 1983), pp. 100-36; E.P. Hennock, 'The Anglo-Catholics and Church Extension in Victorian Brighton' in M.J. Kitch (ed.), *Studies in Sussex Church History* (London, 1981), pp. 173-88; Nigel Yates, '"Bells and Smells": London, Brighton and South Coast Religion Reconsidered', *Southern History* 5 (1983), pp. 122-53.
[396] Golightly, *Letter to Jeune*, pp. 11-3.

feet.[397] Instead Woodard replied with a published statement, denying that crucifixes were distributed at his schools and explaining that confession was 'carefully restricted' – his chaplains did not solicit confessions, and if a boy asked to confess, the chaplain first sought parental consent and afterwards made a report to the bishop. Woodard also insisted that his schools had widespread support amongst the Sussex clergy.[398] Yet Golightly was not satisfied and in *A Second Letter to the Rev. Dr Jeune* he observed that if every case of private confession was reported to the bishop, this would merely encourage any 'weak, vain, and self-conceited lad'.[399] He further alleged that the funeral of a pupil at Hurstpierpoint had been performed according to the guidelines of John Purchas' notorious *Directorium Anglicanum*, and that teachers were bound to secrecy about the institutions' practices. Golightly concluded that the members of Oxford University were 'the victims of as daring a fraud as ever was attempted to be practised upon a public body'.[400] Jeune found himself caught in the cross-fire between Golightly and Woodard, and privately tried to appease both men. He told Woodard that Golightly was 'a very ardent partisan and so not entitled to the weight to which in respect of personal character he might lay claim'.[401] Yet he was also trying to persuade Golightly, 'now that the Puseyite movement has passed away', that people should not be 'held to errors and exaggerations which they fell into when party feelings were warm. On the contrary we ought in defence of our common Christianity to unite as far as we can especially in doing good.'[402]

As so often before, Golightly's charges succeeded in raising a storm. The *Christian Observer* thought the schools 'utterly unworthy of the countenance of a Protestant University'.[403] Lord Radnor mourned, 'we shall soon have to import Protestant feelings & principles from Italy or Spain',[404] and another of Golightly's correspondents declared: 'shame upon the men high in place & power, who ... evidently *rejoiced* in the occasion of giving a stab at Christian Principles by their support of Popish Practices.'[405] Meanwhile Holland described Woodard's scheme as

---

[397] 'Certain Curiosities at 6 Holywell Street, Oxford', 8 April 1878, Stack MS 16a. For John Henry Newman's 'awe and adoration' when Golightly showed him the crucifix, see Goulburn, *Reminiscences of Golightly*, p. 35.
[398] Nathaniel Woodard, *S. Nicolas College and the Handbill Circulated in the Sheldonian Theatre. A Statement* (Oxford, 1861).
[399] Charles P. Golightly, *A Second Letter to the Rev. Dr Jeune, Vice-Chancellor of the University of Oxford, in Reference to the Handbill Distributed at the Doors of the Sheldonian Theatre on Nov. 22, 1861* (Oxford, 1861), p. 4.
[400] Ibid., p. 14.
[401] Jeune to Woodard, 10 December 1861, LCA Woodard Papers (Religion).
[402] Jeune to Golightly, 23 December 1861, LPL MS 1808, fo. 4.
[403] *Christian Observer* (December 1861), p. 980.
[404] Lord Radnor to Golightly, 17 December 1861, LPL MS 1804, fo. 71.
[405] Thomas H. Paddon to Golightly, December 1861, LPL MS 1808, fo. 203.

the most insidious & *effective* confederacy against the Protestantism of the Ch. of Eng. that has been ventured upon since the Reformation, from within or from without her pale. ... there ought to be no *compromise* whatever with the arch conspirators, nor spurious delicacy with their willing dupes.[406]

Criticism centred around Woodard perceived dishonesty and dissimulation. Bishop Trower called him 'thoro'ly Jesuitical in the sense of evasive, shuffling, disingenuous',[407] and John Tucker felt a 'shameless trick' had been played on the University.[408] Richard Twopeny rebuked 'this invidious attempt to pervert the rising generation', observing: 'the endeavours to hide & stifle the truth puts one in mind of Cuddesdon College'.[409] Even a supporter of the schools advised: 'better ten thousand times that they should be known as "extreme men", than suspected as dishonest ones.'[410]

Golightly, in contrast to Woodard, was lauded by his Protestant friends for his integrity. He was praised for upholding 'Protestant Truth',[411] and for his 'continued faithful exposure of the teaching and dishonesty of the Enemies of the Truth within our Camp.'[412] Another emboldened him with the words of St Paul to Timothy, 'Be willing to endure hardness as a good soldier of Jesus Christ' and continued, 'Many of *us look to you* to sound the alarm, when any suspicious measure is broached in Oxford.'[413] Even Provost Hawkins of Oriel, who did not support Golightly's methods, defended him to Woodard as 'a well-meaning man, & seeking the truth'.[414] Other correspondents thanked Golightly for 'constantly withstanding the various insidious approaches of Popery',[415] and for 'boldly grappling with the enemy'.[416] John Shaw, who had provoked the Boyne Hill inquiry, spurred him on in his campaign: 'few, I think, are better qualified for it than yourself'.[417] Yet Golightly's enemies thought that he, not Woodard, was the liar. For example, Sam Brooke (a pupil at Lancing) noted in his diary: 'Mr Golightly adds to his other virtues of informer & slandering [*sic*],

---

[406] Holland to Golightly, 27 January 1862, LPL MS 1807, fos 144-5.
[407] Trower to Golightly, 24 December 1861, LPL MS 1810, fo. 139.
[408] Tucker to Golightly, 14 December 1861, LPL MS 1811, fo. 26.
[409] Twopeny to Golightly, 26 November and 23 December 1861, LPL MS 1811, fos 128, 139.
[410] *St Nicholas and His Schools. A Letter to the Rev. the Vice-Chancellor of the University of Oxford. By a Member of Convocation* (Oxford, 1861), p. 4.
[411] Twopeny to Golightly, 5 December 1861, LPL MS 1811, fo. 133.
[412] Paddon to Golightly, December 1861, LPL MS 1808, fo. 203.
[413] John Langley to Golightly, 7 December 1861, LPL MS 1808, fo. 40.
[414] Hawkins to Woodard, 28 February 1862, LCA Woodard Papers (Bishop's Investigation).
[415] Henry Barne to Golightly, 18 January 1864, LPL MS 1804, fo. 29.
[416] Holland to Glubb, 29 November 1861, LPL MS 1807, fo. 107.
[417] John Shaw to Golightly, 12 December 1861, LPL MS 1809, fo. 72.

the respectable character of a gross & hardened liar.'[418] Likewise the *Guardian* spoke of 'the Golightly libel'[419] and Woodard himself castigated 'the inaccuracies and evil surmises of party spirit'.[420]

Once again a mountain of abusive epithets was heaped upon Golightly. Edward Churton (now Archdeacon of Cleveland) called him 'a self-important busy-body',[421] and his actions were termed 'mean, spiteful, and discreditable'.[422] Meanwhile the *Union* newspaper rebuked 'the malignant attack of some Golightly or other Protestant myrmidon', and praised Woodard's schools for 'raising up a barrier of middle class intelligence against the mendacious or ignorant clamour of Puritanism.'[423] It complained against Golightly's 'ingenious admixture of truth and misstatement, of anonymous delation with avowed invective', and called him the 'Devil's Advocate':

> The office has been self-conferred by its holder. No enthusiastic mass-meeting at Exeter Hall has selected him as its champion, no secret caucus in Mr Westerton's back shop has indicated him as the second leader of the Protestant world, the Vice-President of that Republic of Evil-speaking whose first place is worthily held by an eminent peer. [The first ritualist case tried by the courts was Westerton vs Liddell in the mid-1850s, a Protestant churchwarden's prosecution of his ritualist vicar at St Barnabas', Pimlico. The 'eminent peer' is perhaps a reference to Lord Shaftesbury, who was famous for his anti-ritualism as well as his philanthropy.] ... It mattered little to Mr Golightly whether the middle classes were to be educated at all, but it mattered a great deal if it could be shown that Tommy Smith after leaving school had distinctly refused to eat a mutton chop on a Friday, and that Johnny Robinson had declined to pronounce positively against the salvability of the Pope. The gnats of order, intelligence, sobriety and religion could not be allowed to weigh for a moment against such theological camels as these. ... True to the instincts of his party he could find no remedy but detraction and opposition. He did not propose to found a school for a thousand boys, where each pupil on his departure should be presented with a photograph of Mr Spurgeon [London's leading Baptist preacher], but only that no favour should be shown to one suspected of aiming at a higher ideal. So that Mr Woodard might fail he cared not that any other should succeed. This is our real ground of quarrel with bigots of Mr Golightly's stamp.[424]

However, the *Union* also reserved some of its vitriol for Nathaniel Woodard himself. It thought that he deserved the difficulties in which he found himself,

---

[418] Brooke Diary, 2 January 1862, Corpus Christi College Archives, Oxford.
[419] *Guardian*, 23 December 1863, p. 1191.
[420] *Church Review*, 5 April 1862, p. 214.
[421] Edward Churton to Woodard, 21 February 1862, LCA Woodard Papers (Bishop's Investigation).
[422] *Church Review*, 25 January 1862, p. 46.
[423] *Union*, 6 December 1861, pp. 769-70.
[424] *Union*, 13 December 1861, p. 785.

because he was guilty of compromise (the newspaper's *bête noire*) with non-ritualists. Afraid of being labelled an 'extremist', he had for too long been trying to paper over the deep divisions between rival theological camps:

> High Churchmen of the present day are fain to compromise matters with Low Churchmen. It is so delightful to find everybody agreed and glad to swallow or ignore differences. ... Does the Government purpose an assault on Church Education, Dean Close and Archdeacon Denison are firm allies. Does the Government encourage a raid upon Church Rates, all parties in the Establishment exhibit marvellous concord. Does Lord Ebury menace us with a Puritan Revision of the Prayer Book, there is the same surprising unanimity against him. If it were not for a Poole [suspended from St Barnabas', Pimlico for auricular confession], a Cheyne [dismissed from St John's, Aberdeen for teaching the 'real presence'], a Forbes ['Tractarian' Bishop of Brechin], or a Philpotts [*sic*, octogenarian Bishop of Exeter], the Church would have her note of unity clearly defined and satisfactorily enunciated. Extreme things and extreme people are alike eliminated, and everybody is agreed in denouncing them. ... A very High Churchman who can manage to pass muster as a Broad Churchman, or an Evangelical at a pinch, may expect to get on and win a stall or a mitre at last. Unhappily this system, ingenious as it is, cannot be long carried on without a break down. A Churchman trying to imitate Puritans is at exactly the same disadvantage as a lady of good position who copies 'pretty horsebreakers'.[425]

Cold Feet and a Bishop's Inquiry

The adverse publicity provoked by Golightly's attacks began to damage Woodard's institutions. Edward Lowe (headmaster of Hurstpierpoint) acknowledged: 'Mr Golightly has done us a *little* temporary mischief in checking our numbers'.[426] Twopeny predicted that the schools would 'fall into discredit, & become a mere party institution',[427] and Holland was hopeful that they would shut altogether. He encouraged Golightly:

> Unless W. shd prosecute & convict you of Libel ... with more than farthing damages, I do not see how he can lay a brick at Balcombe [Ardingly], or prevent his present edifices becoming monumental ruins within a few years festooned with ivy, for the sketchbooks of the young Ladies of Brighton & Worthing.[428]

Those in Oxford connected with the Sheldonian Theatre debacle attempted to salvage their reputations and worried that they had been overly hasty in promoting the schools. Vice-Chancellor Jeune and Bishop Wigram, along with

---

[425] *Union*, 14 February 1862, p. 97.
[426] Edward C. Lowe to Woodard, 28 January 1862, LCA Woodard Papers (Religion). See also, letters from parents, *Daily News*, 8, 11, 13-14, 20-21 February 1862.
[427] Twopeny to Golightly, 26 November 1861, LPL MS 1811, fo. 127.
[428] Holland to Golightly, 26 December 1861, LPL MS 1807, fo. 132.

Bishops Gilbert and Wilberforce, were not keen to admit any mistake, but at the same time did not want to be tarred with the same brush as Woodard. Professor Heurtley observed to Golightly: 'people are slow to admit the conviction that they have taken a false step. That wh they would not do, if it was to be done again, having done they vindicate & are ready to fight for.'[429] Wilberforce was the most resilient and tried to persuade his fellow dignitaries not to bow to Golightly's pressure. As in the Lavington case, his influence upon the Bishop of Chichester was evident. Gilbert was called 'a weak & wind-shaken reed',[430] who was 'easily led about by the skilful S. Oxon',[431] his 'guiding coadjutor'.[432] Tucker spoke of 'the rotten palisades – or gabions stuffed with straw, which I suspect the Bp of O. has put up in the night', and lamented:

> public men have such entanglements – & currents & counter-currents, – that I never feel sure what they may do or not do; – & I cannot tell what influence may be brought to bear on the Bp of Rochester by the Bp of Oxford, or others set in motion by him; e.g. 'it is very unwise for a Bp to appear to agitate – or to retract – or to put his brother bishops in an awkward position. Mr Golightly & Mr Twopeny are two of those who caused disturbance in their own Diocese – there is no *necessity* for coming forward – so best to keep quiet – the V.C., you see, is quite indisposed to take such a step' &c &c.[433]

Nevertheless, after much soul searching and delicate negotiations behind the scenes, Wigram and Jeune (called 'hoodwinked Dignitaries'[434]) publicly distanced themselves from Woodard. At the end of January 1862, Wigram stated he now had 'the strongest distrust of the principles by which the Institutions are administered, and the practices which are encouraged or connived at in them', particularly fasting and auricular confession. Jeune withdrew his support until 'after a free and searching inquiry'.[435] John Goring thought their letters 'lame apologies', but observed: 'I am very glad I never had to eat so much dirt.'[436] Trower thought their withdrawal 'a great blow to the most disingenuous scheme of the present Day. They must be an occasion of

---

[429] Heurtley to Golightly, 23 December 1861, LPL MS 1807, fos 39-40.
[430] Stephen Barbut to Golightly, 7 December 1861, LPL MS 1804, fo. 23.
[431] George Ranking to Golightly, 11 December 1861, LPL MS 1808, fo. 2.
[432] Holland to Golightly, 12 December 1861, LPL MS 1807, fo. 122.
[433] Tucker to Golightly, 14 January 1862, LPL MS 1811, fos 33-4.
[434] Holland to Golightly, 3 February 1862, LPL MS 1807, fo. 148.
[435] *Record*, 31 January 1862. For resulting correspondence between Wigram and the English Church Union, see *Church Review*, 15 and 22 March, 12 April, 3 May 1862, pp. 165-6, 198, 229, 278. See also Central Protestant Institute to Wigram, *Guardian*, 16 April 1862, p. 364; *St Nicolas College Middle Schools. A Correspondence between the Right Rev. J.C. Wigram ... and the Rev. F. Jeune ... and the Rev. Popularis Aura, an Impalpable in the Diocese of Rochester* (London, 1862) (copy at Selwyn College Library, Cambridge).
[436] Goring to Golightly, 6 February 1862, LPL MS 1806, fo. 151.

much annoyance – not to say pain – to Bps of Chichester & Oxford – who will *themselves be put upon trial* (!) in any investigation that may take place.'[437] The *Union* was also glad to see Wigram and Jeune's departure and went so far as to hope the Protestant charges against the schools would be proved true. It explained:

> The Shoreham schools are conducted on Church of England principles, or they are not. If they are, they can have no more to do with Bishop Wigram and Dr Jeune than with Mr Spurgeon or Dr Cumming [a Scottish Presbyterian in London]. ... If Mr Woodard has gained them over by allowing them to believe that he cared as little for Anglican doctrine and practice as they, he is undergoing a species of Ecclesiastical retribution. Nothing we confess rouses our indignation more than the muffling our bells, so that at last we begin to think the funeral of the Church system is passing on. Let them ring out sharp and clear.[438]

Likewise the *Church Review* observed:

> that Mr WOODARD ... should know nothing and reckon nothing of schools or parties in the Church, is worthy of his benevolence. But even guilelessness is not always a match for cunning, especially when cunning is backed by jealousy and dislike. ... We confess therefore we had rather see the energetic Provost working away without the checks and drawbacks which come of the hanging on of lukewarm supporters.[439]

Alongside Jeune and Wigram, another high-profile secession was threatened – that of Robert Sanderson, whose appointment as the new headmaster of Lancing was announced in December 1861.[440] He complained to Woodard that because of the practice of auricular confession

> Lancing cannot hope to be a public school or to educate any but the sons of a narrow *section*, I will not say *sect* of the community. It must open its arms, if it is meant to give a training which all plain Churchmen & honest citizens will be willing to use for their children. And if it does not, it is *in spirit* Sectarian.[441]

Lowe believed Sanderson's resignation would be 'a more dangerous matter than the Oxford ferment',[442] but in the event he was persuaded to remain at Lancing, going on to lead the school for 27 years.

Jeune and Wigram were not the only ones to call for a formal inquiry.

---

[437] Trower to Golightly, 3 February 1862, LPL MS 1810, fo. 144.
[438] *Union*, 14 February 1862, p. 97.
[439] *Church Review*, 15 February 1862, p. 90.
[440] M.C. Buck, 'The Appointment of Robert Sanderson', *Lancing College Magazine* 77 (June 1990), pp. 67-9.
[441] R.E. Sanderson to Woodard, 6 December 1861, LCA Woodard Papers (Religion).
[442] Lowe to Woodard, 8 December 1861, LCA Woodard Papers (Religion).

Woodard's friends in Oxford also thought this might be the best way to throw off the persistent and damaging rumours surrounding the schools. Following the meeting in the Sheldonian Theatre, an Oxford Committee had been established to raise subscriptions for the schools, chaired by F.K. Leighton (Warden of All Souls College). The 50-strong committee was 'latitudinarian in the widest sense'.[443] – it included twelve Heads of Houses and people from a broad variety of theological backgrounds.[444] However, Heurtley, Hawkins and Thomson refused to serve on the committee and others began to desert it as Golightly's campaign gathered pace.[445] Peter Medd (secretary to the committee) observed: 'Mr Golightly is not a very formidable opponent, still we know that these statements are damaging us'.[446] He advised Woodard that an official inquiry was 'the only chance of preventing a formidable secession from the Committee', but hoped it would 'settle the thing once for all, & ... show that your Institutions are distinctively Church Institutions worked loyally & honestly in the interest and for the objects of the Church of England.'[447]

At Bishop Wilberforce's suggestion, a series of detailed questions were drawn up by Leighton and others (on behalf of the Oxford Committee) asking about the schools' policies towards auricular confession, crucifixes and fasting.[448] Golightly was invited to comment on these questions before they were sent to Bishop Gilbert, but declined to do so, perhaps because that would limit his ability to criticise the inquiry.[449] Yet ritualist supporters of the schools freely criticised the questions. Members of the English Church Union (founded in 1859 to fight 'against Erastianism, Rationalism and Puritanism' within the Church of England) felt they could not be answered without breaking the seal of the confessional.[450] Henry Liddon (who had been invited to work at Lancing after his resignation from Cuddesdon) thought Woodard should not reply to them.[451] Likewise John Branthwaite (Principal of St Edmund's Hall and former Headmaster of Lancing) believed the schools should not submit to this 'self-appointed Inquisition'.[452] Even Medd soon began to change his tune and doubted the value of the process: 'Of course to think that any enquiry will

---

[443] Heurtley to Golightly, 23 December 1861, LPL MS 1807, fo. 40.
[444] *Oxford Herald*, 7 December 1861.
[445] Leighton to Woodard, 6 December 1861; Medd to Woodard, 6 December 1861, LCA Woodard Papers (Religion).
[446] Medd to Leighton, 5 December 1861, LCA Woodard Papers (Religion).
[447] Medd to Woodard, 6 February 1862, LCA Woodard Papers (Bishop's Investigation).
[448] *Record*, 24 December 1863; Leighton to Woodard, 2 and 18 February 1862, LCA Woodard Papers (Bishop's Investigation).
[449] Golightly to Jeune, 5 February 1862, LPL MS 1808, fo. 10.
[450] *Church Review*, 15 March 1862, p. 166.
[451] Liddon to Woodard, 19 February 1859, LCA Woodard Papers (Masters); Liddon to Woodard, 4 March 1862, Woodard Papers (Bishop's Investigation).
[452] John Branthwaite to Woodard, 6 March 1862, LCA Woodard Papers (Bishop's Investigation).

satisfy Golightly or the Bp of Rochester is absurd.'[453] Robert Moorsom (Chairman of Woodard's Brighton Committee) agreed:

> it is impossible to please Mr Golightly & the Bishop of Rochester unless you put a non natural interpretation on the formularies of the Church & make them of non effect by following Puritan tradition. I trust our Bishop will stand firm & not make a second Cuddesdon of St Nicholas College.[454]

This, however, was precisely what Twopeny feared: 'an inquiry conducted by the Bps of Oxford & Chichester would be quite a sham, & so regarded by the public; we cannot forget Cuddesdon & Lavington'.[455]

Nevertheless, the inquiry went ahead. Bishop Wilberforce had been through this painful process a number of times before and advised Woodard: 'All that I would urge on you is the most complete & out spoken statement of everything. Nothing can hurt you like the appearance of any concealment or want of perfect honesty & openness.'[456] Likewise Lord Cecil counselled: 'the most explicit & unambiguous explanation is our wisest policy.'[457] Answers to the Oxford Committee's questions were duly sent to Bishop Gilbert in March 1862 and his judgment awaited. If Wilberforce's inquiry into Cuddesdon College had been conducted with 'Napoleonic rapidity', Gilbert's inquiry was just the opposite. By November his judgment had still not appeared and Leighton was complaining: 'The delay has been long & I fear mischievous.'[458] Apologising that he had been too busy,[459] the bishop eventually pronounced in May 1863 that he was 'entirely satisfied' with Woodard's schools.[460] In December the suspended operations of the Oxford Committee were revived.[461]

Two years had passed since the famous Sheldonian Theatre meeting and Golightly remained dissatisfied. Gilbert's tardiness had successfully taken the momentum out of his campaign, but he tried to rekindle it. Through the columns of *Jackson's Oxford Journal* and the *Sussex Advertiser*, he complained that the Oxford Committee had not been given direct answers to their questions,

---

[453] Medd to Woodard, 6 February 1862, LCA Woodard Papers (Bishop's Investigation).
[454] Moorsom to Woodard, 8 March 1862, LCA Woodard Papers (1864, Supporters II).
[455] Twopeny to Golightly, 3 February 1862, LPL MS 1811, fo. 153.
[456] Wilberforce to Woodard, 1 February 1862, LCA Woodard Papers (Religion).
[457] Cecil to Woodard, 8 February 1862, LCA Woodard Papers (Bishop's Investigation).
[458] Leighton to Woodard, 1 November 1862, LCA Woodard Papers (Bishop's Investigation).
[459] Gilbert to Woodard, 21 April, 24 June and 18 July 1862, LCA Woodard Papers (Bishop's Investigation); Gilbert to Jeune, 13 May 1863 (Religion).
[460] *Guardian*, 13 May 1863, p. 438. See Leighton to Woodard, 26 May 1863, LCA Woodard Papers (Supporters).
[461] Leighton to Woodard, 8 August 1863, LCA Woodard Papers (Religion); Leighton to Woodard, 10 and 15 December 1863 (Supporters); *Jackson's Oxford Journal*, 19 December 1863.

but only parts of answers embodied in Gilbert's report. It was therefore not the 'free and searching inquiry' which Vice-Chancellor Jeune had requested, and Jeune (now Dean of Lincoln and soon Bishop of Peterborough) refused to renew his support for the schools.[462] This had Woodard immediately writing to the press, chastising Golightly as that 'well-known Oxford censor'.[463] Likewise, from Brighton, Robert Moorsom retorted that Golightly and his allies were 'the exponents of narrow prejudices', and proclaimed: 'The Bishop's judgment, pronounced according to law, is not asked for; but the sentence of a self-constituted and irresponsible Puritan Inquisition, under the presidency of Mr Golightly!'[464] Nevertheless, Holland rejoiced that Golightly had struck 'an effective blow at the resuscitated hydra'. He reckoned the manoeuvres of the Oxford Committee 'insulting to the supposed stupidity & credulity of the public' and a 'transparent sham'.[465] The *Record* thought the true nature of the schools had been 'studiously concealed from the light',[466] while the *Brighton Gazette* complained: 'The only result of his strangled enquiry is to make the public more suspicious than ever.'[467] Golightly also tried to revive his flagging campaign in Sussex by sending a copy of the *Sussex Advertiser*'s report on the affair to every clergyman in Chichester diocese.[468] Yet little interest was taken in his renewed protests.

With his chief Protestant adversary now ignored, Woodard was soon able to return to his high-profile fund-raising and school-building activities. In April 1864 a meeting similar to that in the Sheldonian Theatre was held at Cambridge University, with Holland hoping 'that a Golightly would be raised up for the occasion on the banks of the Cam.'[469] The foundation stone of Ardingly school was laid in July 1864, at a ceremony attended by Bishops Wilberforce and Gilbert, Lords Cecil, Lyttelton and Brougham, and others. Earl Granville laid the first stone, announcing that 'He certainly was not there as representing any political party in the State, and certainly not as representing any particular principle in the Church.'[470] The *Guardian* concluded that the support of 'impartial men' such as Granville and Brougham proved that 'the accusations of the Low Church party' were false.[471] In 1867 Woodard declared: 'Confusion, quarrelling, and party-spirit are obviously out of place in such a scheme as ours,

---

[462] *Jackson's Oxford Journal*, 2 January 1864; *Sussex Advertiser*, 5 January 1864; *Brighton Gazette*, 7 and 28 January 1864.
[463] *Brighton Gazette*, 14 January 1864.
[464] *Brighton Gazette*, 4 February 1864.
[465] Holland to Golightly, 23 December 1863, LPL MS 1807, fo. 157.
[466] *Record*, 16 December 1863.
[467] *Brighton Gazette*, 21 January 1864.
[468] Glubb to Golightly, 7 January 1864, LPL MS 1806, fo. 62.
[469] Holland to Golightly, 16 April 1864, LPL MS 1807, fo. 179; *Times*, 11 April 1864.
[470] *Brighton Gazette*, 14 July 1864.
[471] *Guardian*, 20 July 1864, p. 709.

and destructive of it ... Controversy is not to our mind'.[472] Two years later he was still claiming that his schools were 'very generally approved by all parties in the Church', and that it was possible to raise the £1,500,000 he needed for expansion through 'a union of Church parties'.[473]

Nevertheless the charge of theological extremism, which Golightly had done so much to propagate, was not easily removed. Soon it was freely acknowledged that the schools only represented one sub-section of the Church of England. Brian Heeney concludes that the Oxford Meeting of 1861 and its aftermath saw a decline in the 'national' or 'non-party' prospects of Woodard's scheme, with Golightly and his allies having 'successfully branded Woodard as a Tractarian and his schools as "party establishments".'[474] Bishop Hamilton, for instance, told Woodard: 'I doubt the policy of claiming *general* sympathy for works which professedly rest on distinctive Church teaching. Mr Golightly has if you do so, a right to be heard.'[475] Golightly's pamphlets were cited at a Church Association Conference in 1868 as evidence of the 'theological bias' of Woodard's schools, which were said to be injecting 'the subtle poison of priestcraft into the veins of the very life-blood of English Society.' The Conference heard that education of the 'middle classes' was 'in danger of being monopolized by the Tractarian party', and that Woodard's pupils would 'grow up to be religious partizans of a most pernicious type.'[476] Therefore a committee, including evangelical heavyweights like J.C. Ryle, Edward Hathaway, Edward Auriol and J.C. Colquhoun (Chairman of the Church Association), was formed to consider the establishment of alternative schools 'upon Scriptural principles'.[477] Indeed in 1866 Trent College had already been founded in conscious opposition to Woodard's scheme.[478] The promotion of education for the 'middle classes' was now conspicuously divided along church party lines, and despite his protestations Woodard's schools had gained a widespread reputation for religious partisanship. Golightly bore a large responsibility for the increased clarity of these divisions.

---

[472] Nathaniel Woodard, *Denstone Public School, In Union with S. Nicolas College. A Letter to Sir T. Percival Heywood, Bart.* (London, 1867), p. 4 (copy at LCA).

[473] Nathaniel Woodard, *The Scheme of Education of St Nicolas College, with Suggestions for the Permanent Constitution of that Society, in a Letter to the Most Noble the Marquis of Salisbury* (Oxford, 1869), pp. 15, 19.

[474] Heeney, *Mission to the Middle Classes*, pp. 82-3.

[475] Hamilton to Woodard, 17 March 1864, LCA Woodard Papers (Supporters II).

[476] Church Association, *The Woodard Schools* (second edition, London, 1868), pp. 9, 14-5.

[477] Ibid., pp. 33-6.

[478] M.A.J. Tarver, *Trent College, 1868-1927: A Rough Sketch* (London, 1929), pp. 3-8.

A Predilection for Rome

People seem going crazy about Ritualism. (Bishop Trower, 1867)[479]

The Diocese is in a very agitated state. Alarming rumours circulate even in the most remote villages, to the effect that the Church of England is going back to Rome. (Charles Golightly, 1867)[480]

The nationwide agitation against the spread of ritualism reached fever pitch in the mid-1860s. Battle lines were drawn, prosecutions multiplied, and an array of aggressive organisations fought to reform the Church of England according to their own distinctive theological principles. In response to the work of the pro-ritualist English Church Union, and fearful for the nation's Reformation heritage, the Church Association drew traditional Protestants together from 1865. Their aim was 'to counteract the efforts now being made to pervert the teaching of the Church of England on essential points of the Christian faith, or assimilate her services to those of the Church of Rome' and Golightly became a life member in 1867.[481] Soon the Church Association was helping 'aggrieved parishioners' to take their clergy to court. A lengthy battle was initiated against A.H. Mackonochie of St Alban's, Holborn for illegal liturgical practices during holy communion – for crimes such as elevating the bread and wine, using incense and altar lights, and 'excessive kneeling'.[482] The Church Association also supported the prosecution in the late 1860s of W.J.E. Bennett of Frome Selwood in Somerset and John Purchas of St James, Brighton. Purchas was accused of 35 innovations, including wearing cope and chasuble, using holy water, veiling the crucifix on his altar during Lent, observing feasts not in the *Book of Common Prayer*, blessing candles at Candlemas, imposing ashes on Ash Wednesday, introducing a crib at Christmas and suspending a stuffed dove over the altar at Pentecost. Meanwhile the first Royal Commission set up to investigate ritualism began sitting in June 1867, and Lord Shaftesbury promoted in Parliament his Clerical Vestments Bill which aimed to standardise clergy dress by enforcing the surplice and banning vestments.[483] With thousands of pamphlets and petitions rolling off printing presses across the country on all sides of the debate, Golightly played his part in Oxford diocese by contributing yet another circular and yet another pamphlet. Now Bishop Wilberforce, friend to ritualists, had explicitly become his primary target.

In February 1867 Golightly sent an anonymous circular to all churchwardens in Oxford diocese, signed 'A Clergyman in the Diocese of More Than Thirty

---

[479] Trower to Golightly, 21 February 1867, LPL MS 1810, fo. 182.
[480] Golightly, *Position of Samuel Wilberforce*, p. 87.
[481] *Church Association Annual Report*, 1871, p. clxxxi.
[482] Michael Reynolds, *Martyr of Ritualism: Father Mackonochie of St Alban's, Holborn* (London, 1965).
[483] Nigel Yates, *Anglican Ritualism in Victorian Britain*, ch. 5.

Years' Standing'.[484] He warned them that the recent introduction in many churches across the diocese of stone altars, crosses, crucifixes, vestments, incense, wafer bread, the mixed chalice, candles during the daytime 'and other Romish peculiarities' all tended 'to bring us back to Rome'. Golightly encouraged the churchwardens to oppose every change in their local church services, to remonstrate with their clergy when such changes were made, and if this had no effect, to complain to Bishop Wilberforce and publish their remonstrance in the newspapers. Good examples had recently been set by the parishioners of Banbury and nearby King's Sutton, who in early 1867 organised petitions to their clergy complaining at the introduction of choral services, wafer bread, processions and even the use of bags instead of plates to collect alms.[485] Golightly urged other parishes to follow suit and assured the churchwardens that all costs of replacing stone altars with plain oak tables would be met. He suggested they also petition the Queen to halt ritualism and proclaimed: 'England expects every man to do his duty'.[486]

Unlike his previous inflammatory publications, Golightly's circular had little impact amongst the churchwardens and was hardly noticed by the newspapers. Rare comment came from a churchwarden in Berkshire writing in the *Church Times*. Two hundred laymen from Reading had also recently declared their lack of confidence in Wilberforce, but the churchwarden thought they and Golightly were guilty of 'circulating abuse, slander, and falsehoods ... This 201 uncharitable, narrow-minded, bigoted, small party is as fit to advise the Bishop of Oxford, as a farthing rushlight would be to light the blazing sun.'[487]

The main response to Golightly's circular came from his old adversary, Edward Pusey (still Professor of Hebrew at Oxford University). John Keble had recently died, so Pusey's position as the supreme figurehead of the Catholic Revival was now undisputed. During 1865-66 he had ruffled feathers by republishing *Tract 90* and issuing his first *Eirenicon*, which encouraged closer relations with the Church of Rome. Pusey had survived thirty years of controversy, and his place in the Church of England was increasingly secure, but Golightly could not resist another opportunity to denounce his opinions. In his circular to the churchwardens of Oxford diocese, Golightly claimed that the teaching of Pusey and Newman had been responsible for the secession to the Church of Rome of several hundred people since the early 1840s. He went

---

[484] *Jackson's Oxford Journal*, 2 March 1867.

[485] On Banbury, see *Jackson's Oxford Journal*, 16 and 23 February, 2 and 9 March, 11 May, 22 June 1867; *Oxford Chronicle*, 23 March 1867. On King's Sutton, see *Jackson's Oxford Journal*, 2 and 9 February, 2 March 1867.

[486] Golightly recommended the form of petition adopted by the Lay Members of the Clerical and Lay Association for the Maintenance of Evangelical Principles (Midland Branch): *Record*, 20 February 1867.

[487] *Church Times*, 23 March 1867, p. 100. For the laymen's petition, see *Record*, 11 March 1867. For the bishop's dismissive reply, see *Jackson's Oxford Journal*, 6 April 1867.

further and warned that 'Dr Pusey still professes to belong to the Church of England, but is doing his best to spread amongst us the doctrines of Rome.'[488] Pusey rightly guessed that this anonymous attack was Golightly's doing and wrote privately to remonstrate, but Golightly refused to enter into correspondence about a document to which his name was not attached.[489] Therefore Pusey sent his letter to the *Oxford Chronicle*, in order to provoke a response. He argued that many had been driven out of the Church of England into the Church of Rome not by Tractarian publications, but by 'Evangelical controversialists' who had been 'teaching and teasing people into the opinion that they cannot honestly hold what *we* believe in the Church of England'.[490] Golightly, still signing himself 'A Clergyman of More Than Thirty Years' Standing', retorted: 'The shaking of the apple-tree brings down the ripe fruit, but has no effect in ripening it.'[491]

More seriously, Pusey thought the claim that he was propagating Roman doctrines within the Church of England was 'libellous' and 'clearly actionable'. It was a charge that ought to be decided not by newspaper controversy but by a Court of Law, and must either 'be substantiated or abandoned'.[492] In 1846 Bishop Wilberforce had encouraged Golightly (still then a friend) to prosecute Pusey in the Vice-Chancellor's Court at Oxford for heretical teaching, hoping the charges would be proved. However, in the intervening twenty years the theological sands had shifted, and the bishop now sided more closely with Pusey, fed up with Golightly's ceaseless agitation. Therefore on reading the circular to the churchwardens, Wilberforce encouraged Pusey to challenge Golightly to prosecute him in the Vice-Chancellor's Court. This time the bishop hoped the charges would be thrown out, leaving Golightly embarrassed and defeated. Pusey had recently made a public promise to resign his office if it were decided 'by a competent authority' that his views on holy communion were contrary to the doctrine of the Church of England.[493] Therefore he laid down the gauntlet to Golightly, challenging him to prosecute and insisting that his beliefs were 'an honest exposition of the formularies of the English Church, from which and whose divines I learned my faith, before I read one Roman book.'[494] In May 1867, Pusey wrote to Newman (now at the Birmingham Oratory):

> I am rather waiting to see whether Golightly accepts a challenge of mine ... Of course, I don't care a pin for his abuse; I only did it because he was trying to stir up the Ch. wardens in 3 counties, & the Bp of O. wished something done. I have

---

[488] *Jackson's Oxford Journal*, 2 March 1867.
[489] Pusey – Golightly, 21-22 March 1867, LPL MS 1808, fos 246-50.
[490] *Oxford Chronicle*, 30 March 1867.
[491] *Oxford Chronicle*, 6 April 1867.
[492] *Oxford Chronicle*, 30 March 1867.
[493] Edward B. Pusey, *Will Ye Also Go Away?* (Oxford, 1867), p. 28.
[494] *Oxford Chronicle*, 30 March and 20 April 1867.

staked my office on the result ... But perhaps G. likes hounding others on, rather than fighting himself.[495]

In 1846 Golightly had thought better of prosecuting Pusey and now he came to the same conclusion. Perhaps he sensed sure defeat. After all, as he observed, Pusey himself had recently failed in his attempt to prosecute Benjamin Jowett in the Vice-Chancellor's Court.[496] Instead Golightly issued another pamphlet attack upon his bishop, entitled *The Position of the Right Rev. Samuel Wilberforce in Reference to Ritualism*, using the pseudonym 'A Senior Resident Member of the University of Oxford'. At 112 pages it was the third longest pamphlet of his life (after *Strictures on No.90* and *A Letter to the Bishop of Oxford*) and his most substantial publication on the ritualist question. It bore the motto 'there is no new thing under the sun', and was prefaced by an 'Account of the Romeward Movement in the Church of England in the Days of Archbishop Laud', drawing parallels between the 1630s and the 1860s. Quoting at length from Henry Hallam's *Constitutional History* (1827), Lord Clarendon's *History of the Rebellion* (1702-04) and Joseph Berington's *Memoirs of Gregorio Panzani* (1793), Golightly argued that under the Laudian bishops 'serious and systematic efforts were made, like those which we witness in our own day, to undo the work of the Reformation, and negotiations actually entered into with Papal emissaries for a reunion of the Churches of England and Rome'.[497] The results in the 1630s and 40s had been disastrous, leading to Civil War and the confusion of the Commonwealth, with bishops expelled from the

---

[495] Pusey to Newman, 2 May 1867, BOA Personal Correspondence 108.b.

[496] *Oxford Chronicle*, 6 April 1867. For Pusey's case against Jowett, see *Case as to the Legal Position of Professor Jowett: with the Opinion of the Queen's Advocate thereon* (London, 1862); *Case whether Professor Jowett in his Essay and Commentary has so distinctly contravened the doctrines of the Church of England, that a Court of Law would pronounce him guilty; with the Opinion of the Queen's Advocate thereon* (London, 1862); *Pusey and Others v. Jowett. The Argument and Decision as to the Jurisdiction of the Chancellor's Court at Oxford* (Oxford, 1863); Abbot and Campbell, *Life of Jowett*, i. pp. 309-14; Liddon, *Life of Pusey*, iv. pp. 23-31; Altholz, *Anatomy of a Controversy*, pp. 101-3.

[497] Golightly, *Position of Samuel Wilberforce*, p. i. Golightly's attitude to Archbishop Laud is ambiguous. In 1840 he rejoiced that Laud 'was not ashamed to defend the name of Protestant', *Letter to the Bishop of Oxford*, p. 69, quoting Alexander M'Caul, 'Popish Persecution in the Tyrol – The Exiles of Zillerthal', *Quarterly Review* 64 (June 1839), p. 142. Yet in 1841 he rebuked the Tractarians as 'the Laudian school of divinity', *Strictures on No.90*, part 2, p. 86. There are signs in his historical preface of an attempt to shift the blame for the spread of Roman doctrine and practice from Laud to Bishops Montagu and Goodman. See futher, Peter B. Nockles, 'Anglicanism "Represented" or "Misrepresented"? The Oxford Movement, Evangelicalism, and History: The Controversial Use of the Caroline Divines in the Victorian Church of England' in Sheridan Gilley (ed.), *Victorian Churches and Churchmen: Essays Presented to Vincent Alan McClelland* (Woodbridge, 2005), ch. 16.

House of Lords, the Prayer Book prohibited, and the national church overthrown. It was an appeal to learn the lessons of history, and Golightly later republished his preface as a separate pamphlet in 1873 and 1878.

The main purpose of Golightly's *Position* was to show Wilberforce's 'predilection for the externals of Romanism'.[498] He gave a detailed history of the Cuddesdon College inquiry, the controversy surrounding *Facts and Documents*, and the notorious Woodard Schools meeting in the Sheldonian Theatre, and then went on to illustrate the bishop's attitude to ritualism by a number of more recent facts.[499] For example, Wilberforce had taken to signing his name with a cross ('S. Oxon.✠'), and had posed for a photograph with three fingers raised in blessing and holding a pastoral staff (the gift of John Hubbard of Addington). This photograph was brought to national attention in the *Times* in November 1866 by Lord Sidney Godolphin Osborne,[500] and was initially printed in Golightly's pamphlet, but the photographer gained a court injunction against its reproduction.[501] In the Upper House of Convocation in June 1866, Wilberforce had recommended a notorious collection of ritualist essays, edited by Orby Shipley and entitled *The Church and the World* – a volume which Golightly thought 'disreputable' and 'outrageous'.[502] Wilberforce had also presented to Convocation a petition from the English Church Union in favour of vestments, incense, candles, wafer bread and the mixed chalice.[503] In his own diocese, the bishop had sanctioned the architectural changes at Bloxham church, near Banbury, which reopened in November 1866 with a new stone altar and an alabaster and marble reredos (considered by Arthur Isham to be 'an outrage upon Protestant sentiment').[504] Furthermore, he had invited Pusey to take part in a sermon series at the University Church in Oxford during Lent 1867, despite his noted heterodoxy.[505] Golightly also rebuked Wilberforce for the 'grave moral offence' of using his power to avenge a 'supposed personal affront' by William Acworth.[506] In April 1866 Acworth, an unbeneficed clergyman residing temporarily in Oxford, had complained that St Philip and St James church, Oxford had held a service in imitation of the Roman *Improperia*

---

[498] Golightly, *Position of Samuel Wilberforce*, p. 9.
[499] Ibid., pp. 59-91.
[500] *Times*, 26 and 28 November 1866. Cf. Maurice, *Ritualism of Oxford Popery*, p. 38; Peter Maurice, *Dr Macbride's Legacy, or More about the Ritualism of Oxford Popery* (London, 1869), pp. 128-31.
[501] *Times*, 7 June 1867; letters at LPL CM 23/25.
[502] Golightly, *Position of Samuel Wilberforce*, pp. 61, 65.
[503] *Chronicle of Convocation*, 28 June 1866, pp. 478-82.
[504] *Jackson's Oxford Journal*, 24 November 1866; Isham to Golightly, 31 May 1867, LPL MS 1807, fo. 256.
[505] Edward B. Pusey, 'The Victor, on His Throne, the Object of Divine Worship' in *The Victor in the Conflict. Sermons Preached During the Season of Lent, 1867, in Oxford* (Oxford, 1868).
[506] Golightly, *Position of Samuel Wilberforce*, pp. 70-1.

('The Reproaches'). When Wilberforce refused to act, Acworth published a letter of complaint to Archbishop Longley and immediately had his permission to officiate withdrawn.[507]

Golightly's lengthiest criticisms were reserved for Wilberforce's triennial charge of December 1866, which he called 'an apology for Ritualism'.[508] The bishop had termed the Tractarian Movement 'mighty for good, even with all its drawbacks', and proclaimed that amongst the ritualists were 'men inferior to none in self-devotion, in apparent love to Christ, in tenderness towards His poor, in zeal for His truth, or in the fervour of their own devotion. Such men we can ill afford to lose.'[509] Even the ritualists whom Wilberforce felt bound to condemn, he praised for their 'hearty honesty' and described as 'those whom, for our very love of Him they love, – we cannot choose but love.'[510] The *Record* had called the bishop's charge 'a very studied, artificial, one-sided, and dangerous performance, and slippery in the extreme',[511] while John Tucker considered it 'unsurpassed in its subtilty [sic]'.[512] The *Church Review* meanwhile thought that in it 'the Catholic party may find much to congratulate themselves upon'.[513] In his *Position*, Golightly likened Wilberforce to a commanding officer in a besieged city, who despite professions of loyalty, was actually strongly sympathetic to mutineers within the garrison.[514] He concluded his pamphlet with his conviction that the spread of ritualism throughout the Church of England was 'the result of more than human agency, even of the secret working of him who, as the Scripture warns us, is able to transform himself into an angel of light, and his ministers into ministers of righteousness.'[515]

Bishop Trower thought Golightly's *Position* was composed 'without one word betraying personal animosity, or party bitterness',[516] while Tucker hoped it would 'open the eyes of the semi-deluded' and act 'as a looking glass to shew

---

[507] William Acworth, *The Acts of Uniformity Set at Nought in the Diocese of Oxford. A Letter to His Grace the Lord Archbishop of Canterbury* (Oxford, 1866); *Inhibition of the Rev. W. Acworth, MA, at Christ Church, Plymouth, by the Bishop of Exeter. Report of a Great Public Meeting held at the Royal Hotel, Plymouth, on Thursday, the 30th Day of May, 1867* (Plymouth, 1867). See 'A Member of the University' (Golightly?) in *Jackson's Oxford Journal*, 2 and 9 June 1866; 'An Oxfordshire Clergyman' (Golightly?) in *Record*, 11 March 1867.
[508] Golightly, *Position of Samuel Wilberforce*, p. 77.
[509] Samuel Wilberforce, *A Charge Delivered to the Diocese of Oxford, at his Seventh Visitation* (Oxford, 1866), pp. 33, 35.
[510] Ibid., pp. 36-7.
[511] *Record*, 18 January 1867.
[512] Tucker to Golightly, 15 January 1867, LPL MS 1811, fo. 56.
[513] *Church Review*, 8 December 1866, p. 1169.
[514] Golightly, *Position of Samuel Wilberforce*, pp. 92-3.
[515] Ibid., p. 96.
[516] Trower to Golightly, 18 July 1867, LPL MS 1810, fo. 187.

the Bp to himself'.[517] Golightly's cousin, Frances Green, thought it proved Wilberforce to be 'a Romanist in disguise'.[518] Other friends praised the pamphlet as 'plainly & forcibly written … calm & temperate'[519] and as 'a most crushing exposure of the Bp'.[520] One supporter thought *The Position of Samuel Wilberforce* deserved 'to be circulated among Churchmen from one end of England to the other.'[521] He proclaimed:

> Bishops who halt between two opinions, tamper with Romanism, wink at Popish proceedings, and throw cold water on the Evangelical clergy and laity, must never be surprised if their actions are keenly criticized, and their words unfavourably interpreted.[522]

> What the country desires to see in our Bishops is an increase of scriptural decision and Protestant boldness in their speech and action. We do not of course want them to be party-spirited or one-sided, or persecutors of all who disagree with themselves. But we do want them to lay aside that cold, and cautious, and timid, and vague, and colourless style of language which is now so unhappily characteristic of all their public addresses. We want them to give up speaking as if they thought everything were true and nothing false, – everybody was right and nobody wrong![523]

However, John Peers (vicar of Tetsworth near Thame) had little optimism that Golightly's *Position* would change the situation:

> It is a thorough exposure of the crooked ways, in which our poor miserable Bishop delights to walk. Yet I fear that the world will still admire him, & to a certain extent, believe in him. His great audacity, & shameless impudence, will have a great effect upon many. They cannot imagine that so bold a front covers nothing but 'sounding brass', & so the deceiver triumphs, & his influence remains.[524]

Peers' prediction proved correct. Apart from Golightly's personal friends and close allies few paid attention to his pamphlet. Although it reached a third edition, it failed to achieve the wide publicity of many of his other controversial writings, such as *Facts and Documents* eight years before. Perhaps this was because his allegations about Bishop Wilberforce were already well-known and no longer possessed a 'shock factor'. Moderate ritualism had become more

---

[517] Tucker to Golightly, 16 May and 8 June 1867, LPL MS 1811, fos 72, 79.
[518] Frances W. Green to Golightly, 31 May 1867, LPL MS 1806, fo. 242.
[519] Dear to Golightly, 16 May 1867, LPL MS 1805, fos 89-90.
[520] Tucker to Golightly, 5 June 1867, LPL MS 1811, fo. 77.
[521] *Record*, 29 May 1867.
[522] *Record*, 25 March 1867.
[523] *Record*, 29 May 1867.
[524] John W. Peers to Golightly, 17 May 1867, LPL MS 1808, fo. 210.

firmly established in the Church of England, and in the Oxford diocese the bishop had grown emboldened in his sanction of it. Golightly's *Position* was simply ignored by Wilberforce and by most newspapers and reviews, at a period when there were hundreds of other anti-ritualist pamphlets and petitions to notice around the country, so it soon sank without trace. Golightly had lost his ability to do his bishop serious harm and within a couple of years their paths permanently separated when Wilberforce was translated from Oxford to Winchester. Golightly would need to look for an alternative focus for his agitating energies.

CHAPTER 6

Protecting the University Pulpit

The location for Charles Golightly's theological agitations during his early years had been the University of Oxford. That is where he established his reputation in the 1840s as a fierce opponent of Tractarianism, harnessing the power of the Hebdomadal Board, the Vice-Chancellor, Convocation, tutors and University alumni for his various campaigns. However, after his brief assault upon Benjamin Jowett in 1855-56, Golightly's focus moved away from the University to broader diocesan issues – as witnessed by his persistent attacks upon Cuddesdon College, the Woodard Schools and recalcitrant bishops. He no longer took a prominent lead in University arguments. Yet Golightly had not forgotten his beloved *alma mater*. In 1872, now aged sixty-five, he still had energy for one last campaign in defence of the University's Protestant heritage. It was a rearguard action and a lost cause, but he believed that an important principle was at stake.

The sixteen years since Golightly's failed protest against Jowett had witnessed a continual revolution within University life. Jowett rode out the storm surrounding his New Testament commentary and his part in *Essays and Reviews*, and had grown into one of the most significant personages in Oxford. His broad toleration of diverse religious views was increasingly typical of the University. Jowett had gradually seized control at Balliol College, and was finally elected Master in 1870 when Robert Scott was invited by Gladstone to become Dean of Rochester. He set about turning Balliol into his idea of a model institution, transformed 'from an inconsiderable part of the ecclesiastical establishment into the awesome exemplar of a new educational one'.[1] Clerical fellowships and the necessity for the Master to be in holy orders were abolished. Services in chapel were re-written with a non-denominational slant and Jowett delivered addresses in chapel on non-Christian religions. Tutors were also allowed to retain their fellowships after marriage. Soon Balliol was seen as the pre-eminent Oxford college, with a reputation for efficient management, inspirational teaching and excellent examination results. Jowett's influence spread as his pupils carried his ideas to other colleges and rose to positions of influence throughout the country. In tune with this new mood,

---

[1] John M. Prest, 'Balliol, For Example' in M.G. Brock and M.C. Curthoys (eds.), *The History of the University of Oxford*, vol. 7 *Nineteenth-Century Oxford, Part 2* (Oxford, 2000), p. 161.

Parliament passed the 1871 Universities Tests Act, abolishing subscription to the Thirty-Nine Articles from almost all University teaching positions. Once a strictly Anglican preserve, the University of Oxford had now become officially secular.[2]

A few relics still remained, however, of Oxford's former Anglican status – such as the official 'University sermons'. The orthodoxy of preachers had always been one of Golightly's chief concerns and this was to form the battleground for his last University campaign. When the contest came, it was said to present 'a surprising and somewhat amusing revelation of the theological animosity which smoulders under the suave surface of Oxford life.'[3] The *Morning Post* observed: 'In religion, as in politics, there are Liberals and Conservatives ... In society these two parties are much mingled, and they fuse together very well; but in the Universities their opposition is seen in its concentrated form. It is more clearly defined, more pungent, more incisive.'[4]

On Sundays during term time, sermons before the University were preached according to a strict pattern. On Sunday mornings they were delivered by the Heads of Houses, Dean and Canons of Christ Church, and the six Divinity Professors. In the afternoons it was the turn of younger members of the University to preach – Masters of Arts and Bachelors of Civil Law (whether resident in Oxford or not), in the order by which they graduated. For those who declined to preach when their turn arrived, a 'select preacher' would fill their place. There were ten select preachers at any one time – a combination of university tutors and Church of England dignitaries – each serving for two years. Five nominations were made annually by a small committee comprising the Vice-Chancellor, the two proctors and the Regius and Lady Margaret Professors of Divinity. Nominations were submitted to Convocation for approval, which was usually a mere formality. However, in the late 1860s and early 1870s the procedure began to come under closer scrutiny. The role of select preacher was an honorary position with few duties, but was symbolically significant, so nominations were used as an opportunity to push or resist particular theological agendas. This resulted in a major battle in Convocation, with non-residents called up from around the country to vote, just as they had been against Professor Hampden and John Henry Newman in the 1830s and 40s.

Hints of future trouble began in 1865 when it was rumoured that Vice-Chancellor Lightfoot would nominate Jowett's old friend, Arthur Stanley (now

---

[2] See Ward, *Victorian Oxford*, ch. 11; Christopher Harvie, 'Reform and Expansion, 1854-1871' in M.G. Brock and M.C. Curthoys (eds.), *The History of the University of Oxford*, vol. 6 *Nineteenth-Century Oxford, Part 1* (Oxford, 1997), ch. 23; A.J. Engel, *From Clergyman to Don: The Rise of the Academic Profession in Nineteenth-Century Oxford* (Oxford, 1983).
[3] *Times*, 7 December 1872.
[4] *Morning Post*, 10 December 1872.

Dean of Westminster), as a select preacher. Edward Pusey and his disciple, Henry Liddon, planned to oppose any such appointment and anticipated 'a fierce contest', but nothing came of the rumour.[5] Three years later the two proctors put forward the names of Stanley, Henry Liddell (Dean of Christ Church) and A.C. Tait (the new Archbishop of Canterbury). However, all were rejected by the other members of the committee, who then had to defend themselves from accusations that they acted with 'theological *animus*'.[6]

A major shift in the balance of power took place in 1870 when Dean Liddell began his four year term as Vice-Chancellor. With a small committee of only five men, one change was enough to swing the majority in a different direction. Liddell was known to be sympathetic to a 'broad church' agenda and this was immediately seen the following year by the nomination of Frederick Temple as a select preacher. Temple was notorious as a contributor to *Essays and Reviews* and his elevation in 1869 to Bishop of Exeter had provoked a public outcry, not easily silenced. Now John Burgon (vicar of the University Church in Oxford) protested that Temple's appointment as select preacher was 'improper and even scandalous', part of 'the systematic endeavour which is being made in Oxford to obliterate whatever is distinctive in the teaching of the English Church, as well as to secularise the education of the place in every possible way.'[7] Yet there was no organised campaign to reject Temple's nomination and when Burgon stood up in Convocation to oppose it, he was quashed by the Vice-Chancellor.[8] Golightly's old friend, E.M. Goulburn (now Dean of Norwich and himself a select preacher) complained that the procedure had been rushed through as a matter of course. He thought it 'a miserable apostasy' for the University to commit religious instruction to 'a prelate who labours under grave suspicions of heterodoxy, whose theology is at best hazy, and who will not purge himself from complicity with the attempts of avowed Rationalists to throw doubt upon "those things which are most surely believed amongst us."'[9]

When the annual round of nominations for select preachers arrived in 1872, Burgon, Goulburn and Golightly were determined to put up a better resistance to any suspect name. Burgon and Golightly's close collaboration is at first a surprise. During the diocesan agitation against ritualism in the late 1850s, Burgon had been fiercely loyal to Bishop Wilberforce and had assailed Golightly with harsh words both in private and through the newspapers.

---

[5] Liddon Diary, 13, 18-20 November 1865, PHL.
[6] *Pall Mall Gazette*, 1 December 1868; *Guardian*, 9 December 1868, p. 1363; Leighton to Tait, 7 December 1868, LPL Tait Papers, vol. 85, fos 251-2.
[7] *Guardian*, 29 November 1871, p. 1421.
[8] Burgon to Liddell, 4 December 1872, in *Correspondence between the Very Reverend Henry George Liddell, DD, Vice-Chancellor of the University of Oxford, and Mr Burgon, concerning a privilege of Convocation in Respect of the nomination of Select Preachers* (Oxford, 1872), p. 6.
[9] *Guardian*, 20 December 1871, p. 1505.

However, when they came to know each other better, Burgon found Golightly 'one of the truest and most warm-hearted of friends'.[10] In the *Lives of Twelve Good Men*, he explained how relating to Golightly on a personal level, rather than just via media reports, had changed his perspective:

> He had the reputation of belonging to a school of religious thought greatly opposed to that which I had myself early learned to revere and admire. But when, much later in life, I came to know Golightly somewhat intimately, I found that practically there was very little – if any – difference between us. He was of the school of Hooker – a churchman of the genuine Anglican type. I had heard him spoken of as narrow and bigoted. I will but say that, when I left Oxford, he was every bit as fond of the society of Edward King [former principal of Cuddesdon College], as he was of that of Mr Christopher [evangelical rector of St Aldate's, Oxford]. He was denounced by some as harsh and bitter. Opportunities enough he had for the display of such a temperament in my society, had he been so minded; but I never heard him speak cruelly, or even unkindly, of anybody. Nor have I ever known a man who more ached for confidence, sympathy, kindness; or was more sincere and faithful to his friends. Earnest practical piety had been all his life his prevailing characteristic.[11]

Burgon and Golightly were now ready to fight together to preserve the orthodoxy of the University pulpit. In early November 1872, Burgon wrote to his new friend:

> It is a real consolation to find that one is not the only person in Oxford who cares about the safety of the Ark. I am prepared to oppose – & *promote an organised opposition to* – any improper name. I am glad to be able to add that I *know* there is a growing feeling in the place – (commendable or not) – for not submitting to *that* kind of dictation any longer. Many would say *non placet* in order to show that we have the power to non placet such appointments. Keep a sharp look-out – pray: as *I* am doing. And let us be prepared to act at a moment's notice. We must henceforth build *with a sword in our hand* ...[12]

Burgon and Golightly's worst expectations were fulfilled. At the committee stage, Dean Stanley's name was put forward as select preacher, and with the support of Liddell and both proctors his nomination was inevitable.[13] J.B. Mozley (Regius Professor of Divinity) observed: 'This is an appointment which was to be expected as soon as we had a Liberal V.C., and the V.C. turned from the majority against it ... to a majority for it. Some day there must be, upon the

---

[10] Burgon, *Lives of Twelve Good Men*, i. p. 438.
[11] Ibid., p. xxv.
[12] Burgon to Golightly, 6 November 1872, LPL MS 1804, fos 157-8.
[13] Stanley was proposed by the junior proctor, W.W. Jackson, whose handbill survives at Bodleian MS Eng.th.d.10, fo. 42. For details of voting at the committee stage, see *Times*, 11, 16-19 December 1872.

ordinary chances, two favouring proctors. My predecessor prepared me for it.'[14] As a result, Liddell came under attack for his personal theological bias. In self-defence he maintained that he had 'always endeavoured to act fairly by all parties',[15] and a supporter praised his 'fairness and impartiality' in sanctioning the nomination of men from every section of the Church of England.[16] Nonetheless, the *Record* complained that Liddell tended to exclude evangelicals, so that 'the University pulpit is largely occupied by the dreary negations of the Broad or the mediaeval superstitions of the High Church school.'[17] Golightly's friend, Charles Heurtley (Lady Margaret Professor of Divinity), asked Liddell to withdraw Stanley's nomination for the sake of peace within the University, but it was too late because the dean had already agreed to stand.[18]

Stanley seemed to find himself in theological strife with every year that passed. In 1870 he had provoked controversy by inviting Vance Smith, a Unitarian, to receive communion at Westminster Abbey alongside other members of the committee appointed to revise the Authorised Version of the Bible.[19] He had also supported Charles Voysey, a clergyman from Healaugh near York, who was deprived of his living in 1871 after being found guilty of teaching heresy on topics such as the divinity of Christ, the atonement and the inspiration of Scripture.[20] Now Burgon protested to the Vice-Chancellor:

> I cannot think the advocate of the Westminster Abbey sacrilegious Communion; the patron of Mr Vance [Smith] the Unitarian teacher; the partisan of Mr Voysey the infidel; the avowed champion of a negative and cloudy Christianity which is really preparing the way for the rejection of all revealed Truth, – a fit person to be selected to address the youth of this place from the University pulpit.[21]

Horatio Potter (Bishop of New York) agreed with this assessment and encouraged Burgon:

---

[14] Mozley to Burgon, 14 December 1872, Bodleian MS Eng.th.d.10, fo. 51.
[15] Liddell to Burgon, 3 December 1872 in *Correspondence between Liddell and Burgon*, p. 4.
[16] *Times*, 9 December 1872. For Liddell's appointments, see *Times*, 10 December 1872.
[17] *Record*, 13 December 1872.
[18] Heurtley to Burgon, 7 December 1872, Bodleian MS Eng.th.d.10, fos 43-4.
[19] Prothero and Bradley, *Life of Stanley*, ii. pp. 216-22; John W. Burgon, *An Unitarian Reviser of our Authorized Version, Intolerable: An Earnest Remonstrance and Petition addressed to Charles John Ellicott, DD, Bishop of Gloucester and Bristol* (Oxford, 1872).
[20] Prothero and Bradley, *Life of Stanley*, ii. pp. 374-80; Crowther, *Church Embattled*, pp. 127-37; Garth Turner, 'A Broad Churchman and the Prayer Book: The Reverend Charles Voysey' in R.N. Swanson (ed.), *Continuity and Change in Christian Worship*, Studies in Church History 35 (Woodbridge, 1999), pp. 374-83.
[21] Burgon to Liddell, 4 December 1872 in *Correspondence between Liddell and Burgon*, pp. 7-8.

I look in vain through England for another Ecclesiastic who seems to me to be exerting so evil an influence against all measures that touch the defences of the Faith. That Dean S. is learned & polished & amiable & pure in life is not denied, – but it is nothing to the purpose when in questions between Truth & Error he is continually favouring the wrong side.[22]

As soon as Stanley's nomination was announced, a campaign of resistance began. On 2 and 3 December meetings were held in Burgon's rooms to plan the strategy.[23] First Burgon, Golightly, Montagu Burrows (Chichele Professor of Modern History), Edward Woollcombe (fellow of Balliol College) and Henry Bramley (fellow of Magdalen College) wrote to Liddell announcing their opposition to Stanley's appointment. With a bold hint at their intentions, they asked the Vice-Chancellor to choose a day for Convocation 'convenient for non-resident Members'.[24] Liddell decided upon Wednesday, 11 December, which gave them just a week to get organised. Next they issued a circular encouraging members of the University to come up and vote against Stanley. This circular was signed by fifteen men, including a number of Golightly's old friends who had been allies in previous campaigns – such as Bishop Trower, John Tucker and Richard Cotton (now aged 78, but still Provost of Worcester College).[25] Golightly also helped to recruit the young E.A. Knox (fellow of Merton College and future Bishop of Manchester) for the opposition.[26] A further public letter from Burgon, Golightly, Woollcombe and Edward Hathaway (rector of St Ebbe's) insisted their protest was not against Stanley personally, but aimed 'to anticipate even greater evils' by showing that Convocation would not accept every nomination without murmur.[27] It was soon observed that the organisers of this campaign were drawn together from diverse theological backgrounds. On other issues they would have found themselves strongly divided. For example, Tucker, Cotton, Knox and Hathaway were part of the evangelical movement, while Burrows was a former chairman of the local branch of the English Church Union,[28] and Bramley was Master of the

---

[22] Horatio Potter to Burgon, 6 January 1873, Bodleian MS Eng.th.d.10, fo. 56.
[23] Burgon's memoranda, Bodleian MS Eng.th.d.10, fo. 14; *Jackson's Oxford Journal*, 14 December 1872.
[24] *Correspondence between Liddell and Burgon*, p. 3.
[25] Bodleian MS Eng.th.d.10, fo. 18. According to Burgon, Golightly was Cotton's 'intimate friend'. Golightly ministered to the Provost in the last days of his life (in 1880) and helped to officiate at his funeral: Burgon, *Lives of Twelve Good Men*, ii. pp. 79-80, 85, 87.
[26] Knox to Golightly, 4 December 1872, LPL MS 1808, fo. 28. See also Goulburn to Golightly, 1 December 1872, MS 1806, fos 201-2.
[27] Bodleian MS Eng.th.d.10, fo. 19.
[28] *Autobiography of Montagu Burrows* edited by S.M. Burrows (London, 1908), pp. 210, 218-20.

Brotherhood of the Holy Trinity.[29] It was wryly observed that 'the Ritualists and the Calvinists took sweet counsel together'.[30]

Burgon and his allies were soon receiving letters of support from around the country,[31] and someone proclaimed: 'If necessary the sermons must go altogether, for nothing can be worse than such centres of propagandism in the hands of Broad Churchmen.'[32] However, others mocked Stanley's opponents as an 'army of obscurantists'[33] who were guilty of 'a mere school-boy ebullition of party-feeling'.[34] For example, the *Times* asked:

> If such an appeal is to be made by one party, why not by another? And what is to prevent every nomination of Select Preachers becoming the occasion of a party struggle between the various schools which divide the Church? ... If one party is thus to seize every opportunity of trampling on another, it will become impossible for them to exist side by side.[35]

The newspaper thought the opposition to Stanley was 'ill-judged' and 'indefensible', complaining: 'Cannot religious parties learn more respect for each other, and for the interests they have in charge than to try to win passing victories by a side-wind, or to seek a triumph in the temporary humiliation of an opponent?'[36]

Despite the broad spectrum of support generated by Burgon and Golightly, a number of prominent Oxford leaders who might have been expected to join them were conspicuous by their absence. Professors Pusey and Liddon (Ireland Professor of Exegesis since 1870) were perhaps the most obvious. Pusey (now in his 70s) attended the initial meeting in Burgon's rooms, but declined to add his name to the protest. He thought there was a 'want of practical energy' amongst the attendees – people spoke strongly, but when it came to practical efforts in calling up non-residents 'every one almost seemed busy, & to beg off work'. He told Burgon, 'Voters do not spring up like armed men from the dragon's teeth', and warned: 'You seemed to me to have no organisers, and none willing to give up all their time and energies. In our old battles, we thought nothing of giving up a week or a fortnight of hard work, laying aside all besides.' With only a week before Convocation, Pusey noted: 'You fight,

---

[29] Middleton, *Magdalen Studies*, p. 273.

[30] *Punch*, 21 December 1872, p. 253.

[31] Bishop Christopher Wordsworth to Burgon, 13 December 1872, Bodleian MS Eng.th.d.10, fos 48-9; W.F. Hook to Goulburn, 9 December 1872; Frederick Oakeley to Goulburn, 14 December 1872; J.T. Coleridge to Goulburn, 15 December 1872, Norwich Dean and Chapter Library.

[32] *John Bull*, 7 December 1872, p. 844.

[33] *Daily Telegraph*, 14 December 1872.

[34] *Spectator*, 14 December 1872, p. 1581.

[35] *Times*, 10 December 1872.

[36] *Times*, 12 December 1872.

under tremendous disadvantage, having no time to set the merits of the case before people, or giving them time to think. ... I fear you have no time to organise opposition'.[37]

Support might likewise have been expected from the aged Edward Hawkins (now an octogenarian and in his forty-fifth year as Provost of Oriel). However, he wrote to Burgon:

> The more I think of the step you are discussing against A.P.S. the more indefensible it appears to me. That he may be careless, inaccurate, latitudinarian, dangerous, may be true; but this is all loose and vague, and without specific ground of accusation, such as you can state and maintain. I do not recollect, at least, any specific allegation of false doctrine which you could assert and maintain. And if so, the attack wd be simply regarded as persecution, and wd recoil upon the assailants, and do more harm than good.[38]

Hawkins spoke publicly in the *Times* of his 'sincere respect for the motives and the zeal which have led to the present movement, but ... deep sense of the incalculable mischief of which, if it shall be successful, it may be the precursor to the University and to the Church.'[39] The newspaper's editorial agreed with its correspondent, observing of Burgon and his allies:

> If they are the friends of orthodoxy in Oxford, Dr HAWKINS is the father of it. ... If any one has a right at this day to constitute himself the guardian of orthodoxy at Oxford, it is the Provost of Oriel, and much might have been allowed to his authority had he concurred in such objections as are now raised.[40]

From the Birmingham Oratory, Newman wrote to his sister: 'How strangely Golightly and the Provost come out in their old stage characters at the end of more than thirty years',[41] recalling that Golightly's 'meat and drink is the stocks or the pillory.'[42] He also thought the protest was a mistake: 'you can't bully residents with non-residents – and you know there will be reprisals. Is it not better that Stanley and Pusey should both preach, than that neither should?'[43]

One of those most vocal in his opposition to Stanley was Dean Goulburn. He proclaimed that the only alternative to fighting the appointment was 'to seek a false and hollow peace for the University and the Church by letting everything go by the board, and never raising the voice of protest against what we consider pernicious error.' He declared that Stanley fostered 'the gangrene of

---

[37] Pusey to Burgon, nd, Bodleian MS Eng.th.d.10, fos 32-5.
[38] Hawkins to Burgon, 2 December 1872, ibid., fo. 38.
[39] *Times*, 9 December 1872.
[40] *Times*, 10 December 1872.
[41] Newman to Jemima Mozley, 12 December 1872, *Newman Letters and Diaries*, xxvi. p. 213.
[42] Newman to Liddon, 8 January 1873, ibid., p. 229.
[43] Newman to Rogers, 18 December 1872, ibid., p. 216.

rationalism', which sought to replace Christian doctrine with merely 'an elevated morality'.[44] These were stern words from a former friend. Goulburn and Stanley had been undergraduates together at Balliol College in the 1830s and Goulburn admitted to Golightly that opposing him was 'bitterly painful': 'I really *like him*; and think him a most *amiable* little creature, and one who acts up to his own convictions of right. ... But the Faith of CHRIST before friendship.'[45] In the columns of the *Guardian*, Goulburn explained to Stanley that he felt a duty to oppose 'the rationalistic school', which was 'undermining the faith of many young men, and paving the way for the total rejection of revealed religion.'[46] In private, Stanley replied:

> I only regret that excellent persons, like yourself, should feel it your duty to thwart the efforts of those who (no doubt with many imperfections) are striving to bring out the treasures of the Bible, & enter into the spirit of the Gospel, – to show that Religion & Science need not be opposed to each other, & that Reason is the means which God has given us for arriving at the knowledge of His will. This regret is increased by the reflection that meanwhile little discouragement – I might almost say – much encouragement is given to the return of the grossest superstitions, & to expressions of unchristian uncharitableness.[47]

On Stanley's death in 1881, Goulburn proclaimed: 'Many of his early friends took in after life views entirely antagonistic to his own, and even felt themselves called upon to act against him; but his feeling towards them never chilled, nor did he ever form any but a generous estimate of their motives.'[48] He praised Stanley's intellect and moral character, but lamented that his old friend had substituted sentiment for dogma, and morality for sanctity: 'Arthur Stanley, notwithstanding the large number of attractive religious works which have issued from his pen, was undoubtedly weak, and sometimes alas! worse than weak, as a theologian.'[49]

One of the major questions highlighted by the controversy was the nature of theological 'comprehensiveness' within the Church of England. Where were the limits of orthodoxy? How could a cathedral dean be rejected as heterodox by the University of Oxford and yet welcomed as orthodox by the wider Church of England? One of the proctors observed that to resist Stanley's appointment was to affirm that 'the University should be less tolerant than the National Church, and should be made the mere organ of a party'.[50] Similarly the *Times* proclaimed: 'Either Dr STANLEY has no right to be Dean of

---

[44] *Standard*, 10 December 1872.
[45] Goulburn to Golightly, 1 December 1872, LPL MS 1806, fo. 201.
[46] *Guardian*, 4 December 1872, p. 1518.
[47] Stanley to Goulburn, 2 December 1872, Norwich Dean and Chapter Library.
[48] E.M. Goulburn, *Dean Stanley and his Theology* (London, 1881), p. 11.
[49] Ibid., p. 12.
[50] *Times*, 9 December 1872.

Westminster or he has a perfect right to the University Pulpit'.[51] To censure Stanley would be to prove Convocation's 'dissatisfaction with the laws of the Church of England, and its desire to narrow the pale of her Communion.' Every Sunday, as men like Stanley were invited to preach in other pulpits across the country, there would be ample proof that 'the Church was more comprehensive than the University'.[52] Some even thought this controversy threatened the establishment of the national church, if Stanley's opponents managed to turn the Church of England into 'a sect'.[53] Watching from the sidelines, the Roman Catholic *Tablet* made the most of these tensions. It argued that, in contrast to the Roman Church, toleration of contradictory theological views was an inevitable part of being a member of the Church of England: 'Surely those who remain in communion – some with Archbishops whom they term avowed heretics, others with Ritualists whom they call disguised Papists – need not be so terribly scrupulous about sitting under an unorthodox Dean.'[54]

Another significant issue raised by the controversy was the role of the University in deciding religious questions. By the Universities Tests Act of 1871 it was now officially secular. The *Pall Mall Gazette*, for instance, spoke of the 'ludicrousness' and 'extreme absurdity' of Burgon and Golightly's anachronistic campaign, 'merely a relic of a state of things long since passed away'. It protested:

> The University itself has been secularized, and is actually to be called upon to arbitrate between the opinions of Dean STANLEY and Mr BURGON, when it has lost the right to recognize in any practical way the doctrinal difference between Archbishop MANNING, Mr SPURGEON, Mr CONGREVE [the Positivist philosopher], Mr FRANCIS NEWMAN, and Dr PUSEY.[55]

Triumph or Defeat?

The much-anticipated Convocation met on 11 December 1872. Hundreds of non-residents went up to Oxford to cast their votes, many from country parishes across England and Wales, and the event was called 'a sort of ecclesiastical cattle show'.[56] One of Stanley's notable supporters was Stephen Lushington, former Dean of Arches. Although aged 91, he travelled from his home in Surrey to Oxford and back on the same day, as a result of which he contracted

---

[51] *Times*, 10 December 1872.
[52] *Times*, 12 December 1872.
[53] *Daily Telegraph*, 11 December 1872.
[54] *Tablet*, 14 December 1872, p. 739.
[55] *Pall Mall Gazette*, 9 December 1872.
[56] *Daily News*, 11 December 1872. For details of Convocation, see *Oxford Herald*, 14 December 1872. See also *Graphic*, 21 December 1872, pp. 580, 586. For details of Stanley's supporters, see *Times*, 12 December 1872; *Guardian*, 18 December 1872, p. 1577.

bronchitis and died four weeks later – acclaimed by some as a martyr for religious toleration.[57] Stanley's nomination as select preacher was carried by 349 votes to 287, and Jowett congratulated him: 'I do not think that we could have won with anybody but you. I was surprized to find the number of persons who came up unbidden out of regard & respect for you.'[58]

The result was widely expected. Before Convocation, Goulburn had been predicting defeat, but hoped the action of Stanley's opponents would nonetheless offer a 'salutary warning'.[59] Archdeacon Edward Churton was impressed by the large minority: 'It gives the other side no more than a Cadmean Victory at best, and I hope the lesson will not be lost upon them.'[60] Likewise, Burgon glossed the defeat: 'we reckoned it *a victory*: & well we might. We effected our first purpose – wh was to show that such an appointment shd not pass in future without a formidable protest – & *we liberated our own souls*.'[61] One commentator, however, noted that this 'knot of busy agitators' had 'received a humiliating check': 'The assailants chose their battle-field badly. It would be easy to name more than one Liberal divine over whom they would have gained a certain triumph.'[62] The *Daily Telegraph* rebuked the 'crowd of country parsons, who never rush to their *Alma Mater* so readily as when called by the whistle of bigotry', and argued for reforms to remove the power of non-residents in the affairs of the University.[63]

Others were quick to hail the significance of the vote. It was interpreted as 'a trial of party strength',[64] and therefore was greeted as clear indication that the 'broad church' or 'liberal' party was now dominant in Oxford. During the 1860s there had been a conservative reaction against the cause of reform, which had seen liberals consistently defeated at Convocation. For example, in 1860 Monier-Williams was chosen ahead of Max Müller as Sanskrit Professor. In 1865 the University had declined to re-elect Gladstone as its MP; three years later it had chosen John Mowbray ahead of Roundell Palmer as MP. Convocation had also persistently refused to increase Jowett's salary as Greek Professor from a paltry £40 per annum, primarily because of his theological notoriety. As one observer noted: 'the Liberals had grown so accustomed to defeat that they scarcely hoped for victory'.[65] Yet now there were signs that the situation was changing. The endorsement of Stanley's nomination as select preacher showed, according to the *Daily Telegraph*, 'the triumph at Oxford of

---

[57] S.M. Waddams, *Law, Politics and the Church of England: The Career of Stephen Lushington, 1782-1873* (Cambridge, 1992), pp. 346-7.
[58] Jowett to Stanley, 11 December 1872, BCL IF5/3.
[59] *Standard*, 10 December 1872.
[60] Churton to Burgon, 14 December 1872, Bodleian MS Eng.th.d.10, fo. 52.
[61] Burgon's memoranda, ibid., fo. 15.
[62] *Spectator*, 14 December, 1872, p. 1587.
[63] *Daily Telegraph*, 11 December 1872.
[64] *Daily Telegraph*, 12 December 1872.
[65] *Spectator*, 14 December 1872, p. 1586.

the new order over the old.' In particular the newspaper singled out Jowett and his Balliol disciples for transforming theological opinion within the University:

> In the hour of triumph it would ill beseem the Liberal party to forget those to whom they owe the victory. Yesterday's result is more or less directly due to the personal influence of Professor JOWETT. ... During the last thirty years Baliol [sic] has colonised Oxford; and pupils of Mr JOWETT have been elected to fellowships, tutorships, and professorships, until all Oxford has been filled with a new spirit. ... It was a majority of Mr JOWETT's pupils who yesterday turned the scale in Congregation [sic] ...[66]

However, Jowett himself did not think the result was particularly significant and was resigned to the fact that 'the opposite faction will resort to the same practices again'.[67] Nevertheless, *Punch* was celebrating that

> ... the Broad Church should have laid
> Its basement walls so deep and wide,
> That to her, ev'n in Oxford, aid
> In stress of need is quick supplied –
> That, when the bigot's blast is blown,
> Even though 'STANLEY!' is the cry,
> And Heresy's red cross has flown
> Through cleric England, hot and high,
> They who put trust in truth o'erpower
> Those whom the name of truth appals,
> Till Obscurantism's soldiers cower,
> Beaten, in Convocation's halls ...[68]

Other commentators blamed the failure of Stanley's opponents on the fragility of their theological union. The *Daily Telegraph* labelled Golightly 'the champion of the Evangelicals' and spoke of his 'unnatural alliance' with Professor Burrows, 'the head of the extreme Ritualists': 'The united efforts of Commander BURROWS and of his Evangelical brother-in-arms, the Rev. Mr GOLIGHTLY, have signally failed, and a coalition which would have been comical had it not been so sad has met with a well-merited defeat.'[69] However, as *John Bull* noticed, 'Distinguished Evangelicals and High Churchmen were alike conspicuous by their absence.'[70] In fact the *Record* (oracle of Anglican evangelicalism) argued that the campaign was 'in no sense an Evangelical movement'. Many evangelicals, it explained, had refused to take part because they were opposed to both 'the High Church school' (represented by Burgon)

---

[66] *Daily Telegraph*, 12 December 1872.
[67] Jowett to Stanley, 11 December 1872, BCL IF5/3.
[68] *Punch*, 21 December 1872, p. 254.
[69] *Daily Telegraph*, 12 December 1872.
[70] *John Bull*, 14 December 1872, p. 854.

and 'the Broad Church school' (represented by Stanley): 'Those who love the simple truth of the Gospel ... cannot safely ally themselves with one form of error even in attempting to exclude another.'[71]

The absence of Pusey, Liddon and their circle was more striking. It was the major weakness in the theological alliance brokered by Burgon and Golightly. One observer commented:

> When the leadership of the army passed from the hands of Dr Pusey and Dr Liddon to those of the Dean of Norwich and Mr Burgon, the inevitable defections which followed were ill compensated by recruits gained from the ranks of the Evangelical party. Such coalitions are always hard to cement; and at the present moment the earnest High Churchman or advanced Ritualist must have felt uneasy as he marched to the assault in the ranks of the Church Association, and missed in front the form of his veteran chief, who steadily refused to leave his tent.[72]

According to R.E. Prothero and G.G. Bradley (Stanley's first biographers), Pusey refused to act because he thought Convocation had no authority to decide the orthodoxy of an Anglican clergyman now that, subsequent to the Universities Tests Act, it was no longer an exclusively Anglican body.[73] However, both Pusey and Liddon justified their lack of involvement on the grounds that the campaign would only increase Stanley's following. Pusey admitted Stanley was 'a pioneer for unbelief', yet after the event he explained: 'his appointment will be at the cost of faith and of souls, but I feared that the opposition would only aggravate the evil by enlisting the enthusiasm of the young.'[74] Similarly Liddon wrote of Burgon and his allies:

> My heart was with them; but my judgment as clearly the other way. It was a discreditable nomination; but, having been made, ought, in the interests of the Faith, to have been allowed to pass *sub silentio*. For, if opposed, it must be either defeated or affirmed by Convocation; – a choice, me judice, of nearly balanced evils. To have defeated it would have been to invest Stanley with the cheap honours of a petty martyrdom. To have affirmed it, is, I fear, to have given a new impetus to the barren unspiritual negations which he represents. However, it was impossible to get Burgon &c to see this; so Dr Pusey & I retired ...[75]

Burgon expressed his disappointment to Golightly: 'If we had but numbered 50 more on our side, there wd have been nothing left to be desired. But that 3 times 50 might have been present – & should have been there – all must see.'[76] He later lamented:

---

[71] *Record*, 13 December 1872.
[72] *Times*, 13 December 1872.
[73] Prothero and Bradley, *Life of Stanley*, ii. p. 227.
[74] *Times*, 27 December 1872.
[75] Liddon to C.T. Redington, 23 December 1872, PHL Liddon Papers, box 6/10.
[76] Burgon to Golightly, 7 January 1873, LPL MS 1804, fos 159-60.

What offended me – rather what shocked & disgusted me – was that *not a single Divinity Professor was with* us. Mozley – Bright – Heurtley – Ogilvie – Pusey – Liddon – *not one* appeared. They *all* sunk in my esteem so considerably that, I may truly say, I never entirely respected one of them afterwards: especially as they made no secret that they were with us by conviction – but, for all sorts of worthless reasons, would not help us a bit: would not even vote with us. Liddon came to me & 'wished to say how entirely he was on our side'. 'Very likely', was my reply: 'but you failed to shew it by voting with us.'[77]

For a brief while the controversy rumbled on. The day after Convocation, Dean Goulburn resigned his post as select preacher, unwilling to serve alongside men like Bishop Temple and Dean Stanley. Although 'nearly every serious and thoughtful person is agreed that, however wide our Church's circumference, a line must be drawn somewhere in the interests of truth', Goulburn thought Stanley wanted 'to draw the line nowhere'. He proclaimed: 'If the pulpit of the University is to be turned into a vehicle for conveying to our youth a nerveless religion, without the sinew and bone of doctrine – a religion which can hardly be called faith so much as mere Christianized morality – I for one must decline to stand there'.[78] Stanley retorted that on this reasoning Goulburn 'would feel a difficulty in being the colleague of half the Bishops on the Bench.'[79] One observer lamented that for Goulburn to resign was to 'withdraw the garrison and allow the fortress to be occupied by the enemy unopposed', leaving Oxford to 'descend to the level of a German University'.[80] Likewise the *Guardian* asked: 'If the supporters of a definite creed withdraw from the University pulpit, will not that pulpit, almost of necessity, be turned more and more into what Dr Goulburn fears it is becoming'.[81] Another thought that to be consistent Goulburn should go further and resign his Deanery:

> If the University has manifested by its vote its 'unfaithfulness to God's truth', what is to be said of the Church in which Dean Stanley ministers with impunity? How can Dean Goulburn continue to enjoy its dignities? … I, for one, cannot understand how he can accept Dean Stanley as a fellow-Dean when he refuses to hold office with him as a fellow-preacher.[82]

The *Pall Mall Gazette*, however, observed cynically: '[Goulburn] has drawn the line of sacrifice with a skill which is characteristic of the Church to which he belongs. It includes a duty which pays nothing and excludes a deanery

---

[77] Burgon's memoranda, Bodleian MS Eng.th.d.10, fos 15-6.
[78] *Times*, 13 December 1872.
[79] Stanley to Goulburn, 13 December 1872, Norwich Dean and Chapter Library.
[80] *Oxford Herald*, 21 December 1872.
[81] *Guardian*, 18 December 1872, p. 1561.
[82] *Times*, 14 December 1872.

which pays a great deal.'[83]

When the dust had settled, the *Guardian* concluded that these sorts of theological disputes had become 'ridiculous', winning for the aggressors, whether of one party or another, only the reputation of 'vexatious persecutors':

> The history of Oxford warfare for the last thirty years has been full of such contests; the causes of them have been very different, the actors in them have changed, sometimes their position has been reversed: only one well-known name appears with unvarying consistency and perseverance in all lists of those who have invoked the rigour of University punishment, whether against Dr Hampden, the Tractarians, Dr Newman, or Dr Stanley, – the name of Mr Golightly. It seems to us that it is time to have learned the lessons of this history.[84]

Golightly's name appeared so consistently in these campaigns within the University partly because he had the habit of outlasting both his antagonists and his allies. While they moved away from Oxford, often promoted to other spheres of work, he stayed put. Burgon had been resident in Oxford since 1841, but even he was called away – invited in November 1875 by Prime Minister Disraeli to become Dean of Chichester. When Burgon told Golightly the news, his friend burst into a 'passionate fit of weeping' because he felt Burgon's continued residence in Oxford was important for the Protestant cause.[85] Golightly was resolved to keep up the fight in Oxford to the very end.

---

[83] *Pall Mall Gazette*, 13 December 1872.
[84] *Guardian*, 18 December 1872, p. 1568.
[85] Burgon, *Lives of Twelve Good Men*, i. p. xxvii.

CHAPTER 7

The Final Campaign

> Cuddesdon College has been continually in hot water,
> although we greatly fear *never clean*. (*The Rock*)[1]

Agitation between ritualists and Protestants continued to gather pace throughout the 1870s, affecting every diocese in England, not least the diocese of Oxford. The ritualist controversies had become a characteristic feature of Anglican life in the late-Victorian period. Theological opinion was increasingly polarised and opponents firmly entrenched. In 1874, in a failed bid to stamp out ritualism, Disraeli's Tory government pushed through the notorious Public Worship Regulation Act, which only made matters worse. This new Act was stronger than the 1840 Church Discipline Act and aimed to speed up prosecutions against ritualist clergy. Suits no longer had to be initiated by a bishop, but could now be brought by a churchwarden or three parishioners, so court battles were multiplied. One of the first to suffer was Arthur Tooth, vicar of St James, Hatcham in Rochester diocese, imprisoned in January 1877 for 28 days – the first of five ritualist 'martyrs'. Militant organisations such as the English Church Union (ECU) and the Church Association only deepened divisions and intensified the arguments. They often found themselves in direct conflict in local disputes. The Church Association established a fighting fund to help aggrieved parishioners prosecute errant clergy. The ECU meanwhile adopted a manifesto of 'six points' – seeking to introduce vestments, altar lights, the mixed chalice, wafer bread, incense and the eastward position into every parish in England.[2]

Within Oxford diocese the battle over ritualism was fought partly in the realm of theological education. Rather than use Parliamentary legislation to eradicate the ritualist 'disease', evangelicals combined to deal with what they

---

[1] *Rock*, 11 October 1878, p. 814.
[2] Nigel Yates, *Anglican Ritualism in Victorian Britain*, ch. 5; Bernard Palmer, *Reverend Rebels: Five Victorian Clerics and Their Fight Against Authority* (London, 1993); James Bentley, *Ritualism and Politics in Victorian Britain: The Attempt to Legislate for Belief* (Oxford, 1978); P.P.G. Kitchenham, *The Attempt to Control Ritualism in the Church of England through the use of Legislation and the Courts, 1869 to 1887, with special reference to the Society of the Holy Cross* (PhD thesis, Durham University, 1997).

saw as ritualism's root cause, 'the professional ignorance of the clergy'. Aiming to make ordinands 'mighty in the Scriptures ... prepared to maintain the pure doctrines of the Reformed Church of England in all their simplicity and fulness', they founded Wycliffe Hall theological college in Oxford in Michaelmas term 1877, led by the biblical scholar R.G. Girdlestone.[3] Its sister institution, Ridley Hall in Cambridge, was opened in 1879.[4] However, it was the theological college at Cuddesdon where the battle against ritualism was most acutely seen. Both the Church Association and the English Church Union played a significant part in the renewed attacks which fell upon Cuddesdon in 1877-79. Once again Charles Golightly, a life member of the Church Association, led the assault. Now a septuagenarian, it was to be the final campaign of his colourful career.

Golightly's public exposure of ritualism at Cuddesdon in the late 1850s had met with mixed success. Vice-principal Liddon had been dismissed as a direct result of the uproar, but the college survived and went on to enjoy almost two decades of peace and quiet. When Henry Swinny took over in May 1859 there were just seven ordinands on the books, but gradually public confidence in the enterprise began to return, as did the students. Wilberforce was soon embroiled in new controversies surrounding Darwin's *Origin of the Species* (1859) and the liberal theology of *Essays and Reviews* (1860). Yet now he came forward as a champion of orthodoxy, which won him widespread favour even amongst erstwhile evangelical critics. This in turn revived sympathy for his theological institution. Swinny collapsed and died in December 1862, aged just 49, and Edward King agreed reluctantly to promotion from chaplain to principal.[5] During the decade under his leadership the college continued to avoid public attention and so was free to get on quietly with its task of training clergymen. It was a period of stability and consolidation. King managed to form friendships across a wide theological spectrum and even Golightly became 'sincerely attached' to him. Cuddesdon's arch-opponent later admitted that although he and the principal differed widely, 'in long conversations ... we have found so much in which we agreed, that we never got on to the points in which we

---

[3] Andrew C. Atherstone, 'The Founding of Wycliffe Hall, Oxford', *Anglican and Episcopal History* 73 (March 2004), pp. 78-102. On Wycliffe Hall's first principal, see Andrew C. Atherstone, 'Robert Baker Girdlestone and "God's Own Book"', *Evangelical Quarterly* 74 (October 2002), pp. 313-32.

[4] F.W.B. Bullock, *The History of Ridley Hall, Cambridge* (2 vols, Cambridge, 1941-53).

[5] On King, see George W.E. Russell, *Edward King: Sixtieth Bishop of Lincoln* (London, 1912); Lord Elton, *Edward King and Our Times* (London, 1958); John A. Newton, *Search for a Saint: Edward King* (London, 1977); Geoffrey Rowell, *The Vision Glorious: Themes and Personalities of the Catholic Revival in Anglicanism* (Oxford, 1983), ch. 7; Chadwick, *Spirit of the Oxford Movement*, ch. 13.

differed.'[6] When King was appointed Professor of Moral and Pastoral Theology at Oxford in 1873, he left behind a college more firmly established and better able to withstand future storms.

The renewed Protestant attacks upon Cuddesdon were reserved for King's successor, Charles Furse.[7] Owen Chadwick suggests that this fresh round of controversy was simply 'laughed at' by most observers and that even the Cuddesdon staff thought it 'more frivolous than vexatious'.[8] Certainly the college was not now in danger of folding, as it had been when Liddon was dismissed twenty years before. Nevertheless these renewed criticisms were treated with deadly seriousness and did the college real damage. Cuddesdon's quiet life was replaced by months of intensive and hostile scrutiny.

The troubles began when it was discovered in July 1877 that Edward Willis, Cuddesdon's vice-principal, was a member of the Society of the Holy Cross (SSC). The SSC, exclusively for clergymen, was considered more extreme than the ECU. It had been founded by Charles Lowder and other ritualists in 1855 but obtained widespread notoriety in 1877 when Lord Redesdale exposed in the House of Lords a work entitled *The Priest in Absolution*, an SSC translation of a French Roman Catholic manual for confessors.[9] Protestants across the country, always deeply suspicious of auricular confession, were shocked and outraged that Anglican clergymen should dare to propagate such a book.[10] The bishops led the denunciations, with Archbishop Tait of Canterbury describing the SSC as part of a 'conspiracy' to undermine the doctrine and discipline of the Reformed Church.[11] Soon the national press began to hunt out SSC adherents. As a result of the controversy membership of the organisation fell from an all-time high of 397 in 1877 to just 227 in 1879.[12] Within Oxford, the Bodleian Library banned undergraduates from reading *The Priest in Absolution*, due to its 'obscene' content.[13] The Church Association also launched an Oxford branch in mid-1877, heralded by a series of events in the Town Hall at which prominent evangelical clergymen spoke passionately

---

[6] Golightly, *Letter to the Dean of Ripon*, p. 73. See, however, Golightly's criticisms of King's connection with the ECU: *Position of Samuel Wilberforce* (third edition, London, 1867), pp. 98-100.

[7] On Furse, see Michael B. Furse, *Stand Therefore! A Bishop's Testimony of Faith in the Church of our Fathers* (London, 1953), ch. 1.

[8] Chadwick, *Founding of Cuddesdon*, p. 129.

[9] *Hansard*, 14 June 1877, pp. 1741-53.

[10] L.E. Ellsworth, *Charles Lowder and the Ritualist Movement* (London, 1982), pp. 138-46; Nigel Yates, '"Jesuits in disguise"? Ritualist confessors and their critics in the 1870s', *Journal of Ecclesiastical History* 39 (April 1988), pp. 202-16; Walter Walsh, *The Secret History of the Oxford Movement* (London, 1897), ch. 4.

[11] *Chronicle of Convocation*, 6 July 1877, p. 315.

[12] J. Embry, *The Catholic Movement and the Society of the Holy Cross* (London, 1931), p. 128.

[13] *Oxford Chronicle*, 1 September 1877.

against ritualism.[14]

When Willis' SSC connections were found out, the spotlight fell back on Cuddesdon College. At first Furse was approached in his capacity as vicar of Cuddesdon by his churchwardens and other local laymen, who requested that Willis be banned from ministering in the parish church. Furse dismissed their appeal, surprised that anyone could 'harbour a suspicion against so upright and spotless a Christian man ... a more pure, and holy, and temperate-minded man I cannot reckon among my friends.' However, his parishioners were not to be thus pacified and when Willis next entered the church pulpit in August 1877, many walked out in protest.[15]

Soon Bishop John Mackarness (Wilberforce's successor) was embroiled in the controversy. He was asked how the SSC was allowed to operate under his very nose, in his own parish, in a church which his own family attended. His diocese was described as 'priest-ridden', 'a safe haven for Rome-bound vessels, liable to suffer serious damage in the free and open sea of English public opinion.'[16] Although Mackarness tried quickly to distance himself from the SSC, the *Record* still protested that no other bishop on the bench had approached the issue 'in such a trimming, undecided manner'.[17] One observer remarked on 'the utter inconsistency between Episcopal words and Episcopal actions', declaring that 'while brilliant memories [of Wilberforce] hang about Cuddesdon Palace, the damp and mildewy odour of insincerity has not yet departed from its walls.'[18] Another queried, 'Will our Episcopal rulers be much longer blind to the forecast of the coming storm? ... if the Church of England is to be saved it must be done in the next five years or never.'[19]

Willis was forced to withdraw from the SSC at his bishop's insistence and it seemed that the college might escape further bad publicity. Yet the Cuddesdon parishioners who had refused to listen to his preaching were raised up in the local press as a proud example to emulate. Calls were made for 'a steady persevering agitation' which would show the ritualists 'that a strong and resolute will is possessed by sturdy laymen as well as by meek priests.' One prophesied, 'The farmers of Cuddesdon ... have been the first to resist; the fire has now been lighted, and it will blaze throughout the whole diocese.'[20] The only surprise is that it was a full year before the college was caught up in the conflagration.

Not until September 1878 did the aged Golightly issue *A Solemn Warning Against Cuddesdon College*, which he offered to the public 'as perhaps the last

---

[14] *Oxford Times*, 26 May, 30 June, 15 September and 20 October 1877.
[15] *Oxford Chronicle*, 1 September 1877.
[16] *Oxford Times*, 8 September 1877.
[17] *Record*, 7 and 14 September 1877.
[18] *Oxford Times*, 15 September 1877.
[19] *Record*, 7 September 1877.
[20] *Oxford Times*, 8 September 1877.

service that I may be able to render to my Divine Master'. He argued that Cuddesdon was one of the 'chief nurseries' of that 'conspiracy' to subvert the principles of the Reformation outlined by Archbishop Tait.[21] He called Furse 'a very marked party man' and warned that Willis' withdrawal from the SSC did not prove any change in his sentiments. Golightly calculated that of Cuddesdon's 350 alumni, several had become Roman Catholics, or were members of the SSC or the Confraternity of the Blessed Sacrament, and at least 145 were members of the ECU.[22] To illustrate attempts to overthrow the doctrines of the Church of England, he quoted from the works of two ex-students, Orby Shipley (a Roman Catholic from November 1878) and Frederick Lee (who had been secretly consecrated bishop in 1877 in the bizarre Order of Corporate Reunion).[23]

Golightly's pamphlet re-lit the touchpaper. Former principal Alfred Pott (now Archdeacon of Berkshire) declared:

> I do not think hard words any help in controversy. 'Conspiracy', 'party man', 'secret society', 'paralysis of the clergy', are words which ought not to be used by any clergyman of his brethren. This kind of stone-throwing can only issue in the recoil of the missile on him who casts it: according to the wise proverb, 'Curses, like chickens, come home to roost'.

He thought Golightly's account of the Cuddesdon Affair of 1858-59 'a tissue of inaccuracies', 'calculated to mislead' and 'utterly unhistorical',[24] and Liddon also entered the fray with his version of events.[25] Golightly was called 'an inveterate "accuser of the brethren"',[26] and was mocked in a parody by 'the Unreverend Gohitagain' about 'the bile of Mr Gone Slightly'.[27] Nevertheless he remained unmoved: 'Those who engage in controversy must make up their minds to rough handling.'[28]

By others Golightly was praised as a 'veteran champion of Church of England orthodoxy' and 'one of the few who from the first withstood the Romish movement'.[29] He was applauded by a local branch of the Church

---

[21] Charles P. Golightly, *A Solemn Warning against Cuddesdon College. Addressed to the Laity, and More Particularly to the Lay Members of the Oxford Diocesan Conference* (Oxford, 1878), p. 3.
[22] Ibid., pp. 5-6.
[23] On the OCR see Brandreth, *Dr Lee of Lambeth*, ch. 6; Walsh, *Secret History*, ch. 5; Embry, *Catholic Movement*, pp. 136-45.
[24] *Guardian*, 13 November 1878, p. 1578.
[25] *Guardian*, 20 November 1878, p. 1610.
[26] *Church Times*, 18 October 1878, p. 579.
[27] *An Image of Cuddesdon College, as Reflected in the Bile of Mr Gone Slightly ... by the Unreverend Gohitagain* (np, 1878) (copy at CCA X1/44).
[28] *Guardian*, 13 November 1878, p. 1578.
[29] *Oxford Times*, 21 December 1878; *Rock*, 18 October 1878, p. 829.

Association for drawing the nation's attention to the influence of Cuddesdon,[30] and the *Rock* (an evangelical newspaper) wrote:

> though past the three score years and ten, we are happy to observe [Golightly] again in harness, and in all his pristine vigour. He has now made a brave and powerful onslaught on Cuddesdon College, one of the plague-spots of the Church of England. By this pamphlet the veteran warrior adds another to the long list of important services which during the many years of his ministry he has rendered to the Church of England.[31]

After reading Golightly's *Solemn Warning*, one observer asked: 'Are the bishops slumbering while treason is hatching?'[32] The *Oxford Times* similarly protested: 'The spectacle of professing ministers of the Church of England going forth from Cuddesdon College, under the very shadow of the Bishop's Palace, to proclaim their assent to the dogmas of Rome, and asserting the consistency of this belief with the continued exercise of their ministerial functions, is immoral and offensive.'[33]

The Oxford Diocesan Conference

In his first charge as bishop of Oxford, Mackarness deplored the 'want of active and cordial co-operation' between clergy and laity in the diocese, and announced his intention to establish a diocesan conference, a development which Wilberforce had consistently opposed.[34] In October 1872 the diocesan clergy met together, followed in subsequent years by meetings of a mixed body of clergy and laity.[35] Nigel Yates argues that all sections of the Church of England were divided over ritual and that it is 'a gross over-simplification' to suggest advanced ritual was supported primarily by the clergy and opposed primarily by the laity.[36] Nevertheless, it was said of Wilberforce that he left Oxford diocese 'with nine out of ten of the clergy High Churchmen, and nine out of ten of the laity the other way'.[37] The first diocesan conference of 1873, with its debates on Parochial Church Councils and the Public Worship Facilities Bill, was said to reveal 'the rising impatience, the overflowing

---

[30] *Church Association Monthly Intelligencer* 12 (December 1878), p. 438.
[31] *Rock*, 4 October 1878, p. 802.
[32] *Times*, 8 October 1878.
[33] *Oxford Times*, 28 September 1878.
[34] John F. Mackarness, *A Charge Delivered to the Diocese of Oxford, at his Primary Visitation* (Oxford, 1872), pp. 37-9.
[35] *Oxford Diocesan Conference Minutes*; C.C. Mackarness, *Memorials of the Episcopate of John Fielder Mackarness* (Oxford, 1892), pp. 12-7.
[36] Yates, *Anglican Ritualism in Victorian Britain*, p. 152.
[37] 'Life of Bishop Wilberforce', *Edinburgh Review* 157 (April 1883), p. 557.

indignation' of the laity at the ritualism of the clergy.[38] As has been seen, it was the lay parishioners of Cuddesdon who first blew the whistle on Willis. This tension was harnessed by Golightly. In 1867 he had sent a circular to the churchwardens of the diocese, encouraging them to prosecute their clergy. Now he addressed his *Solemn Warning* exclusively to the laity, particularly the lay members of the Oxford diocesan conference:

> Because in this Diocese at all events the Clergy are paralysed. Some of the more excellent of my Clerical brethren are so absorbed in their parishes, as hardly to have time or inclination to attend to anything else; some are indifferent; and others, moderate High Churchmen with no Ritualistic inclinations, – a class of Clergy of whose supineness the Archbishop of Canterbury has more than once publicly complained, – lament over the widespread mischief, but do nothing; only whispering one to another that nothing should induce them to take a Curate from Cuddesdon.[39]

Golightly asked his young friend, E.A. Knox, to initiate a debate at the diocesan conference of 1878 about Cuddesdon College. Knox agreed to broach the issue out of 'a plain sense of duty and nothing else',[40] and tabled a motion that the teaching at Cuddesdon did not 'deserve the confidence of members of the Church of England.'[41] Professor Montagu Burrows (who had been chairman of the Oxford branch of the ECU but resigned because of its extremism[42]) refused to second Knox's motion, despite his own concerns about Cuddesdon, because he thought it 'a vote of censure'.[43] Instead Alfred Christopher (chairman of the Oxford branch of the Church Association) agreed to do so, observing: 'Now that persecution has ceased I think that one of the greatest trials to which Christ's servants are exposed is to be required by faithfulness to oppose publicly an extreme party, towards some of whom ... one feels a sincere regard'.[44] Before the conference began, letters in the *Record* and the *Times* encouraged those alarmed at 'Mediaeval Romanism' or 'the present Romeward movement' to attend the debate.[45] In reply Knox and his supporters were challenged whether they could

> in the face of Oxford immorality and Oxford free thought, afford to throw a

---

[38] John W. Burgon, *The Oxford Diocesan Conference; and Romanizing Within the Church of England* (Oxford, 1873), p. 17.
[39] Golightly, *Solemn Warning*, p. 8.
[40] E.A. Knox, *An Address Respecting Cuddesdon College, Intended to Have Been Delivered at the Oxford Diocesan Conference, October 10th, 1878* (London, 1878), p. 4
[41] *Times*, 24 September 1878.
[42] *Autobiography of Montagu Burrows*, pp. 210, 218-20.
[43] *Record*, 11 October 1878.
[44] Christopher to G.N. Freeling, nd, in John S. Reynolds, *Canon Christopher of St Aldate's, Oxford* (Abingdon, 1967), p. 214.
[45] *Record*, 7 October 1878; *Times*, 8 October 1878.

stumbling block in the way of a diocesan college (patronized, be it remembered, by your own Bishop) which at least trains her sons to go out into the world like valiant soldiers of the Cross, and combat these two crying evils of the day?[46]

In his opening address to the conference in Oxford's Sheldonian Theatre on 9 October 1878, Bishop Mackarness tried to defuse the situation. He announced his pleasure that the assembly had never been 'divided into parties' and hoped they had better things to do than attack one another.[47] As one observer later wrote: 'Diocesan conferences are not courts of heresy; directly you allow votes of censure and declarations of want of confidence to be discussed in them their death-warrant is sealed. They must need become a simple nuisance to the Church.'[48] The debate on Knox's motion was set for the afternoon of 10 October.[49] As delegates left the Sheldonian after the morning session they were handed an article from the *Rock* exhibiting two coloured woodcuts of the 'altar' in Cuddesdon College chapel, purporting to show 'the striking progress made by Cuddesdon in the race to Rome'. This revealed that the simple altar cross ('itself illegal') had been replaced by a triptych; the altar cloth now displayed a chalice and host ('Nothing can be more detestable'); and two golden angels were suspended over the altar ('doubtless designed to suggest the notion of cherubim overshadowing and protecting – as in the Holy of Holies – the ark of GOD').[50]

The Sheldonian Theatre was crowded for the afternoon session. Before Knox could speak, however, Sir Robert Phillimore rose to denounce the 'irrelevancy and impropriety' of his motion. He considered it 'unjust to the individuals intercated ... discourteous and unfair to the Lord Bishop ... very injurious to the Conference itself'. Mackarness agreed that if Knox were heard it would be difficult to refuse any censorious motion in the future. John Hubbard, John Mowbray (MP for Oxford University) and the three archdeacons of the diocese spoke in support of Phillimore, one of them mocking Golightly's pamphlet as not worth its price of thrupence.[51] Arthur Purey-Cust (Archdeacon of Buckingham) appeared to be in 'a paroxysm of rage' and 'in a state approaching frenzy'.[52] He claimed the conference was too heated to consider the question, due to the agitation of 'Mr Golightly and his friends', and rejected the *Rock*'s handbill on the two altars as 'a disgrace even to that disgraceful periodical'. Knox recalled that Purey-Cust waved the handbill 'with wild

---

[46] *Times*, 9 October 1878.
[47] *Record*, 16 October 1878. For episcopal concerns that diocesan assemblies should not become a focus of party division, see Crowther, *Church Embattled*, pp. 205-18; Burns, *Diocesan Revival*, ch. 9.
[48] *Guardian*, 23 October 1878, p. 1470.
[49] For details of the debate, see *Record*, 11 October 1878.
[50] *Rock*, 11 October 1878, pp. 814-5.
[51] *Record*, 14 October 1878.
[52] *Rock*, 18 October 1878, pp. 829, 832.

gesticulations' and denounced him 'with passionate fervour'.[53] The archdeacon concluded his diatribe: 'There is a right way and a wrong way of bringing every matter forward. Mr Golightly has gone to work the wrong way – he has mistaken his time, he has mistaken his instruments, he has made a mess of the whole thing. (Laughter.) Do not allow him to make a mess of this Conference. (Cheers.)' Phillimore's motion that Knox be not heard, described as 'a deplorably shuffling, Jesuitical mode of evading the matter', was carried by 252 votes to 75.[54] The appeals of Christopher and Sir Harry Verney (a vice-president of the Church Association) for open discussion fell on deaf ears and the bishop pronounced his pleasure at the result.

During the course of the debate Knox had referred to Mackarness' dismissal of complaints against M.H. Noel (the ritualist vicar of St Barnabas', Oxford) because Noel worked hard. The bishop sarcastically apologised for

> the offence of saying that somebody was a hard-working man. (Laughter.) ... I frankly confess that whenever I see any brother in the diocese who is really devoting all his energies, his time, and his money to the welfare, as he believes, of his flock ... I feel inclined not to be too nicely curious as to some matters which, perhaps, if he were a mere trifler, I should be inclined to notice with much more severity. (Cheers.)

Such toleration, according to Handley Moule (later bishop of Durham), dispensed with the Bible as 'the one infallible instrument for forming and testing belief and teaching'. He lamented:

> such is now the length which toleration goes in the direction of Rome, of Jesuit Rome, the Rome of the Curia, that under an English Bishop, firm in his own personal allegiance to the Bible, the disciples of thorough-going mediaeval and post-mediaeval tradition can teach nearly what they like, if they will only do it like men in right earnest.[55]

While acknowledging his duty as Visitor of Cuddesdon, Mackarness played down the seriousness of the charges levelled at the institution:

> no one has a deeper interest in its welfare and in its conduct than I have, but I do not write to the newspapers whenever I see something which I do not entirely approve of. (A laugh.) Perhaps if I happen to see anything which I do not entirely approve of, I have a few minutes quiet talk with a dear old friend about it, and he may take a hint from me without laying the matter before his visitor in solemn court. (A laugh.) I hope this is not wrong. (Cheers.)

And so the conference closed in what the *Oxford Times* called 'a barren victory

---

[53] Knox, *Reminiscences of an Octogenarian*, p. 116.
[54] *Truth*, 24 October 1878, p. 465.
[55] *Record*, 21 October 1878.

for the Ritualists'.[56]

Golightly's work for that day, however, was not yet finished. At the famous Woodard Schools event in Oxford in 1861 he had used circulars distributed at the doors of the Sheldonian Theatre to good effect. Now he repeated the same stratagem. Having calculated that Knox would be silenced, he had positioned helpers at each door of the Sheldonian with printed copies of Knox's speech, resulting in its wide circulation. Knox reflected: 'The old tactician had once more out-manoeuvred his adversaries.'[57] By the *Church Review* Golightly was rebuked for his 'inconceivable folly'. The newspaper proclaimed: 'This is the end, we should suppose, of "the Oxford spy", and foreshadows the end of all the conspiracy-mongers. We do not regret the miserable attempt. It has cleared the air, and the stupid party in the Church of England are a league nearer common sense.'[58]

It was far from the end of the affair, however. Many objected to Golightly and Knox's methods, but did not want the subject 'quietly quashed as an unpleasant subject'.[59] Even Edward Elton of Wheatley, a long-time supporter of Cuddesdon College, would have welcomed formal investigation:

> Had Mr Golightly, instead of writing an inflammatory pamphlet, manfully grappled with the question whether the teaching of the college exceeded that of the great Anglican divines, he would have been listened to with interest, and good might have come out of the inquiry. ... Had Mr Knox, instead of listening to mere newspaper gossip, and like sources of information, come over to Cuddesdon, mixed with the students, as I have, I am sure his testimony would have been different.[60]

There were growing calls for an open inquiry, perhaps even a Royal Commission established by Parliament.[61] The *Oxford Times* declared that a theological college 'can afford, less than Caesar's wife, to bear for an hour the shadow even of stain upon its fair name.'[62] Another observer stated: 'It is no mere "Evangelical craze" that is at work to make men disquieted. There is really and truly, perhaps groundlessly, but no less actually, a very uneasy feeling about Cuddesdon among many High Churchmen in the diocese of Oxford.'[63] Further fuel was added to the fire by John Burgon (now Dean of Chichester), who preached at the University Church three days after the

---

[56] *Oxford Times*, 12 October 1878.
[57] Knox, *Reminiscences of an Octogenarian*, p. 116.
[58] *Church Review*, 19 October 1878, p. 501.
[59] *Standard*, 12 October 1878.
[60] *Guardian*, 16 October 1878, p. 1452.
[61] Church Association Committee Minutes, 25 October 1878, p. 21 (at LPL); *Rock*, 13 December 1878, p. 995.
[62] *Oxford Times*, 21 December 1878.
[63] *Guardian*, 23 October 1878, p. 1470.

diocesan conference against

> a miserable endeavour to familiarize our people with Romish dresses, Romish gestures, Romish practices, Romish phraseology, Romish doctrines; as if *this* were the legitimate aim of English Divines in these last days; instead of being as it is, nothing else but a crime. ... O do ye beware of this miserable counterfeit, this pitiful caricature rather, of true Religion, 'pure and undefiled', – this unhealthy yearning after the corrupt method of a Church which is branded in the Apocalypse with infamy and a most tremendous doom.[64]

Cuddesdon Teaching and Secessions

More than a month after his *Solemn Warning*, Golightly wrote to Mackarness reiterating his charges. Despite the fact that he was a member of the Church Association, he felt able to declare, as often before: 'I am no party man. ... I protest as strongly against one part of the Church appropriating to itself the name of Evangelical, as against another appropriating to itself the name of Catholic.' Golightly reminded the bishop of his duty 'to banish and drive away all erroneous and strange doctrine', and implored him to dismiss the teaching staff at Cuddesdon and close the college until suitable replacements could be found.[65] The *Oxford Times* agreed: 'Excision is now the only remedy equal to the emergency.'[66] Likewise the *Rock* wrote: 'At present Cuddesdon College is infected with sacerdotal fever in its most virulent form; therefore the sooner it is fumigated the better for the spiritual health of the Church of England.'[67]

One of the chief complaints against Cuddesdon was that the staff were 'members of disloyal, discreditable and Romish Societies'.[68] Furse, Willis and Herbert Barnett (the chaplain) were all members of the ECU. Meanwhile Willis was forced to defend his former links with the SSC: 'I joined it with no party aims, still less with any shadow of a thought of disloyalty to the Church of England, but with a view to my own life before God. I have never been able to understand by what right outsiders have interfered with my personal and religious liberty.'[69] He assured his critics that none had 'a more profound horror of Romanism' than himself, and his aim was to make his students 'on the one hand, intelligent, uncompromising opponents of the encroachments and unauthorised developments of the Roman Church, and, on the other, steadfast,

---

[64] John W. Burgon, *Nehemiah, a Pattern to Builders: Counsels on the Recommencement of the Academical Year* (Oxford, 1878), pp. 18-9.
[65] *Record*, 25 October 1878. Mackarness' reply was conciliatory: Henry Linton to Golightly, 12 November 1878, LPL MS 1808, fo. 57.
[66] *Oxford Times*, 21 December 1878.
[67] *Rock*, 4 October 1878, p. 802.
[68] *Oxford Times*, 30 November 1878.
[69] *Guardian*, 23 October 1878, p. 1470.

hearty, and loyal members of the Church of England'.[70] Willis' friend, H.T. Morgan (a former chaplain at Cuddesdon), defended him as 'entirely moderate and sound is his teaching', with no tendency 'to lay stress on externals, or to encourage Romanism in any way' but rather to 'discourage men from party strife'.[71] Likewise the *Church Times* defended Furse as 'a very moderate, not to say cautious, Anglican Churchman'.[72]

In order to explain publicly the nature of teaching and discipline at Cuddesdon, Furse published a report on his five years as principal.[73] Yet the *Rock* remained dissatisfied with such self-justification: 'They have not a single independent witness to place in the box, nor a tittle of evidence to disprove the charge.'[74] Similarly the *Record* wanted an open inquiry rather than this vain attempt with a 'little handful of dust ... to still the angry buzzing'. It warned that Mackarness was

> surrounded by a knot of shrewd, unscrupulous intriguers who, in a spirit of ultra-partisanship, are managing the diocese with the comfortable assurance that if these proceedings are questioned they will simply have to give any account they please of themselves, and that the Bishop will assure the public that they are all honourable men.[75]

Nevertheless, Furse received encouragement from Liddon. In the light of the debacle surrounding Golightly's attacks in 1858-59, he urged Furse to ensure

> no changes whatever will be so made as to give an appearance of yielding to pressure. There may of course be changes, which, on consideration, *are* desirable; none of us pretends to be practically infallible. But they should be carried out, if at all, in utter independence of forms of opinion which in reality are hostile, not to the accidents, but to the substance, of all true Church work, & which never will be satisfied by partial concessions. As for the Puritan temper ... you do it no kindness by teaching it to think itself reasonable & right.[76]

Liddon concluded that the hostile reaction to Cuddesdon was a result of 'evangelicalism' feeling pressurised:

> From time to time, it becomes more than commonly conscious of its weakness, & it relieves itself by a burst of irritation. ... In fact modern English puritanism is human nature placed under trying circumstances, & acting as most men would be

---

[70] *Guardian*, 6 November 1878, p. 1548.
[71] *Guardian*, 30 October 1878, p. 1503.
[72] *Church Times*, 13 December 1878, p. 706.
[73] Charles W. Furse, *Cuddesdon College. A Report for the Five Years ending Trinity Term, 1878* (Oxford, 1878).
[74] *Rock*, 6 December 1878, p. 957.
[75] *Record*, 9 December 1878.
[76] Liddon to Furse, 15 October 1878, LPL MS 4122, fo. 15.

tempted to act. Only in this way can one explain the conduct of a kindly old man like Mr Golightly, & of others who side with him.[77]

It is striking that after twenty years of open hostility, Liddon's antipathy towards Golightly's methods was still mixed with respect and even a hint of personal affection for Golightly himself. In his *Life of Pusey*, Liddon later called Golightly an authority on the 'gossip ... of Puritan Oxford', but also 'a kind-hearted and in his way an earnest man, if somewhat self-important'.[78]

The *Record* advised that the teaching at Cuddesdon College should be 'a prophylactic against Romanism'.[79] However, there were concerns about instruction on auricular confession and that the *Cuddesdon Manual of Intercession for Missions* included prayers 'for the fuller restoration of the religious life' and for God's blessing in 'hearing confessions' and 'exorcising evil spirits'.[80] When the *Rock*'s 'special correspondent' visited Cuddesdon village, he found in the parish church an altar 'of the most repulsive and Popish kind' and a stone reredos with a striking portrait: '*It was that of a Pope in full Pontifical garments, and with the unmistakable Papal tiara on his head!!!* Therefore when a Ritualistic worshipper bends before the "altar" in Cuddesdon Church he actually bows before the image of a Pope which a former principal of Cuddesdon has set up!' On infiltrating the college chapel the correspondent found a stained glass window representing fourteen saints: 'It will be observed that all the male "saints" were thorough-going *Papists*. ... Dominick the murderer, Xavier the Jesuit, and Bonaventura the blasphemer – these are the men whom Cuddesdon delighteth to honour!' He also spotted a processional cross inscribed with the letters A. M. D. G. (the motto of the Jesuits), 'stations of the cross', and the college prayer book with 'canonical hours' given Roman names such as prime, terce, sext, none and compline.[81]

Another major complaint against Cuddesdon was that approximately twenty ex-students had converted to Roman Catholicism.[82] Willis thought such secessions 'simply irrelevant' since the same could be said of Balliol College or Exeter College, to which came the predictable retort: 'Mr Willis forgets that Cuddesdon is distinctly a *theological* college'.[83] Supporters of Cuddesdon argued that some students arrived on the brink of secession, so the college

---

[77] Ibid., fos 14-5.
[78] Liddon, *Life of Pusey*, ii. pp. 12, 444.
[79] *Record*, 1 November 1878.
[80] *The Cuddesdon Manual of Intercession for Missions* (Oxford, 1876), pp. 31, 42-3 (copy at CCA C1/12); *Rock*, 13 December 1878, p. 990; *Guardian*, 4 and 24 December 1878, pp. 1677, 1803.
[81] *Rock*, 13 December 1878, p. 997. On the stained glass and processional cross, see *Cuddesdon College Annual Record* (1877), pp. 33-4.
[82] Knox, *Address*, pp. 7-8. Knox had to apologise for errors in his list of seceders: *Oxford Times*, 19 October 1878; *Guardian*, 6 November 1878, p. 1548.
[83] *Guardian*, 23 and 30 October 1878, pp. 1470, 1504.

could not be held responsible for failing to keep them all within the Anglican Communion. Pott explained that four of the first seven seceders were judged unfit for ordination, a fifth never proceeded beyond deacon's orders, and the other two converted after many years working within the Church of England. This satisfied Bishop Mackarness that there was not 'a tittle of evidence' to connect Cuddesdon with the secessions.[84] The teachers could not be blamed simply for failing to cure student errors: 'When patients die in a hospital during the prevalence of an epidemic, we do not lay their deaths to the charge of the hospital staff.'[85]

Others defended the college in like manner. For instance, Elton stated: 'Those who went from us were mostly weak and ill-instructed minds, who brought their Romanism to Cuddesdon, and did not find it there'.[86] Similarly Morgan argued:

> A theological college has to deal, not with machines, but with human minds, which often refuse to be moulded after a given type. Some young men came to us, from time to time, of an unquiet, restless spirit, often full of devotion, but with little intellectual power or grasp of facts, longing for a peace, or a reverence, or seeming certainty, which they could not find in the Church of England. ... Who will, in these troubled days, give a specific for scrupulous conscience? If Mr Knox or his friends are able to provide a perfectly satisfactory cure for persons troubled with Romanizing fears and doubts, let them tell it to us, and we shall be too glad to apply it.

With similar logic, another observer asked: 'Is then the Evangelical party to be cast out because such a very large per-centage of Roman perverts were originally Evangelicals?'[87] In a variation on this theme, a correspondent in the *Church Times* declared that the Church Association, 'that most disgraceful caucus', was itself to blame for conversions to Rome.[88] It is one of the ironies of family life that Knox's own son, Ronald, was to become an influential Roman Catholic.

With less than twenty secessions from Cuddesdon to Rome in 24 years, the *Guardian* thought that 'the evil is absurdly exaggerated'. Likewise Mackarness wrote: 'For one recruit to Rome, there have probably been fifty deserters from the Church of England to the forces of unbelief, and a still larger number, alas! of victims to the fatal seductions of immorality and vice. Here are our greatest

---

[84] Furse, *Cuddesdon College*, p. iii. See *Cuddesdon College, 1878. Address of Old Students to the Right Rev. the Lord Bishop of Oxford, Visitor, on the Subject of Recent Charges Brought Against the College: Together with his Lordship's Reply* (Oxford, 1878), pp. 5, 15.
[85] *Guardian*, 24 December 1878, p. 1796.
[86] *Guardian*, 20 November 1878, p. 1610.
[87] *Guardian*, 30 October 1878, p. 1503.
[88] *Church Times*, 18 October 1878, p. 581.

perils, our most serious losses.'[89] Unlike other theological colleges, he proclaimed, Cuddesdon did not 'admit only the straitest adherents of a special system of theology', but rather 'men of wide and varied sympathies, who would have refused to be bound by party tests of any kind.' He believed that residence at Cuddesdon always produced a change for the better.[90] The bishop was addressed by 284 ex-students who repudiated 'with indignation, the imputations of unfaithfulness and disloyalty to the Church of England' which had been cast upon them and their college tutors.[91] Ironically, at least six of these signatories were themselves to secede to the Church of Rome in later years.

Address from the Laity

At a lecture against ritualism in Oxford in early November 1878 given by Walter Walsh (a representative of the Protestant Reformation Society, now notorious for his *Secret History of the Oxford Movement*), it was announced on Golightly's authority that a large demonstration against Cuddesdon College was being arranged, at which Lord Macclesfield, a major landowner in the village, would take the chair.[92] This planned demonstration was soon replaced by an Address to the bishop. After the diocesan conference, Golightly had asked the council of the Church Association whether an appeal to the Queen might be organised, but was advised to address Mackarness as Cuddesdon College's Visitor.[93]

The Address was headed by Lord Jersey, but was said to have originated with the Oxford branch of the Church Association and Christopher was involved in co-ordinating it.[94] It complained that Golightly and Knox's charges had been ignored, expressed concern that the teaching staff at Cuddesdon were members of the ECU, and appealed to the bishop to find 'a remedy to the serious evil'.[95] At Christopher's request, the Church Association helped to generate support for the Address by distributing to all JPs and churchwardens in Oxford diocese pamphlets entitled *The English Church Union Proved to be a*

---

[89] *Guardian*, 24 December 1878, pp. 1793, 1796.

[90] Furse, *Cuddesdon College*, p. iv. For praise of Cuddesdon curates, see *Guardian*, 16, 23 and 30 October 1878, pp. 1452, 1470, 1503.

[91] *Cuddesdon College, 1878*, p. 5.

[92] *Oxford Times*, 16 November 1878. See Walter Walsh, *'Is Ritualism Loyal to the Church of England?' Report of a Lecture and Discussion* (Oxford, 1879).

[93] Church Association Committee Minutes, 11 October 1878, pp. 10-1 (at LPL); W.C. Palmer to Golightly, 14 October 1878, LPL MS 1808, fos 206-7.

[94] *Guardian*, 18 December 1878, p. 1766; Mackarness to Christopher, 18 December 1878, in Reynolds, *Canon Christopher*, p. 215; *Record*, 23 December 1878.

[95] *An Address to the Right Reverend the Lord Bishop of Oxford, from Peers, Magistrates, Lay Members of the Diocesan Conference, and Churchwardens, Resident Within his Lordship's Diocese, Concerning Cuddesdon College* (Oxford, 1878), p. 4.

Romanizing Confederacy and *Twelve Reasons for Not Joining the English Church Union*.[96] The protest was eventually signed by 827 peers, JPs, churchwardens and lay members of the diocesan conference.[97] The *Rock* concluded that the affair was 'a turning-point in the history of the great struggle between lay endurance and ecclesiastical tyranny and assumption.'[98]

The signatories were said to be mostly from 'the old moderate High Church party'[99], but were dismissed as neither 'leaders in religious opinion' nor 'peculiarly conversant with Anglican theology'.[100] The *Church Review* remarked: 'it would be interesting to know how many are not communicants, how many of the ordinary aggrieved parishioner sort, how many members of the Church Association, how many liturgical revisionists, how many not even Churchmen.'[101] The wide spectrum of opinion represented by the Address was freely acknowledged by the *Church Times*:

> Its signatories are partly men of such notorious character that a little more discretion would have prompted the suppression of their names; partly old-fashioned Evangelicals who cannot bear to think that their hey-day is over, and would like to deal a blow at the competition who is driving them out of the field; and partly of country peers and squires who find that the High Church parson is the only one who does not treat them as petty kings, with supreme jurisdiction over ecclesiastical as well as temporal causes within their domains; whereas a Low or Broad Churchman is usually far more docile, obsequious, and squeezable.[102]

In reply to the Address, Mackarness expressed sorrow that the laity had chosen to act alone, without the advice of the clergy of the diocese. He announced that Furse, Willis and Barnett had all withdrawn from the ECU of their own volition and therefore the memorialists' only charge against the college had been removed. Unless more than 'vague imputations' were put forward, with specific charges and citations of laws allegedly broken, no case could be heard in the visitorial court 'without absurdity'.[103] The *Oxford Times* thought the bishop's response 'disengenuous [sic] and superficial ... a dodge and an artifice ... Why not face the question like a man?'[104] Some suggested the laity should press the matter further, but Lord Jersey decided the

---

[96] Church Association Committee Minutes, 13 December 1878, pp. 68-9 (at LPL).
[97] *Record*, 23 December 1878.
[98] *Rock*, 3 January 1879, p. 2.
[99] *Record*, 2 December 1878.
[100] *Guardian*, 1 January 1879, p. 7.
[101] *Church Review*, 28 December 1878, p. 626.
[102] *Church Times*, 13 December 1878, p. 705.
[103] *Guardian*, 24 December 1878, p. 1796
[104] *Oxford Times*, 4 January 1879.

correspondence should cease.[105]

The English Church Union and the Church Association

Members of the ECU and the Church Association played a prominent part throughout the renewed Cuddesdon controversy. The local branches of these organisations continued to stoke the fire at their rival meetings. In November 1878 T.H. Gill of Manchester spoke at the Oxford branch of the Church Association, criticising Pusey's recent adaptation of the Abbé Gaume's *Manual for Confessors*.[106] Three days later C.L. Wood (national president of the ECU and later Viscount Halifax) told ECU's Oxford branch that the Cuddesdon furore was about 'no mere question of ritual ... but the whole principle of the sacramental system'.[107] The *Church Times* asked why the ECU, with approximately 3,000 clerical members and 15,000 lay members, should not have one theological college out of twenty which was sympathetic to its aims, 'on mere grounds of demand and supply'.[108] Likewise the *Guardian* thought that if colleges with Low Church sympathies were allowed, such as St John's, Highbury and St Aidan's, Birkenhead, then a High Church tendency at Cuddesdon should be tolerated.[109]

The debate was characterised by heated polemics, and after only a couple of months one observer appealed: 'I really think it is time to cry truce'.[110] Another concluded: 'There is ample room for both parties to work side by side with charity and with mutual trust; the present want of this is the great evil of the day. If it is not too late, let all parties agree to pursue their work in their own way, and to cease cutting one another's throats, or we know what the result will be.'[111] A plea for tolerance was issued: 'The heathen of old was able to say, "See how these Christians love one another!" The English infidel of to-day is able to say the same, but, alas! with a large qualification if he is unfortunate enough to observe the spirit of the Church Association, the *Rock*, or the *Church Times*.'[112] The *Guardian* went further and encouraged the dissolution of both the ECU and the Church Association: 'It would be a happy and hopeful Christmas for the Church of England if both parties were disbanded. Parties in

---

[105] See letters between Hubbard and Jersey, *Oxford Times*, 18 January and 1 February 1879.
[106] T.H. Gill, *Dr Pusey and the Abbé Gaume: or, the Latest Development of the Confessional in the Church of England* (London, 1878). See correspondence between Christopher, Liddon and Pusey in Reynolds, *Canon Christopher*, pp. 380-93; Bodleian MS St Edmund Hall 88, fos 1-27.
[107] *Oxford Times*, 30 November 1878.
[108] *Church Times*, 13 December 1878, p. 706.
[109] *Guardian*, 24 December 1878, p. 1793.
[110] *Guardian*, 20 November 1878, p. 1610.
[111] *Church Times*, 18 October 1878, p. 581.
[112] *Guardian*, 30 October 1878, p. 1503.

the Church there always have been. Organisations for party purposes exclusively, and for party warfare, are an unhappy and disastrous novelty of these days of ours.'[113]

Numerous other appeals were issued for an end to such conflict. For instance, in October 1878 William Ince (Regius Professor of Divinity) asked an Oxford congregation:

> If men are deep-rooted in the love of God and imitation of Jesus Christ, why should they bite and devour one another? ... Surely, in the presence of a blighting infidelity, and a despairing scepticism all around us, we who profess the faith of Christ are bound, above all things to abstain from internecine controversy.[114]

In December Purey-Cust preached what the *Rock* called a 'peace-at-any-price sermon',[115] on *Harmony in Spite of Differences*, lamenting the prevalence of 'rabid and savage strife', 'mutual insinuations and imprecations' and 'hereditary prejudices and watchwords'.[116] He appealed for mutual toleration:

> My brethren, I believe that one crying need in our day, that in a Church, *where parties must be tolerated*, party spirit on all sides should be discouraged and frowned down. Such hateful imputations are condemned in politics, why are they tolerated and encouraged in religion, until weak men are driven out, and thoughtful men are rendered sick at heart, and the love which might, and I believe would, redress many of the evils which the law cannot touch, and restrain those whom the law only goads into mad rebellion, is evaporated in the crucible of controversy and mutual recrimination?[117]

Purey-Cust further advised the clergy of Buckinghamshire archdeaconry:

> My friends, if we are ever to have peace in our distracted Church, our first step must be to relinquish and set our face against the use of hateful party names. ... Party cries have been the bane of the seventeenth and eighteenth centuries, – are they to be the bane of the nineteenth also? ... Are we so stupid? Have we learned nothing by experience? Must history ever repeat itself to our shame?[118]

He described the ECU and the Church Association as 'grinding millstones, between which the very heart of our Holy Faith will be inevitably crushed

---

[113] *Guardian*, 24 December 1878, p. 1793.
[114] William Ince, *The Internal Duties of the University in Prospect of External Changes* (Oxford, 1878), p. 16.
[115] *Rock*, 3 January 1879, p. 9.
[116] A.P. Purey-Cust, *Harmony in Spite of Differences* (London, 1878), pp. 6, 8.
[117] Ibid., p. 9. See also, A.P. Purey-Cust, *Unity with Division in the Established Church Possible and Essential* (London, 1874).
[118] A.P. Purey-Cust, *A Charge Delivered at his Third Visitation of the Archdeaconry of Buckingham* (London, 1879), pp. 37-9.

out.'[119] Yet the *Rock* objected that 'Religion itself sinks to the level of a "cat's concert" if Romish and Reformed tunes are to be played simultaneously in the National Church.'[120]

Bishop Mackarness' attitude to the ECU and the Church Association came under close scrutiny during the controversy. Some praised his 'impartial conduct, tact and temper',[121] but the *Record* thought him at best guilty of weak leadership:

> Bishop MACKARNESS has the reputation of being a very kindly, genial man, who would be very anxious, if he possibly could, to make all things pleasant for everybody all round, probably even for Mr GOLIGHTLY himself if he could. His notion seems to be that the Church of England is well able to take care of herself without any intervention on the part of Bishops.[122]

By others Mackarness was seen as strongly biased towards the ritualists. It was discovered that he had himself once been a member of the ECU, resigning in 1869 shortly before his consecration as bishop.[123] This explained why he had appointed more than twenty members of the ECU to livings of which he held the patronage, but few evangelicals.[124] He had also written prefaces to 'Romeward-propelling books' and prevented prosecutions of ritualistic clergy at Clewer, Reading and Dorchester.[125] Three years later Golightly described Mackarness as having a 'mitigated dislike' for Low Churchmen, to which the bishop replied:

> I do not quite see why you should suppose that I entertain a 'dislike' – even of a 'mitigated' kind – to Low Churchmen. I learned much from Divines of that school in my younger days: and I have always been grateful for the good they taught me. There are Low Churchmen now in Oxford, for whom I have a sincere regard. If I do not like those who are factious and intolerant, I can only say that I dislike a factious and intolerant spirit in any Christian, 'High', or 'Low'.[126]

However, Golightly's friend William R. Fremantle (Dean of Ripon since 1876) retorted: 'The Bishop ... is wofully [*sic*] ignorant of himself – there is a great deal of difference between a cold shoulder and a hearty shake of the hand. When has he ever given this latter to an Evangelical?'[127]

---

[119] Ibid., p. 40.
[120] *Rock*, 3 January 1879, p. 9.
[121] *Oxford Times*, 12 October 1878.
[122] *Record*, 9 December 1878.
[123] *Guardian*, 8 January 1879, p. 45.
[124] *Record*, 13 November 1878.
[125] *Rock*, 6 December 1878, p. 981.
[126] Golightly, *Letter to the Dean of Ripon*, p. 68; Mackarness to Golightly, 29 September 1881, LPL MS 1808, fo. 71.
[127] Fremantle to Golightly, 25 October 1881, LPL MS 1805, fo. 295.

In his reply to the Address of the laity concerning Cuddesdon College, Mackarness publicly assailed both the ECU and the Church Association:

> As to the English Church Union, if they [the memorialists] regret its methods of action, I go further, and regret that it exists. Excellent as were the purposes of its foundation twenty years or more ago, it has resulted in a state of things injurious to the welfare of the Church. Stirring up rival organisations, it has divided Churchmen into hostile camps, and has brought many good men, who have no real share in its counsels, though they are counted among its 17,000 members, into indiscriminate and unmerited obloquy. Fruitless litigation has been encouraged, charity grievously impaired. The heaviest indictment against the Church Union is, that it called the Church Association into life. Until both societies are dissolved there will be, in my judgment, small hope of peace for the Church.[128]

Predictably, such statements produced a stern reaction from both organisations. G.A. Denison, one of the original founders of the ECU and a former curate of Cuddesdon, thought the claim it had stirred up rival organisations was 'historically ludicrous'.[129] Meanwhile Thomas Andrews (chairman of the Church Association) argued that 'A truce with the enemy while within the walls (actually daily sustained by the supplies and wearing the uniform of our Church) is not "peace", but a shameful surrender from which true Churchmen cannot but shrink with the deepest aversion'. To this Mackarness responded:

> I have no sympathy with your appetite for condemnations. Too often they do but provoke men to revolt. In things indifferent liberty, and neutral toleration, are more to my taste. In things really objectionable, as ministering to superstition, we might have trusted the good sense and sound feeling of Churchmen to prevail, if polemical confederacies had not almost banished reason and charity from the sphere of their discussion.[130]

By the end of January 1879, the controversy over Cuddesdon College had died down. The attention of Oxford diocese moved instead to the ritualistic practices of T.T. Carter at Clewer, where the ECU and the Church Association were again prominently involved.[131] Only briefly did Cuddesdon regain the lime-light when Charles Elliott (vicar of Winkfield, near Bracknell) attacked *The Communicant's Manual*, a book 'tainted with Roman error' to which King had contributed a preface when principal.[132] The *Rock* immediately proclaimed

---

[128] *Guardian*, 24 December 1878, p. 1796.
[129] Quoted in *Oxford Times*, 18 January 1879.
[130] *Church Association Monthly Intelligencer* 13 (February 1879), pp. 46-7.
[131] W.H. Hutchings, *Life and Letters of Thomas Thellusson Carter* (London, 1903), pp. 150-79; Mackarness, *Memorials*, pp. 86-98.
[132] Charles J. Elliott, *Some Strictures on a Book Entitled 'The Communicant's Manual'* (London, 1879), p. 29. See also Edward King, *A Letter to the Rev. Charles J. Elliott*

once more that Cuddesdon had 'no right whatever to call itself in any true sense a Church of England institution', and concluded that if Mackarness were a man of honour he would resign his see and secede to Rome.[133]

Unlike with their attacks upon Liddon and Pott in the 1850s, Golightly and his allies failed to provoke substantial changes in the teaching at Cuddesdon during the affair of 1878-79. Willis remained until 1880 when he became a founding member of the Oxford Mission to Calcutta, replaced as vice-principal by Charles Gore. Furse continued in charge until 1883 when he was appointed a canon of Westminster. Nevertheless the controversy received nationwide attention and its outcome was seen as of vital import to the future direction of Anglicanism. The *Rock* described it as 'a struggle which – despite all attempts to localize it – is rapidly assuming an importance co-extensive with the Church of England'.[134] The achievement of Oxford's Protestants was assessed differently by observers. The *Guardian* maintained: 'Mr Golightly and his henchman Mr Knox have led their too credulous followers – as the former gentleman has more than once done before – into something very like "a mare's nest".'[135] In contrast the *Record* judged that they had gained 'a substantial victory' because of the extensive publicity: 'Forewarned is to be forearmed, and parishes which receive Cuddesdon curates will know what to expect.'[136]

Re-writing History

Golightly's *Solemn Warning Against Cuddesdon College* spearheaded the final campaign of his life, but it was not quite his final pamphlet. He still had within him one more polemical publication, primarily written in self-defence. It was called forth by the authorized biography of his old antagonist, Bishop Samuel Wilberforce. Golightly had lived long enough to begin already appearing in the history books and he wanted to ensure that the historical accounts of his part in the ritualist agitations in Oxford diocese were true and fair. It was another lost cause.

When Bishop Wilberforce was killed in a fall from his horse in July 1873, plans were immediately put in place (as with most Victorian notables) for a multi-volume *Life*.[137] William Gladstone was invited to write it, as was James

---

(Oxford, 1879); Elliott, *Some Remarks Upon a Letter to the Rev. C.J. Elliott* (London, 1879).

[133] *Rock*, 14 March 1879, p. 206.
[134] *Rock*, 6 December 1878, p. 957.
[135] *Guardian*, 24 December 1878, p. 1793.
[136] *Record*, 8 January 1879.
[137] For correspondence and reviews concerning the *Life of Samuel Wilberforce*, see Bodleian MS Wilberforce c.26-c.29 and e.22.

Randall (former Archdeacon of Berkshire), but both declined.[138] Instead the task was given to Arthur Ashwell, principal of Chichester Theological College, who had previously worked under Wilberforce as principal of the Oxford Diocesan Teacher Training College at Culham.[139] Volume I, covering Wilberforce's life from birth to 1848, was published at the end of 1879 and was warmly received by the reviewers.[140] Golightly thought Ashwell had 'praised the Bishop through thick and thin', yet even he admitted: '*On the whole* the book leads me to think better of the Bishop than I did before. It shews that there was more good in him than I had thought.'[141] However, Ashwell died in October 1879 as Volume I was passing through the press, so the search for a biographer had to begin again. Gladstone was again mentioned, as was Alfred Pott, but the bishop's son, Reginald Wilberforce, was determined to take up the project himself.[142] John Murray, publisher of the *Life*, pleaded that Wilberforce was unqualified because of his lack of knowledge of church affairs and lack of experience in literature: 'I feel quite convinced that no friend of yours or your Father will be found to encourage you to attempt [the work]. You would certainly not obtain the confidence of the Public, more especially not of the Clerical portion of it.'[143] Understandably Golightly did not want Archdeacon Pott to be chosen, but still preferred him to Reginald Wilberforce whom he considered 'utterly unequal to the task'.[144] Wilberforce, however, refused to be dissuaded, despite acknowledging that 'as a general rule, a son is the person least capable of writing his father's life'.[145]

Volume II was published in April 1881 and, despite the publisher's foreboding, was also well received. Rare criticism came from the *Athenaeum* ('with the best intentions, Mr Reginald Wilberforce has failed'[146]) and from the

---

[138] Henry D. Gordon to Golightly, 6 October 1881, LPL MS 1806, fo. 133; James Randall to Reginald G. Wilberforce, 22 November 1873, Bodleian MS Wilberforce c.26, fos 80-3; Ashwell and Wilberforce, *Life of Samuel Wilberforce*, ii. p. 1.

[139] Arthur R. Ashwell, 'Samuel Wilberforce', *Quarterly Review* 136 (April 1874), pp. 332-71; *Church Quarterly Review* 9 (January 1880), p. 541.

[140] For example, 'Ashwell's Life of Wilberforce', *Church Quarterly Review* 10 (April 1880), pp. 229-59; John W. Burgon, 'Bishop Wilberforce', *Quarterly Review* 149 (January 1880), pp. 84-125; R.M. Milnes, 'Samuel Wilberforce, Bishop of Oxford and Winchester', *Fortnightly Review* 27 (March 1880), pp. 335-57; James H. Rigg, 'Bishop Wilberforce', *London Quarterly Review* 54 (July 1880), pp. 331-58; George A. Simcox, 'Bishop Wilberforce', *Macmillan's Magazine* 41 (March 1880), pp. 395-404; Arthur P. Stanley, 'The Oxford School', *Edinburgh Review* 153 (April 1881), pp. 325-35.

[141] Golightly to Burgon, 22 January 1880, Bodleian MS Eng.th.d.12, fos 84-7.

[142] *Dundee Advertiser*, 28 January 1880; John Murray to Reginald G. Wilberforce, 3 March 1880, Bodleian MS Wilberforce c.26, fos 171-2.

[143] Murray to Wilberforce, 17 February 1880, ibid., fos 169-70.

[144] Golightly to Burgon, 20 February 1880, Bodleian MS Eng.th.d.12, fo. 105.

[145] Ashwell and Wilberforce, *Life of Samuel Wilberforce*, ii. p. v.

[146] *Athenaeum*, 16 April 1881, p. 517.

Record, which thought 'the whole tendency of the second volume ... anti-Protestant, if not Romeward', and that it was 'ministering to a love of gossip'.[147] The most passionate objections, analysed below, came from Golightly, a warning of the storm which was to break over the *Life* on the publication of Volume III.

The third and final volume appeared in December 1882, and unlike the previous two was vociferously slated by reviewers. A dominant feature of the volume was the large number of extracts from the bishop's diary, in which he had the habit of recording private conversations and his personal opinions of contemporaries. When these were printed wholesale in the *Life* there was uproar.[148] One critic observed: 'If directly a man of distinction is dead his literary heirs are allowed to publish every anecdote he knows, however depreciating, of his surviving contemporaries, a fresh terror will be added to human intercourse.'[149] The *Times* remarked: 'We can only marvel at the audacity of the revelations, some of which, if they do not make dead men turn in their graves, will, at least, make living men very uncomfortable.'[150] Similarly, the *Edinburgh Review* commented:

> If opportunity had been given, many of these judgments on men, much of this trivial gossip which are now enshrined in a widely circulated book, would have been condemned to the fire. The mischief can never be repaired. ... The book is inaccurate, as gossip always is.[151]

A more serious crime, perhaps, than printing too much of a private diary was Reginald Wilberforce's careless style of writing. For example, in one chapter he gave the impression that he was quoting a letter from Dean Burgon slating the new lectionary, although no such letter existed. When challenged, Wilberforce replied that it was only meant as 'a good story', upon which Burgon expostulated: 'the framework of society would become hopelessly out of gear in less than a week if such a proceeding could be allowed to pass

---

[147] *Record*, 2 and 6 May 1881.
[148] For controversial passages, see Ashwell and Wilberforce, *Life of Samuel Wilberforce*, iii. pp. 24-6, 69, 248-9, 268-9, 294. For related correspondence, see *Times*, 2, 4, 6, 9 and 11 January, 6 February 1883; *Guardian*, 10 January 1883, p. 56; W. Edwards to Reginald G. Wilberforce, January – February 1883, Bodleian MS Wilberforce c.27, fos 172-83.
[149] Quoted in *Tablet*, 30 December 1882, p. 1049.
[150] *Times*, 20 December 1882.
[151] 'Life of Bishop Wilberforce', *Edinburgh Review* 157 (April 1883), p. 530. For an alternative perspective, see Herbert Cowell, 'Bishop Wilberforce', *Blackwood's Edinburgh Magazine* 133 (February 1883), p. 291; George W. Dasent, 'Samuel Wilberforce', *Fortnightly Review* 33 (February 1883), p. 196.

without grave public remonstrance.'[152] Such revelations only increased suspicions surrounding the accuracy of the *Life*. The *Westminster Review* spoke for many when it asked: 'the question arises, what other statements of alleged facts by Mr Wilberforce may be exaggerated or wholly unfounded.'[153] These severe strictures indicated, according to Liddon, *'the utter loss of a true sense of proportion'*,[154] while Basil Wilberforce (Reginald's brother) advised: 'let them jabber & be hanged'.[155] Reginald Wilberforce brazenly stood his ground and responded to his critics: 'Could you see the materials which I have not yet published, you might marvel at my amazing moderation.'[156]

Warning of the furore surrounding Volume III can be seen in Golightly's complaints, fifteen months before, about the way in which he had been treated in Volume II. At the time, however, he was a lone voice of protest and few took notice. The second volume, covering the period 1848 to 1860, included important issues in Bishop Wilberforce's career such as the Gorham Judgment and the 'Papal Aggression', the revival of the Church of England's Convocation, F.D. Maurice's *Theological Essays*, and controversies with T.W. Allies, E.B. Pusey and G.A. Denison. In the midst of these events, the account between 1857 and 1859 of the Cuddesdon affair and Golightly's *Facts and Documents shewing the Alarming State of the Diocese of Oxford* was given only twenty out of 465 pages.[157] This was seen by the *Guardian* as illustrative of the proper perspective gained with hindsight:

> It is not without its wholesome and sobering effect on the mind to recall the hot volleys of pamphlets and newspaper letters and articles with which those who knew Oxford in those days were familiar. How insignificant the net result of all the worry and excitement seems now to be! Not Mr Golightly himself – most persistent and unappeasable of pamphleteers – cuts any very conspicuous figure even in this copious collection of the Bishop's memoranda and of the words and deeds of his opponents.[158]

On the other hand, the *Church Times* thought the Cuddesdon crisis had been underplayed, and that it was 'an episode which Mr Reginald Wilberforce passes over much more lightly than an wholly unbiased biographer would have felt

---

[152] Ashwell and Wilberforce, *Life of Samuel Wilberforce*, iii. p. 249; *Times*, 7 February 1883; Burgon, *Lives of Twelve Good Men*, ii. pp. 423-4.

[153] Edward C. Whitehurst, 'The Late Bishop Wilberforce', *Westminster Review* 63 (April 1883), p. 379.

[154] Liddon to Anna M. Wilberforce, 24 January 1883, Bodleian MS Wilberforce c.28, fo. 45.

[155] Basil Wilberforce to Reginald G. Wilberforce, 19 December 1882, ibid., fo. 117.

[156] *Times*, 22 December 1882.

[157] Ashwell and Wilberforce, *Life of Samuel Wilberforce*, ii. pp. 358-73, 415-9.

[158] *Guardian*, 25 May 1881, p. 760.

free to do.'[159]

The *Life*'s version of events surrounding Cuddesdon College and *Facts and Documents* was certainly one sided. Indeed Liddon was asked to proof-read the chapters and concluded: 'All that concerns myself is as just as any one could wish; or rather it errs on the side of generosity.'[160] On learning that Reginald Wilberforce had replaced Ashwell as biographer, Henry Gordon (son of Golightly's friend, Richard Gordon, a former rural dean) withdrew permission for his father's correspondence to be used in the *Life*, and when he warned that personal remarks should not be directed at Golightly, Wilberforce became 'most violent & obstinate ... Never was man more pig-headed.'[161] When Volume II appeared it was peppered with abuse of Golightly. It spoke of his 'inaccurate and sweeping accusation' against Cuddesdon College, and of the 'Golightly faction'. It described *Facts and Documents* as fostered by his 'malignant hostility'.[162] This was hardly dispassionate history and Dean Burgon agreed that his friend had been 'maligned and ungenerously misrepresented'.[163]

In a vain attempt to re-write the history books in his own favour, Golightly published the final pamphlet of his life in September 1881. It was primarily an act of self-defence against Reginald Wilberforce's 'personal attacks', but included a last stab against Cuddesdon College and Bishop Mackarness.[164] Running to 99 pages, it took the form of a letter to one of Golightly's close allies during the agitation against ritualism in the 1850s, William R. Fremantle, entitled *A Letter to the Very Reverend the Dean of Ripon, containing Strictures on the Life of Bishop Wilberforce*. Golightly emphasised that he had known the Wilberforce family for more than fifty years and was a 'personal friend' of the bishop, who had often shown him kindness.[165] Although the two men had sometimes exchanged sharp words in public, this was no indication of personal antipathy between them.[166] Golightly announced: 'I trust that I duly appreciated his many and great excellences, whilst I was not blind to his defects',[167] although he was happy to delineate defects at far greater length. He described Samuel Wilberforce as 'always craving after preferment', 'very impatient of opposition' and guilty of 'flinging about words at random, and saying what was convenient, without stopping to consider whether it was true.' He called the bishop 'chameleon-like', with a lively imagination and treacherous memory.[168]

---

[159] *Church Times*, 6 May 1881, p. 296.
[160] Reginald G. Wilberforce to Liddon, 21 and 23 December 1880, KCL Liddon Papers; Liddon to Wilberforce, 22 December 1880, Bodleian MS Wilberforce c.27, fo. 35.
[161] Gordon to Golightly, 6 October 1881, LPL MS 1806, fo. 134.
[162] Ashwell and Wilberforce, *Life of Samuel Wilberforce*, ii. pp. 363, 366, 415.
[163] Burgon, *Lives of Twelve Good Men*, i. p. xxiv.
[164] Golightly, *Letter to the Dean of Ripon*, pp. 1, 68-71, 81.
[165] Ibid., pp. 3-8.
[166] Ibid., pp. 15-6.
[167] Ibid., p. 64.
[168] Ibid., pp. 15, 55, 64-6, 68.

However, Golightly reserved some of his sternest rebukes for the bishop's son, in a foretaste of the type of criticism Reginald Wilberforce would receive over Volume III of the *Life*. For example, Wilberforce had published to the world a passage from his father's private diary about Golightly's 'sinful revenge', which left Golightly embarrassed and smarting at the biographer's 'thoughtless cruelty'.[169] Likewise two letters from the bishop to Golightly from 1857 were quoted in the *Life*, signed 'very truly yours' and 'ever sincerely yours'. Yet the originals (which still survive amongst Golightly's correspondence at Lambeth Palace Library) read 'ever yours affectionately' and 'affectionately yours'.[170] Golightly suggested they had been '*not unintentionally altered*', in an attempt to show that he was not on intimate terms with the bishop.[171] His family and friends agreed that such adaptation was 'disgraceful'[172] and amounted to 'editorial forgery',[173] but Reginald Wilberforce categorically asserted: 'A more unfounded and reckless charge was never made, and I distinctly affirm that I never altered a single word.'[174]

Golightly also challenged several other statements of fact in the *Life*. For instance, Reginald Wilberforce wrongly claimed that the archdeacons' inquiry into Cuddesdon College in 1858 had 'refuted' the charges of the *Quarterly Review*, and that Liddon's resignation as vice-principal had no connection with the affair. The biographer also gave the impression that during the *Facts and Documents* crisis, the Oxford diocese had been wholeheartedly behind their bishop. Yet he failed to mention significant clergy protests against ritualism and wrongly portrayed one major anti-ritualist address from 4,000 laymen as sympathetic to the bishop.[175] The *Record* opined: 'It is charitable to suppose that Mr WILBERFORCE did not know what he was writing about.'[176] Wilberforce also maintained that Golightly had 'taunted' his father over the secession of his relatives to Rome, to which Golightly complained: 'I indignantly deny that I was ever guilty of such malicious wickedness, and challenge him to the proof.'[177]

The *Life of Samuel Wilberforce* was an immediate best-seller, but

---

[169] Ashwell and Wilberforce, *Life of Samuel Wilberforce*, ii. p. 415; Golightly, *Letter to the Dean of Ripon*, p. 19.

[170] Ashwell and Wilberforce, *Life of Samuel Wilberforce*, ii. pp. 360-1; Wilberforce to Golightly, 23 September and 4 October 1857, LPL MS 1811, fos 211, 218.

[171] Golightly, *Letter to the Dean of Ripon*, pp. 21-3.

[172] Frances W. Green to Golightly, 5 October 1881, LPL MS 1806, fo. 248.

[173] Gordon to Golightly, 6 October 1881, LPL MS 1806, fo. 134.

[174] Reginald G. Wilberforce, 'Remarks on Some of My Reviewers', *Fortnightly Review* 34 (July 1883), p. 91.

[175] Ashwell and Wilberforce, *Life of Samuel Wilberforce*, ii. pp. 363, 366, 416-9, 424; Golightly, *Letter to the Dean of Ripon*, pp. 45, 51-2, 56-7, 61.

[176] *Record*, 26 October 1881.

[177] Ashwell and Wilberforce, *Life of Samuel Wilberforce*, ii. p. 415; Golightly, *Letter to the Dean of Ripon*, pp. 28-9.

Golightly's *Letter to the Dean of Ripon* sank almost without trace. If he was hoping to alter the judgment of history, he was fighting a losing battle. His friends, however, welcomed the pamphlet and praised its 'wonderful lucidity and force'.[178] Arthur Isham (who had been threatened with dismissal as rural dean in 1859 for challenging the bishop) spoke of its 'Christian fair spirit'.[179] William Acworth (who had his licence to officiate revoked by the bishop in 1866) wrote: 'Mr R.W. must be παχοδερμος [thick-skinned] if he does not feel the lash you have administered.'[180] Likewise the *Record*, one of the few newspapers to notice the pamphlet, thought it 'animated by a spirit of Christian and gentlemanlike courtesy', and 'full of salutary teaching and matter of reflection for those who are willing to be warned.'[181] Professor Heurtley, though, was more tentative: 'I am not sure that it was worth while to stir the water again now that the mud has so long settled at the bottom.'[182] The responsibility for opening old wounds was seen by others, however, to lie at the biographer's door. For instance, the *Edinburgh Review* commented: 'It is a pity that Mr Wilberforce has roused the slumbering wrath of Mr Golightly, and revived the bitterness of the past.'[183]

A similar perspective came from Golightly's old friend from Oriel days, Thomas Mozley. Although they had fallen out in the 1840s because of their arguments over Tractarianism, the two men had renewed their acquaintance in old age, in the mid-1870s.[184] As Mozley's sister recalled, 'time, that wondrous healer, brought about *more* than a reconciliation – a forgetfulness apparently on both sides of the old wrong.'[185] In his *Reminiscences Chiefly of Oriel College and the Oxford Movement* (1882), Mozley came to the defence of his friend:

> Golightly, with most other people, was evidently willing to merge old feuds and long reckonings in the more agreeable sentiment of a loving admiration for Samuel Wilberforce's genial nature and many useful qualities. But he was not allowed to do this. The biographer as it were diverted the funeral train from its proper course that the mourners might break Golightly's windows as they passed.[186]

Perhaps Reginald Wilberforce took note, because when Volume III of the *Life* appeared it made no reference to Golightly. It spoke blandly of 'the

---

[178] Charles Hill to Golightly, 10 October 1881, LPL MS 1807, fo. 87.
[179] Arthur Isham to Golightly, 28 September 1881, LPL MS 1807, fo. 257.
[180] William Acworth to Golightly, 29 September 1881, LPL MS 1804, fo. 1.
[181] *Record*, 26 October 1881.
[182] Heurtley to Golightly, 5 October 1881, LPL MS 1807, fo. 74.
[183] 'Life of Bishop Wilberforce', *Edinburgh Review* 157 (April 1883), p. 539.
[184] See letters of Mozley to Golightly, 1876-81, LPL MS 1808, fos 168-75.
[185] *Letters of the Rev. J.B. Mozley*, p. 124.
[186] Mozley, *Reminiscences Chiefly of Oriel College and the Oxford Movement*, ii. p. 114.

attacks' on Cuddesdon College and only mentioned the notorious Woodard Schools meeting of 1861 in passing. Although a whole chapter was given to the circumstances surrounding the bishop's 'pro-ritualist' diocesan charge of 1866 and the work of the Ritual Commission, no account was made of Golightly's controversial pamphlet, *The Position of the Right Rev. Samuel Wilberforce in Reference to Ritualism*.[187]

Golightly's *Letter to the Dean of Ripon* was to be the final pamphlet of his life – the last of fifteen pamphlets stretching back forty-five years. In fact it was his last public utterance and shortly afterwards he was taken to a private lunatic asylum in London – Brooke House Asylum in Upper Clapton, Hackney.[188] No letter survives amongst his correspondence from after October 1881. With little sympathy, Reginald Wilberforce announced to the world that Golightly's pamphlet was 'the last unfettered act of his life, and almost immediately after its publication his friends found it necessary to put him under restraint'.[189] E.M. Goulburn thought that the strain of composing the *Letter to the Dean of Ripon*, 'probably contributed to the mental derangement which preceded his end'.[190] When his old adversary, Cardinal Newman, heard the news, he declared: 'Poor Golightly!'[191]

It is difficult to discern the nature of Golightly's illness. Possibly, as Newman hinted, it ran in the family. His younger brother, Edward, had suffered with mental illness throughout his life, from as early as his teenage years, and experienced periods of confinement. When he came of age in 1830, the family considered taking out a Commission of Lunacy in case during 'a fresh attack of his complaint' he might throw away his property.[192] Three friends of the Golightly family, John Tucker, Walter Trower and Charles Heurtley, were given legal responsibility for his affairs.[193] Edward managed to work for a while as a barrister, but he died, emaciated, in 1856 at the Retreat Asylum in Clapham, aged only 47.[194]

It would be tempting, perhaps, to see some connection between Golightly's 'mental derangement' and his lifelong Protestant agitation. Indeed many of his

---

[187] Ashwell and Wilberforce, *Life of Samuel Wilberforce*, iii. pp. 22, 74, ch. 7.

[188] On Brooke House Asylum, see *Survey of London* 28: *Parish of Hackney (part 1): Brooke House* (London, 1960); C.G. Ethelston, *A Private Lunatic Asylum Exposed* (np, 1885).

[189] Wilberforce, 'Remarks on Some of My Reviewers', p. 91.

[190] Goulburn, *Reminiscences of Golightly*, p. 10.

[191] Newman to Church, 6 March 1882, *Newman Letters and Diaries*, xxx. p. 65.

[192] Golightly to Mozley, 12 January 1830, BOA Thomas Mozley Papers. For further discussion of Edward Golightly's health and peculiar habits, see Golightly to Mozley, 25 July 1827 and 6 May 1830. Charles summed him up as 'a source of great perplexity to the whole family'.

[193] Codicil (1837) to the will of Margaret Golightly, proved 24 November 1842, Prob 11/1970, fos 367-70.

[194] Death certificate of Edward Richard Golightly, 1856.

opponents down the years, and a few of his friends, alluded to the fact that he must be mentally unhinged. For example, during the early 1840s, Newman wrote: 'Poor Golightly's friends (entre nous) are seriously alarmed for his mind ...'[195] Likewise Goulburn concluded that during the *Tract 90* crisis, Golightly's mind had been 'momentarily thrown off its pivot'.[196] Others spoke of his 'monomania'[197] or described him as a 'restless spirit'[198] working with 'restless energy',[199] with 'a brain so notedly restless'.[200] Such criticisms of Golightly's mental state can largely be dismissed as anti-Protestant polemic, though they do reveal him to be a character of unusual intensity.

According to Heurtley, Golightly was 'haunted by distressing illusions' for the last three years of his life.[201] The medical records from Brooke House Asylum do not survive and the nature of these 'illusions' is not known. It would be foolish to speculate on whether or not they had a theological dimension. Possibly they were connected with the insomnia from which Golightly began to suffer in his early 70s. Various cures had been suggested, such as drinking 'liquid coffia',[202] eating lettuce,[203] and altering the orientation of his bed ('It depends on the currents of Electricity').[204] Towards the end of Golightly's time in Oxford, Heurtley sympathised with his 'distressing malady & of your apprehensions (I earnestly hope unfounded) in connexion with it'. He recommended Golightly consult the Queen's physician, Sir George Burrows, author of *On Disorders of the Cerebral Circulation and the Connection Between Affections of the Brain and Diseases of the Heart*.[205]

There was clearly no anticipation amongst Golightly's family and friends that he would recover. The contents of his home in Holywell Street were auctioned off in February 1884 – including his mahogany furniture, dozens of framed pictures and engravings, 250 bottles from his cellar (mainly port and sherry), and more than 1,600 volumes from his library (mainly works of theology, history, poetry and classics).[206] Quickly forgotten by the public, he spent the last four years of his life locked up at Brooke House. After a bout of

---

[195] Newman to Jemima Mozley, 5 December 1841, *Newman Letters and Diaries*, viii. p. 364.
[196] Goulburn, *Reminiscences of Golightly*, p. 32.
[197] *Morning Post*, 22 December 1841 and 10 March 1859.
[198] *Morning Post*, 15 June 1859.
[199] *Union*, 8 July 1859, p. 424.
[200] Keon, 'Catholic Man of Letters', p. 240.
[201] *Guardian*, 6 January 1886, p. 26.
[202] Burgon to Golightly, 19 July 1879, LPL MS 1804, fo. 191.
[203] Goring to Golightly, nd, LPL MS 1806, fo. 169.
[204] Burgon to Golightly, 23 September 1880, LPL MS 1804, fos 197-8.
[205] Heurtley to Golightly, nd, LPL MS 1807, fos 78-9.
[206] Auction Sales Catalogue for 6 and 7 Holywell Street, Oxford (25-26 February 1884), Bodleian 2591.f.2 (1).

pneumonia, he died on Christmas Day 1885, aged 78.[207] Few noticed Golightly's passing, but his body was brought back home to the city where he had made his name and was buried in a quiet ceremony at Holywell Cemetery.

---

[207] Death certificate of Charles Portalès Golightly, 1885.

Epilogue

Partisan or Protestant?

Throughout this study of Charles Golightly's controversial career, amidst all the torrent of petitions and pamphlets, the temporary alliances and the theological arguments, one important question has remained perpetually unanswered: How should Golightly be categorised? Was he an 'evangelical', or would he prefer to be called an 'Anglican'? Was he a 'high churchman' or a 'low churchman'? To which church party, if any, did he belong? What is the best way to sum up his theological outlook?

Since Golightly's own day, the Church of England has often been interpreted using a framework of 'church parties'. As has been seen in previous chapters, many of the heated ecclesiastical disputes in which he was involved in Oxford were portrayed at the time, and since, as high church versus low church, or Tractarian versus evangelical – competing and antithetical ideologies, battling tooth and nail to win supremacy. As William Wordsworth once put it,

> HIGH and LOW
> Watch-words of Party, on all tongues are rife;
> As if a Church, though sprung from heaven, must owe
> To opposites and fierce extremes her life ...[1]

Others interpreted these disputes with a tripartite model of church divisions, such as anglo-catholic, evangelical and liberal, or William J. Conybeare's influential designation, outlined in his famous *Edinburgh Review* article of 1853, of high church, low church and broad church.[2] By the end of Golightly's life it had become generally accepted that most people belonged to one of these three parties. For example, a commentator wrote in 1878:

> the result of forty years of controversy and litigation has been that each of the three great theological parties has made good its position in the Church of England, and has established an indefeasible title to the peaceful and unmolested enjoyment of its share of the ecclesiastical territory. The existence side by side of three parties in the Church of England is now, therefore, an acknowledged fact, almost a part of her constitution. They, of course, shade off into each other, and there is a certain amount of neutral territory in which peace-loving souls still

---

[1] *The Sonnets of William Wordsworth* (London, 1838), p. 415.
[2] Conybeare, 'Church Parties', pp. 213-385.

contrive to escape from the fray, though there is a kind of Commons Enclosure Commission at work, by which the neutral ground is being rapidly narrowed.[3]

Golightly was quick to take sides and can hardly be described as 'neutral' on any church question of importance, so does he fit into one of these three categories? Or is a different title necessary?

Of course, only a moment's reflection is needed to realize that dividing the Church of England into three parties is too simplistic to take into account theological diversity and human idiosyncrasy. Therefore many have tried to develop a more complicated model. Conybeare himself noticed the problem, and so subdivided his three main church parties into 'normal', 'exaggerated' and 'stagnant' types. Others posit alternative solutions. For example in 1858, when Golightly's first agitation against Cuddesdon College was at its height, the *English Churchman* divided the Church of England into twelve categories – 'Romanists', 'Romanizers', 'Semi-Romanizers', 'Consistent Anglicans', 'Wavering Anglicans', 'Old Fashioned High Churchmen', 'Neutrals', 'Broad Churchmen', 'Tolerant Evangelicals', 'Intolerant Evangelicals', 'Semi-Dissenters' and 'Rationalists or Latitudinarians'.[4] Likewise, by the early twentieth century Ronald Knox could declare: 'I suppose nobody is now so old-fashioned as to think of the Church of England as divisible into three parties – High, Low, and Broad. It was never true, and what meaning it ever had has long since disappeared.' Instead he identified nine parties, called 'Active Protestants', 'Evangelicals', 'Neo-Evangelicals', 'Evangelical Liberals', 'High Church Liberals', 'High Churchmen', 'Anglo-Catholics', 'Ultramarines' and 'The Rest'.[5]

No matter how sophisticated the model of 'church party', one stubborn fact remains – it is notoriously difficult to develop sensible criteria by which to place real men and women into these categories. Obvious exceptions become immediately apparent – such as Golightly standing shoulder to shoulder with the Tractarians, against his natural allies, to maintain Oxford University's censure of Professor Hampden in 1842. As Arthur Burns rightly observes, the history of nineteenth century Anglicanism is littered with numerous errors in the attribution of party allegiance and 'individuals who, chameleon-like, appear in different colours according to the occasion.'[6] Similarly Peter Marsh writes:

> In both Church and State, mid-Victorian individualism played havoc with party lines. ... Again and again a clergyman whose party leanings were otherwise clear would agree with his enemies against his friends on a particular issue as proof of

---

[3] Robert E. Bartlett, 'On the Position of the Evangelical Party in the Church of England', *Fraser's Magazine* 17 (January 1878), pp. 25-6.
[4] *English Churchman*, 26 August 1858, pp. 801-2.
[5] Ronald A. Knox, 'Tendencies of Anglicanism', *Dublin Review* 162 (January 1918), pp. 25-6.
[6] Conybeare, 'Church Parties', p. 229.

his impartiality ... Party tags could never denote anything more precise than schools of thought or than generalizations riddled with exceptions.[7]

Indeed Frances Knight warns that real people tend to transcend stereotypes: 'it may be a flawed notion to suppose that churchmanship can be labelled and pinned down by an historian. The reality of human experience is more complicated'.[8]

Yet if there is one churchman who it should be possible to label and pin down, it is Charles Golightly. Unlike many of his contemporaries, he was as different to a 'chameleon' as can be imagined. His theological views altered little throughout his adult life, and he gained the reputation in his latter years of being stuck in a time-warp, a rare example of constancy when all around him was changing. For example, in the late 1870s E.M. Goulburn writing to Archbishop Tait remarked that although a 'revolution' had 'passed over the old University, its institutions, its education, its theology, its ἦθος', still Golightly remained the same as always, except now with white hair.[9] Elsewhere Goulburn reflected that there was 'but little growth or expansiveness in his mind'.[10] Tait agreed, speaking of Golightly's 'immovability & unchangeableness in the midst of this whirl of change.'[11] Likewise, writing in the early 1880s, Thomas Mozley called Golightly 'the most unchangeable member of Oriel, not to say Oxford society', an 'iron bridge' spanning almost sixty years of Oxford affairs.[12] He continued:

> while all is change around him, and nowhere is change so rapid and so revolutionary as at Oxford, Golightly has remained as fixed as the rock against which Virgil describes the winds and waves beating in vain. Generations of undergraduates, of tutors, and even of heads of houses, have passed by him, and he remains. Oaths, subscriptions, clerical fellows, lay fellows, Tutors, halls, have passed away, but Golightly still lives to tell of Oxford, and of Rome too, as they were in the first quarter of this century. Ordinary natures might succumb under the sense of an ineffectual struggle against the law of change, not to say deterioration. Fortunately a fact so painful and depressing seems almost out of Golightly's ken ...[13]

Other contemporaries made the same observation. For example, recalling Golightly's old-age, E.A. Knox asserted: 'I do not imagine that either in mental

---

[7] Peter T. Marsh, *The Victorian Church in Decline: Archbishop Tait and the Church of England 1868-1882* (London, 1969), p. 11.
[8] Frances Knight, *The Nineteenth-Century Church and English Society* (Cambridge, 1995), p. 210.
[9] Goulburn to Tait, nd [1878], LPL Tait Papers, vol. 98, fo. 229.
[10] Goulburn, *Reminiscences of Golightly*, p. 10.
[11] Mozley to Golightly, 12 November 1879, LPL MS 1808, fo. 170.
[12] Mozley, *Reminiscences Chiefly of Oriel College and the Oxford Movement*, ii. p. 108.
[13] Ibid., pp. 112-3.

outlook or even in costume Golightly had departed from the days in which he took his degree'.[14] More recently Owen Chadwick has concluded that Golightly's 'mind ran on tram-lines'.[15] Golightly himself would have agreed with these assessments and probably would welcome them as a compliment. As has been seen, he once told John Henry Newman: 'I abandon any views which I have once deliberately taken up with extreme reluctance and look with suspicion at every new view ... which interferes with them.'[16]

Yet despite his fixed opinions, historians have found it difficult to decide upon a suitable label for Golightly's churchmanship. Many from the 1880s to the present have called him an 'evangelical'.[17] For example, at the turn of the twentieth century Hurrell Froude's biographer, Louise Guiney, termed Golightly the 'King of the "Peculiars"',[18] while in the 1920s Yngve Brilioth called him 'a pugnacious and wire-pulling Evangelical'.[19] More recently, Vivian Green says that he 'veered more and more towards the Evangelical position', although given Golightly's dissociation from his early evangelical friends, it would be possible to argue the exact opposite.[20] Other writers prefer to give Golightly the label 'high church'. For example, in 1908 G.R. Balleine, author of *A History of the Evangelical Party in the Church of England*, called him 'a High Churchman of the older school'.[21] Likewise in the 1930s L.E. Elliott-Binns labelled him an 'old-fashioned High Churchman'.[22] The original *Dictionary of National Biography* maintained that he 'gloried in the traditions of the old high church party',[23] while Martin Murphy in the new *Oxford*

---

[14] Knox, *Reminiscences of an Octogenarian*, p. 114.

[15] Chadwick, *Founding of Cuddesdon*, p. 69.

[16] Golightly to Newman, 6 June 1836, BOA Miscellaneous Letters.

[17] For example, Robert Ornsby, *Memoirs of James Robert Hope-Scott of Abbotsford* (2 vols, London, 1884), i. p. 267; C.A. Heurtley, *Wholesome Words. Sermons on Some Important Points of Christian Doctrine* edited with a memoir by William Ince (London, 1896), p. lvii; Abbott and Campbell, *Life of Jowett*, i. p. 238; W.J. Baker, *The Attitudes of English Churchmen, 1800-1850, toward the Reformation* (PhD thesis, Cambridge University, 1966), p. 116; F.J. Thomson, *William Palmer and the Orthodox Church* (PhD thesis, Cambridge University, 1964), p. 235; Herring, *What Was the Oxford Movement?*, p. 59; James C. Whisenant, *A Fragile Unity: Anti-Ritualism and the Division of Anglican Evangelicalism in the Nineteenth Century* (Milton Keynes, 2003), pp. 35, 75.

[18] Louise I. Guiney, *Hurrell Froude: Memoranda and Comments* (London, 1904), p. 188.

[19] Yngve Brilioth, *The Anglican Revival: Studies in the Oxford Movement* (London, 1925), p. 156.

[20] Green, *Religion at Oxford and Cambridge*, p. 220.

[21] G.R. Balleine, *A History of the Evangelical Party in the Church of England* (London, 1908), p. 218.

[22] L.E. Elliott-Binns, *Religion in the Victorian Era* (London, 1936), p. 111.

[23] W.P. Courtney, 'Charles Pourtales Golightly', *Dictionary of National Biography* (63 vols, London, 1885-1901)

Dictionary of National Biography says he was 'devoted to the vigorous and vigilant defence of traditional high-church principles'.[24] Other scholars like W.R. Ward, Peter Nockles, Peter Toon and Standish Meacham have chosen similar descriptions for Golightly such as 'High Church',[25] 'High and Dry Anglican',[26] or 'Protestant High Church'.[27]

Golightly is difficult to pin down partly because although his views did not change, the meaning of churchmanship labels and the relationship between church parties is constantly changing. As a number of recent historians have shown, before the rise of the Tractarian Movement in the 1830s there was considerable overlap between different parties within the Church of England, both theologically and socially. For example, William Gibson argues that the Church of England in the eighteenth century was 'marked by a strong sense of political, religious, cultural and national unity'. High church and low church were not exclusive categories but 'blurred and broad streams within Anglicanism that often merged, overlapped and coincided.' He warns that the heat and light generated by controversial figures likes Francis Atterbury, Benjamin Hoadly and Henry Sacheverell 'has blinded us to the comparative agreement of High and Low Churchmen on matters of Church doctrine, liturgy, ceremony and pastoralia.'[28] Likewise John Walsh and Stephen Taylor observe that 'On the eve of the Oxford Movement the centripetal forces within the Church were still vastly more powerful than the centrifugal.' They point to the 'massive Anglican consensus and solidarity in the eighteenth-century Church. Even those who appear to stand for highly distinctive styles of churchmanship often show cross-bench attachments which make it difficult to label them as partisans.'[29] Peter Nockles has come to a similar conclusion. His ground-breaking study of high churchmanship before the rise of the Tractarians concludes that its 'theological party character ... remained indistinct'.[30] Instead attitudes to church questions were determined by 'personality and social connexions as much as "party" allegiance to a set of distinct doctrinal principles', with a cohesion due more to 'the ties of location, family and

---

[24] Martin Murphy, 'Charles Pourtalès Golightly', *Oxford Dictionary of National Biography* (60 vols, Oxford, 2004).

[25] Ward, *Victorian Oxford*, p. 112; Toon, 'Parker Society', p. 325.

[26] Standish Meacham, *Lord Bishop: The Life of Samuel Wilberforce, 1805-1873* (Cambridge, MA, 1970), p. 198.

[27] Ward, *Victorian Oxford*, p. 143; Nockles, 'Lost Causes and ... Impossible Loyalties', p. 236.

[28] William Gibson, *The Church of England 1688-1832: Unity and Accord* (London, 2001), pp. 2, 242-3.

[29] John D. Walsh and Stephen Taylor, 'The Church and Anglicanism in the "Long" Eighteenth Century' in John D. Walsh, Colin Haydon and Stephen Taylor (eds.), *The Church of England c.1689-c.1833: From Toleration to Tractarianism* (Cambridge, 1993), pp. 51-2.

[30] Nockles, *Oxford Movement in Context*, p. 272.

friendship' than has previously been assumed.[31]

This broad consensus is seen clearly in Golightly's early Oxford years, particularly in his personal friendships with 'radical evangelicals' like Charles Brenton and John Hill. Reflecting on this complicated network of relationships, Timothy Stunt concludes that Golightly and Walter Trower are 'good instances of the dissatisfied evangelical, uncertain which way to turn and associating with a fairly wide variety of churchmanship.'[32] Yet Stunt warns:

> Just as sixteenth-century church historians have to resist the temptation of reading back into the early days of the Reformation the hardened attitudes of Tridentine Rome and full-fledged Protestantism, so we have to strive to recreate the uncertainties and ambivalence of pre-Tractarian Oxford. Party labels and loyalties were far from precise, and 'high-church' and 'evangelical' could mean a variety of things to different people. ... there was, for a while, a remarkable amount of common ground shared by evangelicals and their high-church contemporaries. Inevitably attitudes polarised in the thirties, but in the preceding decade the wings of Anglicanism were by no means mutually exclusive.[33]

A similar point is made by John Wolffe when he observes that 'In the early nineteenth century, there were considerable signs of crosscurrents between ecclesiastical groups that must not be obscured by the teleological tendencies inherent in an awareness of later party spirit.'[34]

The Church of England's theological consensus on the eve of the Oxford Movement might loosely be described as 'Protestantism', and Paul Avis explains it as follows:

> What united them was an unquestioned, tacit consensus with regard to the protestant character of the Anglican church – a character that was evidenced above all in the doctrines of justification by faith and the paramount authority of scripture, in a fraternal regard for the continental churches of the Reformation, in esteem of the Reformers both English and foreign, and in loyalty to the standards of the Church of England – the Thirty-nine Articles and the Book of Common Prayer, as well as unofficial secondary standards among which Richard Hooker's *Ecclesiastical Polity* stands pre-eminent. The Tractarians set out to challenge the consensus on each of these points.[35]

---

[31] Peter B. Nockles, 'Church Parties in the Pre-Tractarian Church of England 1750-1833: the "Orthodox" – some Problems of Definition and Identity' in Walsh, Haydon and Taylor, *The Church of England c.1689-c.1833*, pp. 355-6.
[32] Stunt, *From Awakening to Secession*, pp. 204-5.
[33] Ibid., pp. 183-4.
[34] John R. Wolffe, 'Anglicanism' in D.G. Paz (ed.), *Nineteenth-Century English Religious Traditions: Retrospect and Prospect* (Westport, Connecticut, 1995), pp. 15-6.
[35] Paul D.L. Avis, *Anglicanism and the Christian Church: Theological Resources in Historical Perspective* (Edinburgh, 1989), p. 166. See also, Paul Avis, 'The Tractarian

This Protestant consensus was destroyed by the dramatic events at Oxford University in the 1830s and 40s, in which Golightly was actively involved. The Tractarian crisis had serious repercussions for the whole of the Church of England, leading to an increased polarization and fragmentation of church parties which continued to grow deeper throughout the rest of the century. Peter Nockles warns that the divisive impact of the Oxford Movement should not be exaggerated, but yet he states: 'the Tractarians came to challenge, then shatter, the doctrinal consensus of the earlier High Church Anglicanism, seeming to dissolve the Church of England into its constituent parts as never before'.[36] They provocatively forced churchmen to take sides and to adopt a more rigid dogmatic position.[37] Furthermore, the Tractarians radically and irrevocably altered the nomenclature of Anglican church parties, which makes the historian's attempt to categorise Golightly and his contemporaries all the more doomed to failure. For example, Nockles details the shifting sands of party terminology between 1760 and 1857, with the varied use of 'high church', 'low church', 'orthodox', 'Tractarian', 'Anglican' and 'Anglo-Catholic', and shows that each has had multiple definitions which often overlapped with one another.[38]

If recent scholars have not been able to agree on a churchmanship label for Golightly, his contemporaries came to no more of a consensus. In part this is because party ascriptions are often distorted by each writer's personal theological bias. As Arthur Burns notes, many accounts of Victorian church party were 'no dispassionate sociological exercise' but rather 'written with polemical intent from within the party traditions themselves'. Even Conybeare's influential *Edinburgh Review* article was 'a polemical intervention in a debate about the future of English christianity.'[39] This is seen, for example, in the names most often chosen for Golightly by his opponents – 'Evangelical', 'Puritan', 'Ultra-Protestant', 'Low Church' or 'Recordite'. They were intended not as an impartial assessment of his theological views, but as terms of abuse and an attempt to raise questions about his loyalty to the Church of England. Likewise Thomas Mozley, no friend to evangelicals, wrote that Golightly 'remained always, a decided, not to say extreme, Evangelical, showing more sympathy for Puritans than for High Churchmen.'[40] Yet this verdict, like much

---

Challenge to Consensus and the Identity of Anglicanism', *King's Theological Review* 9 (Spring 1986), pp. 14-7.

[36] Nockles, 'Oxford, Tract 90 and the Bishops', p. 31.

[37] Nockles, *Oxford Movement in Context*, pp. 307-27; Nockles, 'Church Parties', pp. 355-8.

[38] Nockles, *Oxford Movement in Context*, pp. 25-43. See also Raymond Chapman, *Faith and Revolt: Studies in the Literary Influence of the Oxford Movement* (London, 1970), pp. 280-9.

[39] Conybeare, 'Church Parties', pp. 217-8, 251.

[40] Thomas Mozley, *Reminiscences Chiefly of Towns, Villages and Schools* (2 vols, London, 1885), i. p. 12.

in Mozley's *Reminiscences*, is highly questionable and says more about Mozley than it does about Golightly. E.M. Goulburn in his own *Reminiscences* retorted that Mozley did not put Golightly's 'ecclesiastical temperature as "High" as it really was.'[41] Due to Golightly's persistent opposition to the Tractarians, Goulburn continued, 'his Churchmanship was considerably under-rated. ... He was, indeed, a most staunch Protestant at all times, but certainly ... he was anything but a Low Churchman.'[42]

With no agreement on an appropriate theological label, Golightly's associates tried to identify his theological heroes, again without success. Mozley pointed back to the eighteenth-century evangelicals and their predecessors: 'His religion was that of Scott, and Newton, and Cecil, and Baxter, and Owen, and certain select Puritans, not without a little High Church seasoning, when not quite too high.'[43] Yet Goulburn insisted Golightly's theological outlook was more in line with the thought of Richard Hooker – indeed that his mind was 'profoundly imbued' with Hooker's teaching.[44] Both Burgon and Heurtley concurred that he was 'of the school of Hooker'.[45] In contrast, Newman recalled that Golightly's 'favourite divine' was the Caroline theologian, Henry Hammond.[46] However, part of Hammond's attraction may have been merely sentimental rather than theological – like Golightly he had also ministered in the parish of Penshurst in Kent, as incumbent in the 1630s.

Unable to fit Golightly exclusively into either 'high church' or 'evangelical' categories, Goulburn was not prepared to leave him unlabelled. Instead he chose the hybrid title 'evangelical high church', writing in 1886:

> A distinction has been drawn between a High Church Evangelical and an Evangelical High Churchman to this effect – that in the first, the Evangelicalism is the basis of the man's religious mind, and the High Churchism is super-induced, and the growth of a later age; in the second, the views are fundamentally High Church, and the Evangelicalism is the colour subsequently given to them. To this latter class rather than the former I should say that Golightly belonged, though I doubt not that the controversy with the Tractarian school in which his better years

---

[41] Goulburn, *Reminiscences of Golightly*, p. 13.
[42] Ibid., p. 22.
[43] Mozley, *Reminiscences Chiefly of Oriel College and the Oxford Movement*, ii. p. 110. Yet Golightly once distanced himself from Charles Brenton by likening Brenton's opinions to 'as nearly as possible those of Scott': Golightly to Newman, 10 August 1831, BOA Miscellaneous Letters.
[44] Goulburn, *Reminiscences of Golightly*, p. 14.
[45] Burgon, *Lives of Twelve Good Men*, i. p. xxv; Heurtley in *Guardian*, 6 January 1886, p. 26.
[46] Newman's memorandum (1860) in *Letters and Correspondence of John Henry Newman*, ii. p. 105.

were spent, drove him into a more pronounced Low Church attitude than was strictly congenial with his nature. He was bred in High Church traditions.[47]

The term 'evangelical high church' had been coined in 1840 by Henry Christmas, editor of the *Church of England Quarterly Review* and the *Churchman*.[48] 'Evangelical high churchmen' were said to have a concern for both 'evangelical truth and apostolic discipline', and should expect 'to be disowned by all *parties*, and be acknowledged only by those free from party spirit.'[49] Theologians as different at Bishop Blomfield of London, Archbishop J.B. Sumner of Canterbury, G.S. Faber and Archbishop Laurence of Cashel were claimed as examples of the type.[50] Faber was one of Golightly's regular correspondents and an influential ally in the anti-Tractarian cause. His *Provincial Letters* (1842), an exposé of Tractarian principles, were first published in the *Churchman*, and he explained privately to Golightly that 'evangelical high churchmanship' was 'a just medium' between Tractarianism and Ultra-Protestantism.[51] Christmas made clear that the views of his journals would be

> those of the Church of England – not as expounded by 'The Tracts for the Times' – still less as understood by the Calvinistic divines who still remain in the communion of our Church; but as taught in her own Liturgy – as elucidated by Hooker, and Bramhall, and Hammond, and Hall, and Sanderson, and Blackall, and Comber, and Waterland, and Wheatley, and Mant, and many more whose names are enshrined in the hearts of good men: in a word, our views are those of EVANGELICAL HIGH CHURCHMEN. We acknowledge the supremacy of Scripture – the great doctrines of the Atonement and of Justification by Faith only; while we hold the personal Episcopal Apostolical Succession – the TRUTH OF OUR BAPTISMAL, VISITATION, AND BURIAL SERVICES – and the right of the Church to decree rites and ceremonies, and to decide in controversies of Faith.[52]

Golightly fits well into this definition offered by Christmas. His dependence on the Caroline divines was evident in his two most weighty theological works, *A Letter to the Bishop of Oxford* and *Strictures on No.90* from 1840-41. He was said to have a 'profound deference' to the formularies of the Church of England,[53] as witnessed by his passionate defence of the Thirty-Nine Articles against Newman's *Tract 90* and his appeals for Edward Pusey and Benjamin

---

[47] Goulburn, *Reminiscences of Golightly*, p. 13.
[48] Toon, *Evangelical Theology*, pp. 41-3; Nockles, *Oxford Movement in Context*, pp. 284-5.
[49] 'The Office of a Bishop', *Church of England Quarterly Review* 8 (July 1840), p. 24.
[50] Ibid., p. 23.
[51] Faber to Golightly, 4 March 1841, LPL MS 1805, fos 229-30.
[52] *Churchman* 5 (July – December 1841), p. iv.
[53] Goulburn, *Reminiscences of Golightly*, p. 19.

Jowett to be brought into line by renewed subscription. His final split with Newman and Pusey occurred over the crucial issue of justification by faith alone and he campaigned for the orthodox understanding of the atonement against the novel views in Jowett's New Testament Commentary. His antipathy to the *Tracts for the Times* was legendary, and although 'well versed in the works of Calvin',[54] his disapproval of Calvinism was one cause of the breach with his early 'radical evangelical' friends. Nevertheless, as Peter Toon observes, 'evangelical high churchmen' are as hard to pin down as any other churchmanship category – they were little different from traditional 'high churchmen' who opposed the Tracts, and yet were also hard to distinguish from 'evangelicals' with 'a high doctrine of the visible, episcopally governed, national Church'.[55]

What is clear is that Golightly rejected both the labels 'evangelical' and 'high church'. Partly this was for polemical reasons. He did not want to be identified with any particular 'party' within the Church of England, because 'partisan' in the nineteenth century, as much as today, was a term of abuse and chastisement – it signified small-mindedness, bias, aggression and an over-dependence on human leaders. A popular form of rhetoric in theological disputes between the 1830s and the 1880s was to deny that one's allies were motivated by 'party spirit' but to label one's opponents as 'partisans'. Golightly frequently used this polemical devise in his campaigns – while insisting that he himself belonged to no party, he was quick to denounce Tractarians and ritualists as 'extreme party men'. He exposed their distinctive 'party badges', whether Newman's habit of mixing water and wine at holy communion, or the eccentric clothing and posture of students at Cuddesdon, or the practice of auricular confession at the Woodard Schools. Furthermore Golightly knew that his campaigns would have greater success if he could unite diverse theological opinion against a specific and isolated opponent, and therefore it was of benefit not to be too closely identified with one particular grouping.

Yet there are also signs that Golightly rejected the terms 'high church' and 'evangelical' because he was genuinely ill at ease with them. Although he could write in 1831 of his 'high church' prejudices,[56] that title was soon taken hostage by the Tractarians and ritualists, and ceased to be appropriate. Likewise, it was perhaps his early Oxford experiences which permanently coloured his view of the name 'evangelical'. He had watched in horror as evangelical convictions drove men like Henry Bulteel and Charles Brenton out

---

[54] Ibid., p. 22.
[55] Toon, *Evangelical Theology*, p. 5. The *Record*, 24 August 1840, thought high churchmen and evangelicals had little in common: 'We may as well say that there are Evangelical Papists, as that there are Evangelical-High-Churchmen. Possibly there may be some rare exceptions; but they must be very rare indeed – they must be almost a new race in the world.'
[56] Golightly to Mozley, 21 December 1831, BOA Thomas Mozley Papers.

Epilogue 319

of the Established Church. Reflecting on these secessions, Grayson Carter observes:

> Seen in the intense atmosphere of Oxford in the late 1820s and early 1830s, Evangelicalism could be understood as given over to eccentricity, waywardness and irregularity; it could be plausibly seen as high or hyper in its Calvinism, antinomian in its tendencies, and extremely ambivalent about, if not actively disloyal to, the formularies of the Church of England.[57]

Golightly had no intention of being identified with such a movement. Throughout life he shared many friendships and alliances with Anglican evangelicals, but refused to be counted as one of them. For example, in 1840 he advised Bishop Shuttleworth to conciliate the evangelicals in Chichester diocese, but added:

> I am not, I repeat it, one of them – they wd not own me, and I have not always received kind usage from them. It gives me much pain to differ from them on points of some importance. But I know their worth, believe them to be on the whole the salt of the diocese, and that it is deeply indebted to their labours.[58]

Likewise, writing forty years later in his final pamphlet, Golightly declared that he had always thought 'evangelical' was 'a very unfortunate designation of a religious body. It has a touch of Pharisaism in it. It is surely as indecorous for one party in the Church of England to appropriate to itself the name of Evangelical, as for another to lay exclusive claim to the title of Catholic.'[59] Bishop Knox, who knew Golightly well in the 1870s and 80s, stated emphatically:

> Golightly was not an Evangelical. Again and again he has said ... with the contemptuous snort peculiar to many Dons of his generation: 'The name Evangelical stinks in my nostrils.' To the end of his life he refused to identify himself with the leading Evangelicals of Oxford, seldom preached in their churches, attended their services or meetings, or associated himself with any of their activities.[60]

Knox perhaps overstates the case. For example, Golightly was a life member of the Church Association, an organization dominated by evangelicals. He was also a co-founder with John Hill of the Oxford Union for Private Prayer, which again had a large proportion of evangelical members. Although Golightly refused to join national 'evangelical' organizations such as the Church Missionary Society and the British and Foreign Bible Society, he served

---

[57] Carter, *Anglican Evangelicals*, p. 311.
[58] Golightly to Shuttleworth, 29 December 1840, LPL MS 1809, fo. 50.
[59] Golightly, *Letter to the Dean of Ripon*, p. 62. See also *Record*, 25 October 1878.
[60] Knox, *Tractarian Movement*, p. 252.

alongside Knox and other local evangelical leaders on the committee of the Oxford and Oxfordshire auxiliary society for Promoting Christianity Amongst the Jews.[61] Golightly remained in high honour amongst evangelical friends. Therefore A.C. Downer (an evangelical undergraduate at Brasenose College in the 1860s), while noting Knox's verdict, gives Golightly a chapter to himself in his book, *A Century of Evangelical Religion in Oxford*.[62]

If a theological label must be given to Golightly, it is perhaps best to adopt his own choice – not 'evangelical' or 'high church' or even 'evangelical high church', but simply 'Protestant'.[63] It is the title above any other that Golightly's friends and allies usually gave him, and one in which he delighted. Francis Close, for instance, termed him 'a truly Protestant Brother',[64] and Lord Harcourt said he was 'a friend of the Protestant Church'.[65] Walter Walsh called him a leader of the 'Oxford Protestant Crusade'[66] and Goulburn praised him as 'a most staunch Protestant at all times'.[67] As Golightly himself explained in *Facts and Documents* in the 1850s, he was 'neither a High Churchman, nor a Low Churchman', but 'simply a Protestant, and a true son of the Church of England.'[68] This one word is an appropriate summary of Golightly's colourful life and controversial career – passionate and ceaseless protest against the dangerous encroachments of both the Church of Rome and of Infidelity upon his beloved Church of England. A man of extreme methods and often reviled, but a staunch Protestant right to the end.

---

[61] Golightly was on the committee of this Oxford auxiliary from the 1850s until he was taken to London in 1881; see the auxiliary's annual reports. It was not uncommon for non-evangelicals to support these 'evangelical' societies: Martin, *Evangelicals United*, pp. 89-90; Mark A. Smith, *Religion in Industrial Society: Oldham and Saddleworth, 1740-1865* (Oxford, 1994), pp. 86, 276-8.
[62] A.C. Downer, *A Century of Evangelical Religion in Oxford* (London, 1938), ch. 12
[63] See Georgina Battiscombe, *John Keble: A Study in Limitations* (New York, 1964), p. 208; Green, *Religion at Oxford and Cambridge*, p. 270.
[64] Close, *Mystery of Iniquity*, p. 18.
[65] Harcourt to Golightly, 9 December 1874, LPL MS 1807, fo. 19.
[66] Walter Walsh, *The History of the Romeward Movement in the Church of England 1833-1864* (London, 1900), p. 393.
[67] Goulburn, *Reminiscences of Golightly*, p. 22.
[68] Golightly, *Facts and Documents*, p. [3].

Sources

Select Manuscript Collections

Balliol College Library, Oxford
Jowett Papers
Jowett – Stanley Correspondence

Birmingham Oratory Archives
Jemima Mozley Papers
Thomas Mozley Papers
Newman Papers

Bodleian Library, Oxford
Burgon Papers
Hill Diary
Liddon – Christopher Correspondence
Martyrs' Memorial Papers
Oxford Prayer Union Papers
Rigaud Papers
Shuttleworth Papers
Wilberforce Papers
Wynter Papers

British Library, London
Gladstone Papers
Lord Holland Papers

Corpus Christi College Archives, Oxford
Brooke Diary

Cuddesdon College Archives
Liddon Diary (1855-57)
Liddon Papers

Guildhall Library, London
Bishop of London's Registers

Keble College Library, Oxford
Liddon Papers
Keble Papers

Lambeth Palace Library, London
Archbishop of Canterbury's Act Books
Church Association Papers
Furse Papers
Golightly Papers
Keble Papers
Tait Papers
Williams Papers

Lancing College Archives
Woodard Papers

Lincoln College Archives, Oxford
Pattison Papers

Lincolnshire Record Office
Kaye Papers

Norwich Dean and Chapter Library
Goulburn Papers

Oriel College Archives, Oxford
Hampden Papers
Hawkins – Gladstone Correspondence
Miscellaneous Letters (mostly Hawkins Papers)
Newman Papers

Oxford University Archives
Hebdomadal Board Minutes

Oxfordshire Record Office
Visitation Returns
Survey of Diocese (1846)
Wilberforce's Notes on Parishes (1854-64)
Parish Records for Elsfield, Headington, Marston, Marsh Baldon, Toot Baldon and St Mary Magdalen's Oxford

Pusey House Library, Oxford
Bagot Papers
Bricknell Papers
Churton Papers
Gresley Papers
Liddon House Papers
Liddon Papers and Diary (1858-90)

Paget – Eden Letters ('Introduction to the Bishop Bagot Correspondence')
Perceval Papers
Pusey Papers
Randall Papers
Scott Papers
Woodgate Papers
Wynter Papers

Southampton University Library
Wellington Papers

Surrey History Centre, Woking
Parish Records for Godalming and Kingston-on-Thames

Wadham College Archives, Oxford
Symons Papers
Martyrs' Memorial Papers

Papers in Private Hands

Cossington MSS
Graham – Golightly Papers

Stack MSS
Dodd Papers
Golightly Papers
Graham Papers

Pamphlets Identified as by Charles Golightly

Brief Observations upon Dr Hampden's Inaugural Lecture (Oxford, 1836) 7pp
Look at Home, or Short and Easy Method with the Roman Catholics (Oxford & London, 1837) 39pp
A Letter to the Right Reverend Father in God, Richard, Lord Bishop of Oxford, Containing Strictures upon Certain Parts of Dr Pusey's Letter to his Lordship. By a Clergyman of the Diocese, and a Resident Member of the University (Oxford, 1840) 115pp
Strictures on No.90 of the Tracts for the Times. By a Member of the University of Oxford, part 1 (Oxford, 1841) 76pp
Strictures on No.90 of the Tracts for the Times. By a Member of the University of Oxford, part 2 (Oxford, 1841) 95pp
New and Strange Doctrines Extracted from the Writings of Mr Newman and His Friends, in a Letter to the Rev. W.F. Hook, DD. By One of the Original Subscribers to the Tracts for the Times (Oxford & London, 1841) 27pp

Brief Remarks Upon No.90, Second Edition, and Some Subsequent Publications in Defence of It (Oxford & London, 1841) 19pp

Correspondence Illustrative of the Actual State of Oxford with Reference to Tractarianism, and the Attempts of Mr Newman and His Party to Unprotestantize the National Church (Oxford & London, 1842) 36pp

Facts and Documents shewing the Alarming State of the Diocese of Oxford. By a Senior Clergyman of the Diocese (Oxford & London, 1859) 38pp

A Letter to the Rev. Dr Jeune, Vice-Chancellor of the University of Oxford, in Vindication of the Handbill Distributed at the Doors of the Sheldonian Theatre on Nov. 22, 1861 (Oxford & London, 1861) 16pp

A Second Letter to the Rev. Dr Jeune, Vice-Chancellor of the University of Oxford, in Reference to the Handbill Distributed at the Doors of the Sheldonian Theatre on Nov. 22, 1861 (Oxford & London, 1861) 15pp

The Position of the Right Rev. Samuel Wilberforce, DD, Lord Bishop of Oxford, in Reference to Ritualism, together with a Prefatory Account of the Romeward Movement in the Church of England in the Days of Archbishop Laud. By a Senior Resident Member of the University of Oxford (Oxford & London, 1867) xv + 97 pp

A Brief Account of the Romeward Movement in the Church of England in the Days of Archbishop Laud. By Oxoniensis (Oxford, 1873) 17pp

A Solemn Warning against Cuddesdon College. Addressed to the Laity, and more Particularly to the Lay Members of the Oxford Diocesan Conference (Oxford & London, 1878) 8pp

A Brief Account of the Romeward Movement in the Church of England in the Days of Archbishop Laud (Oxford & London, 1878) 17pp

A Letter to the Very Reverend the Dean of Ripon, containing Strictures on the Life of Bishop Wilberforce, Vol.II with special reference to the Cuddesdon College Enquiry and the Pamphlet 'Facts and Documents' (Oxford & London, 1881) 99pp

Newspaper Letters Identified as by Charles Golightly

Morning Post, 14 January 1839; to the editor, signed C.P. Golightly

Oxford Herald, 12 December 1840; to the editor, signed 'A Resident MA of this University'

Oxford Herald, 6 February 1841; to the editor, signed 'A Resident MA'

Oxford Herald, 16 October 1841; to the editor, signed 'C.P.G.'

Standard, 13 November 1841; to the editor, signed 'A Master of Arts'

Standard, 29 November 1841; to the editor, signed C.P. Golightly

Morning Herald, 14 February 1842; to the editor, signed C.P. Golightly

Morning Herald, 7 January 1843; to the editor, signed 'An Oxford Master of Arts'

Morning Herald, 13 January 1843; to the editor, signed 'An Oxford Master of Arts'

Morning Herald, 16 January 1843; to the editor, signed 'An Oxford Master of Arts'

Oxford Herald, 11 February 1843; to the editor, signed 'A Master of Arts'

Oxford Herald, 25 February 1843; to John Henry Newman, signed 'A Member of Convocation'

Oxford Herald, 1 April 1843; to John Henry Newman, signed 'A Member of Convocation'

Standard, 26 October 1843; to the editor, signed 'A Master of Arts'

Standard, 31 October 1843; to the editor, signed 'A Master of Arts'

Standard, 7 November 1843; to the editor, signed 'A Master of Arts'

Standard, 18 September 1844; to the editor, signed 'A Resident Master of Arts'

Standard, 6 December 1844; to the editor, signed 'A Senior Member of the University of Oxford'

Standard, 10 December 1844; to the editor, signed 'Academicus'

Standard, 5 November 1845; to the editor, signed C.P. Golightly

Standard, 11 November 1845; to the editor, signed C.P. Golightly

Standard, 6 January 1846; to the Vice-Chancellor, signed C.P. Golightly

Oxford Herald, 15 December 1855; to the Vice-Chancellor, signed C.P. Golightly (with J.D. Macbride)

National Standard, 18 September 1858; to the editor, signed 'MA Oxon'

Jackson's Oxford Journal, 2 January 1864; to the editor, signed C.P. Golightly

Oxford Chronicle, 2 March 1867; to the churchwardens of Oxford diocese, signed 'A Clergyman in the Diocese of More Than Thirty Years Standing'

Oxford Chronicle, 6 April 1867; to the editor, signed 'A Clergyman of More Than Thirty Years Standing'

Record, 25 October 1878; to the Bishop of Oxford, signed C.P. Golightly

Guardian, 13 November 1878; to the editor, signed C.P. Golightly

INDEX OF NAMES

Abbott, Evelyn 165, 171
Acworth, William 258-9
Alleyne, Arthur 199
Allies, T.W. 302
Anderson, Charles 185, 188, 196
Andrewes, Lancelot 52, 87, 182
Andrews, Thomas 298
Aquinas, Thomas 207
Arnold, Matthew 164
Arnold, Thomas 42, 63, 143, 164-5, 173
Ashley, Lord, see Lord Shaftesbury
Ashwell, Arthur 300, 303
Atterbury, Francis 313
Auriol, Edward 253
Austen-Leigh, James 225
Avis, Paul 314
Bagot, Richard 19, 35, 51-2, 63, 67, 69-74, 94, 96-7, 102, 116, 129
Balleine, G.R. 312
Barff, Albert 200
Baring, Charles 22, 174-5
Barnett, Herbert 289, 294
Baxter, Richard 316
Bayley, W.G. 210
Belchier, Frances 8
Bennett, W.J.E. 254
Berington, Joseph 257
Bernard, Thomas 174
Beveridge, William 52, 95
Bickersteth, Edward 63, 124
Bickersteth, Edward (archdeacon) 225
Bingham, Joseph 52
Bird, C.S. 128
Blackall, Ofspring 317
Blencowe, Edward 22, 29
Blomfield, Charles 17, 24-5, 69, 74, 90, 96-7, 99, 129, 235, 317
Blore, John 78
Bloxam, John 109-10, 120
Böhler, Peter 8
Bonner, Edmund 42, 81-2, 158
Bowden, J.W. 113

Bowyer, George 183
Boyd, Henry 176
Bradley, G.G. 275
Bramhall, John 52, 95, 317
Bramley, Henry 268
Brancker, Thomas 91
Branthwaite, John 250
Brendon, Piers 57
Brenton, Charles 12, 15, 19-20, 22, 45, 159, 314, 316, 318
Bricknell, W.S. 81, 103, 105, 112, 120, 128-30, 134, 144-5, 147, 155
Bridges, R.E. 124, 126
Bright, William 276
Brilioth, Yngve 312
Brooke, Lord 55
Brooke, Sam 245
Brougham, Lord 241, 252
Browne, J.H. 111, 125, 127, 158-9
Brunel, I.K. 161
Buckler, J.C. 78
Budd, Susan 166
Bull, George 52
Bulteel, Henry 12-3, 18-20, 92, 318
Burgon, J.W. 4, 194, 198, 201-2, 204, 208-9, 212, 218, 222-4, 232, 265-70, 272-5, 277, 288, 301, 303, 316
Burnand, Francis 197, 200
Burnet, Gilbert 95
Burns, Arthur 310, 315
Burrows, George 307
Burrows, Montagu 268, 274, 285
Burton, Edward 36, 54-5
Bury, Arthur 40
Butler, William 182, 188, 203-4, 225
Campbell, J.M. 178
Campbell, Lewis 165, 171
Canning, George 152
Cardwell, Edward 113
Carnarvon, Lord 240
Carter, Grayson 319
Carter, T.T. 298

Cecil, Richard 316
Cecil, Robert 240, 242, 251-2
Chadwick, Owen 4, 38, 232, 281, 312
Chamberlain, Thomas 129, 220-1
Chambers, William 86
Chandler, George 54-5
Chantrey, Francis 79
Chapman, J.M. 175
Cheyne, Patrick 247
Christie, J.F. 11, 35, 110
Christmas, Henry 317
Christopher, Alfred 266, 285, 287, 293, 295
Church, R.W. 55, 63, 85, 89-91 93, 145, 147, 200
Churton, Edward 63, 68, 104, 106, 110, 136, 143, 158, 246, 273
Churton, T.T. 91
Churton, Whitaker 62, 70
Clarendon, Lord 257
Claughton, Thomas 106
Clerke, Charles 117
Close, Francis 63, 150-1, 247, 320
Clough, A.H. 164
Cochrane, A.B. 148, 156
Cockey, Edward 91, 144
Colenso, J.W. 167
Coleridge, S.T. 176
Colquhoun, J.C. 253
Comber, Thomas 317
Congreve, Richard 272
Conybeare, W.D. 106
Conybeare, W.J. 164-5, 167, 175, 309-10, 315
Copeland, William 27, 57, 85, 120
Copleston, Edward 10, 54, 59, 63, 118, 127, 139, 141, 145
Corsi, Pietro 165
Cotton, Richard 61, 133, 170-2, 174-5, 268
Cox, G.V. 161
Cox, W.H. 144, 147
Cox, William 79
Cramer, J.A. 66, 118
Cranmer, Thomas 58-9, 61, 65, 67-8, 71-2, 74-6, 79-80, 82, 142
Crowther, Margaret 4
Cumberlege, Arthur 200

Cumming, John 249
Curme, Thomas 227
Curteis, G.H. 197
Dalgairns, J.D. 132
Davey, W.H. 204
Dayman, E.A. 93
Dear, W.S. 169
Denison, Edward 54
Denison, G.A. 247, 298, 302
Derick, John 78
Disraeli, Benjamin 147-9, 156, 277, 279
Dodd, Philip 17-8, 110
Dodd, William 17
Downer, A.C. 320
Dungannon, Lord 64
Ebury, Lord 247
Eden, Charles 11, 63, 91, 136, 146
Ellacombe, Henry 10
Ellerton, Edward 144-5, 147
Elliott, Charles 298
Elliott, H.V. 238
Elliott-Binns, L.E. 312
Ellis, Ieuan 178
Elton, Edward 203, 288, 292
Elwin, Whitwell 192-3
Endicott, John 158
Faber, F.A. 120
Faber, Frederick 55, 148, 156, 161
Faber, Geoffrey 63, 165
Faber, G.S. 63, 104, 108, 110, 117, 317
Farrar, Frederic 176
Faussett, Godfrey 58, 75-6, 133, 144-5, 147
Flesher, J.H. 199-200
Forbes, Alexander 247
Foxe, John 64
Fremantle, William H. 176
Fremantle, William R. 176, 181, 226, 228-9, 297, 303
French, T.V. 55, 155
Froude, J.A. 153, 155, 163
Froude, R.H. 11, 25, 29, 33-4, 53, 57-9, 62-4, 153, 312
Furse, Charles 281-3, 289-90, 294, 299
Garbett, James 81, 103-6, 111, 143, 213, 236, 239
Gardiner, Stephen 81-2
Gibbon, Edward 117

Index of Names

Gibson, William 313
Gilbert, A.T. 1, 74, 80, 101, 103-4, 106-7, 113, 129, 132-3, 145, 207-10, 212-2, 219, 234, 236, 238-42, 248-52
Gill, T.H. 295
Gilley, Sheridan 4
Girdlestone, Charles 27
Girdlestone, R.G. 280
Gladstone, William 63-4, 106, 136, 164, 193, 242, 263, 273, 299-300
Glubb, Matthew 239
Golightly, Charles 1-320 *passim*
Golightly, Edward 9, 28, 306
Golightly, Frances, senior 9, 28
Golightly, Frances, junior 9, 28
Golightly, William 9
Golightly, William C. 9, 28
Gooch, John 108
Goode, William 127
Goodman, Godfrey 257
Gordon, Henry 303
Gordon, Richard 225, 303
Gore, Charles 299
Gorham, G.C. 164
Goring, John 238-9, 248
Goulburn, E.M. 46, 55, 88, 95, 174-5, 265, 270-1, 273, 275-6, 306-7, 311, 316, 320
Gower, J.A. 29
Graham, James 129
Grant, Anthony 146
Granville, Lord 252
Greaves, Richard 21
Green, Frances 260
Green, V.H.H. 3, 312
Gresley, William 106, 120, 131, 136, 143, 219
Greswell, Edward 40
Greswell, Richard 40, 68, 75
Grey, Lord 149
Griffiths, John 91-2, 135, 144
Guillemard, H.P. 147
Guillemard, James 112
Guiney, Louise 312
Hadfield, M.E. 78
Hall, George 66
Hall, Joseph 52, 95, 317
Hallam, Henry 257

Hamilton, W.K. 62, 64, 136, 184, 253
Hammond, Henry 52, 87, 316-7
Hampden, R.D. 1, 10, 36-45, 50, 57, 59, 60, 85, 118-22, 128, 133, 140, 264, 277, 310
Hansell, Edward 91
Harcourt, Edward 69
Harcourt, Lord 320
Harding, Henry 210, 216
Hare, Julius 236-7, 239-40
Harington, Richard 139
Harrison, Benjamin 62-3, 66-7
Hathaway, Edward 253, 268
Hawkins, Edward 10, 92, 118, 135, 245, 250, 270
Heathcote, William 73
Heeney, Brian 4, 235, 237, 253
Helmore, Thomas 185
Herbert, George 114
Heurtley, C.A. 12, 15, 159, 170-1, 174, 248, 250, 267, 276, 305-7, 316
Hewett, J.W. 240
Heylyn, Peter 73
Hill, Francis 100
Hill, John 12-3, 21, 40-1, 55, 75, 119, 314, 319
Hilton, Boyd 176
Hinchliff, Peter 165-6, 169, 173
Hoadly, Benjamin 313
Holland, T.A. 239, 242, 244, 247, 252
Hook, W.F. 63-4, 97-101, 104, 106, 120, 131, 136, 139-40, 145
Hooker, Richard 52, 87, 95 182, 266, 314, 316-7
Hoper, Henry 159, 238-9
Hopkins, Matthew 158
Hoskyns, Hungerford 13
Howley, William 38, 69-70, 72, 74, 90
Hubbard, John 200, 258, 286, 295
Hughes, James 117
Hume, Joseph 85
Hussey, Robert 91
Ince, William 296
Inglis, Robert 16
Ingram, James 68
Isham, Arthur 191, 225-6, 258, 305
Jackson, John 170, 199
Jackson, Thomas 52

Jackson, W.W. 266
Jacobs, Henry 237
Jersey, Lord 293-4
Jeune, Francis 242-4, 247-9, 252
Jewell, John 82, 95
Johnson, George 48, 91
Jowett, Benjamin 1, 164-78, 257, 263-4, 273-4, 318
Kaye, John 123, 129
Keate, John 9-10
Keble, John 10, 17, 22, 24-5, 46, 57, 59, 63-4, 66, 70, 73, 88, 101-4, 110, 116, 120, 123, 130, 140, 183, 206, 255
Kennedy, Pitt 63
Kenyon, Lord 44, 63
Keon, M.G. 149-54, 156-7
King, Edward 198, 201, 266, 280-1, 298
Kingsley, Charles 156
Kirk, Charles 78
Knight, Frances 311
Knott, John W. 238
Knox, E.A. 32, 56, 77, 268, 285-8, 291-3, 299, 311, 319-20
Knox, Ronald 292, 310
Lake, W.C. 164
Lamb, John 43
Lambert, William 19-20, 22
Lancaster, T.W. 132
Lathbury, Thomas 74
Latimer, Hugh 58, 61, 65, 67, 72, 75, 79, 81-2, 89
Laud, William 141, 143, 223, 257
Laurence, Richard 317
Lee, F.G. 183, 220, 283
Leighton, F.K. 250-1
Liddell, Henry 164, 171, 265-8
Liddell, Robert 190, 214, 246
Liddon, H.P. 58-9, 92, 182-5, 189-90, 194, 196-205, 211, 250, 265, 269, 275-6, 280-1, 283, 290-1, 295, 299, 302-4
Lightfoot, J.B. 175
Lightfoot, J.P. 264
Lindley, Charles 78
Litton, E.A. 176, 186, 205, 226, 228
Lloyd, Charles 54
Lockhart, John 106
Longley, Charles 98, 241, 259
Lowder, Charles 281

Lowe, E.C. 247, 249
Loyola, Ignatius 109
Lushington, Stephen 272
Lyttelton, Lord 241, 252
Macaulay, T.B. 154
Macbride, J.D. 66-7, 72, 74-5, 77, 79, 170, 172
Macclesfield, Lord 293
Mackarness, John 282, 284, 286-7, 289-90, 292-4, 297-9, 303
Mackonochie, A.H. 254
Mahony, Francis 151
Mair, G.J.J. 78
Manners, John 147-50, 156, 241
Manning, Henry 54, 116, 131, 136, 139, 182, 206, 236, 241, 272
Mant, Richard 317
Marigold, William 210
Marriott, Charles 27, 54, 61, 120, 145
Marsh, Peter 310
Martineau, James 168
Martyn, Henry 206
Maude, J.A. 199-200
Maurice, F.D. 35, 100-1, 106, 143, 166-7, 175-6, 232, 302
Maurice, Peter 57
Meacham, Standish 313
Medd, Peter 250
Melbourne, Lord 36, 38-40
Mendham, Joseph 128, 151
Menzies, Alfred 28
Meyrick, Frederick 175-6, 201
M'Ghee, Robert 24
Mill, William 23-4
Miller, George 53, 90, 102, 117, 128
Miller, John 104
Milman, Robert 201
Miremont, Marquis de 7-8
Moberly, C.E. 237
Moberly, George 139
Monier-Williams, Monier 273
Montagu, Richard 257
Montgomery, James 17
Moorsom, Robert 251-2
Morgan, H.T. 290, 292
Morris, J.B. 133, 153, 161
Morse-Boycott, Desmond 4
Moule, Handley 287

Index of Names

Mowbray, John 273, 286
Mozley, J.B. 27, 140, 144-6, 160, 266, 276
Mozley, Thomas 5, 11, 13-7, 19-21, 24, 26-8, 31, 48, 93, 109-10, 121, 130-2, 305, 311, 315-6
Müller, Max 273
Murphy, Howard 166
Murphy, Martin 312
Murray, John 192, 300
Napoleon Bonaparte 115
Nelson, Horatio 71
Newcastle, Duke of 65
Newman, F.W. 13, 15, 169, 227, 272
Newman, Harriett, 14-5, 87
Newman, Jemima, senior 13-4, 29-30
Newman, Jemima, junior 14, 25, 126
Newman, J.H. 1-2, 10-1, 13-5, 18, 20-3, 25-33, 35-6, 40-1, 45-52, 54-5, 57-65, 67-70, 72-3, 75, 80-3, 85-7, 89-99, 101-5, 108-10, 113, 115-6, 119-20, 123, 126-33, 137, 139, 141-2, 145-7, 150, 152, 159, 161, 163, 168, 179, 190, 200, 220, 235, 244, 255-6, 264, 270, 277, 306-7, 312, 316-8
Newman, Mary, 14-5
Newsome, David 3, 58
Newton, Benjamin 12, 19, 22, 177
Newton, John 313
Nockles, Peter 3, 36, 313, 315
Noel, M.H. 287
Nowell, Alexander 95
Oakeley, Frederick 61, 82, 87-8, 90, 101-2, 130, 136, 140, 147, 150, 152, 159, 161
Oates, Titus 216-7
O'Connell, Daniel 141
O'Connell, Marvin 4
Ogilvie, C.A. 147, 276
Osborne, S.G. 258
Otter, William 54-5
Owen, John 316
Paget, Francis 63, 116, 131
Paley, William 173
Palmer, Roundell 115, 273
Palmer, William (Magdalen College) 81, 108, 114-5, 120
Palmer, William (Worcester College) 26, 33, 40, 85, 92, 94, 127, 130-2, 137, 143
Pattison, Mark 110, 163, 171, 177
Paz, Denis 64
Pearson, John 52
Peel, Robert 16, 65, 107, 147, 156
Peers, J.W. 260
Perceval, Arthur 33, 53, 73
Perry, T.W. 220
Phillimore, J.G. 122
Phillimore, Robert 286-7
Phillpotts, Henry 24, 63, 90, 145, 164, 193, 236, 247
Philpot, Joseph 12, 19
Pinder, J.H. 197
Plumptre, E.H. 200
Plumptre, Frederick 79-80, 133
Poole, Alfred 236, 247
Poole, John 2
Portalès, Charles 7-8
Pott, Alfred 182, 185, 187, 189-91, 193, 198-201, 203, 225, 283, 292, 299-300
Potter, Horatio 267
Powell, Baden 39
Prest, John 4
Prevost, George 11, 63
Prothero, R.E. 275
Prynne, G.R. 236
Pugin, A.W.N. 73-4, 110
Purchas, John 220, 244, 254
Purey-Cust, A.P. 196, 201, 225, 233, 286-7, 296
Pusey, E.B. 1, 10, 23, 30-1, 34-7, 39-42, 44-54, 58, 60-3, 66-8, 70, 72-3, 87, 93-4, 101-4, 107-8, 114, 116-7, 120, 126, 128-30, 133, 137, 140-2, 150, 153, 158-61, 169-72, 176, 182, 203, 235, 238, 255-8, 265, 269-70, 272, 275-6, 295, 302, 317-8
Radnor, Lord 244
Randall, Edward 206-10, 218
Randall, James 206, 208, 300
Randall, R.W. 206-13, 216, 218
Rawlinson, George 153-5
Redesdale, Lord 241, 281
Reed, J.S. 236
Reeve, J.W. 214
Reynolds, John 12
Richards, Joseph 89, 92-3, 139, 153

Ridley, Nicholas 58-9, 61, 65, 67, 72, 75, 79, 81-2, 89, 95
Rigaud, S.J. 153, 175
Robertson, Frederick 55
Rogers, Frederic 58, 72, 104, 146
Routh, Martin 66, 68
Ryder, Henry 11
Ryle, J.C. 253
Sacheverell, Henry 313
Sanderson, R.E. 249
Sanderson, Robert 317
Sandford, John 185
Sargent, John 206
Scholefield, James 129
Scott, Gilbert 74, 78
Scott, Robert 87, 164, 173-4, 263
Scott, Thomas 78, 316
Secker, Thomas 95
Selwyn, William 208
Semler, Johann 167
Sewell, William 40-1, 53, 66-8, 70, 87, 106
Shaftesbury, Lord 63, 145, 166, 208-9, 246, 254
Shaw, John 219, 245
Shipley, Orby 258, 283
Short, Thomas 71
Shute, Hardwick, 194
Shuttleworth, Philip 53-5, 59, 66-9, 72, 76, 90, 107-8, 118, 206, 319
Sibthorp, R.W. 12, 15, 107-9
Sidney, Philip 18
Simeon, Charles 22, 168, 206
Smith, Bernard 122-3, 126
Smith, Sydney 107
Smith, Vance 267
Smythe, George 147-9, 152, 156
Spurgeon, C.H. 246, 249, 272
Stanhope, Philip 17
Stanley, A.P. 1, 38, 93, 126, 146, 164-6, 168, 171-2, 175-6, 264-77
Stanley, Edward 129
Stephenson, George 161
Stowell, Hugh 186, 216
Street, G.E. 181
Stunt, T.C.F. 12, 314
Sue, Eugène 149
Sumner, J.B. 57, 63, 90, 178, 317

Sumner, C.R. 63, 80, 90, 198
Surin J.J. 142
Swinny, H.H. 202, 280
Symons, Benjamin 89, 92, 132-8, 145, 147, 153, 159-60, 186
Symons, Lydia 135
Tait, A.C. 48, 63, 91, 93, 113, 120, 143, 164, 184, 189, 198, 236, 265, 281, 283, 311
Tatham, Edward 59
Taylor, Jeremy 95
Taylor, Stephen 313
Temple, Frederick 87, 164, 167, 177, 265, 276
Thirlwall, Connop 143, 240
Thomas, Vaughan 40, 44, 65, 79-80, 120-1
Thomson, William 166, 242, 250
Toon, Peter 61, 64, 313, 318
Tooth, Arthur 279
Torquemada, Tomás de 158
Townsend, George 82
Trower, Walter 13, 15, 184, 187, 189, 194, 238-9, 245, 248, 254, 259, 268, 306, 314
Tucker, John 28, 169, 173, 226, 228, 230, 245, 248, 259, 268, 306
Tulloch, John 178
Turner, Frank 4
Twiss, Travers 91
Twopeny, Richard 190, 193, 226, 228, 231, 245, 247-8, 251
Tyler, James 106
Ussher, James 52, 95
Van Mildert, William 52
Verney, Harry 286
Voltaire 117
Voysey, Charles 267
Wackerbarth, F.D. 107, 109
Wagner, A.D. 243
Waldegrave, Samuel 55
Walsh, John 313
Walsh, Thomas 109-10
Walsh, Walter 293, 320
Ward, G.R.M. 132
Ward, W.R. 163, 313
Ward, W.G. 91, 101-2, 108-9, 114, 130, 136-41, 143, 146-7, 150, 152, 161, 170

Index of Names

Waterland, Daniel 52, 95, 317
Weekes, Henry 79
Wellington, Duke of 16, 65, 71, 78, 135, 147
Wesley, John 8
West, R.T. 219
Wetherell, Charles 78
Wharton, Hannah 8
Whately, Richard 10, 54, 139, 145, 174
Wheatly, Charles 317
White, Blanco 37
Wigram, George 12
Wigram, J.C. 242, 247-9, 251
Wilberforce, Basil 302
Wilberforce, Henry 11, 13-5, 36, 106, 182, 206
Wilberforce, Reginald 300-6
Wilberforce, Robert 11, 29, 106, 111, 136, 182
Wilberforce, Samuel 1-2, 11, 15, 35, 39, 62, 160, 173, 175-6, 179-85, 187, 191-97, 201-6, 208-13, 218-21, 223-5, 227-33, 236, 242-3, 248-52, 254-61, 265, 280, 282, 284, 299-305
Wilberforce, William 11, 206, 232
Williams, Isaac 29, 31, 33, 52, 61, 73, 81, 102-6, 111, 115, 120
Willis, Edward 281-3, 285, 289-91, 294, 299
Wilson, Daniel 63, 227
Wilson, H.B. 91, 144
Wilson, H.H. 23-4
Wilson, J.H., 190
Wilson, William 227
Winchilsea, Earl of 65
Wiseman, Nicholas 41, 109, 128
Wolffe, John 64, 80, 314
Wood, C.L. 295
Woodard, Nathaniel 234-53
Woodgate, Henry A. 105
Woollcombe, E.C. 91, 268
Wordsworth, William 106, 309
Wynantz, Francis 8
Wynter, Philip 92, 120, 132-4, 137, 153, 155
Yates, Nigel 284

Studies in Evangelical History and Thought
(All titles uniform with this volume)
Dates in bold are of projected publication

Andrew Atherstone
Oxford's Protestant Spy
The Controversial Career of Charles Golightly
Charles Golightly (1807–85) was a notorious Protestant polemicist. His life was dedicated to resisting the spread of ritualism and liberalism within the Church of England and the University of Oxford. For half a century he led many memorable campaigns, such as building a martyr's memorial and attempting to close a theological college. John Henry Newman, Samuel Wilberforce and Benjamin Jowett were among his adversaries. This is the first study of Golightly's controversial career.
***2006** / 1-84227-364-7 / approx. 324pp*

Clyde Binfield
Victorian Nonconformity in Eastern England
Studies of Victorian religion and society often concentrate on cities, suburbs, and industrialisation. This study provides a contrast. Victorian Eastern England—Essex, Suffolk, Norfolk, Cambridgeshire, and Huntingdonshire—was rural, traditional, relatively unchanging. That is nonetheless a caricature which discounts the industry in Norwich and Ipswich (as well as in Haverhill, Stowmarket and Leiston) and ignores the impact of London on Essex, of railways throughout the region, and of an ancient but changing university (Cambridge) on the county town which housed it. It also entirely ignores the political implications of such changes in a region noted for the variety of its religious Dissent since the seventeenth century. This book explores Victorian Eastern England and its Nonconformity. It brings to a wider readership a pioneering thesis which has made a major contribution to a fresh evolution of English religion and society.
***2006** / 1-84227-216-0 / approx. 274pp*

John Brencher
Martyn Lloyd-Jones (1899–1981) and Twentieth-Century Evangelicalism
This study critically demonstrates the significance of the life and ministry of Martyn Lloyd-Jones for post-war British evangelicalism and demonstrates that his preaching was his greatest influence on twentieth-century Christianity. The factors which shaped his view of the church are examined, as is the way his reformed evangelicalism led to a separatist ecclesiology which divided evangelicals.
2002 / 1-84227-051-6 / xvi + 268pp

Jonathan D. Burnham
A Story of Conflict
The Controversial Relationship between Benjamin Wills Newton and John Nelson Darby

Burnham explores the controversial relationship between the two principal leaders of the early Brethren movement. In many ways Newton and Darby were products of their times, and this study of their relationship provides insight not only into the dynamics of early Brethrenism, but also into the progress of nineteenth-century English and Irish evangelicalism.

2004 / 1-84227-191-1 / xxiv + 268pp

Grayson Carter
Anglican Evangelicals
Protestant Secessions from the Via Media, c.1800–1850

This study examines, within a chronological framework, the major themes and personalities which influenced the outbreak of a number of Evangelical clerical and lay secessions from the Church of England and Ireland during the first half of the nineteenth century. Though the number of secessions was relatively small—between a hundred and two hundred of the 'Gospel' clergy abandoned the Church during this period—their influence was considerable, especially in highlighting in embarrassing fashion the tensions between the evangelical conversionist imperative and the principles of a national religious establishment. Moreover, through much of this period there remained, just beneath the surface, the potential threat of a large Evangelical disruption similar to that which occurred in Scotland in 1843. Consequently, these secessions provoked great consternation within the Church and within Evangelicalism itself, they contributed to the outbreak of millennial speculation following the 'constitutional revolution' of 1828–32, they led to the formation of several new denominations, and they sparked off a major Church–State crisis over the legal right of a clergyman to secede and begin a new ministry within Protestant Dissent.

2007 / 1-84227-401-5 / xvi + 470pp

J.N. Ian Dickson
Beyond Religious Discourse
Sermons, Preaching and Evangelical Protestants in Nineteenth-Century Irish Society

Drawing extensively on primary sources, this pioneer work in modern religious history explores the training of preachers, the construction of sermons and how Irish evangelicalism and the wider movement in Great Britain and the United States shaped the preaching event. Evangelical preaching and politics, sectarianism, denominations, education, class, social reform, gender, and revival are examined to advance the argument that evangelical sermons and preaching went significantly beyond religious discourse. The result is a book for those with interests in Irish history, culture and belief, popular religion and society, evangelicalism, preaching and communication.

2005 / 1-84227-217-9 / approx. 324pp

Neil T.R. Dickson
Brethren in Scotland 1838–2000
A Social Study of an Evangelical Movement

The Brethren were remarkably pervasive throughout Scottish society. This study of the Open Brethren in Scotland places them in their social context and examines their growth, development and relationship to society.

2003 / 1-84227-113-X / xxviii + 510pp

Crawford Gribben and Timothy C.F. Stunt (eds)
Prisoners of Hope?
Aspects of Evangelical Millennialism in Britain and Ireland, 1800–1880

This volume of essays offers a comprehensive account of the impact of evangelical millennialism in nineteenth-century Britain and Ireland.

2004 / 1-84227-224-1 / xiv + 208pp

Khim Harris
Evangelicals and Education
Evangelical Anglicans and Middle-Class Education in Nineteenth-Century England

This ground breaking study investigates the history of English public schools founded by nineteenth-century Evangelicals. It documents the rise of middle-class education and Evangelical societies such as the influential Church Association, and includes a useful biographical survey of prominent Evangelicals of the period.

2004 / 1-84227-250-0 / xviii + 422pp

Mark Hopkins
Nonconformity's Romantic Generation
Evangelical and Liberal Theologies in Victorian England
A study of the theological development of key leaders of the Baptist and Congregational denominations at their period of greatest influence, including C.H. Spurgeon and R.W. Dale, and of the controversies in which those among them who embraced and rejected the liberal transformation of their evangelical heritage opposed each other.
2004 / 1-84227-150-4 / xvi + 284pp

Don Horrocks
Laws of the Spiritual Order
Innovation and Reconstruction in the Soteriology of Thomas Erskine of Linlathen
Don Horrocks argues that Thomas Erskine's unique historical and theological significance as a soteriological innovator has been neglected. This timely reassessment reveals Erskine as a creative, radical theologian of central and enduring importance in Scottish nineteenth-century theology, perhaps equivalent in significance to that of S.T. Coleridge in England.
2004 / 1-84227-192-X / xx + 362pp

Kenneth S. Jeffrey
When the Lord Walked the Land
The 1858–62 Revival in the North East of Scotland
Previous studies of revivals have tended to approach religious movements from either a broad, national or a strictly local level. This study of the multifaceted nature of the 1859 revival as it appeared in three distinct social contexts within a single region reveals the heterogeneous nature of simultaneous religious movements in the same vicinity.
2002 / 1-84227-057-5 / xxiv + 304pp

John Kenneth Lander
Itinerant Temples
Tent Methodism, 1814–1832
Tent preaching began in 1814 and the Tent Methodist sect resulted from disputes with Bristol Wesleyan Methodists in 1820. The movement spread to parts of Gloucestershire, Wiltshire, London and Liverpool, among other places. Its demise started in 1826 after which one leader returned to the Wesleyans and others became ministers in the Congregational and Baptist denominations.
2003 / 1-84227-151-2 / xx + 268pp

Donald M. Lewis
Lighten Their Darkness
The Evangelical Mission to Working-Class London, 1828–1860
This is a comprehensive and compelling study of the Church and the complexities of nineteenth-century London. Challenging our understanding of the culture in working London at this time, Lewis presents a well-structured and illustrated work that contributes substantially to the study of evangelicalism and mission in nineteenth-century Britain.
2001 / 1-84227-074-5 / xviii + 372pp

Herbert McGonigle
'Sufficient Saving Grace'
John Wesley's Evangelical Arminianism
A thorough investigation of the theological roots of John Wesley's evangelical Arminianism and how these convictions were hammered out in controversies on predestination, limited atonement and the perseverance of the saints.
2001 / 1-84227-045-1 / xvi + 350pp

Lisa S. Nolland
A Victorian Feminist Christian
Josephine Butler, the Prostitutes and God
Josephine Butler was an unlikely candidate for taking up the cause of prostitutes, as she did, with a fierce and self-disregarding passion. This book explores the particular mix of perspectives and experiences that came together to envision and empower her remarkable achievements. It highlights the vital role of her spirituality and the tragic loss of her daughter.
2004 / 1-84227-225-X / xxiv + 328pp

Don J. Payne
The Theology of the Christian Life in J.I. Packer's Thought
Theological Anthropology, Theological Method, and the Doctrine of Sanctification
J.I. Packer has wielded widespread influence on evangelicalism for more than three decades. This study pursues a nuanced understanding of Packer's theology of sanctification by tracing the development of his thought, showing how he reflects a particular version of Reformed theology, and examining the unique influence of theological anthropology and theological method on this area of his theology.
2005 / 1-84227-397-3 / approx. 374pp

July 2005

Ian M. Randall
Evangelical Experiences
A Study in the Spirituality of English Evangelicalism 1918–1939
This book makes a detailed historical examination of evangelical spirituality between the First and Second World Wars. It shows how patterns of devotion led to tensions and divisions. In a wide-ranging study, Anglican, Wesleyan, Reformed and Pentecostal-charismatic spiritualities are analysed.
1999 / 0-85364-919-7 / xii + 310pp

Ian M. Randall
Spirituality and Social Change
The Contribution of F.B. Meyer (1847–1929)
This is a fresh appraisal of F.B. Meyer (1847–1929), a leading Free Church minister. Having been deeply affected by holiness spirituality, Meyer became the Keswick Convention's foremost international speaker. He combined spirituality with effective evangelism and socio-political activity. This study shows Meyer's significant contribution to spiritual renewal and social change.
2003 / 1-84227-195-4 / xx + 184pp

James Robinson
Pentecostal Origins
Early Pentecostalism in Ireland in the Context of the British Isles
Harvey Cox describes Pentecostalism as 'the fascinating spiritual child of our time' that has the potential, at the global scale, to contribute to the 'reshaping of religion in the twenty-first century'. This study grounds such sentiments by examining at the local scale the origin, development and nature of Pentecostalism in Ireland in its first twenty years. Illustrative, in a paradigmatic way, of how Pentecostalism became established within one region of the British Isles, it sets the story within the wider context of formative influences emanating from America, Europe and, in particular, other parts of the British Isles. As a synoptic regional study in Pentecostal history it is the first survey of its kind.
2005 / 1-84227-329-1 / xxviii + 378pp

Geoffrey Robson
Dark Satanic Mills?
Religion and Irreligion in Birmingham and the Black Country
This book analyses and interprets the nature and extent of popular Christian belief and practice in Birmingham and the Black Country during the first half of the nineteenth century, with particular reference to the impact of cholera epidemics and evangelism on church extension programmes.
2002 / 1-84227-102-4 / xiv + 294pp

Roger Shuff
Searching for the True Church
Brethren and Evangelicals in Mid-Twentieth-Century England

Roger Shuff holds that the influence of the Brethren movement on wider evangelical life in England in the twentieth century is often underrated. This book records and accounts for the fact that Brethren reached the peak of their strength at the time when evangelicalism was at it lowest ebb, immediately before World War II. However, the movement then moved into persistent decline as evangelicalism regained ground in the post war period. Accompanying this downward trend has been a sharp accentuation of the contrast between Brethren congregations who engage constructively with the non-Brethren scene and, at the other end of the spectrum, the isolationist group commonly referred to as 'Exclusive Brethren'.

2005 / 1-84227-254-3 / xviii+ 296pp

James H.S. Steven
Worship in the Spirit
Charismatic Worship in the Church of England

This book explores the nature and function of worship in six Church of England churches influenced by the Charismatic Movement, focusing on congregational singing and public prayer ministry. The theological adequacy of such ritual is discussed in relation to pneumatological and christological understandings in Christian worship.

2002 / 1-84227-103-2 / xvi + 238pp

Peter K. Stevenson
God in Our Nature
The Incarnational Theology of John McLeod Campbell

This radical reassessment of Campbell's thought arises from a comprehensive study of his preaching and theology. Previous accounts have overlooked both his sermons and his Christology. This study examines the distinctive Christology evident in his sermons and shows that it sheds new light on Campbell's much debated views about atonement.

2004 / 1-84227-218-7 / xxiv + 458pp

Kenneth J. Stewart
Restoring the Reformation
British Evangelicalism and the Réveil at Geneva 1816–1849
Restoring the Reformation traces British missionary initiative in post-Revolutionary Francophone Europe from the genesis of the London Missionary Society, the visits of Robert Haldane and Henry Drummond, and the founding of the Continental Society. While British Evangelicals aimed at the reviving of a foreign Protestant cause of momentous legend, they received unforeseen reciprocating emphases from the Continent which forced self-reflection on Evangelicalism's own relationship to the Reformation.
2006 / 1-84227-392-2 / approx. 190pp

Martin Wellings
Evangelicals Embattled
Responses of Evangelicals in the Church of England to Ritualism, Darwinism and Theological Liberalism 1890–1930
In the closing years of the nineteenth century and the first decades of the twentieth century Anglican Evangelicals faced a series of challenges. In responding to Anglo-Catholicism, liberal theology, Darwinism and biblical criticism, the unity and identity of the Evangelical school were severely tested.
2003 / 1-84227-049-4 / xviii + 352pp

James Whisenant
A Fragile Unity
Anti-Ritualism and the Division of Anglican Evangelicalism in the Nineteenth Century
This book deals with the ritualist controversy (approximately 1850–1900) from the perspective of its evangelical participants and considers the divisive effects it had on the party.
2003 / 1-84227-105-9 / xvi + 530pp

Haddon Willmer
Evangelicalism 1785–1835: An Essay (1962) and Reflections (2004)
Awarded the Hulsean Prize in the University of Cambridge in 1962, this interpretation of a classic period of English Evangelicalism, by a young church historian, is now supplemented by reflections on Evangelicalism from the vantage point of a retired Professor of Theology.
2006 / 1-84227-219-5 / approx. 350pp

Linda Wilson
Constrained by Zeal
Female Spirituality amongst Nonconformists 1825–1875
Constrained by Zeal investigates the neglected area of Nonconformist female spirituality. Against the background of separate spheres, it analyses the experience of women from four denominations, and argues that the churches provided a 'third sphere' in which they could find opportunities for participation.
2000 / 0-85364-972-3 / xvi + 294pp

Paternoster
9 Holdom Avenue,
Bletchley,
Milton Keynes MK1 1QR,
United Kingdom
Web: www.authenticmedia.co.uk/paternoster

July 2005

www.ingramcontent.com/pod-product-compliance
Lightning Source LLC
Chambersburg PA
CBHW061424300426
44114CB00014B/1522